SLAVES AND SLAVERY IN ANCIENT GREECE

Slavery in ancient Greece was commonplace. In this book Sara Forsdyke uncovers the wide range of experiences of slaves and focuses on their own perspectives, rather than those of their owners, giving a voice to a group that is often rendered silent by the historical record. By reading ancient sources "against the grain," and through careful deployment of comparative evidence from more recent slave-owning societies, she demonstrates that slaves engaged in a variety of strategies to deal with their conditions of enslavement, ranging from calculated accommodation to full-scale rebellion. Along the way, she establishes that slaves made a vital contribution to almost all aspects of Greek society. Above all, despite their often brutal treatment, they sometimes displayed great ingenuity in exploiting the tensions and contradictions within the system of slavery.

SARA FORSDYKE is Josiah Ober Collegiate Professor of Ancient History at the University of Michigan. She has published widely on ancient democracy, slavery and the law.

KEY THEMES IN ANCIENT HISTORY

EDITORS

P. A. Cartledge
Clare College, Cambridge
G. Woolf
Institute of Classical Studies, London

EMERITUS EDITOR

P. D. A. Garnsey
Jesus College, Cambridge

Key Themes in Ancient History aims to provide readable, informed and original studies of various basic topics, designed in the first instance for students and teachers of Classics and Ancient History, but also for those engaged in related disciplines. Each volume is devoted to a general theme in Greek, Roman, or where appropriate, Graeco-Roman history, or to some salient aspect or aspects of it. Besides indicating the state of current research in the relevant area, authors seek to show how the theme is significant for our own as well as ancient culture and society. It is hoped that these original, thematic volumes will encourage and stimulate promising new developments in teaching and research in ancient history.

Other books in the series

Death-Ritual and Social Structure in Classical Antiquity, by Ian Morris
978 0 521 37465 1 (hardback) 978 0 521 37611 2 (paperback)
Literacy and Orality in Ancient Greece, by Rosalind Thomas
978 0 521 37346 3 (hardback) 978 0 521 37742 3 (paperback)
Slavery and Society at Rome, by Keith Bradley
978 0 521 37287 9 (hardback) 978 0 521 37887 1 (paperback)
Law, Violence, and Community in Classical Athens, by David Cohen
978 0 521 38167 3 (hardback) 978 0 521 38837 5 (paperback)
Public Order in Ancient Rome, by Wilfried Nippel
978 0 521 38327 1 (hardback) 978 0 521 38749 1 (paperback)
Friendship in the Classical World, by David Konstan
978 0 521 45402 5 (hardback) 978 0 521 45998 3 (paperback)
Sport and Society in Ancient Greece, by Mark Golden
978 0 521 49698 8 (hardback) 978 0 521 49790 9 (paperback)
Food and Society in Classical Antiquity, by Peter Garnsey
978 0 521 64182 1 (hardback) 978 0 521 64588 1 (paperback)
Banking and Business in the Roman World, by Jean Andreau
978 0 521 38031 7 (hardback) 978 0 521 38932 7 (paperback)

Roman Law in Context, by David Johnston
978 0 521 63046 7 (hardback) 978 0 521 63961 3 (paperback)
Religions of the Ancient Greeks, by Simon Price
978 0 521 38201 4 (hardback) 978 0 521 38867 2 (paperback)
Christianity and Roman Society, by Gillian Clark
978 0 521 63310 9 (hardback) 978 0 521 63386 4 (paperback)
Trade in Classical Antiquity, by Neville Morley
978 0 521 63279 9 (hardback) 978 0 521 63416 8 (paperback)
Technology and Culture in Greek and Roman Antiquity, by Serafina Cuomo
978 0 521 81073 9 (hardback) 978 0 521 00903 4 (paperback)
Law and Crime in the Roman World, by Jill Harries
978 0 521 82820 8 (hardback) 978 0 521 53532 8 (paperback)
The Social History of Roman Art, by Peter Stewart
978 0 521 81632 8 (hardback) 978 0 52101659 9 (paperback)
Ancient Greek Political Thought in Practice, by Paul Cartledge
978 0 521 45455 1 (hardback) 978 0 521 45595 4 (paperback)
Asceticism in the Graeco-Roman World, by Richard Finn OP
978 0 521 86281 3 (hardback) 978 0 521 68154 4 (paperback)
Domestic Space and Social Organisation in Classical Antiquity, by Lisa C. Nevett
978 0 521 78336 1 (hardback) 978 0 521 78945 5 (paperback)
Money in Classical Antiquity, by Sitta von Reden
978 0 521 45337 0 (hardback) 978 0 521 45952 5 (paperback)
Geography in Classical Antiquity, by Daniela Dueck and Kai Brodersen
978 0 521 19788 5 (hardback) 978 0 521 12025 8 (paperback)
Space and Society in the Greek and Roman Worlds, by Michael Scott
978 1 107 00915 8 (hardback) 978 1 107 40150 1 (paperback)
Studying Gender in Classical Antiquity, by Lin Foxhall
978 0 521 55318 6 (hardback) 978 0 521 55739 9 (paperback)
The Ancient Jews from Alexander to Muhammad, by Seth Schwartz
978 1 107 04127 1 (hardback) 978 1 107 66929 1 (paperback)
Language and Society in the Greek and Roman Worlds, by James Clackson
978 0 521 19235 4 (hardback) 978 0 521 14066 9 (paperback)
The Ancient City, by Arjan Zuiderhoek
0 521 19835 6 (hardback) 978 0 521 16601 0 (paperback)
Science Writing in Greco-Roman Antiquity, by Liba Taub
978 0 521 11370 0 (hardback) 978 0 521 13063 9 (paperback)
Politics in the Roman Republic, by Henrik Mouritsen
1 07 03188 3 (hardback) 978 1 107 65133 3 (paperback)
Roman Political Thought, by Jed W. Atkins
978 11 07 10700 7 (hardback) 9781107514553 (paperback)
Empire and Political Cultures in the Roman World, by Emma Dench
978 0 521 81072 2 (hardback) 978 0 521 00901 0 (paperback)
Warfare in the Roman World, by A.D. Lee
978 1 107 01428 2 (hardback) 978 1 107 63828 0 (paperback)

SLAVES AND SLAVERY IN ANCIENT GREECE

SARA FORSDYKE
University of Michigan

CAMBRIDGE
UNIVERSITY PRESS

University Printing House, Cambridge CB2 8BS, United Kingdom

One Liberty Plaza, 20th Floor, New York, NY 10006, USA

477 Williamstown Road, Port Melbourne, VIC 3207, Australia

314–321, 3rd Floor, Plot 3, Splendor Forum, Jasola District Centre, New Delhi – 110025, India

79 Anson Road, #06–04/06, Singapore 079906

Cambridge University Press is part of the University of Cambridge.

It furthers the University's mission by disseminating knowledge in the pursuit of education, learning, and research at the highest international levels of excellence.

www.cambridge.org
Information on this title: www.cambridge.org/9781107032347
DOI: 10.1017/9781139505772

© Cambridge University Press 2021

This publication is in copyright. Subject to statutory exception and to the provisions of relevant collective licensing agreements, no reproduction of any part may take place without the written permission of Cambridge University Press.

First published 2021

A catalogue record for this publication is available from the British Library.

ISBN 978-1-107-03234-7 Hardback
ISBN 978-1-107-65889-9 Paperback

Cambridge University Press has no responsibility for the persistence or accuracy of URLs for external or third-party internet websites referred to in this publication and does not guarantee that any content on such websites is, or will remain, accurate or appropriate.

*For my dear daughter, Sophie, with love and thanks for
your spirited companionship.*

Contents

List of Figures	*page* x
List of Tables	xii
Acknowledgments	xiii
Note on Translations, Dates and Abbreviations	xv

1	Approaching Slavery in Ancient Greece: Motivations, Methods and Definitions	1
2	Becoming a Slave: "The Day of Slavery"	52
3	Being a Slave: Experiences of Slavery	102
4	Slaves and Status	161
5	Resourceful Slaves and Controlling Masters	200
6	Why Should We Care?	247

Bibliographical Essay	252
Bibliography	255
Index	271

Figures

1.1	Map of ancient Greece and the Mediterranean region.	*page* xvi
1.2	Fifth-century vase from Lokris, showing a slave tied up in a pottery workshop.	2
1.3	Tombstone of Aulos Kapreilios Timotheos with representation of a slave coffle.	16
1.4	Aristotle's conception of the associations that comprise the city-state (polis).	24
1.5a	Juan Ginés de Sepulveda.	28
1.5b	Bartolomé de las Casas.	29
2.1	Close-up of slave coffle from tombstone of Aulos Kapreilios Timotheos.	72
3.1	Attic black-figure cup, c.530 BCE, showing ploughing and sowing grain.	105
3.2	Attic black-figure amphora, c.520 BCE, showing slaves (?) harvesting olives.	108
3.3	Slaves (?) working in a blacksmithing shop specializing in bronze sculptures (Side A). Red-figure vase, c.490–480, found at Vulci, Italy.	115
3.4	Slaves (?) working in a blacksmithing shop specializing in bronze sculptures (Side B). Red-figure vase, c.490–480, found at Vulci, Italy.	116
3.5	Slaves (?) in a clay pit or mine. Corinthian ceramic plaque.	121
3.6	Woman grinding grain. Terracotta, c.450 BCE, from Kameiros, Rhodes.	126
3.7	Phallus procession in honor of Dionysus. Attic black-figured cup, c.550 BCE.	128
3.8	Slaves (?) spinning and weaving wool. Black-figure oil flask (lekythos), 550–530 BCE.	134

3.9	Slaves (?) kneading dough with a slave (?) flute player setting the pace. Terracotta model from Thebes, Boeotia, 525–475 BCE. CA804.	156
4.1	Grave marker of Sostratus.	167
4.2	Peter, a slave in Louisiana, photographed April 1863.	169
5.1	A dung beetle rolling a pellet of dung.	208
5.2	Advertisement for a reward for capture of a runaway slave, 1853.	212
5.3	Topographical map of Greece.	218
5.4	View of Mt. Taygetus.	219
5.5	Toussaint L'Ouverture, the leader of a successful slave rebellion that led to the establishment of the modern state of Haiti in 1804.	222

Tables

1.1	Aristotle's analogies reinforcing the naturalness of slavery.	*page* 27
1.2	Standard distinctions between slavery and serfdom.	42

Acknowledgments

My sincere gratitude to the series editors, Paul Cartledge and Greg Woolf, for their patience with the delayed production of the manuscript and especially for their careful reading of it when it finally appeared. Their suggestions and corrections have strengthened the book considerably. Thanks also to Michael Sharp for his support for this project and to both Michael and Katie Idle for their skillful shepherding of the manuscript through the production process. Alexander Macleod copyedited the book with a sharp eye for errors and inconsistencies. I am very grateful for his care and skill.

This book began as a series of lectures that I was kindly invited to give at the École des Hautes Études en Sciences Sociales in Paris in 2011. I thank François Hartog for the invitation, and both François and Cléo Carastro for hospitality during my stay. Paulin Ismard and Pauline Schmitt-Pantel provided helpful commentary on and critique of my ideas, and I thank them heartily for their engagement.

Welcome opportunities to try out my ideas were generously offered by Peter Hunt at the University of Colorado, Adam Rabinowitz at the University of Texas, Austin, and by Adriaan Lanni at Harvard Law School. Peter Hunt's own work on slavery has enlightened me on many points, and I draw on his ground-breaking work throughout this book. Conferences at Oxford University (organized by Samuel Gartland and David Tandy) and Tel Aviv (a Symposion conference on Greek law organized by Uri Yiftach and Rachel Zelnick-Abramowitz) have provided important opportunities for feedback from expert audiences.

The group that has endured my presentations on slavery the longest is the Midwestern Consortium of Greek Historians and Political Theorists. This lively group of friends has been a source of great fun and intellectual stimulation for many years and I thank them all most warmly: Ben Akrigg, Greg Anderson, Ryan Balot, Matthew Christ, Judith Fletcher, Adriaan Lanni, Eric Robinson, Robert Tordoff, Bernd Steinbock and Victoria

Wohl. Josh Ober continues to be a source of inspiration for me, and I affectionately thank him for his mentorship – and friendship – for almost thirty years.

David Lewis read and generously commented on a chapter of this book. He has also been unstintingly responsive to my repeated inquiries about various aspects of slavery in the ancient Mediterranean and I thank him for his intellectual generosity.

I thank my students and colleagues at the University of Michigan for providing a sounding board on many occasions for the ideas presented in this book.

My father, Donald Forsdyke, a biochemist and historian of science, read the entire manuscript and corrected many errors of spelling and style. While it is quite humbling for a humanist to be corrected by a scientist on points of style, I lovingly thank him for his interest in my work over many years.

None of the above are responsible for the flaws that remain in this book.

This book is dedicated to my teenage daughter, Sophie, who sketched one of the illustrations for this book and who has also contributed her spirited companionship. May you never lose your lively spirit, dearest Sophie. Thanks also to my husband, Finn, for his love, and to our wonderful son, Thomas, who is finding his own way now as a mathematician and computer scientist, and contributes daily through his cheerful presence.

Note on Translations, Dates and Abbreviations

All translations are mine, unless otherwise noted, and dates are BCE, unless otherwise noted.

In the interests of transparency for the general reader, and where it is not too cumbersome, I have provided the names of ancient authors and titles of their work in English translation. Occasionally, I resort to the standard abbreviations of the field, which can be found in the *Oxford Classical Dictionary*, third edition, edited by S. Hornblower and A. Spawforth, 1996.

For abbreviations of modern works of scholarship, see the Bibliography.

Fig. 1.1 Map of ancient Greece and the Mediterranean region.

Fig. 1.1 (cont.)

CHAPTER I

Approaching Slavery in Ancient Greece
Motivations, Methods and Definitions

At some date in the fourth century BCE, a slave laboring in a metal-casting workshop engraved (or had someone engrave for him) a short letter on a piece of lead. The letter reads:

> Lesis sends [this letter] to Xenocles and his mother, [asking] that they not overlook at all the fact that he is perishing in a foundry, but that they go to his masters and find a better situation for him. For I have been handed over to a thoroughly wicked man, and I am perishing from being whipped. I am tied up. I am treated like dirt ... more and more![1]

This letter is exceptional in that it provides direct access to the voice of a slave who lived almost two and a half thousand years ago. As we shall see, such direct evidence is exceedingly rare.[2] We learn in this letter that Lesis is a slave whose masters have put him to work in a metal-casting workshop where he is treated so brutally that he believes he will die.[3] Lesis writes to his mother, presumably also a slave, and Xenocles, her partner, asking that they approach his masters and find new employment for him.

The letter raises many questions. Most generally, we might ask whether Lesis' situation is typical of slaves in ancient Greece.[4] Notable features of Lesis' condition are that he seems to have more than one master, and that he is being rented out to work in a metal-casting workshop. Moreover, he is treated brutally, whipped and tied up (Fig. 1.2). We might further wonder

---

[1] Trans. E. Harris (2004) (with slight modifications).
[2] Other examples are questions put by slaves to the oracle at Dodona (Eidinow 2007, 100–104) and an ancient graffito scratched on a rock in Attica by a shepherd who was probably a slave (Langdon 2015, 53; with Lewis 2018, 121 n.59).
[3] Fischer (2012, 118) suggests that Lesis' treatment is strongly reflected in a scene on a fifth-century vase from Locris. The vase (Fig. 1.2) shows a pottery workshop in which a figure is tied up (suspended?) with ropes around his neck, foot, hands and even his penis.
[4] I follow Harris, in accepting that Lesis is in fact a slave. Not only is the use of the word "master" indicative of a master-slave relationship but also the use of the whip is characteristic of slavery. Jordan (2000) followed by Maffi (2014) doubts that Lesis is a slave, while Harris (2004) and Harvey (2007) argue for this interpretation.

Fig. 1.2 Fifth-century vase depicting a figure tied up (suspended?) and beaten (?) in a pottery workshop. Black-figure skyphos from Exarchos, Lokris. Athens, National Archaeological Museum A 442. Hellenic Ministry of Culture and Sports / Archaeological Resources Fund.

whether slaves typically labored in manufacturing workshops or were employed primarily in other sectors of the economy; for example, in agriculture and domestic service. Similarly, we might ask whether Lesis' overseer at the workshop was a particularly "wicked man," as Lesis claims, or whether such brutal treatment was typical. Finally, we might wonder whether Lesis was literate. Did he actually write the letter that he "sends" to Xenocles and his mother, or did he find someone else to write it for him? Given that teaching slaves to read was illegal in some slave-owning societies (e.g., the American South), this question broaches the larger issue of whether slaves were literate in ancient Greece.

These are just a few of the issues raised by this exceptional document. But these queries provide an entry point into some of the big questions that this book aims to answer. In particular, we will ask what it was like to be a slave in ancient Greece, and how the experience of slavery in ancient Greece was different from or similar to the experiences of slaves in other times and places. Key questions here include how individuals became enslaved, how they worked and lived, and the nature of their relations with other slaves – as well as their masters. As far as possible, this book will attempt to answer these questions from the point of view of the slaves themselves rather than from that of their masters. This aim, however, raises a crucial methodological challenge since most of our sources derive from slave-owners rather than slaves. This is a challenge that I address in more detail below.

Before proceeding further, however, it is necessary to specify more precisely the chronological and geographical scope of this study. The term "ancient Greece" is a general one that can refer to a broad span of time from the great palace cultures of the Late Bronze Age (c.1500–1200 BCE) to the kingdoms of the successors of Alexander the Great (c.323–30 BCE). Within this time span, ancient Greek culture spread across a huge swath of territory from southern Italy and Sicily to Egypt and the Middle East. While slavery existed in all of these times and places, the focus of this study will be on the society of the ancient Greeks as it existed in the classical period – that is, roughly 500–300 BCE – in the city-states of mainland Greece and the islands and coasts of the Aegean Sea. The reasons for this choice are pragmatic. This is the period and these are the places for which we have the best evidence and therefore for which we can understand the workings of slavery best.

A central question that this book poses is the question of the degree to which slave labor contributed to what we identify today as the culture and society of ancient Greece. This question can be posed in two ways. On the one hand, we might ask to what extent was the labor of slaves crucial to the prosperity that allowed free Greeks the leisure to engage in politics, warfare and the intellectual and artistic pursuits for which they are so famous? In other words, we might ask whether any of the well-known features of ancient Greece would have been possible without the labor of slaves, including Athenian democracy, the Spartan army or the literary and philosophical works of intellectuals such as Sophocles and Aristotle?

Another, equally important way of posing the question is to ask what direct contribution slaves made to the culture that we tend to attribute to the (free, citizen) Greeks? Here we might ask, who painted the vases that sit in our museums as prime examples of the artistic achievement of the Greeks? Who carved the stones that adorn the architectural wonders of the ancient Greeks? Were these products of free labor, the labor of enslaved groups or a combination of both? As we will see, in each of these areas – and even in relation to the literary and intellectual culture of Greece – slaves made a significant direct contribution. In asking these questions, moreover, this book aims not only to bring to the foreground the central role of slaves in almost every sphere of Greek culture and society but also to underscore the ways that the achievements of Greece are inextricably tied to a system of brutal exploitation.

That said, a key argument of this book is that slaves themselves were active in shaping the conditions of their enslavement. While forceful control by others was obviously the most fundamental aspect of the slave condition, this study shows that slaves were very resourceful in exploiting whatever opportunities existed for improving their situation. The most important such opportunity, as we shall see, was the dependence of slave-owners themselves on the slaves' labor and – most crucially – slave-owners' frequent need to acknowledge their slaves' human capacity for rational self-direction (paradoxically, the very thing that the ideology of slave-ownership attempts to deny). This book, therefore, will examine not only the most well-known types of slave resistance such as flight and rebellion, but also the myriad ways that slaves maneuvered to improve their conditions by exploiting some of the tensions and contradictions within the system of slavery itself.

The chapters of this book will address these questions and many others. Like most historical questions worth asking, however, the answers are complex and must be approached by recognizing the diverse experiences of slaves in ancient Greece. Generalizations *can* be made, but they should not be allowed to obscure the startling range of experiences of slaves in the ancient world. This book will therefore tread a fine line between highlighting some fundamental features of slavery in ancient Greece, and giving the reader a sense of the rich diversity of experiences of individual slaves both within particular Greek city-states and across the Greek landscape. Some of this intriguing complexity can been grasped by the following sample of a few aspects of slavery in ancient Greece that may be surprising to some.

- Slavery was not primarily based on notions of racial difference, and the Greeks enslaved their fellow Greeks, along with other ethnic groups.
- Some slaves lived and worked independently from their masters and were able to keep a portion of their earnings. Some of these slaves even accumulated considerable personal fortunes.
- Some slaves were publicly owned by the state and performed important civic roles. For example, publicly owned slaves were responsible for ascertaining the authenticity of coins used in the marketplace and others served as a police force to keep public order.
- Some slaves escaped their masters by seeking asylum in religious sanctuaries and either becoming "slaves of a god" or requesting sale to a new master.

This list of some features of slavery in ancient Greece is not comprehensive, of course, and is certainly not intended to diminish our understanding of the cruelty, violence and inhumanity of slavery. We will have plenty of opportunity to observe the brutality of Greeks towards their slaves in the chapters that follow. What the list does do, however, is to caution us against simplistic readings of slavery in ancient Greece that emphasize its violence without doing justice to the complex relations between slaves and their owners. It is altogether appropriate to feel moral outrage at the hypocrisy of the ancient Greeks, who championed freedom in their political discourse yet denied it to many members of their own communities. Yet, frank acknowledgement of the failings of Greek society must be carefully contextualized and balanced with an examination of all the evidence in its perplexing diversity.

Why Should We Care?

Why should we care about slavery in ancient Greece, beyond intellectual curiosity at best, or mere antiquarianism at worst? In fact, there are two principal reasons why we should strive to understand the role of slavery in ancient Greece.

The first reason is closely related to the point made above about the diversity of the slave experience. Slavery is an important aspect of the history of ancient Greece, and by ignoring it not only do we fail to provide a complete picture of Greek society but we also risk giving an unduly positive (or negative) representation of it. Long gone are the days when scholars heralded the "glory that was Greece," yet ancient Greece still occupies a privileged place in history. What if, as hypothesized above, the great achievements attributed to the free Greeks were underwritten by the brutal exploitation of other human beings? Even if we do not discount these achievements because of their entanglement with an unjust and inhumane system of unfree labor, nevertheless, acknowledgement of slavery puts ancient Greece in a more balanced historical perspective. As Keith Bradley, an historian of ancient Rome, puts it:

> Ancient societies depended on slave labor. It does not follow that what is admirable from the past is any less admirable; it simply means that the price of the admirable – an incalculable degree of human misery and suffering – is given its full historical due.[5]

---

[5] Bradley 1994, 181.

A second reason for studying ancient slavery is that it provides a useful point of comparison and contrast to better-known slave societies such as those arising from the transatlantic slave trade. While there are considerable similarities between ancient slave societies and their more recent counterparts, the differences are as illuminating as the similarities. For example, while in the American South in the nineteenth century, racial ideas were the primary mode of distinguishing free from slave, the Greeks (as we have already mentioned) were in fact rather indiscriminate in subordinating individuals and groups to slavery. Indeed, they frequently enslaved one another – that is their fellow Greeks – and often found their largest sources of slaves among fellow Europeans and peoples inhabiting the broadly defined region of the eastern Mediterranean and Middle East. These peoples were often not visibly different from Greeks in skin color and other physical features, and their submission to slavery, as we shall see, was not primarily justified along racial lines.[6]

The larger point for current purposes is that the example of ancient Greece illustrates the diverse ways that slavery was justified in historical societies, and shows that biologically based racist thought is not a given in slave owning societies. Indeed, although nineteenth-century race-based slavery looms large in modern historical consciousness, it is in fact the exception rather than the norm among historical slave societies. Recognition of the various forms of discrimination that have underwritten slavery in historical societies, moreover, allows us to better understand and acknowledge the shifting contours of discriminatory thought in our own times. As Benjamin Isaac puts it:

> Racism has been with us for a long time and in various cultures, adopting various different shapes. It continues and will continue to be with us. If we recognize only one variety that belongs to a restricted period, we may fail to recognize it as it emerges in altered guise.[7]

In other words, the study of slavery in ancient Greece can contribute to contemporary discussions of racism by illustrating some of the myriad ways that constructions of difference have been used to justify the unequal distribution of power in society. Moreover, as we shall see, the patent artificiality of these ideological structures in ancient Greece, and the ways that they changed over time, are an important reminder of the

---

[6] This is a controversial claim, and the evidence is complex. For further discussion, see below and Chapter 4.
[7] Isaac 2004, 3.

susceptibility of all societies – including our own – to patterns of prejudicial thought. We will return to this point in Chapter 6.

Sources and Methods

A key question in the study of slavery in ancient Greece is one of evidence. Apart from a few sources such as the letter from the slave with which this chapter began, there are no first-person accounts of slavery surviving from ancient Greece. We have no Solomon Northrup or Harriet Jacobs from Greek antiquity.[8] What we *do* have are the material remains and literary works produced by the free-citizen population, and – an important qualification – usually the most elite strata within the citizen population. As we shall see, while evidence of slavery is very scant in the material record, slaves and slavery appear in literature with considerable frequency, confirming the impression of the pervasiveness of slavery in ancient Greece. Yet, as we might expect, neither do these depictions give a complete account of slave life nor are they written from a slave's perspective. How, then, can we study the lives of slaves given that our primary informants are free Greeks who had no particular interest in recording the experiences and perspectives of slaves? A few examples will illustrate the difficulties of grasping the slaves' experience from ancient Greek literature.

In his epic poem *The Odyssey*, Homer provides a portrait of one of Odysseus' few loyal slaves, the swineherd Eumaeus. Although this poem predates classical Greece by a few centuries and therefore reflects a form of slavery that was in some ways distinct from those of classical Greece, the figure of the slave Eumaeus will serve to illustrate the methodological issues at stake in understanding slavery from literary sources.[9] When we first meet Eumaeus in Book 14 of the poem, he is desperately longing for the return of his master from the Trojan War. In a brilliant deployment of dramatic irony, Homer constructs a scene in which Eumaeus bemoans the absence of Odysseus in the presence of Odysseus himself. The latter, of course, is disguised as a wandering beggar in order to avoid the risk of being murdered on his return by the suitors of his wife, who believe him long dead. In this scene, Eumaeus speaks of Odysseus as if he were a loving father, and laments the loss of the benefactions that he believes that Odysseus would have granted him on his return.

---

[8] For these and other first-person accounts of slavery in the modern era, see Gates 1987; Andrews and Gates 2000; Yetman 2002; Northrup 2013.
[9] For a recent discussion of slavery in the Homeric epics (eighth–seventh centuries) that emphasizes continuities with classical Greece, see Lewis 2018, 107–24.

> Indeed, the gods prevented the return of the man
> who would love me kindly and would have given me property,
> the sort that a benevolent master gives his slave
> – a house and a plot of land, and a much-wooed wife –
> who toils a great deal for him.[10]

Contrary to what we might expect, Eumaeus not only seems to accept the necessity of working as a slave for Odysseus, but even praises Odysseus for his generosity and kindness. Later on in the story, Eumaeus makes several general criticisms of his fellow slaves, noting their tendency to shirk work and behave reprehensibly.

> Slaves, when their masters cease to have power,
> No longer want to do their fair share of work,
> For, far-thundering Zeus takes away half of the excellence
> of a man when the day of slavery overtakes him.[11]

It strikes the reader as odd that such criticism of slaves is put in the mouth of a slave, albeit a loyal one. As scholars of ancient slavery, we might ask if such words are a genuine reflection of the voice or perspective of slave, or if they better represent what Homer and his fellow free Greeks wanted to believe about slaves?

These passages are most often interpreted as a reflection of the paternalistic ideology of slave-owners who wished to encourage a submissive attitude among their slaves.[12] This ideology included the notion that slaves not only needed rational direction from their masters in order to live productive and satisfying lives, but that their hard work and loyalty would ultimately be fairly rewarded. On this reading, the passage is a very partial reflection of the system by which slaves were controlled. As we shall see in Chapter 5, although a system of rewards was utilized by slave-owners to incentivize hard work among their slaves, it existed alongside a system of deprivation and punishment that played an equal or perhaps even greater role in extracting labor from slaves. On this interpretation, Eumaeus is a character thoroughly shaped by the needs of Homer's slave-owning audience, and certainly not a reflection of the perspectives of real slaves concerning the conditions of their servitude.

On the other hand, it is possible, of course, that Homer's character Eumaeus was created to appear historically plausible and thus recognizable to Homer's audience. Accordingly, we might conclude that Eumaeus is representative of a certain group of hardworking and loyal slaves who

---

[10] 14.61–65. [11] 17.320–23. See below n.23. [12] See, for example, Thalmann 1998, 13–107.

willingly accepted their slavery in return for the promise of concrete rewards. Furthermore, one could even detect an attempt, in Eumaeus' first speech, to shape the institution of slavery in ways that were beneficial to slaves. By articulating an ideal image of a benevolent master, while not questioning his subordinate status, the character of Eumaeus encourages his master to provide benefits that come very close to the perquisites usually reserved for the free – a family, house and land of their own. Furthermore, by suggesting that this treatment is the proper way that a master should reward a loyal slave, Eumaeus' character may reflect the strategies of actual slaves to shape the system of rewards by which, at least in part, they were controlled.[13] If this interpretation is correct, then, we see in this passage an example of the slave agency that I highlighted as a theme of this book.

But which of these two interpretations of the passage is more plausible? Let's look at a few more examples before answering. At the beginning of Euripides' tragic play *Medea* of 431 BCE, the male slave-tutor of Medea's children addresses Medea's slave-nurse as "the possession of my mistress" and asks the slave-nurse why she is so upset. The nurse responds by saying that "good slaves are disturbed by the misfortunes of their masters and feel it in their hearts."[14] The Greek word for "possession," *ktema*, is a term that usually denotes movable property – furniture, money, livestock and, of course, slaves.[15] We might wonder, nevertheless, whether an actual slave – rather than a slave character in a play written by and for free Greeks – would address another slave with such an impersonal and dehumanizing form of address? Did some slaves openly accept and affirm their status as property or does this word choice express the slave-owners' perspective on slaves as mere pieces of property? As we shall see in more detail shortly, Aristotle, a free and leisured Greek intellectual, provides perhaps the most blunt expression of this conceptualization of slaves as property when he classifies slaves as "living tools" (ὄργανα ἔμψυχα) and "animate property" (κτῆμα ἔμψυχον).

Returning to Euripides' play, we might further question the nurse's dictum that "good slaves" sympathize with the sufferings of their masters. Again, we must ask whether this saying expresses a slave's perspective on slaves or only what slave-owners wished to believe about (or encourage in) their slaves? Alternatively, we might speculate that both the form of address

---

[13] For the shaping of slavery to create a "living space" for slaves, in ancient Greece and modern slave-owning societies, see Forsdyke 2012, 37–89; Bergad 2007, 165–201; and Chapter 5.
[14] Euripides, *Medea* 49–55. See also Plato's *Laws* (776–77) where contrasting depictions of slaves are presented – slaves as loyal and slaves as deficient in rationality and moral character.
[15] Isaeus 5.43.

and the dictum represent the ways that actual slaves might address one another, *but only as they would speak in the presence of slave-owners themselves*. That is to say, this form of speech represents what the political scientist James Scott calls the "public transcript" – namely, the ways that subordinate individuals speak in the presence of their superiors in order to put on display their submission to the existing power structure.[16] When slaves speak among themselves, Scott posits, they express a much more critical attitude towards their masters and the institution of slavery. While there are no free characters on the stage when the two slaves speak to one another in the play, it is reasonable to consider the audience of free Greeks watching the play as the target of this form of subordinate speech. On this interpretation, then, the slave-tutor and slave-nurse provide a window on to a particular slave strategy – the performed deference that was aimed at securing rewards for slaves from masters.

Whichever interpretation we choose, we are once again confronted with the problem of literary evidence that is produced by and for free Greeks. How are we to decide which, if any, of this material is realistic and which is a product of the slave-owners' fantasies, desires and ideological needs?

A final example comes from the Athenian comic playwright Menander. In his fourth-century play *Aspis*, or "The Shield," Menander depicts a loyal slave named Daos. When Smikrines, a free character, tries to solicit the slave Daos' help in his scheme to marry his niece – who is due an inheritance of land – Daos demurs in the following way:

> Smikrines, this saying appears to me
> To be thoroughly worth meditating upon:
> "Know who you are!" Permit me to obey it
> and refer to me those matters which are
> appropriate for a good slave.

Daos then lists the knowledge that is appropriate for a slave, and again refuses to play a role in matters that are above his pay grade. These matters include marriages and their resulting inheritances of land and other goods.

> I am able to demonstrate that the seals are on the goods,
> and show you the contracts my master made
> with some men while abroad. These things, if someone
> should command me, I will expound them one by one:
> where they were made, how, and with what witnesses.
> Concerning a piece of land, Smikrines, or, by Zeus, an heiress,

---

[16] Scott 1990. For further discussion of Scott's ideas, see Chapter 5.

> And marriages and kin affairs and disputes – don't involve Daos.
> You yourself engage in the matters of free men
> for whom such matters are appropriate.[17]

Significantly, Daos acknowledges that slaves had considerable knowledge of their masters' business affairs. For example, Daos claims precise knowledge of the contents of his master's property. Moreover, he claims that he has accurate knowledge of all aspects of his master's foreign business deals: "where they were made, how and with what witnesses." This representation of the role of slaves in the financial transactions of free Greek men accords well with a variety of other evidence, as we shall discuss in Chapter 3, and seems to capture one aspect of the reality of master-slave relations.

On the other hand, Daos' repudiation of any role in the marriage schemes of his master is not so easy to interpret, and an understanding of the literary context and particularly, the nature of ancient comedy is needed to grasp the scene's significance for interpreting Greek slavery. As in many Greek comedies, there is a reversal of the normative hierarchy of slave and master. Smikrines has asked his nephew's slave for help in matters of marriage and inheritance – matters that were normally considered the prerogative of the free alone. Furthermore, while Smikrines is driven by greed to transgress the norms of master-slave relations, Daos, the slave, is principled and refuses to become involved in matters that are not within his sphere of competence according to Greek slave-owners' own ideology.

In observing these reversals, we might question whether a real slave would be so eager to reinforce an ideology that kept him firmly in a subordinate position. Or, is it possible that this comic reversal aims to reinforce the normative order precisely by reversing it in absurd ways? The ridiculousness of the whole scene is particularly underlined by the depiction of the slave rebuking a free Greek by deploying a celebrated piece of Greek wisdom. Indeed, the saying – "Know who you are" – was inscribed on the temple of Apollo at Delphi, an oracular shrine that served as the religious center of the Greek world.

The interpretative dilemmas of this play are only increased in the subsequent lines in which Daos both signals his rejection of the morality of free Greeks, and affirms (albeit sarcastically) the superior rationality of the free.

> I am a Phrygian. Much of your "good" morality
> appalls me and vice versa.

---

[17] Lines 189–204.

> Why worry about my opinions? You are
> more rational than I, of course.[18]

In this passage, we seem to get a slave's perspective on the cultural differences between his master and himself. Yet in the next line, Daos affirms his acceptance of his own subordination by acknowledging the master's greater claim to the supreme human quality of rationality. Or, is this another example of Scott's "public transcript" – namely, the way subordinates speak in the presence of their superiors? Once again, we are faced with the difficulties of deciding whether the depiction of slavery in Greek literature reflects slave-owners' perceptions or projections, or, in fact, captures some aspects of the actual lived experience of slaves in ancient Greece.

The three examples that we have just analyzed from three different texts – Homer's *Odyssey*, Euripides' *Medea* and Menander's *Aspis* – illustrate the general problem and challenge of the study of ancient slavery.[19] Epic poetry, tragedy, comedy and other genres of Greek literature all feature slaves, but none aims primarily to explain the origins, roles and experiences of slaves per se, let alone represent slavery from the slaves' perspective. We are on slightly better ground with philosophical and economic treatises of authors such as Plato and Xenophon, since these works sometimes discuss the role of slavery in society and the economy. But even so, this evidence is written from a particular perspective (elite, free, male) and usually forms part of an ideological or philosophical agenda, rather than an historical one.

Furthermore, the scant evidence of archaeology provides only meager insight into the living conditions of slaves.[20] There are no clearly identifiable slave quarters or workshops, since slaves often lived and worked in rooms that were used interchangeably with the free. With a few exceptions, the closest we come to the voice of a slave in the archaeological record is the lead letter with which this chapter began. The funeral monuments of skilled slaves and ex-slaves augment this meager record since these sometimes recorded the ethnic identity and occupations of the deceased.[21] Vase painting and the sculptural arts sometimes depict figures that might be slaves, but identification is often problematic, since it is not always easy to distinguish between free Greek and slave by dress, occupation, ethnicity or race.[22]

---

[18] Lines 206–209. [19] McKeown (2007) is centrally concerned with this question.
[20] Thompson 2003; Morris 1998, 2011; Morris and Papadopoulos 2005.
[21] Bäbler 1998, especially #35, #69; Taylor 2015; Hunt 2015; and see Chapter 4.
[22] Himmelmann 1971; Wiedemann and Gardner 2002; Lewis 2002, 79; Osborne 2011, 107–8, 133–53; Wrenhaven 2012, 75–89; and Chapter 4 . Osborne, however, concludes that slave status was something that was sometimes "important to show" and that ethnic markers were the primary

With these meager or indirect pieces of evidence, what options remain for the historian interested in understanding the experience of slaves in ancient Greece?

First of all, the available evidence, though often indirect, is still valuable. Most obviously, the views of slave-owners themselves are revealed through their representations of slaves. By understanding how slave-owners viewed – or wished to view – their slaves, we can better see how slave-owners' ideological needs (to maintain and justify the slave system) distort the actual experience of slavery. For example, a constant theme in Greek literature is that slaves are foolish and lazy and therefore need to be guided and disciplined in order to live productive lives. This theme runs throughout Greek literature from Homer's *Odyssey*, as we have just seen, to Aristotle's notorious theory of natural slavery (discussed below) according to which slaves lack reason and are better off if their labor is subject to the rational direction of a free citizen male.[23]

If we set aside the obvious justificatory aim behind the frequent representation of slaves as foolish and lazy, however, we might argue, as one scholar has done, that this portrait of slaves reflects slave resistance to their masters, rather than their actual inability to perform tasks without direction.[24] As we know from comparative evidence from countries like Brazil, Cuba and the United States, slaves often resisted their masters by purposely breaking tools, working slowly and otherwise impeding the work that they were forced to perform.[25] In other words, the representation of slaves as foolish and lazy does reflect some aspects of the behaviors of slaves, but does not accurately capture the reasons for these behaviors. This is just one example of how careful consideration of the ideological context of representations of slaves in Greek literature can reveal the experiences of slavery from the slaves' perspective. It also shows how comparative evidence from more recent and better-documented slave-owning societies can shed light on the partial evidence that we have for slavery in ancient Greece.

---

indication of slave status (2011, 153). As we shall see further in Chapter 4, ethnic markers were sometimes used in the visual arts and literature to indicate slave status, despite the practice of enslaving both Greeks and non-Greeks.

[23] Homer, *Odyssey* 17.323 (cited above): ἥμισυ γάρ τ' ἀρετῆς ἀποαίνυται εὐρύοπα Ζεὺς ἀνέρος, εὖτ' ἄν μιν κατὰ δούλιον ἦμαρ ἕλῃσιν. Plato in *Laws* (777a) quotes this line with a few changes of vocabulary: ἥμισυ γάρ τε τοῦ νόου, φησίν, ἀπαμείρεται εὐρύοπα Ζεὺς ἀνδρῶν, οὓς ἂν δὴ κατὰ δούλιον ἦμαρ ἕλῃσι ("Zeus deprives men of half their sense (rationality: νόος) when the day of slavery takes them"). Earlier in *Laws*, Plato states: "there can be neither equality nor friendship between masters and slaves, since they are not equal with regards to virtue (ἀρετή)" (756e–57). Nevertheless, Plato gives contradictory views of slaves in *Laws* and recognizes the tensions between different views of slavery (see below).

[24] McKeown 2010, 167.   [25] Bergad 2007, 166; and Chapter 5.

A further source of information on slavery in ancient Greece is inscriptions – that is, writings engraved on stone and sometimes on other hard surfaces. This type of evidence has some of the same biases as literary sources in so far as inscriptions were often composed by and for the free male citizen population. For example, we have lists of property – including slaves – confiscated from citizens who had committed crimes. Similarly, we have lists of payments to skilled craftsmen – including slave-craftsmen – who worked on various public building projects, as well as lists of rowers – including slave-rowers – in the navy.[26] Despite the primary purpose of these documents to provide a public record of the judicial, civic and military activities of the state – that is, the community of free male citizens – these texts nevertheless reveal key facts about slaves. For example, these public documents reveal slave names, slave occupations and slave sale prices, not to mention the fact of slave labor in some key areas of the economy and civic life.

While these public records reveal a lot about slaves in one particular Greek city-state – namely, Athens – other types of public inscriptions come from a variety of Greek communities and reveal aspects of slave experience throughout Greece. For example, slaves freed at religious sanctuaries and theaters sometimes left a permanent record of their liberation. The best-known records of this type are a set of over one thousand inscriptions from the temple of Apollo at Delphi, relating to the grant of freedom to some thirteen hundred slaves.[27] Although these inscriptions are later in date than the primary period under consideration in this book (they date between 201 BCE and c.100 CE), they are nevertheless an invaluable source of information for how some slaves secured their freedom. Furthermore, these inscriptions may be supplemented by records from other parts of Greece which date anywhere from the sixth to the fourth century BCE. Among these records is a set of inscriptions from fourth-century Athens recording the dedication of silver bowls to Athena by emancipated slaves.[28]

---

[26] Naval lists recording names of slaves as well as free rowers: *IG* i³.1032; Erechtheion building accounts, including slave stonemasons: *IG* i³.474–79; lists of confiscated property, including slaves and their sale prices: *IG* i³.421–30. For discussion, see Chapter 3.

[27] Delphic manumission lists: *SGDI* 1689, 1772, 1779, 1804, 1878, 1909, 2317 discussed by Zelnick-Abramowitz (2005); see also the Thessalian manumission documents dating to the second century BCE (Zelnick-Abramowitz 2013).

[28] See, for example, the sixth-century list of freed slaves from Chios (Robert 1938, 118–26); the inscriptions recording freedom of slaves at Tainaron dating from the fifth century (*IG* v².1228–32); and finally the dedications of silver bowls by slaves at Athens dating to the last third of the fourth century (*IG* ii².1553–78). There are also inscriptions of manumissions in Boeotia, with dates beginning in the fourth century (*IG* vii.3081, 3204, 3322).

In the Peloponnesian city of Epidaurus, an inscription provides the names of slaves who were declared free in the theater.[29] As already mentioned, we have tombstones erected for slaves or recently liberated slaves, who sometimes mention their profession, ethnic origin and other personal qualities.[30] Even monuments erected by free men can sometimes attest to slave experiences. For example, a tombstone for an ex-slave slave-dealer depicts slaves linked by neck chains, and other funeral monuments depict a master alongside his slaves (Fig. 1.3).[31]

By combining different types of evidence (literary, epigraphical, archaeological), moreover, one can often make more of the evidence than would be possible by relying on one type alone. For example, sometimes the inscriptional evidence provides confirmation of the testimony of literature, or provides details of aspects of slavery that we know of only in general terms from literature. On other occasions, the inscriptional evidence can even correct the representations of slavery in the literary sources. This is not to say that inscriptions are factual "documents," or that Greek literature is merely literary or ideological fiction. Inscriptions, just as literature, are a subjective representation of reality, and literature does sometimes represent slavery in historically realistic ways. Careful consideration of all the evidence, however, can provide a more solid base for reconstructing aspects of slavery than reliance on one type of evidence alone.

Beyond the use of all types of ancient evidence, a final approach to understanding slavery in ancient Greece is to compare and contrast the evidence for ancient slavery with that from other, often better attested, slave societies. Comparison with societies such as ancient Rome, and nineteenth-century Brazil, the Caribbean and the Southern United States can reveal many illuminating similarities and differences. Furthermore, such comparisons can help us understand what was distinctive about slavery in ancient Greece, and what was more typical of slave-owning societies. For example, comparison with these other societies shows that Greece was fairly typical of slave societies in terms of the infrequency of slave rebellions.[32] In Greece, as in most slave-owning societies except for

---

[29] *IG* iv².353–66.
[30] For example, a tombstone of a slave or ex-slave who worked in mining (*IG* ii².10051; cf. Lauffer 1979; Braund 2011, 131–33; Bäbler 1998; Hunt 2015; and Chapter 3).
[31] See Duchêne (1986, Figure 1) for a photograph of the original monument, which was destroyed in World War II; for slaves depicted on funeral monuments of their masters, see Wrenhaven 2012, 101–9.
[32] Cartledge 1985; and Chapter 5.

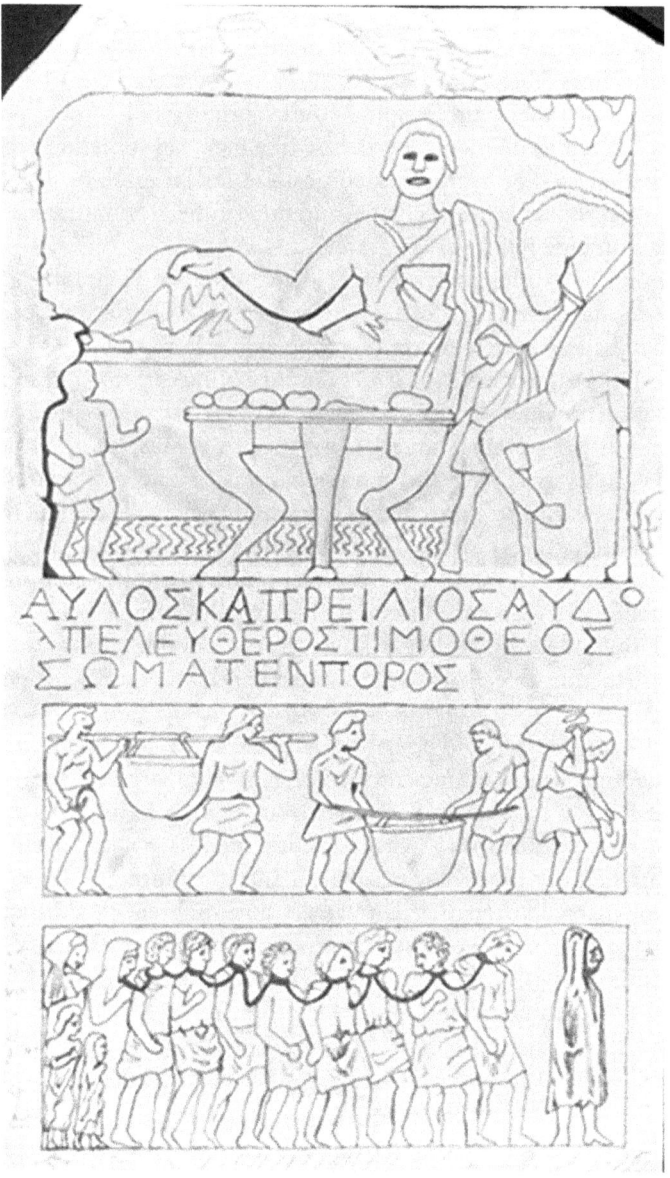

Fig. 1.3 Tombstone of Aulos Kapreilios Timotheos, a slave-trader. Aulos is depicted on the upper register, while scenes from his profession – including a group of slaves being transported – appear in the lower registers. For a discussion and close-up image of the slaves, see Chapter 2 and Fig. 2.7. (Line drawing by Sophie Forsdyke Larsen.)

the Caribbean, conditions were not conducive to major slave rebellions.[33] Instead, slaves resorted to less risky forms of resistance, including working slowly, breaking tools and otherwise thwarting the will of their masters.[34] By contrast, ancient Greece, along with Rome, seems to be distinctive in permitting and even encouraging literacy and numeracy in its slave population. For example, some slaves served as archivists, accountants and bankers, and, as we saw in the case of the comic Daos above, managed the financial affairs of their owners.

One method which has been used to study more recent slave-owning societies is not possible for ancient Greece – namely, the quantitative, or, as it is known among scholars of slavery in the American South, the "cliometric" method.[35] This approach, introduced in the 1970s, attempts to study slavery using the methods of formal economics rather than "softer" sociological and historical methods. By attempting to quantify aspects of slavery such as the productivity of slaves, scholars employing this method challenge orthodox interpretations of slavery in the American South as an inefficient system of labor that would have fallen out of favor even without the Civil War. While the particular conclusions of this "quantitative turn" in slave studies are controversial, and indeed rejected by many scholars today, the attempt to establish the basic parameters of a system of slavery in terms of numbers could potentially be illuminating.[36] Unfortunately, however, quantitative analysis of slavery in ancient Greece is next to impossible for lack of sufficient data.[37] We do not have accurate population figures for slaves, let alone productivity figures.[38] Even if we had reliable numbers for economic output, it would be hard to determine which portion of that output was generated by slaves, since, as we shall see, slaves and free persons often labored alongside one another in ancient Greece.

---

[33] Genovese 1979; and Chapter 5. [34] Hodkinson and Geary 2012; and Chapter 5.
[35] Fogel and Engerman 1974.
[36] For recent discussion of the "quantitative turn," the productivity of slave labor, and its connections to the rise of capitalism, see, for example, Parry (2016) discussing the debate arising from Baptist (2014).
[37] Some historians have attempted to determine "ballpark" figures. See, for example, Scheidel's attempt to calculate the numbers of Spartan helots based on "parametric models of production and consumption" (Scheidel 2003a, 240).
[38] A few population figures for slaves are recorded in ancient Greek literature, but these seem so obviously inaccurate that they give little ground for confidence. For example, one ancient Greek source claims that there were 460,000 slaves in Corinth, another that there were 470,000 slaves in Aegina, and another that there were 400,000 slaves in Athens c.310 BCE (Athenaeus, *Learned Banqueters* 272b–c). These figures are far too high, since they result in impossible population densities in these city-states (Fisher 1993, 34). For discussion of numbers of slaves, see Chapter 2.

What Is Slavery?

The ancient Greeks have not, for the most part, provided modern scholars with neat definitions of the various groups in their communities. The Greeks "lived" their social categories, rather than theorized about them (Aristotle and a few other intellectuals are exceptions). Modern historians, however, generally require that fundamental concepts be clearly defined as part of historical analysis. The historian is therefore faced with the daunting task of trying to reconstruct the underlying concepts behind a variety of different types of evidence concerning slavery in ancient Greece.

Modern Definitions and Debates

One starting point is to look at modern definitions and determine how far they apply to the ancient world. Modern definitions of slavery, however, have themselves been subject to debate and evolution. While originally based on ancient Roman legal concepts of slavery – that is, of legal ownership of one person by another – a strong movement of legal scholars, historians and journalists has been lobbying to broaden the definition of slavery to include the domination by force of one person by another, whether or not legal ownership is involved. This expansion of the definition of slavery is a result of the recognition of the continued existence of slave-like conditions despite the abolition of legal slavery throughout the modern world.

Modern definitions of slavery begin with the League of Nations Slavery Convention of 1926. Article 1 (1) of the convention defined slavery as

> The status or condition of a person over whom any or all of the powers attaching to the right of ownership are exercised.

While it is clear that the framers of the convention had the genuine right of legal ownership in mind, it soon became a matter of debate as to whether actual legal ownership was required to constitute slavery or simply the exercise of "the powers attaching to the right of ownership" without any legal ownership.[39] At stake was the question of whether practices analogous to slavery where no legal ownership was involved – such as forced labor, debt bondage and servile forms of marriage – could be classified as slavery and hence regulated by the convention.

---

[39] Allain 2012.

What Is Slavery?

This question was partially resolved in 1956 when the United Nations enacted the Supplementary Convention on the Abolition of Slavery, the Slave Trade, and Institutions and Practices Similar to Slavery. This resolution maintained the definition of slavery from the 1926 convention, but added other forms of "servitude" – debt bondage, serfdom, servile forms of marriage and the exploitation of children and adolescents – as institutions and practices so similar to slavery that they were to be subject to similar legal regulation by international law. Since 1956, moreover, the United Nations has enacted further resolutions; for example, on forms of child labor (1989) and child prostitution (2000) and trafficking in persons (2000) that lead to enslavement.[40]

As part of the process that led to the 1956 supplementary convention, the "powers attaching to the right of ownership" were defined for the first time and provided criteria for distinguishing between slavery and the "lesser servitudes" regulated in the supplementary convention and the subsequent resolutions. These powers included the right to purchase, use and dispose of a person, as well as the ownership of the products of the labor of the individual "without any compensation commensurate to the value of the labour." Further criteria included the permanence of servile status (i.e., the individual subject to it cannot terminate it by his own will) and the transmission of servile status to the descendants of an individual having such a status.[41]

This action on the international legal stage has been accompanied by calls by scholars, activists and journalists to recognize a broader array of forms of exploitation as slavery. The most influential reconceptualization of slavery in scholarship has been that of the Harvard historical sociologist Orlando Patterson. Patterson's 1982 book *Slavery and Social Death* was based on a comparative study of slavery in historical societies ranging from ancient Mesopotamia to the slave systems of the modern Atlantic. Patterson's goal was "to define and explore empirically ... the nature and inner dynamics of slavery and the institutional patterns that supported it."[42] The definition of slavery that emerged from this comparative sociological analysis is based on three features: violence, natal alienation and dishonor. For Patterson, "slavery is the permanent, violent domination of natally alienated and generally dishonored persons."[43] Legal ownership –

---

[40] UN General Assembly, Resolution 44/25, Convention on the Rights of the Child, A/RES/44/25 (November 20, 1989); Resolution 54/263, Optional Protocols to the Convention on the Rights of the Child, A/RES/54/263 (May 25, 2000); Resolution 55/25, UN Convention Against Transnational Organized Crime, A/RES/55/25 (November 15, 2000).

[41] Allain 2012, 208–9.   [42] Patterson 1982, ix.   [43] Patterson 1982, 13.

rather than being the essence of slavery – is, according to Patterson, simply one of the cultural mechanisms through which slave-owners disguised the violence of slavery, and tried to legitimize or naturalize its existence.

Along with the violence at the core of slavery, Patterson pointed to the ways that slave-owners denied slaves a social identity by destroying their ties to their birth families and by not allowing any social or legal recognition of their relationship to ancestors and descendants. This "natal alienation" was accomplished in the first instance by the removal of the slave from his or her birth family, culture or country, and was also achieved by the renaming of the slave and the denial of legal protections regarding their person or property. Patterson's focus on dishonor is based on the observation not only that slaves lack honor in the societies in which they are held but, more strikingly, that slaves played a vital role in conferring honor upon their owners. In many slave-owning societies, Patterson noted, the struggle for prestige among the free requires a supply of honor-conferring dishonored peoples – that is, slaves. The state of total dishonor of slaves in these societies, therefore, played a crucial role in defining the honor of the free. For Patterson, then, slavery entails social death for the slave, and the condition of the slave is analogous to death. Indeed, it is a sort of "living death."

Similarly, Kevin Bales, a scholar and activist against modern forms of slavery, argues in his 1999 book *Disposable People: New Slavery in the Global Economy* that modern slaves include all those who are "held against their will for the purposes of exploitation." As Bales notes, the abolition of slavery entailing the legal ownership of one person by another has meant that in all but a few countries, slavery in the traditional sense no longer exists.[44] Yet, Bales maintains that there are over 27 million slaves in the world today, if we count all those who "are held by violence or the threat of violence for economic exploitation."[45] For Bales, then, it is the use of violence and the lack of free will that defines the slave.

Journalists have also begun to call for "a new abolitionist movement against twenty-first-century slavery."[46] A New York Times article from 2009, for example, describes the trafficking of girls into brothels in Thailand under the title "If This Isn't Slavery, What Is?"[47] The article

---

[44] According to Bales (1999, 15, 19, 80–120), "old slavery" (i.e., chattel slavery) still exists today in northern and western Africa, (e.g., Mauritania) and some Arab countries. While the ownership of one person by another has been abolished legally in countries such as Mauritania, it nevertheless flourishes due to a lack of enforcement.
[45] Bales 1999, 280.
[46] Nicolas D. Kristoff, *New York Times*, January 4, 2009. Cf. Allain 2012; and Bales 1999.
[47] Nicolas D. Kristoff, *New York Times*, January 4, 2009.

describes in horrific detail how young girls are kidnapped and sold to brothels in Phnom Penh, where they are beaten, tortured, confined and forced to have sex with customers. Another article from 2013 entitled "Indentured Servitude in the Persian Gulf" describes the plight of foreign workers from the Philippines who come to countries such as Qatar with the belief that they have a contract to work for wages, only to find that their employers have almost total control over them. These workers are often forced to labor seven days a week, with little or no wages, and no ability to change or leave their jobs without their employers' permission.[48] Instances of "new slavery," furthermore, are not confined to developing nations: individuals who are held by violence and whose labor is exploited have been found, for example, in the cities and farms of Western Europe and the United States.[49]

The existence of forms of unfree labor that are slavery in everything but legal ownership has led some scholars and activists to call for further revision of the legal definitions of slavery.[50] For example, a group of scholars and activists who call themselves the Research Network on the Legal Parameters of Slavery have issued guidelines for the revision of international laws on slavery. Included in this manifesto is a call to recognize as slavery any form of possession of another person in ways that result in "control over a person in such a way to significantly deprive that person of his or her individual liberty," regardless of whether "the state supports a property right in respect of persons."[51] Furthermore, the Research Network calls on the international community to put emphasis on whether the "substance" of slavery exists – namely, whether "the powers attaching to the right of ownership" are exercised – rather than the particular "form" of slavery or slave-like institutions, whether debt bondage, serfdom, child labor, or slave-like marriage practices.

Ancient Greek Conceptions and Debates

It is against the backdrop of the ongoing debate about the nature of slavery that we must approach slavery in ancient Greece. For, on the one hand, the idea of slaves as property is well attested in ancient Greece, and is further developed as a legal concept under the Romans. On the other hand, however, the new perspectives raised by scholars about the fundamental nature of slavery as one of violent domination seem also relevant to

---

[48] Richard Morin, *New York Times*, April 14, 2013. [49] Bales 1999, 22; Scott 2012.
[50] Allain 2012. [51] Research Network on the Legal Parameters of Slavery 2012, 2.

understanding and explaining the practice of slavery in ancient Greece, not least because many slaves were produced through conquest in war. Furthermore, slave-like practices, including debt bondage, serfdom and child labor certainly existed in ancient Greece, and hence the question arises of defining slavery, just as it does in the modern world.

It is conventional to start with Aristotle, since, as a philosopher known for his systematic analyses of aspects of Greek culture, he provides reasonably clear and convenient categories. Yet Aristotle's strength – the way that his classifications help to make sense of the messy empirical data of the behavior of individuals and states – is also his weakness: he imposes order on material that is not necessarily so clear and ordered in actual lived experience. Perhaps even more problematic is the fact that Aristotle looks at slavery from the perspective of a wealthy slave-owner. Indeed, Aristotle moved in the highest social circles of ancient Greece. His father was a court physician for Amyntas III, the grandfather of Alexander the Great, and Aristotle himself was sent to Athens – the cultural and intellectual center of ancient Greece – to study at the Academy of Plato. Highlights of his adult life included his position as tutor of Alexander the Great amidst the wealth of the Macedonian court, and the foundation of his own school of philosophy in Athens.[52] While we have little reliable information about his private life, it is highly likely, as a Roman-era Greek source claims, that he owned slaves, and that his leisured lifestyle was made possible at least in part by the exploitation of slaves.[53]

It is therefore vital at the outset that we recognize that Aristotle's status results in emphasis on particular concerns related to slavery – for example, his classification of slavery as a feature of property rights – and neglect of other aspects – for example, the violence that frequently sustained the relationship between master and slave. Indeed, to read Aristotle is almost to forget that many slaves were beaten and tortured, and to think that slaves always gratefully accepted their subordinate status. We only have to look at other sources, however, to rectify this oversight. The beating of a slave was always good for a laugh in Greek comedy, and Plato himself remarks that masters often morally degrade their slaves by subjecting them to constant whippings as if they were animals.[54]

Furthermore, Aristotle's account of slavery – one of the longest and most notorious discussions of slavery surviving from antiquity – is, like most of

---

[52] For Aristotle's biography, see Natali 2013. [53] Diogenes Laertius 5.13–14.
[54] For comedy, see, for example., Aristophanes, *Wasps* 3, 1292–95, *Peace* 747; cf. Plato, *Laws* 777a–b. For further discussion, see Chapter 5.

our evidence for slavery, not primarily concerned with slavery. Slavery comes up almost inadvertently, as it often does in Greek literature, as necessary only for the understanding of the author's real concern, which, in Aristotle's case, is the question of the best life for human beings. According to Aristotle, various forms of association are required to achieve the good life, starting from the association of man and woman that allows for the perpetuation of life itself and ending with the political formation of the city-state (*polis*) in which alone the truly good life is possible.

Since the city-state is the final form of association and the one in which the highest good is achieved, it is this form of association that is the goal and end (*telos*) of all other associations. Crucially for Aristotle, this final form of association and all the other subordinate associations that precede its formation exist "by nature;" that is, are natural formations tending towards the highest human goal – namely, the good life. Accordingly, man naturally strives to form the political association of the city-state and consequently is a "political animal" by nature. For Aristotle, the relationship of the subordinate forms of association to the highest form of association is like the relationship between a part of the body, such as a foot or hand, and the whole body. Just as in the case of a foot or hand, the subordinate associations cannot function properly except in relation to the whole association that is the city-state.

How does slavery fit into this analysis? The master-slave relationship is one of the subordinate forms of association that is deemed necessary for the formation of the city-state. Thus we might acknowledge from the outset that, at least for Aristotle, Greek civilization in its highest form (the city-state) cannot exist without slavery. Furthermore, it turns out that for Aristotle not all men are naturally suited to full participation in this highest form of association. Rather, some men are possessed of the capacity for rule, while others are naturally suited to be ruled. The difference, for Aristotle, lies in the quality of the mind or soul as opposed to the qualities of the body:

> For the one who has the ability to foresee things with his mind is naturally ruler and naturally master, and the one who can do things with his body is naturally subject and slave.[55]

Those who are by nature suited to do things with their bodies, therefore, partake of the one of the subsidiary associations – namely, the master-slave relationship – that contributes to the highest form of association – namely,

---

[55] Aristotle, *Politics* 1252a33–34.

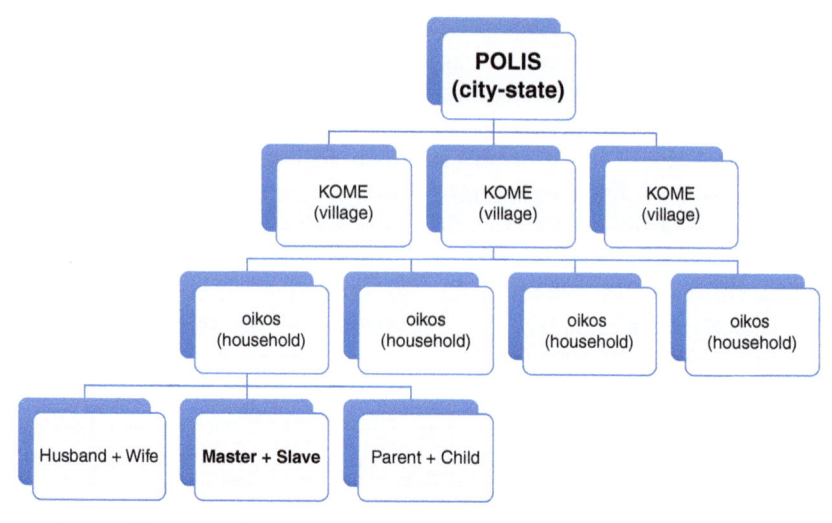

Fig. 1.4 Hierarchy of associations comprised by the city-state (*polis*), according to Aristotle.

the city-state. The hierarchy of associations can be mapped according to the diagram in Figure 1.4.

The master-slave partnership is therefore a key component of the association of the household, alongside the associations of husband and wife, and parent and child. In this analytical framework, then, the slave is conceptualized *as a person* partaking of a *human relationship* with his master, albeit an unequal one. This classification is reflected in a common Greek term for a slave, *oiketes* (οἰκέτης), or "member of the household (οἶκος)."[56]

At this point, however, Aristotle shifts his analytical frame slightly to focus on the art of household management, *oikonomia* (οἰκονομία) – the ancient word that became the modern term for "economics." Aristotle's particular concern is the production of material goods that are needed for life. In this analytical framework, slaves are classified as part of the property of the household that is used for producing goods.

> Of tools, some are inanimate, and others are animate. For example, for a helmsman, the rudder is an inanimate tool, while the lookout man is an animate tool ... so also property is a tool for the purpose of living, and

[56] Morrow 1939, 25.

property is a collection of tools, and the slave is an animate piece of property.[57]

In equating a slave to a tool (ὄργανον) and a piece of property (κτῆμα) analogous to the inanimate possessions of a master, Aristotle here dehumanizes the slave and conceptualizes him as an object capable of being possessed and put to use by another human being. Indeed, it is the classification of the slave as the object of ownership that allows Aristotle to draw the sharpest distinction between free men and slaves.

> The term "article of property" is used in the same way as the term "part." For a part not only is part of something else, but also completely belongs to that other thing. It is the same with an article of property. Therefore, a master is the master of a slave alone, and does not belong to the slave. A slave, on the other hand, is not only the slave of a master but also completely belongs to the master.[58]

Aristotle continues in the same vein,

> From these considerations it is clear what the nature of a slave is and what his essential quality is. For the human being who is a slave by nature is a human being who belongs not to himself by nature, but to another man. A human being belongs to another man whenever he is an article of property, although a human being.[59]

Interestingly, Aristotle's definition focuses on complete possession of the slave by the master. Aristotle does not, however, put forth any legal standards of ownership, and it is reasonable to assume that he would accept as slavery any situation in which a master had possession and therefore control over another human being. This interpretation is strengthened by consideration of Aristotle's description of the attributes of a free man in another treatise, *Rhetoric*. Here Aristotle defines a free man in part by contrast to the situation of a slave. According to Aristotle, a free man is "one who does not live in the service of another."[60] Aristotle's focus on "service" rather than "ownership" in this passage is suggestive for modern attempts, discussed above, to redefine slavery in terms of control rather than legal ownership.

Stepping back from this discussion, we can therefore see that Aristotle classifies slaves both *as persons* partaking of one of the human associations that make up the association of the city-state, and *as objects* possessed by free men in order to make the good life possible. While Aristotle justifies

---

[57] Aristotle, *Politics* 1253b29. [58] Aristotle, *Politics* 1254a9. [59] Aristotle, *Politics* 1254a14.
[60] Aristotle, *Rhetoric* 1367a27: ἐλευθέρου γὰρ τὸ μὴ πρὸς ἄλλον ζῆν.

this theoretical scheme through his goal of discovering the foundations of the best possible life for mankind, it is equally true that these foundations include – indeed require – the denial of the best possible life to *all* of mankind. Aristotle meets this objection with an argument that was to be reutilized again and again by slaveholders in later ages. According to this argument, slaves actually benefit by being governed by the free, just as the body is governed by the mind.

> Authority and subordination are not only necessary, but also expedient ... It is clear that it is natural and expedient for the body to be governed by the soul, and for the emotional part to be governed by the mind and the part possessing reason. For it is harmful for the two to be equal or to be opposed to one another. And it is the same for man in relation to the other animals ... It is better for all these animals to be ruled by man, for thus security is achieved. And again, men are by nature the stronger and women the weaker and therefore men are the rulers and women are subjects. Furthermore, as some men differ from one another in as much as the soul differs from the body, and man from beast ... these men are slaves by nature. For these men, it is better to be governed by this kind of authority, in as much as it is advantageous to the subjects already mentioned.[61]

The reason that slavery is advantageous to some human beings, as Aristotle goes on to elaborate, is that they lack the capacity for rational judgment, although (conveniently) they can apprehend the rational judgments of others and therefore obey the rational command of their masters.[62] While slaves' minds are ill-suited to rule, however, their bodies are (again conveniently) designed by nature to provide the necessities of life. Whereas a free man, according to Aristotle, has an erect body unsuited to manual labor, the slave's body is strong and capable of productive use .

Here, we see Aristotle naturalizing the enslavement of some individuals on the basis of a pseudoscientific theory of inborn differences between human beings, strengthened by analogy with man's relations with other species, as well as differences between genders Table 1.1 These observations of "nature" provide the justification for Aristotle's proposition that slavery is not only natural but also expedient and just.[63]

Aristotle's argument continued to have currency in later time periods. Indeed, slave-owners have frequently called upon the authority of Aristotle to grant legitimacy to their arguments for slavery. For example, in the famous debate that took place in Valladolid, Spain, in 1550, regarding the justice of enslaving the native peoples of the Americas, the Spanish

---

[61] Aristotle, *Politics* 1254a22. [62] Aristotle, *Politics* 1254b23. [63] Aristotle, *Politics* 1255a2.

Table 1.1 *Aristotle's analogies reinforcing the naturalness of slavery.*

RULING ELEMENT	SUBORDINATE ELEMENT
master	slave
mind	body
rationality	emotionality
man	beast
male	female

humanist Juan Ginés de Sepúlveda was clearly drawing on Aristotle when he wrote that such native peoples were

> barbarous, uncivilized, and inhuman people who are natural slaves, refusing to admit the superiority of those who are more prudent, powerful and perfect than themselves. Their subordination would bring them tremendous benefits and would, besides, be a good thing by natural right as matter conforms to a mold, as the body to the soul, the appetite to reason, brutes to gentlemen, the wife to the husband, children to parents, the imperfect to the perfect, the worse to the better, all for the universal betterment of the whole. This is the natural order for which divine and eternal law requires unqualified acceptance.[64]

The resonances with Aristotle's *Politics* are obvious, even without the further knowledge that Sepúlveda was the author of a translation into Latin of Aristotle's *Politics* published in 1548. Fortunately, Sepúlveda was opposed in the debate by a fellow Spaniard, the bishop Bartolomé de las Casas, who at least articulated the idea that natives deserved to be treated as free men, even if he was not successful in changing Spanish policy in the Americas (Figs. 1.5a, b).

Returning to Aristotle himself, we might sum up the discussion so far by stating that he created a theory of the origins of human society that justified and legitimized the existence of slaves. Yet tensions are immediately evident. For example, Aristotle acknowledges that "while nature intends to make the bodies of free men and slaves different . . . it often happens that slaves have the bodies of free men, and free men possess only the souls."[65] In other words, Aristotle has to admit that nature does not always conform

---

[64] Juan Ginés de Sepúlveda, *Demócrates Segundo*. The translation is from Knight and Hurley (2003, xxxii). For further examples of using Aristotle to justify slavery, see de Bivar Marquese and Duarte Joly (2008)
[65] Aristotle, *Politics* 1254b25.

Fig. 1.5a Juan Ginés de Sepúlveda. Universal History Archive / Universal Images Group via Getty Images.

to slave-owners' ideological preferences, since slaves are often born with bodies of free men, and free men with the bodies of slaves. Furthermore, Aristotle's attempt to categorize slaves as articles of property analogous to livestock conflicts with the distinctions that he also makes between humans

Fig. 1.5b Bartolomé de las Casas. Bildagentur-online / Universal Images Group via Getty Images

and animals. As we have seen, Aristotle classifies slaves alongside other pieces of property, such as livestock, that are required for the functioning of the household. This was in fact a common way of classifying slaves, as is shown by the appearance in Greek literature of the word *andrapodon* (ἀνδράποδον), meaning "man-footed creature," a coinage apparently based on the similar word *tetrapoda* (τετράποδα), or "four-footed creatures," used of livestock.[66] Yet, Aristotle recognizes that mankind is different from other animals in so far

---

[66] Homer, *Iliad* 7, 475. For the use of this word in inscriptions, see, for example, *IG* ii².2747, 2748, 2749 = Finley 1952 #88, 89, 90.

as human beings have the capacity not only for speech but also for moral judgment.

> Mankind is unique in this in relation to the other animals, for mankind alone has perception of good and evil, justice and injustice, as well as all the other moral judgments. And the participation in these moral judgments is what makes possible the household and the city-state.[67]

In so far as slaves, as human beings, have the capacity for moral judgment that Aristotle views as the key to civic life, it becomes unclear why they are excluded from the highest form of association – namely, political life in the city-state.[68] The classification of all human beings as moral beings in contrast to the other animals, furthermore, is in conflict with Aristotle's distinction between men and beasts as justification for his distinction between masters and slaves.

The most striking contradiction of all, however, is found in Aristotle's attempt to distinguish between what he calls "natural slaves" and "slaves by convention." This distinction is Aristotle's response to those who object to the idea of natural slaves by saying there is no difference by nature between human beings that would justify making some free and others slaves.[69] Aristotle reports this view before attempting to refute it.

> Some men believe that to be a master is contrary to nature (φύσις) since one man is a slave and another man free by convention (νόμος) only. And since there is no difference by nature, mastership is not just but based on force.[70]

Aristotle responds to this argument first by conceding that it has some merit, and by acknowledging that in fact many men who are enslaved by force are not suited to slavery by nature. On the other hand, Aristotle insists, the distinction between free and slave by nature does in fact exist in some instances. Just because nature and convention do not always coincide, Aristotle asserts, there is no need to conclude that they never do. Indeed, this coincidence between what is natural and what is conventional occurs, Aristotle seems to imply, when Greeks conquer non-Greeks, since, as he says elsewhere, non-Greeks are slaves by nature.[71] In such cases,

---

[67] Aristotle, *Politics* 1253a15.
[68] Compare Hesiod (*Works and Days* 274–81) and Plato (*Protagoras* 322a–d) for the idea that all men have a sense of justice and that this capacity in part distinguishes human beings from other animals.
[69] For some indication of the arguments of these anonymous ancient critics of slavery, see Chapter 4; and Garnsey 1996, 75–86.
[70] Aristotle, *Politics* 1253b20–23.
[71] Aristotle, *Politics* 1252b5–9. Cf. Plato *Rep.* 469b–c; and discussion in Chapter 4.

Aristotle argues, slavery is not only advantageous, but also just and proper.[72]

These tensions and contradictions in Aristotle's discussion illustrate the difficulty of creating a convincing conceptual framework that classifies certain human beings as natural slaves and as the legitimate property of others. They also illustrate an early Greek attempt to define slavery on racial lines, even though the practice of slavery in ancient Greece clearly did not coincide in any comprehensive way with race. Indeed, even to the extent that Greeks in general (and not just Aristotle) considered non-Greeks as appropriate subjects for slavery, it seems that the Greeks believed that the slavish nature of non-Greeks was not due to any innate biological inferiority but to environmental and cultural factors – such as monarchical rule – that had diminished the human capacities of non-Greeks by accustoming them to slavish behavior.[73]

Ancient Greek Laws and Legal Conceptions of Slavery

The same tensions between treating slaves as pieces of property and as persons with human capacities are evident in extant laws of Greek states relating to slavery.[74] While the Greeks never defined a slave in law, as did the Romans, the conceptualization of slaves both as property and as human beings may be gleaned from particular laws that treat property rights of owners and offenses that involve slaves.[75] Such laws survive from classical Athens, our best-attested city-state, but there is also a smattering of laws concerning slaves from other city-states. One particularly extensive source for slavery in Greek law is a lengthy law code inscribed on a wall in the city of Gortyn, Crete, sometime in the fifth century BCE.[76]

In examining the treatment of slavery in surviving Greek laws, it is immediately clear that – at least at Athens and at Gortyn – slaves were conceptualized as property. The first indication of this conceptualization is that slaves could be bought and sold, just like any other piece of property, including land, houses and farm animals. Laws regulating sales were concerned to establish principles of fair dealing, which, in the case of slaves, involved measures to

---

[72] Aristotle, *Politics* 1255b8. [73] For further discussion, see Chapter 4.
[74] Textbooks on Greek law treat slaves variably under the law of persons or the law of property. Harrison (1968) treats slavery under the law of family, but acknowledges that "to some extent this is an arbitrary choice"(p. 163). Morrow (1939, 25–26) acknowledges the ambiguity of the law in this respect. For recent discussion, see Ismard 2019.
[75] For Roman legal definitions of slavery, and the Roman law of slavery generally, see Watson 1987.
[76] On the Gortynian law code, see Gagarin and Perlman 2016.

ensure that the seller was in fact the legal owner of the slave as well as the disclosure of any disabilities that might not be apparent to the purchaser.[77] The first objective was secured through the requirement that sales be proclaimed in a public place, or declared, and sometimes preregistered, before a magistrate.[78] In order to attain the second objective, sellers were required to reveal diseases, such as epilepsy or diabetes, or any other mental or physical disorders from which the slave might suffer.[79] If the seller failed to disclose any such disabilities, the sale was rendered invalid.

A further area in which the status of the slave as a piece of property is evident is in testamentary bequests. In Athens, slaves were items of property that could be passed on to one's descendants and therefore are frequently listed along with other assets such as land, houses and furniture in legal cases having to do with inheritance. For example, the Athenian orator Demosthenes, in his suit against his guardians for their mismanagement of his inheritance, provides the following list of goods that he should have inherited from his father:

> My father left me two workshops … In one workshop, there were thirty-two or thirty-three slaves who manufactured knives. These slaves were worth about five or six minas each, and not less than three minas. They brought in a revenue of thirty minas net per year. The other workshop had twenty slaves who made couches, given to my father as security for a debt of forty minas. These slaves brought in a net profit for him of twelve minas per year … Apart from these things, my father left behind the following: ivory and iron, for the factories, and wood for chairs, worth eighty minas; gall and bronze which he had bought for seventy minas; a house worth three thousand drachmas; furniture and tableware; jewelry and clothing; my mother's ornaments, all worth ten thousand drachmas; and silver in the house worth eighty minas.[80]

In many other legal cases from Athens in which litigants have cause to list their assets, slaves are counted among the items of property. For example, Aeschines, Demosthenes' political rival, once accused a man of squandering his considerable inheritance, the contents of which he recited in detail.

> His father left behind property that would have caused another man to be liable to expend his money for the good of the state [i.e, be taxed heavily].

---

[77] Our evidence for Greek laws of sale is exiguous, but includes a valuable passage in Hyperides, *Against Athenogenes* 15; cf. Plato, *Laws* 915c–918a. Theophrastus' work *The Laws* is valuable also for its non-Athenocentric perspective, but is concerned mainly with sale of land. Cf. Szegedy-Maszak 1981.
[78] Theophrastus fr. 21 (Szegedy-Maszak 1981).   [79] Plato, *Laws* 916a–c.
[80] Demosthenes 27; *Against Aphobus* 1.9–10.

But this man was not even able to preserve his money for himself! [The property consisted of:] a house outside the city; a piece of land in the deme [i.e., district] of Sphettos, and another piece of land in Alopeke; nine or ten slaves skilled in leatherwork ... in addition to these, a slave woman skilled at weaving linen ... and a male slave skilled in embroidery.[81]

At Athens again, we have lists of property surviving in the records of the state auctioneers, whose job it was to sell off the assets of citizens convicted of treason or those who owed money to the public treasury. In one list, the property of men convicted of treason or impiety in 414 BCE is recorded.[82] Slaves feature prominently among their assets, as is clear from the example below.

[Property sold from the assets] of Kephisodorus, a non-citizen, residing in the Piraeus:

Thracian woman	165 drachmas
Thracian woman	135 drachmas
Thracian man	170 drachmas
Syrian man	240 drachmas
Carian man	105 drachmas
Illyrian man	161 drachmas
Thracian woman	220 drachmas
Thracian man	115 drachmas
Scythian man	144 drachmas
Illyrian man	121 drachmas
Colchian man	153 drachmas
Carian youth	174 drachmas
Carian child	72 drachmas
Syrian man	301 drachmas
Lydian woman	85 drachmas[83]

This list not only illustrates in stark terms the fact that slaves at Athens were considered part of a free person's property alongside other material "goods," but also gives us a sense of their monetary values in relation to these other goods. It is distressing, for example, to read in these lists that a wooden box or chest (κιβωτός) was sold for 180 drachmas, approximately the average price for a slave.[84]

---

[81] Aeschines 1.97. [82] *Stelae Atticae* = *IG* i³.421–30.
[83] *IG* i³.421, col. 1, lines 33–49. The price for the Lydian woman is hard to decipher, but ranges probably between 85 and 88 drachmas. Cf. Osborne 1995, 29.
[84] *IG* i³.422, col. 3.

Another striking illustration of the status of slaves as property is the fact that they could serve as collateral to a loan.[85] Besides the example of Demosthenes' knife workshop mentioned above, we have three inscriptions on stone publicizing the fact that the physical structure of a workshop as well as the slaves who worked there were security for a loan.[86] In another example, we have a legal case concerning a loan contracted on the security of an ore-crushing facility and its thirty slaves.[87]

One consequence of the treatment of slaves as property is that they had no legal personhood and could neither prosecute nor defend themselves in court.[88] As Plato says, "It is the condition of slaves, for whom it is better to die than to live, to be wronged. For when they are wronged and humiliated they are neither able to help themselves nor to help someone whom they care about."[89] In Athens, even the (often crucial) testimony of slaves was not presented in court by the slaves themselves, but read out from a transcript that was recorded while the slave was questioned under torture. In fact, it was a requirement that the testimony of slaves be extracted by torture since otherwise it was thought that the slave would not tell the truth. If the torture resulted in the death of the slave, moreover, then monetary compensation had to be given to the owner.[90]

The legal non-personhood of the slave meant that wrongs done to a slave were subject to a suit for damage of property, and it was up to the owner of the slave to initiate such a procedure against the third party who caused the damage. If the master chose not to prosecute, then the slave had no legal redress. It follows, furthermore, that if the master harmed his own slave, then the slave had no legal means of redress against his master.[91]

The flip side of the legal non-personhood of the slave was that masters were liable for wrongs committed by their slaves. Just as in the case of animals that caused damages (e.g., to a neighbor's property), it was the owner, not the slave, who was required to pay the damages.[92] This principle is stated explicitly in an Athenian law, according to a speaker in a legal case at Athens.

---

[85] Harrison 1968, 229.
[86] *IG* ii².2747, 2748, 2749 = Finley 1952, 88–90. These workshops seem to be related to mining operations, in so far as two of them were found in mining districts.
[87] Demosthenes 37.4 et passim.
[88] At Athens, there appear to be a few exceptions to the legal non-personhood of slaves, and these involve the actions of a privileged class of slaves, who often lived independently of their masters and/or acted as agents for their masters in commercial affairs. For discussion, see Chapter 4.
[89] Plato, *Gorgias* 483b. Cf. Demosthenes 53.20.   [90] See Chapter 4 for evidence and discussion.
[91] Antiphon 5.47 claims that a master did not have the right to kill his own slave without a trial. The speaker in this case, however, is falsely applying a rule about the murder of free citizens in allied states to the case of slaves. Cf. de Ste. Croix 1981, 271.
[92] Plato, *Laws* 936.

> [The Athenian lawgiver] Solon ... passed a law, which everyone admits is just, stating that any offences or crimes committed by a slave shall be the responsibility of the master who owns him at the time.[93]

The speaker in this case is concerned to show that some debts owed by slaves he has just purchased were contracted before he became owner and that therefore the previous owner, not he, is liable for their repayment. A law from Gortyn in Crete, however, suggests that in some city-states, an owner's liability could even encompass acts committed before he became owner. According to this law, a person who purchases a slave and does not terminate the sale within sixty days is liable for wrongs committed by the slave both before and after he became owner of the slave.[94]

Other legal cases from Athens, however, suggest that the law made some distinction between wrongs committed by slaves with their owners' knowledge or consent, and those committed without the knowledge of their masters. For example, the speaker, in one case from Athens, argues that he cannot have commanded his slave to take some silver from the prosecutor's slave, since he was out of town at the time.[95] The speaker then claims that it is not possible to accuse a slave but sue his master. The implication, then, is that the master is not liable for wrongs committed by his slave without his knowledge. This argument shows that some ambiguity existed, at least in Athenian law, regarding the status of a slave as a piece of property belonging wholly to his master. Indeed, the speaker in this case seems to acknowledge the slave as a human being with a will of her own. For, if a slave can act without the knowledge of her master, then she is not merely an extension of the master himself, but a person in her own right.

Furthermore, a master could limit his liability for an offence committed by a slave by handing over the offending slave to the victim.[96] In Roman law, this principle is known as noxal surrender.[97] Moreover, just as in Roman law, this provision opened the way for collusion between a slave and the "victim." For an enterprising slave might collude with a third party to be transferred to the third party in order to escape her master or gain her freedom. If such cases of collusion were detected, however, the original owner of the slave could sue the allegedly injured party and, if successful, win twice the value of the slave in compensation.[98] For our purposes, such laws against collusion not only attest to the existence of clever slaves who

---

[93] Hyperides, *Against Athenogenes* 22. This is the only reference to this law in our sources. Cf. Demosthenes 53.20: "Arethousios, as master, gave and received compensation whenever Kerdon [his slave] did some wrong."
[94] Gortyn Code, col. VII, lines 10–15.   [95] Demosthenes 37.23–25; cf. 37.57.
[96] Plato, *Laws* 878, 936.   [97] Frier 1989, 124.   [98] Plato, *Laws* 878, 936.

were knowledgeable about the law and capable of manipulating it to their own advantage, but also constitute tacit admission once again that slaves were not just extensions of the will of their masters (see Chapter 5).

The laws dealing with murder reveal further tensions between the status of the slave as a piece of property and as a human being. In Athens, for example, cases of murder of a slave were held in one of the special courts for homicide rather than in a regular court, where trials for damages took place.[99] Furthermore, just as in cases of the murder of a free person, the law required that the killer of a slave be purified so as not to bring religious pollution into the community.[100] The particular homicide court that dealt with cases of murder of a slave – the Palladion – reveals, however, that the murder of a slave was considered less serious than the murder of a free person. The Palladion was the court for unintentional homicide, and penalties imposed in such cases were less grave (temporary exile or a fine) than those imposed in cases of intentional homicide (death or permanent exile).[101] So, even while classifying the death of the slave alongside those of free persons, the law counted the death of a slave as less serious than that of a free person. While a master might seek compensation for the murder of his slave by a third party, there was no legal protection for a slave murdered or otherwise assaulted by her own master. In this case, the slave, as the property of her master, could be used (abused) as the master saw fit.

But, again this failure to recognize the personhood of the slave is complicated by another law that protected slaves by including them in laws covering certain types of assaults. For example, at Athens it seems that in cases of gross assault on the dignity of a person – free *or slave* – a third party (i.e., a free citizen who was not the owner of a slave) could prosecute on behalf of the slave. In this law then, as in the law dealing with murder, slaves are classified as persons, alongside free citizens.

> If anyone commits an outrage (*hybris*, ὕβρις) against anyone, whether child or woman or man, whether slave or free, or if he does anything unlawful against any of these, *let anyone who wishes* of the Athenians to whom this is permitted bring an action before the magistrates.[102]

This Athenian law of hubris is often viewed as quite extraordinary, since it seems to offer protection of the basic human dignity of the slave. Indeed, if the essence of slavery is a lack or deprivation of honor, as Orlando Patterson has argued, then this law would suggest that slaves in ancient

---

[99] [Aristotle] *Constitution of the Athenians* 57.3.
[100] Antiphon 6.4. Cf. Plato, *Laws* 865d, 868a, 872a.
[101] Isocrates 18.52ff; pseudo-Demosthenes 59.9ff. [102] Demosthenes 21.47.

Athens, at least, were quite extraordinary in the legal protection they (in principle) enjoyed.[103] No other such law survives from ancient Greece and our ancient sources even suggest that the law was exceptional and characteristic of the unusual mildness of Athenian democratic rule.[104] Therefore we should be cautious in claiming that such recognition of the human dignity of slaves was widespread in ancient Greece.[105]

Yet, there does seem to be one universal Greek institution that protected slaves from excessive abuse, and that is the religious sanctuaries that offered refuge to slaves. The best-known slave sanctuary is the precinct of the hero Theseus at Athens, but several others are attested and it is likely that such slave refuges were quite widespread in the Greek world.[106] While the evidence is meager, it appears that these sanctuaries received slaves who fled from their masters due to extreme abuse. At Athens, at least, it seems that some sort of trial was held within the precincts and, depending on the outcome, the slave could be subject to one of the following results: she could be returned to her master; she could be sold to a new master; she could be kept as a temple slave; and finally, it is even possible that she could be liberated. What is important for the present discussion, however, is that the institution of religious refuges recognized the personhood of the slave by granting him the same right to asylum that was enjoyed by free individuals. Once again, the conception of the slave as a piece of property wholly belonging to a master is destabilized by the existence of laws that recognize the personhood – and in this case, apparently, the basic human dignity – of the slave.

Yet, before we jump to conclusions about the humanity of the Greeks towards their slaves, it is important to put these slave refuges as well as the Athenian law of hubris in the wider context of societal goals. Societal interest in stability can be reasonably argued as the rationale of these practices rather than the well-being of slaves per se. Extreme abuse of slaves, like that of free people (note that the law of hubris covers both free and slave), could be socially disruptive. Abusive acts might lead to a generalized slave revolt (see Chapter 5), or, in the case of citizens, tyranny or civil war. By banning such behavior – whether towards slaves or citizens – overall social stability was prioritized. Significantly, both the existence of slave refuges and the inclusion of slaves in the hubris law suggest that states were willing at times to subordinate the interests of

---

[103] Patterson 1982. [104] Demosthenes 21.48–49.
[105] Ober ([2000] 2005) argues, in fact, that such protection for slaves, women and children is a result of the extension of negative liberties under a democratic system.
[106] For the evidence and full discussion, see Chapter 5.

particular slave-owners to the good of the larger community of slave-owners.

It is important to remember, however, that slave refuges and the law of hubris were designed to prevent the potentially unpleasant consequences of the most extreme forms of abuse and did nothing to diminish more routine physical punishment of slaves. Whipping and other everyday forms of violence towards slaves were the accepted modes of dealing with recalcitrant slaves, and do not seem to have led to a flood of slaves seeking refuge at shrines or, in Athens, to public suits for outrage (hybris, ὕβρις) against owners. The commonplace assumption in Greek literature that whipping was the main instrument of a master vis à vis his slaves shows that the law of hubris and the existence of slave refuges were not viewed as mechanisms for escaping the routine violence of slavery.[107] The key point for the present discussion, however, is that the law of hubris and the right of asylum for slaves at certain sanctuaries introduces more conceptual fuzziness in Greek thinking about slaves, since they seem to allow for – albeit only as a side effect of their main goal of social stability – a modicum of human dignity for slaves.

Consideration of the legal evidence is similarly revealing about another aspect of the conception of slaves in ancient Greece – namely, the lack of correlation between race and slave status. This fact is especially evident from the legal cases in which the status of an individual as free citizen, non-citizen resident or slave is in question (see Chapter 4). For example, in a speech against a man named Pancleon, the speaker argues that Pancleon is a slave, while Pancleon himself claims that he is an Athenian citizen.[108] In another case, a litigant tries to prove that he is in fact, a citizen, while his opponent alleges that he is not.[109] In a third case, a speaker argues that his opponent is an ex-slave prostitute who has been illegally living in marriage with an Athenian citizen.[110] According to her opponent, this woman even passed off her ex-slave daughter as a citizen and married her off to another unsuspecting citizen.

In one of these cases, a foreign accent is alleged as a sign that the person in question is a slave.[111] In none of the cases, however, is race or physical appearance used as grounds for confirming or denying a person's slave status. Indeed, the very fact these possible instances of "passing" flew under the radar of the Athenian state for some time suggests that there was no

---
[107] Sexual violence perpetrated by male slave-owners on female slaves is also attested widely in our sources and is discussed further in Chapters 3 and 5.
[108] Lysias 23. Cf. Lysias (3) in which the status of a young male prostitute is disputed.
[109] Demosthenes 57.   [110] Demosthenes 59.   [111] Demosthenes 57.18.

obvious way to tell who was a slave and who was not. Indeed, one ancient source confirms this indistinguishability when he writes (with some disgust) that you cannot identify a slave at Athens since "the mass of citizens is no better dressed than slaves."[112] Furthermore, it is remarkable that just as a slave might "pass" as a free person, it was possible for a free person to be falsely held as a slave. In fact, the Athenians developed a special legal procedure for asserting the freedom of an individual who was unjustly being held as a slave, known as "removal to freedom" (ἐξαίρεσις εἰς ἐλευθερίαν).[113] Finally, we might recall that even Aristotle, in his theory of natural slavery, admitted that often nature and legal status do not coincide: it often happens that slaves have the bodies of free people, and conversely that free people have the bodies of slaves.[114] It is clear from Aristotle's admission that even for a stalwart believer in the physical and mental differences between free men and slaves, there were no convincing empirical grounds for this distinction.

Ancient Greek Conceptions of Slavery

Summing up the Greek conception of slaves, we might conclude that the Greeks primarily thought of them as pieces of property that could be bought and sold just as livestock and other material possessions. We have also observed, however, a certain anxiety in our sources arising from a tension between the conception of slaves as pieces of property and as human beings. In political thought, law and some aspects of religion, the human capacities of slaves continued to resurface and disrupt the neat conceptual distinctions between slaves and free men. The resulting anxiety may be attributed in part to the fact that there was no empirical evidence upon which to base this ideological distinction. There was no physical marker of the difference between slave and free, and there was certainly no consistent "racial" marker such as skin color. While philosophers such as Aristotle insisted on the category of natural slaves – and by the middle of the fifth century, many Greeks seem to have thought of non-Greeks as naturally suited to slavery – in practice, the Greeks enslaved other human beings, including their fellow Greeks, indiscriminately.[115]

A definition of slavery that seems implicit to the functioning of slavery in Greek society, might run something like this: "The state of being

---

[112] Pseudo-Xenophon (or the "Old Oligarch"), *Constitution of the Athenians* 1.10–12; see Chapter 4 for discussion.
[113] Lysias 23.9–10.   [114] Aristotle, *Politics* 1254b35.   [115] Plato, *Republic* 469b–471c.

controlled by force and/or by social consensus (as expressed by laws, institutions and other cultural practices) by another human being who makes use of one's labor and has total power to use, enjoy and abuse one as they see fit."

Following Orlando Patterson and other critics of definitions of slavery that focus on legal ownership, this definition makes use of the broader idea of "control" that can be exercised by violence, or the threat of violence, and also by all sorts of legitimizing social practices including not only laws of property but, as we shall see in more detail in Chapter 4, the distinctions that are made in the everyday social, political and religious life of the city-state.

On the other hand, this definition leaves out several key aspects of Orlando Patterson's cross-culturally derived definition – namely, natal alienation and dishonor. There are several reasons for these omissions. Firstly, while it is true that most slaves in the Greek world were displaced from their native lands and denied a social identity in their new Greek communities, not all were. The fact that some chattel slaves were ethnically Greek, and some others were born to slave parents in Greece, meant that a number of slaves belonged to kinship networks and participated in communal life in ways that gave them a social identity.[116] Furthermore, slaves who were displaced to new communities often maintained memories of their kinship relations and ethnic origins, and also strove to create new bonds with slaves of similar ethnic origins in their new communities.[117] For these reasons, I suggest that although natal alienation was a key method deployed by slave-owners for controlling their slaves, natal alienation was not characteristic of all slaves.

Secondly, as the discussion of the law on hubris and slave refuges above has already hinted, slaves in Greece were not necessarily without honor altogether. The existence, moreover, of wealthy slaves and slaves who held positions of responsibility in workshops, banks and in the administration of the city-state (see Chapter 3) shows that while slaves lacked political and legal rights, they could hold some social status. Again, distinctions of honor and dishonor were cultural mechanisms for

---

[116] For evidence and discussion, see Chapter 2.
[117] Patterson (1982, 5–6); however, Patterson himself acknowledges that slaves struggled to maintain their social identity or create new ones but that such relationships "were never recognized as legitimate or binding" (p. 6). As Bodel and Scheidel (2017) note, Patterson's concept of "social death" is an ideal type, asserted by masters but never fully realized or internalized by slaves themselves. For slaves' retention of their ethnic identity in Athens, see Hunt 2015 and Chapter 4.

reinforcing the ability of slave-owners to dominate their slaves, but were not fundamental to maintaining slavery.

With this definition of slavery in hand, we can now address two further definitional problems that have plagued the study of slavery. Firstly, what (if anything) is the difference between slavery and other forms of unfree labor such as serfdom, debt bondage and indentured servitude? Answering this question will require examining the Spartan helots whose status is sometimes equated with slavery and sometimes with serfdom. Secondly, we must address the question of what makes a society a "slave society" – a phrase that has been used to designate societies in which slavery is thought to play a highly significant, if not determining, role in contrast to those for which slavery is judged to be of lesser significance. As we shall see, although the term "slave society" has been very influential in elevating ancient Greece to an exclusive yet "macabre hall of fame" (as one scholar puts it), nevertheless, the definition of what constitutes a "slave society" is fraught with imprecision and arguably obscures rather than clarifies the analysis of slavery in historical societies.[118] Consequently, some scholars are calling for the abolition of the term, and the creation of a new model that puts societies on a spectrum that allows for consideration of various factors.[119]

Serfdom and Other Forms of Unfree Labor

Modern discussions of unfree labor delineate five basic categories: slavery, serfdom, debt bondage, indentured servitude and penal servitude.[120] Of these five categories, the last three were of minor importance in the systems of labor in ancient Greece. The Athenians banned debt bondage in the sixth century BCE, and, while it persisted in some other parts of Greece, it seems have been marginal among the forms of labor utilized.[121] Indentured servitude – that is, contracting out one's labor for a set period of time – is also attested but similarly rare.[122] Finally, penal servitude is attested only for the Roman period.[123] The two main categories of unfree labor in

---

[118] Lenski 2018.
[119] Bodel and Scheidel 2017; Lewis 2018; Lenski 2018. Hunt (2018b) makes the case for retaining the concept.
[120] Bush 1996; Engerman 1996; Archer 1988. Cf. de Ste. Croix 1981, 133–74.
[121] Debt bondage existed in Crete, as the Gortynian Code reveals (col. I, line 56 to col. II, line 2 (see below)), and seems not to have been entirely eradicated even in Athens. For example, the character Plangon in Menander's *Heros* is described as enslaved as a result of debts at 36–38. See discussion and further examples in Harris 2006, 256–63.
[122] Gagarin and Perlman 2016, 81; and discussion below on indentured slavery at Gortyn.
[123] De Ste. Croix 1981, 170.

Table 1.2 *Standard distinctions between slavery and serfdom.*

SLAVERY	SERFDOM
Human property	Status as a person: payment of taxes and performance of military service
Usually imported, ethnically different from masters	Indigenous, not ethnically different from masters
No legal rights	Some legal rights, e.g., property ownership
Full-time labor for master	Part-time labor for lords, part-time labor for state, part time for self
No family life	Family life
Use of force to control	Cooperation/reciprocity
Rural and urban; range of occupations	Rural, predominantly agricultural

ancient Greece, therefore, were slavery and serfdom. Table 1.2 summarizes the main distinctions between these two categories according to the standard classification.

Yet, once we begin to examine any particular group of "slaves" or "serfs," these neat distinctions seem to break down. For example, as we have just seen, Greek laws exhibit some confusion as to whether slaves were property or persons. Furthermore, slaves in Greece were often, but not always, ethnically distinct from their masters. Finally, some slaves in Greece enjoyed de facto property rights, even if legally speaking their possessions belonged to their masters. Most strikingly, one class of slaves in classical Athens known as "slaves of the *demos* (people)" (δημόσιοι) –that is, publicly owned slaves – seem to have enjoyed special privileges including the right to own goods and possibly even to initiate legal proceedings on their own behalf. There is also evidence not only that such slaves had families but that their children were granted freedom and even citizenship.[124]

When we turn to the category of "serfdom" the contradictions between the ideal type and historical realities are especially glaring. This is particularly true of the most famous category of "serfs," the Spartan helots. The helots are most commonly characterized as a sort of state owned, serf-like, mainly agricultural population. This view is coupled with the (ancient) conjecture that the status of helots originated when the Spartans invaded and conquered the territory in which this population lived. At that time (tenth century BCE), the

---

[124] Ismard 2015, 95–130. Lewis 2016b, however, emphasizes that these were not legal rights but rather privileges extended by the state to incentivize good work. For evidence and full discussion of publicly owned slaves, see Chapter 3.

conquering Spartans subjected these people en masse and distributed their land among the Spartans. Helots then worked the land, handing over a fixed proportion of the fruits of their labor to their Spartan overlords. On this traditional interpretation, then, Spartan helots were distinct from slaves in that they were collectively, not individually owned, and were tied to the land on which they worked. As serfs, they enjoyed certain minimal rights that elevated them above slaves: they worked only part time for their masters, they could own property, and they lived in family and village settings that allowed them a certain independence from their masters.[125]

Yet, as scholars have recently observed, this view is at least partially based on a preconception of what helots were like (i.e., like medieval serfs) rather than a direct reflection of what the ancient evidence suggests.[126] For example, our sources often refer to the helots with the same term that is elsewhere used to designate slaves (δοῦλοι), sometimes with a qualifier to designate that they were commonly or publicly owned, rather than privately owned as was typical of slaves. The second-century travel writer Pausanias, for example, calls them "commonly held slaves" (δοῦλοι τοῦ κοινοῦ),[127] while the fourth-century BCE historian Ephorus suggests that the helots were held privately by individual Spartans but – in so far as there were restrictions on the right of individual Spartans to liberate or sell them – they were a kind of publicly owned slave.

> The helots were defeated by force in war and were made into slaves (δούλους) on specific conditions – namely, that the person who possessed them could neither free them nor sell them beyond the borders ... The Spartans held the helots as sort of public slaves (δημοσίους δούλους) and appointed them to certain settlements and tasks.[128]

Aristotle gives similarly ambiguous evidence, when he implies that helots were privately owned, but shared in practice as the need arose.

> In Sparta, people use one another's slaves (δούλοις) as if they were their own ... It is clear therefore that it is better if property is privately owned but made available for common use.[129]

What the ancient sources seems to reflect, then, is considerable confusion about the kind of slavery represented by the helots.[130] The evidence that the

---

[125] The strongest proponent of this view is Cartledge (1979, 164–65; 1988, 33–41; 2003, 12–30), though see also de Ste. Croix (1981, 133–73).
[126] Ducat 1990, 19–29; Hodkinson 2000; Luraghi 2002, 2003; Kennell 2010, 82–88; Lewis 2013, 393–96.
[127] Pausanias 3.2.6.   [128] Ephorus (*BNJ* 70) F117 = Strabo 8.5.4.   [129] Aristotle, *Politics* 1263a35.
[130] Further arguments for the helots as collectively owned are, firstly, the equal number of helots (seven) assigned to each Spartan at the battle of Plataea (Herodotus 9.28) and, secondly, evidence

Spartan helots shared characteristics with slaves – for example, "possession" by individual Spartans – is so strong that some scholars have proposed that they were not, in fact, a different category.[131] These scholars stress that the prohibition of sale beyond the borders of Laconia implies that they could, like other chattel slaves, be sold within Spartan territory, and were not, as were serfs, tied to specific pieces of land. Furthermore, these scholars point out that helots were not simply agricultural slaves, but also performed other types of servile labor characteristic of slaves, especially domestic service.[132] Finally, some of our sources suggest that helots were treated even more brutally than chattel slaves, and were controlled by force rather than the reciprocity that characterizes serf-like arrangements in other societies.[133]

Yet, on the other hand, certain aspects of the condition of the helots seem to distinguish them from slaves in other parts of Greece. Most crucially, our sources suggest that the helots were required to hand over one half of their crop to their Spartan overlords, and therefore did not labor full time for their masters.[134] Furthermore, the helots were an indigenous, self-reproducing population, rather than imported through capture or purchase as chattel slaves were.[135] Finally, at least some of the helots seem to have lived in family units and participated in communal life in nucleated settlements or villages.[136]

Some of the lack of clarity in the portrayal of the helots in our sources can be accounted for by the notorious secrecy of Spartan society.[137] Indeed, most of our sources for Spartan history are non-Spartan, and, furthermore, they are influenced by the Spartan myth of a brutally tough, militarized

---

that the Spartan state had the power to liberate helots for good service (e.g., in the military) or kill them as a preventative measure against rebellion (Thucydides 3.8, 4.26, 80; Xenophon, *History of Greece* 6.5.28–29). However, even in Athens, where slaves were predominantly privately owned, the state could reward slaves with freedom for military service (Aristophanes, *Frogs* 33; with Hunt 1998, 92) or other outstanding service to the state (e.g., as witnesses in treason trials; see Andocides 2.23 and discussion in Chapter 5).

[131] See references in n.126 above.   [132] Ducat 1990, 53–55.
[133] Most strikingly, through periodic purging of the helot population: Thucydides 4.80.
[134] Tyrtaeus fr. 6 West; Plutarch, *Moralia* 214a; Xenophon, *Constitution of Sparta* 7.1–6; Isocrates, *Busiris* 20; Nicolaus Damasc. *FGrH* 90 F114; Josephus, *Against Apion* ii.229; Aelian, *Varia Historia* vi.6; Athenaeus, *Learned Banqueters* 657d; Plutarch, *Spartan Institutions* 41.
[135] Ducat 1990, 64. If the list of liberated slaves *IG* v¹.1228–33 records the names of helots, then their names (Kleogenes, Nearetas, Lyhippos, Nikarchidas, Thorax, Kleomenes and Nicaphoris) are clearly Greek in ethnicity and no different from Spartiate names. On the problematic nature of slave names as testimony for ethnicity, however, see Chapter 2.
[136] Alcock 2002 and 2003.
[137] Thucydides, for example, complains of the secrecy of the Spartan political system or way of life (πολιτεία, 5.68.2).

society in which wealth was banned and property was shared. While much of this "mirage" has been dismantled in recent years, it is still difficult to reconstruct a detailed picture of the realities of relations between Spartans and the helots. Some further confusion might be due to the failure to distinguish between the helots of Laconia – that is, the territory occupied by the Spartans – and those of Messenia – a territory first conquered by the Spartans sometime in the eighth century BCE. While the Laconian helots may have been more similar to slaves in that they served in the households of their Spartan masters as well as in agricultural and other roles, Messenian helots lived in a fertile plain separated from Laconia by a major mountain range, and were primarily engaged in agriculture. The distance separating Messenian helots from their masters, moreover, would have been a key factor in their relative autonomy and, as we shall see in Chapter 5, their propensity for revolt.

Yet, these distorting factors are not sufficient to obscure the general conclusion that Spartan helots do not neatly fit into either modern category of slaves or serfs. While the ancient sources suggest that there was something distinctive about Spartan helots, the particular collocation of attributes belies easy classification.

Another, more vague, ancient classification is perhaps useful here. The second-century CE Greek scholar Pollux, who wrote a thesaurus of Greek terms and phrases, identifies a class of persons "between free and slave" and provides the Spartan helots, the Penestae of Thessaly and the Cretan Klarotae, among others, as examples.[138] In fact, many other ancient authors, including earlier ones such as Plato and Aristotle, categorized the helots alongside these other groups of dependent labor.[139] While different authors cite different criteria for this grouping, and some cite none at all, it is clear that the ancients themselves felt that these groups were distinct from slaves.

In fact, once we start to look, we can see that there were many gradations of status between free and slave, and that the helots were just one such category.[140] For example, freed slaves in many city-states did not become fully free, but continued to be subject to certain duties towards their

---

[138] Pollux 3.83. Other groups mentioned in this category include the "spear-bearers" of the Mariandyni in Heraclea Pontica on the Black Sea, the Gymnetai of Argos and the "cloak-bearers" (κατωνακοφόροι) of Sicyon.
[139] Plato, *Laws* 776; and Aristotle, *Politics* (1369a–b); with discussion of van Wees 2003.
[140] Kamen (2013, 1–7) adopts Finley's (1981) concept of a spectrum of statuses between slave and free. Ismard (2015, 118–28) rejects the idea of a rigid hierarchy of legally defined statuses in favor of the notion of "un espace social pluridimensionnel, traversé par un kaleidoscope de status."

masters, as we shall discuss in more detail in Chapter 5. Newly freed helots at Sparta were known as "newly-enrolled members of the people" (νεοδαμώδεις) and freed slaves elsewhere in Greece were given special labels derived from the Greek root meaning "free" or "liberated" (ἀπελεύθερος, ἐξελεύθερος, ἀπελευθερόμενοι). These labels show that these groups were considered to be different from freeborn Greeks, and were subject to a range of restrictions on full freedom, as the following remarkable passage from Plato's *Laws* suggests (while Plato is creating laws for an imaginary state in this work, his legislation is based on historical Greek laws, especially those of his native state of Athens[141]):

> A freedman (ἀπελεύθερος) may be arrested if he fails to perform his services to the one who freed him, or fails to perform them adequately. The services are these: three times a month a freedman must proceed to the home of the person who freed him and offer to do anything lawful and practicable; and as for marrying he must do whatever his former master thinks right. He must not grow wealthier than his master; if he does, then the excess becomes the property of his master. The freedman must not stay in the state longer than twenty years, but like the other foreigners he must then take all his property and leave, unless he has gained permission from the state and his former master to remain ... If a freedman disobeys these regulations and is taken to court and convicted, he must be punished by death and his property confiscated by the state.[142]

The case of the island of Crete provides a fascinating window into the possible range and complexities of status distinctions between fully free and fully enslaved in ancient Greece. Thanks to the preservation of a legal code at the Cretan city-state of Gortyn dating to the fifth century BCE, we have a unique window on the various categories and privileges of residents of this city-state. Within the category of free residents (ἐλεύθεροι), for instance, there were both fully enfranchised citizens (πολῖται) and lower-status free persons, those "not of a *hetaireia*" (ἀπεταῖροι) – that is, not belonging to the male citizen association known as the *hetaireia* (ἑταιρεία). The category of slave (δῶλος – Cretan for the standard Greek term,

---

[141] For discussion of the relation of Plato's *Laws* to historical Greek laws, see Morrow 1938; and Chapter 5.

[142] Plato, *Laws* 915a (trans. Saunders (1970), slightly adapted). Although in this work Plato is setting forth laws for an imaginary colony, it is widely agreed that much of his work is based on actual Greek, and especially Athenian, legislation (e.g., Morrow 1960). For historical examples of the continuation of obligations of slaves towards their masters after emancipation, see pseudo-Demosthenes (59.46–47) and the Delphic manumission inscriptions, which frequently require slaves to continue to serve their owner for a set number of years or the lifetime of the owner before claiming full freedom. See Chapter 5; and Zelnick-Abramowitz 2005.

δοῦλος), moreover, seems to include not only chattel slaves but also higher-status unfree laborers known as "ϝοικεῖς" and commonly referred to as "serfs." Fascinatingly, these serfs are able to inherit a free person's estate in the absence of relatives, and both slave and serf in Gortyn had the right to marry and enjoyed certain legal capacities that far exceeded what was accorded to slaves in classical Athens.[143]

It is at Gortyn, finally, where we have some rare evidence for a category of "temporary servitude" or a "kind of indentureship or debt-bondage" persisting into the classical period.[144] The laws show that free persons or slaves could pledge themselves to another person for a certain period of time until a debt was paid. If previously free, the pledged person returned to freedom after a certain period of time. If previously enslaved, the pledged person simply returned to permanent slavery under his previous master. Persons who were subject to this sort of temporary servitude for debt were referred to as "*katakeimenoi*" or "those who lie under [an obligation]."

The example of Gortyn should make us wary of assuming a simple dichotomy between free and slave, or a fixed set of privileges attached to each status. Gortyn illustrates not only the complex range of statuses that might exist in a city-state, but also the variation in privileges that could be attached to a particular status in different parts of Greece. As we have seen, slaves in Gortyn seem to have enjoyed a higher status and significantly greater legal protection than the vast majority of slaves in classical Athens. If we had more evidence from other city-states, we might recognize even greater diversity of statuses and more variation in the array of "rights" accorded to each status.

The inevitable conclusion of this brief survey is that the historian should avoid general conclusions about "slaves" in Greece and even about "slaves" within a particular Greek city-state. Tremendous variation existed both between and within Greek city-states, and a single category (slave or serf) could encompass a range of different levels of honor and privilege or their opposites. The historian must therefore take each community on a case-by-case basis, looking for commonalities but always sensitive to the specificities of time and place. While the terms slave, serf and freedman reflect fundamental distinctions made in our sources and therefore shall be used in this book, the reader should be aware that they represent a simplification of a rather more messy reality, a theme that will be emphasized throughout this book.

---

[143] Gagarin 2010; Gagarin and Perlman 2016. Lewis (2013), by contrast, argues that slaves in Gortyn were not granted extraordinary privileges.
[144] Gagarin and Perlman 2016, 81.

Slave Societies

A second concept that has recently come under attack is the notion of a "slave society" as opposed to a "society with slaves." According to a commonly accepted distinction, "slave societies" are those in which slaves not only comprise a substantial proportion of the total population (above 20 percent) but also play a significant role in production of wealth.[145] M. I. Finley, who developed the concept as a tool of analysis, judged that five historical societies met the criteria for a slave society: classical Athens, Rome, the U.S. South, the Caribbean and Brazil.

As a number of scholars have recently pointed out, Finley's definition of a slave society is problematic for several reasons. Firstly, given the lack of reliable demographic information for the ancient world, it is difficult to be sure of the percentage of slaves relative to the total population. Estimates of numbers of slaves in classical Athens range from 60,000 to over 300,000, and, depending on the estimates of the total population one adopts, Athens either falls within or outside Finley's category of a "slave society."[146] Secondly, it is unclear what constitutes a "significant" role in the production of wealth and – even if we had better evidence for the economy of ancient states – this is still a vague criterion that makes it difficult to discriminate objectively between societies.

Finley's delineation of five historical states as fulfilling the criteria for a slave society has also been criticized. Firstly, it has been noted that this selection reflects a Western bias, granting this dubious distinction to five Western states and denying it to the many Eastern states that would seem to qualify.[147] Secondly, there are many Western states – both ancient and modern – that probably ought to be included in the category of a slave society. For example, several other ancient Greek states beyond classical Athens seem to have had large numbers of slaves and – if we had more information – would probably be judged "slave societies." Just to mention a few, we might include Chios, Sparta, Corinth, Corcyra, Aegina, Carthage and even pre-classical (Homeric) Greece.[148] To this list, one should probably add ancient Israel and Babylonia, though again definitive evidence is

---

[145] This definition combines the quantitative measure developed by Hopkins (1978, 99–102) with Finley's qualitative criterion (1980, 79–82, 145–160).
[146] Lewis 2018, 95. For discussion of the size of the slave population at Athens, see Chapter 2.
[147] Lenski 2018, 24–38.
[148] Lewis 2018, 96. It is important to acknowledge that Finley did not include Sparta in the five historical slave societies because he was concerned with chattel slave-systems rather than serf-like systems such as the helots (see below).

lacking. In the modern world – that is, the nineteenth century – dozens of states in Africa, the Middle East and Asia would qualify as slave societies.[149]

Given these valid criticisms of Finley's concept of a slave society, we are left with the choice of either accepting the definition and expanding the number of states that qualify or abandoning the concept altogether. If we abandon the concept, we must ask what we should replace it with? Noel Lenski has proposed a new model that takes better account of the differences between slave societies, not just their similarities. Even more importantly, this new model measures slave societies in terms of their negative effects on slaves, and not just their positive effects on masters. Recognizing that slavery is a relationship between two parties, Lenski proposes a more nuanced model that allows for different vectors of comparison. In particular, Lenski is interested in measuring not just "the benefits that the slave offers to the master" but also "the disadvantages imposed by the master on the person of the slave."[150] Under the first category, Lenski considers the use and exchange value of the slave as a commodity and the slave's labor. Under the second category, Lenski quantifies various factors affecting the slave, including the permanence of the slave condition, the level of violent domination, the degree of natal alienation and the level of dishonor. While for ancient societies, these measures must be based on estimates, for more recent societies quantitative date could be marshaled. The resulting measures can then be aggregated and plotted against one another to gauge the "degree of intensity of a slave society." Lenski adds a final measure – namely, the "demographic significance" of slavery that indicates the proportion of slaves relative to the total population without imposing a strict cutoff point below which a society does not qualify as a "slave society."

On this new definition, classical Athens and – if we had more evidence – many other Greek city-states would be classified as "intensive slave societies." This new index, however, also allows us to acknowledge differences as well as similarities in intensive slave systems. Slavery in classical Greece, for example, resulted in less disadvantage to slaves, than did slavery in the American South, primarily because slaves in Greece were subject to less dishonor. Similarly, slavery in Rome was also less disadvantageous to slaves than in the American South, not only on the measure of dishonor but also on the degree of permanence of the slave condition.

The new model is an improvement on Finley's concept in that it allows for comparison without flattening out distinctions between slave societies. On the other hand, this new model is vulnerable to criticism on the same

[149] Patterson 1982; Lovejoy 2012.   [150] Lenski 2018, 50.

grounds as Finley's original definitions in that – at least for the ancient world, and arguably for much of the modern world – it relies on educated guesses rather than accurate numbers. Despite this weakness, Lenski's model results in a more nuanced and less biased assessment of ancient Greece in relation to other slave societies. Furthermore, following Orlando Patterson's lead, it opens up a much wider array of slave systems for comparison. And most importantly of all, it gives full weight to the negative effects of slavery on the slave in its analysis of the intensity of a slave system.

Conclusion

In sum, this book aims to provide a synchronic account of the experiences of slaves and the systems of slavery in mainland Greece and the Aegean islands in the central period of Greek history from about 500–300 BCE. Such an account is valuable because it demonstrates the key role that slaves played and therefore provides a more complete and unvarnished picture of ancient Greece. It is also valuable because it provides an illuminating point of comparison to the systems of slavery and discrimination of later periods, including our own.

In this book, moreover, particular attention is paid to the experiences and perspectives of slaves themselves, and not just slave-owners. While this goal is difficult to attain given the nature of our sources, a consistent consideration of the evidence from the slave point of view, along with perspectives gained from better-attested modern slave-owning societies, can reveal much about the lives of slaves in ancient Greece. One of the important results of this approach, moreover – besides acknowledging the extraordinary amount of cruelty and suffering perpetrated on slaves – will be to show that slaves in ancient Greece often acted strategically to improve their conditions within the system of slavery and sometimes even to escape slavery altogether. In other words, this study will present slaves not just as passive victims of the system of slavery but as active agents who used every means at their disposal – including sometimes even the religious and legal institutions of the Greek city-state itself – to reclaim their basic freedoms and dignity as human beings.

In this chapter, ancient and modern conceptualizations of slavery have been surveyed and the difficulties of classifying certain human beings as slaves have been highlighted. It was demonstrated that ancient conceptualizations of slaves vacillate between the idea of slaves as property and the recognition that slaves are persons with distinctive capacities that they share with other human beings. Moreover, it has been shown that, although legal concepts of ownership often underwrote distinctions between slave and free, domination and control – with or without legally enforceable property rights – were fundamental to ancient understandings of the master-slave relationship. Finally, it was recognized that distinctions between slave and free and between slavery and other forms of unfree labor were not always clear cut in lived experience and that there was a range of statuses between these categories.

While this book makes some broad claims about the experience of slaves and the systems of slavery in ancient Greece, it is important to acknowledge at the start that it is difficult to generalize. There was no single slave experience, but rather a multitude of individual experiences. This book, therefore, does not attempt to tell a simple story, but a complex one in which there are rebellious slaves and accommodating slaves, privileged slaves and oppressed slaves, educated slaves and laboring slaves. Similarly, some masters were kind, and some brutal; many were both.

CHAPTER 2

Becoming a Slave
"The Day of Slavery"

> While sailing along the shore, [the Athenians] conquered Hykkara, a Sikanian city which was hostile to the Egestaeans... After enslaving the population, they handed over the city to the Egestaeans. They themselves [the Athenians] went back through Sikanian territory on foot until they reached Katane, while the ships sailed around bringing the slaves... The Athenians then sold the slaves and made a profit of one hundred and twenty talents from them.
>
> Thucydides 6.62.3–4

Our sources for the experience of enslavement typically reflect the perspective of the enslavers, rather than the enslaved. In the brief account above, for example, we are told that the Athenians conquered and enslaved a native Sicilian city, but we learn nothing of what the experience was like for the enslaved Sicilians. Only the barest of practical details are reported: the Sicilians were captured, transported to market by ship and sold for a certain amount of money.

Modern scholars have also largely approached the question of enslavement in Greece from the perspective of the slave-owners. They ask how the Greeks acquired their slaves, and address the question of "the slave supply."[1] While it is certainly true that this focus simply reflects the bias of our sources, it is not true that we cannot recover anything of the experience of the slaves themselves. We can reconstruct their experience through, firstly, the practical details of their enslavement: the means of enslavement, mode of transport and conditions of sale. In addition, cautious use of comparative evidence can suggest possibilities for interpreting the evidence that we have. Finally, free (i.e., non-enslaved) elite Greek

---

[1] See, however, now Braund (2011, 127–32) although his chapter bears the traditional title, "The Slave Supply in Classical Athens." To frame the topic in this way not only considers the issue from the slave-owners' perspective but reproduces the discriminatory ideology of slave-owners by equating the human beings who were enslaved with other commodities that they acquired.

poets and other writers sometimes represented the experience of enslavement in their works, thereby providing a contemporary perspective on this most dire of human experiences. While the writers themselves for the most part never experienced enslavement, some Greeks were enslaved in Greece and elsewhere – as we shall see. Greek representations of the enslavement of Greeks and non-Greeks, therefore, are not without value.

This chapter will address two key questions: How did one become a slave in ancient Greece? What was the experience of enslavement like? While the next chapter will address the broader question of the experience of slavery over time, we here examine the moment of enslavement itself. In addition, we will address key questions about the slave population – namely, the age profile, gender ratio and the ethnic origins of slaves.

Capture in Raids by Bandits, Pirates or Soldiers, and Sale into Slavery

Probably the most common way of becoming a slave in the ancient world was to be captured in a raid by bandits or pirates (ληστῆρες/λησταί) and then sold on the slave market. Armies on campaign, moreover, also often conducted raids as a side venture to the principal conflict in which they were engaged.

Enslavement by bandits and pirates was so common that it appears as an element of the plot of early Greek myths and heroic legends, as well as the later literary genres of Greek New Comedy and the Greek novel.[2] For example, in one version of the myth of Demeter and Persephone, the goddess Demeter arrives in the town of Eleusis in search of her daughter Persephone, who had been kidnapped by Hades and taken to the Underworld. Not wanting to reveal her identity, Demeter invents a plausible story by evoking what would have been a familiar occurrence in ancient Greece.

> My name is Doso – that's what my revered mother called me.
> Yet now from Crete I've come upon the broad back of the sea,
> Not willingly but rather unwillingly, through violence and compulsion,
> pirate men carried me off.[3]

---

[2] The Homeric epics (probably reflecting conditions in Greece in the eighth century) are full of such accounts. For example, Odysseus, in his Cretan lies, tells of a plundering mission in Egypt in which his men raided the fields, carried off the women and children and killed the men (*Odyssey* 14.261–65). Odysseus also recounts several near escapes from enslavement himself (*Odyssey* 14.295–97, 14.339–59). At the other end of the chronological spectrum, in the fourth century, Menander's play *Sicyonians* 7–16 tells of a four-year-old girl and her slave kidnapped from the coast of Attica and transported for sale to Mylasa in Caria.

[3] *Homeric Hymn to Demeter*, lines 121–24.

In Demeter's fictive but plausible tale, she further recounts how she anticipated being sold by her new masters but took the opportunity to flee as soon as she had the chance:

> when they beached their swift ship
> At Thorikos, there the women together
> Disembarked onto the land and the men
> Were preparing a meal by the stern of the ship;
> However, I felt no desire for the sweet savor of supper,
> but instead, setting out secretly through the dark land,
> I fled my arrogant commanders, so that they would not enjoy my sale price,
> Bringing me overseas without having purchased me.
> So here I've arrived in my wanderings, and I do not even know
> What land this is and who lives here.[4]

While this story is a part of a myth and is furthermore a lie intended to deceive the goddess's host, it achieves its dramatic goals by presenting a plausible scenario based on realistic details drawn from the world of its audience. The tale not only attests to the presence of pirates who carried off people from one part of Greece to another, but it also imagines what this experience was like from the perspective of the victim. Here we catch a glimpse of what it might have been like to be violently removed from one's city and family, and to experience a dramatic change of status from free to enslaved. Demeter evokes the anger and even the indignation of the captive towards her captors (note her description of her captors as "arrogant"), as well as the bewildering loss of orientation that comes from being lifted from one's own territory and transferred to an unknown land ("I don't even know what land this is and who lives here").

Demeter's captors apparently intend to sell her and enjoy the profits, but the goddess represents herself as escaping this fate by running away while her captors were not paying attention. As we shall see, there are historical examples of captives choosing to take their chances on flight rather than be subject to sale. In Demeter's case, she says that she wandered from Thorikos to Eleusis (some seventy-five kilometers), before offering to serve as trusted housekeeper for the local ruling family. While this outcome still entails slavery, it is a privileged kind of servitude, and represents an improvement on the uncertain and potentially much worse conditions of sale on the open market. Flight, as we shall see in Chapter 5, was one of the most common ways of resisting slavery and, even when it did not end

---

[4] *Homeric Hymn to Demeter*, lines 127–33. The crucial lines 131–32 are "as hard to follow in the Greek as they are in English" (Foley 1994, 43), but this translation captures its generally agreed meaning.

slavery, it gave some control to slaves over the conditions of their enslavement.

Demeter's tale of capture by bandits reflects on an individual scale an experience that must have been undergone by many – both within and beyond Greece. In a legal speech from 399, a speaker observes that during the Peloponnesian War (431–404), many Greeks were seized by pirates and spent the rest of their lives in slavery.[5] Another speech from 368/7 refers to the fate of one Nicostratus, an Athenian who was brought to the island of Aegina (a well-known slave market) and sold into slavery after being captured by a trireme (warship) while chasing after some of his own runaway slaves.[6] In this latter case, we know that Nicostratus, although apparently "in bad shape," was able to send letters to his brother seeking rescue from slavery. Eventually, Nicostratus was ransomed at an enormous price (26 minae, more than ten times the average price of a slave).[7] Nicostratus was able to return to Athens a free man, though now burdened by a large debt to his friend who had contributed to the ransom price.

While these anecdotes show that Greeks within Greece were subject to the predations of pirates and brigands, it is likely that a much larger number of non-Greeks suffered this fate on the margins of the Greek world. Both literary and archaeological evidence suggests that large numbers of individuals from the hinterlands of Thrace, the Black Sea, and Anatolia (including Phrygia, Caria, Cappadocia, Lydia and Paphlagonia) were captured and sold to slave-dealers before being transported to Greece. Xenophon provides an example of how a local leader along with his hired army of Greek mercenaries might contribute to the flow of slaves from inland regions to coastal cities and then on to Greek city-states.

Xenophon's story falls within his larger account of his travels through Anatolia with a group of Greek mercenaries. Originally hired by Cyrus, the younger brother of the Persian King, he and his fellow soldiers marched as far as Babylonia, before Cyrus was killed and the mission aborted. Towards the end of their long march back to Greece, Xenophon describes how Seuthes, a Thracian prince, hired Xenophon and his fellow soldiers to help him regain his ancestral lands, which had been usurped by another Thracian potentate. According to Xenophon, the deal struck was that Xenophon and his men would be paid from the proceeds generated by the sale of the plunder they collected under Seuthes' direction. As part of this bargain, Seuthes promised that he would never lead the men more than seven days march inland, a restriction that nevertheless indicates the

---

[5] Andocides 1.138.   [6] Pseudo-Demosthenes 53.6.   [7] Braund 2011, 118.

direction of these raids. Xenophon describes how Seuthes led them to a cluster of villages up in the mountains and together they captured the villages and burned them to the ground, leaving not a single house standing. In the process, he adds, "they gathered together 1000 slaves, 2000 cattle, and 10,000 sheep and goats." Seuthes then sent this human and animal plunder to the city of Perinthus on the northern coast of the Propontis (Sea of Marmara) to be sold to raise money for paying the men.[8]

While this is only a minor episode in Xenophon's account, it illustrates how rivalries among local leaders in Thrace resulted in raids on inland villages and enslavement and sale of Thracian captives into Greece via coastal cities around the Propontis and Black Sea. The prevalence of such raiding activity is suggested by Herodotus, who in his ethnography of the Thracians, observes that among the Thracians farming was considered dishonorable, whereas to make one's living from war and banditry was esteemed (5.6.2). While Herodotus aims to shock his audience through such cultural reportage, it is likely that his observation is based on the prominence of such activity among the Thracians with whom the Greeks came into contact – namely, the suppliers of slaves (i.e., bandits or their agents).[9]

With the same almost clinical detachment from the human suffering caused by such raids, Polybius, writing several centuries later, observes how productive the Black Sea region was for high quality slaves:

> In regard to necessities, the regions around the Black Sea supply both livestock and slaves in the greatest abundance and of the best quality. In regard to luxuries, they bring a never-ending supply of honey, wax and salt fish. And from the surplus in our lands they receive olive oil, and every type of wine. As far as grain is concerned, sometimes they supply it and sometimes they import it.[10]

Archaeological evidence confirms that wine from Greece was arriving deep into the hinterlands of the Black Sea region. Amphoras, the ancient storage and transport vessels for wine, are not only archaeologically visible, but traceable back to their original source. On this basis, we know that wine

---

[8] Xenophon, *Anabasis* 7.3.44–48. An earlier raid on villages in Bithynia in Anatolia follows the same pattern, though without the intercession of local leaders: Xenophon and his men march one day and one night inland and collect "many slaves, sheep and goats," which they then transport to Chrysopolis on the Bosporus for sale and transport (*Anabasis* 6.6.38).

[9] For Herodotus' view of other cultures as the inverse of Greek culture, see Hartog 1988; Cartledge 2002. While there is much validity to this interpretation, Pelling (1997) and others have shown that Herodotus' representations of non-Greek cultures are not simply "mirrors" of Greek culture and sometimes contest Greek claims of superiority and difference.

[10] Polybius 4.38.4–5; cf. Paulus Orosius 3.13.4.

from Ionia and Aeolis, and particularly the offshore islands of Chios and Lesbos, was being imported to the regions around the Black Sea as early as the seventh century BCE.[11] Archaeological evidence for Greek luxury goods, including not just Chian wine, but also fine Attic pottery, is found from the eighth century onward at Gordion, the capital of Phrygia, one of the primary sources for slaves in Greece.[12] Even the remote eastern end of the Black Sea, the region of Colchis and home of the legendary Golden Fleece, was connected to this trade in slaves. In exchange for slaves, the Colchians sought salt, among other necessities. Salt was also the item of choice for the Thracians, who allegedly went so far as to sell their own children in exchange for it.[13]

The literary and archaeological evidence together allows scholars to conclude that a flourishing trade took place between Greeks and non-Greek populations of Thrace and Anatolia by which slaves were exchanged for both necessary and luxury goods. It is likely, moreover, that the demand for slaves and the goods for which they could be exchanged stimulated raids in the interior and contributed to conflicts between the inhabitants of these regions.[14] This is precisely how the African slave trade flourished, as C. R. L. James describes:

> The slavers scoured the coasts of Guinea. As they devastated an area they moved westward and then south, decade after decade, past the Niger, down the Congo coast, past Loango and Angola, round the Cape of Good Hope, and, by 1789, even as far as Mozambique on the eastern side of Africa. Guinea remained their chief hunting ground. From the coast, they organized expeditions far into the interior. They set the simple tribesmen fighting against each other with modern weapons over thousands of square miles.[15]

We may compare this modern description with the account of a native of the Black Sea region, Strabo of Amaseia, writing in the late first century BCE, who provides the fullest ancient account of the role of piracy and banditry in supplying slaves to the Greeks. In this passage, he describes the

---

[11] Braund and Tsetskhladze 1989; Gavriljuk 2003; Braund 2008, 2011, 121.
[12] Lewis 2016a. The comic poet Hermippus, for example, observes that this region is remarkable for its slaves (fr. 63 K-A).
[13] Braund and Tsetskhladze (1989) citing Pollux (7.14) s.v. *halonetos*. Cf. Herodotus (5.6), who reports that the Thracians sell their children for export, leaving out the detail that they exchange them for salt.
[14] Braund 2011, 115. A similar pattern is attested for the Great Lakes region (Miles 2017): indigenous peoples engaged in intertribal warfare and enslaved one another, while French and British tapped into this slave supply for their own needs.
[15] James 1963, 6.

activities of the tribes of the inland regions east of the Black Sea, a part of Colchis.

> After the Sindic and Gorgippian territory, along the coast, is the land of the Achaei, the Zygi and the Heniochi. The majority of their land is without harbors and mountainous, since it is part of the Caucasus. These people gain their livelihood through piracy on the sea, having boats that are light and narrow, holding up to twenty-five people and occasionally up to thirty. The Greeks call these boats "*camarae*" ... After equipping fleets of *camarae*, they attack cargo vessels or territories or cities. Sometimes those who control the Bosporus aid them, providing them with a harbor and a market to dispose of the goods they have seized ... And they do the same thing also in the countries of others, since they know this wooded territory well. Hiding their boats away, they wander on foot at night and during the day for the sake of kidnapping and enslaving people.[16]

Despite such descriptions of the role of indigenous tribes in procuring slaves, it is important to stress that the Greeks themselves were often instigators of such raids, and frequently conducted them independently without the cooperation of local groups. For example, Xenophon mentions that an Athenian naval commander, on duty off the coast of Ionia in 409, made a spontaneous raid into Lydia.

> The next day, they sailed to Notion, and from there, after making preparations, they marched over to Colophon. And the Colophonians joined them in alliance. When night fell, they made a raid into Lydia, where the grain was just ripening. They burned down many villages and they seized money, slaves and much other booty.[17]

Since such raids were a standard side activity of Greek military campaigns, they were seldom deemed worthy of mention in our sources. We can therefore only assume that such events happened with much more regularity than appears in our evidence.

One other chance mention of such raids appears in Thucydides' account of the Athenian invasion of Sicily (see epigraph above). Thucydides' brief narrative reminds us that such raiding activities were not confined to the East, and, moreover, that captives were usually sold at market rather than being kept as slaves of their captors. It is noteworthy that, while this raid takes place during the Peloponnesian War, the target is not one of the principal combatants. Rather, the Athenians take the opportunity provided by their passage from one part of the island to another to attack Hykkara, a city of non-Greek Sicilians. In doing so, they capture and

---

[16] Strabo 11.2.12.   [17] Xenophon, *History of Greece* 1.2.4–5.

enslave the entire population. After transporting them to the nearest market, they then sell them for a profit. Assuming a sale price of 100 drachmas per slave, there would have been over 7,000 people who became slaves as a result of this raid.[18]

Although the Athenian attack on Hykkara was not one of the principal engagements of the Peloponnesian War, it does illustrate the close connection between warfare and enslavement in ancient Greece.[19] If we now turn to warfare proper, however, it is worth asking to what extent wars were conducted for the purpose of acquiring slaves. First, however, we must determine the extent to which wars did produce slaves, since not all defeated combatants were enslaved.

Defeat in War and Enslavement by Captors or Sale into Slavery

Enslavement was one of a number of possible fates for those defeated in war. Those who lost battles could be killed, held captive for ransoming or prisoner exchange, become the slave of their captors or be sold into slavery.[20] Some scholars have argued that enslavement was in fact less common than other outcomes – namely, a return to freedom through a prisoner exchange or ransoming.[21] These scholars point to the fact that often the terms of a peace treaty between hostile states included a provision to return or exchange captives. For example, when the Athenians captured the Boeotian city of Chaeronea in 447/6, they agreed, after suffering a reversal, to exchange prisoners.[22] Similarly, when the Athenians captured two hundred and ninety-two men, including one hundred and twenty Spartans, at Sphacteria in 425, they brought them to Athens for safekeeping until they could exchange them for some of their own men by the terms of a peace treaty in 421.[23]

If no enemy captives were available for exchange, sometimes captives could be ransomed. The hundreds of Boeotians and Chalcidians captured alive by the Athenians in 506 BCE were held in captivity and eventually released at the price of 200 drachmas per man.[24] Most famously, it appears

---

[18] Pritchett 1991, 243; Finley 1962; Hornblower 2008, 465.   [19] Braund 2011, 120.
[20] Ducrey 1999; Panagopoulos 1978; Pritchett 1991; Bielman, 1994.
[21] Ducrey 1999, 74–75. Ducrey tabulates that of 120 known battles 28 resulted in enslavement en masse of the conquered population. Note, however, that Ducrey includes in his tabulation episodes of repression of revolts, raiding and civil war (1999, 54).
[22] Thucydides 1.113.3; Hunt 1998, 42–52.   [23] Thucydides 4.38.5, 4.41.1, 5.18.7. Cf. 4.118.
[24] Herodotus 5.77. This price is above the average attested price of an adult male slave, which makes sense given that it would have been easier to sell a captive than arrange for ransom. The average price of the slaves auctioned off in *IG* i^3.21–30 is 157 drachmas (Schmitz 2011, 55). For discussion of slave prices, see Chapter 3.

that the few hundred Athenians who survived and were held in captivity at Syracuse after their disastrous defeat in Sicily in 413 were eventually ransomed and returned to freedom in Athens. Thucydides vividly depicts the dire conditions of these captives, who were held for eight months in a quarry and deprived of both shelter and basic sanitation.[25] Nevertheless, we know from a commemorative inscription and several literary sources that many of these men returned to Athens after being ransomed. The inscription honors a wealthy trader from Cyrene, by the name of Epikerdes, who gave money to prevent the Athenians from dying in captivity in Sicily.

> Epikerdes of Cyrene, benefactor.
> The Council and the People decided ...
> to commend Epikerdes of Cyrene, because
> he is a good man and he was responsible
> for preventing the death of the captive
> citizens from Sicily during the war,
> since he willingly donated one hundred
> minas for their salvation.[26]

The Athenian politician, Demosthenes, recalls this honorary decree in a speech from 355/4, and suggests that Epikerdes' donation was used to provide food for the captives until they could eventually be ransomed by their families.[27]

Raising ransom money was sometimes difficult, and some families were forced to rely on the generosity of wealthier citizens to help them recover their relatives. In return, these wealthy citizens could put their magnanimity towards fellow citizens on display in public speeches for political gain or even favor from jurors in their legal battles. For example, Demosthenes, in his famous legal conflict with his political rival Aeschines, boasts of having paid the ransom of many fellow citizens.[28] In reality, most families were probably forced to contract loans to pay ransom. Strikingly, at Athens there was even a law that a person ransomed from the enemy belonged to the ransomer if he did not pay back the amount of the ransom to his creditor.[29] In this case, it would seem that the ransomed soldier became a slave again, at least temporarily in his home state, until he eventually paid back the ransom. This outcome was particularly likely if the price of the ransom was extortionate – as was allegedly the case with the Athenian Nicostratus, mentioned above, who was captured by pirates, and was ransomed with help from one Apollodorus for the extraordinary sum of 26 minae.[30]

---

[25] Thucydides 7.87. [26] IG i³.125 with Bielman 1994, 3–7. [27] Demosthenes 20.41–44.
[28] Demosthenes 19.166. [29] Pseudo-Demosthenes 53.11. [30] Pseudo-Demosthenes 53.6–11.

Defeat in War and Enslavement by Captors or Sale into Slavery 61

The Athenians captured in Sicily were held in a known location. The difficulties of ransoming one's relative, however, were compounded if the location was unknown. Such uncertainty obviously arose when captives were sold into slavery and transported away from the site of the battle, before being ransomed. In such cases, it could be years before relatives might locate their lost family member and arrange for ransom. This was apparently the case with the father of a man, Euxitheus, who found his citizenship questioned. In a legal appeal, Euxitheus refutes one of his opponent's items of proof of his non-citizenship: the fact that his father spoke with a foreign accent. The reason for his father's accent, says Euxitheus, was that he was captured by the enemy during the Decelean War (413–404) and sold into slavery on Leucas, a relatively remote island in northwest Greece. It was only after a chance encounter with a renowned Athenian actor that his relatives learned of his location and he was ransomed "after a great deal of time had passed."[31] According to the speaker, then, his father had lived for many years as a slave in Leucas and acquired a northwestern Greek accent, before he was fortuitously located and, presumably, ransomed.[32]

A final example serves as a reminder that non-Greeks as well as Greeks could be ransomed, rather than enslaved, after capture in war. In another legal speech we learn that some Thracians captured by the Athenians were taken on a boat back to Thrace in order to exchange them for ransom.[33] Presumably, the ransom offered was so lucrative that it was more worthwhile for the Athenians to return the Thracians than sell them into slavery or keep them as slaves themselves.

These cases of ransoming and prisoner exchanges demonstrate that some captives in war regained their freedom and found their way back to their homes. There is, however, considerable evidence for the enslavement of captives by their captors, or their sale into slavery. In these cases, captives did not return to freedom, unless, of course, they were voluntarily freed by their owners, or ran away – as seems to have frequently happened.

The case of the Athenian defeat in Sicily is again instructive. We have already seen that the Athenians kept in quarries were eventually ransomed. However, these were not the only captives. Thucydides tells us that the total number of captives in the quarries was not less than seven thousand, and that all were sold into slavery after seventy days except for the

---

[31] Demosthenes 57.18–20.
[32] Even those captured by pirates could be ransomed: on Amorgos, a ransom was paid to pirates in c.250: *Syll.* 3.521; with de Souza 1999, 61.
[33] Antiphon 5.20; with Braund 2011, 118; and Gagarin 1997, 187.

Athenians and some of their Italian and Sicilian allies.[34] If we imagine the latter group to number not more than one thousand, then the Spartans and their allies sold more than six thousand of the soldiers captured in the war. In addition to these captives sold by the state, however, many others apparently were seized and held captive by their captors privately. This was the fate of many of the men who retreated overland under the command of the Athenian general Nicias, according to Thucydides' account.

Thucydides describes how Nicias' men, after being harassed relentlessly by the Spartans and Syracusans, were eventually surrounded as they attempted to cross a river. Thucydides paints the gruesome scene as many of Nicias' men were slaughtered in the riverbed and notes that the killing was stopped only when Nicias made a personal plea to the Spartan commander, Gylippus. After this, the survivors were rounded up, including a renegade band of three hundred men who had deserted Nicias' army during the night. Significantly, Thucydides observes that "the number of captives gathered together as the property of the state was not large, but the number stolen was very large, and all of Sicily is full of them."[35] We can infer from the distinction made by Thucydides that the vast number of those defeated during the retreat were "stolen" by individual soldiers in Gylippus' army and sold as slaves in markets in Sicily. That said, we should also note that Thucydides mentions that many of the defeated escaped slavery, some at the moment of defeat and others after serving as slaves for a while. These men fled to Catane, a city on the coast, some fifty kilometers to the north of Syracuse, from where they presumably hoped to find passage back home.

If we turn now to the capture of entire cities, rather than defeated armies, we can see that enslavement again was one of several possible outcomes. Sometimes only the women and children of a conquered city were sold into slavery. In these cases, the men were held captive for ransoming or for a prisoner exchange. For example, after the Athenians took Torone in Chalcidike in northern Greece in 422 BCE, they enslaved the women and children but sent back to Athens any men who had not been killed in the initial assault. Some of these men were released under the terms of the Peace of 421, while others were exchanged for Athenian prisoners held by the Olynthians.[36] In other more extreme cases, the women and children were enslaved while the men were executed. This was the fate of the people of Scione in 421 and Melos in 415.[37]

---

[34] Thucydides 7.87.3.   [35] Thucydides 7.85.3.   [36] Thucydides 5.3.4
[37] Thucydides 5.32.1, 5.116.4.

These examples illustrate the many possible outcomes for captured soldiers and conquered populations – only some of which entailed enslavement. Yet thousands of men and women *were* sold into slavery as a result of war, some by the state and some by private individuals. Many were also kept as slaves by individual soldiers in the victorious army. Such evidently was the case with many of the Hykkarians captured by the Athenians in 415 (discussed above). Indeed, Nicias, the Athenian commander in Sicily, complained in a letter from the field that his navy was being depleted by desertions and substitutions of Hykkarian slaves as rowers in the place of their owners.[38] On the basis of this brief survey, we may conclude that the production and acquisition of slaves was a significant outcome of war. The question remains, however, whether this outcome was a *goal* of war or a secondary *effect*.[39]

The prospect of acquiring slaves among other booty is frequently presented as an incentive for war in our sources. For example, Herodotus, writing in the middle of the fifth century, tells the story of the Greek ruler of Miletus, one Aristagoras, who in c.500 enticed the Persian general Artaphernes to help him restore some exiles to Naxos through the prospect of "a great deal of money and slaves."[40] When this mission failed, Aristagoras then made a similar appeal to the Spartans to attack the Persian Empire. He tells the Spartans that "The men who live there possess more good things than all other men put together, including gold, silver, bronze, fancy clothing, cattle and slaves. If you desire them, you yourselves could have these things."[41] According to Herodotus, Aristagoras brought with him a bronze plaque on which all the lands, seas and rivers had been engraved. Pointing to this map, he enumerated the various lands and their resources, beginning with the Phrygians and running through other Asiatic populations such as the Syrians and Cilicians, all of whom were familiar sources of slaves for Herodotus' audience. Aristagoras ends his speech by pointing to the Persian administrative capital of Susa, and suggests that, if the Spartans conquer it, "you may take heart that you will rival Zeus in wealth."[42]

Aristagoras' claim is intended to trigger notions of hubris in Herodotus' audience since it was well known that mortals should never try to rival the gods. Yet, according to Herodotus' account, the Spartans were deterred from attempting to obtain such wealth only when they learned how far

---

[38] Thucydides 7.13.2.
[39] Ducrey (1999) is skeptical about booty as primary motive, but Braund (2011, 118–19) is much more inclined to see booty as primary.
[40] Herodotus 5.31.   [41] Herodotus 5.49.4.   [42] Herodotus 5.49.7.

inland from the sea they would have to march to capture Susa. Aristagoras himself, despite his rejection in Sparta, went on to Athens and successfully persuaded the Athenians with the same arguments for material gain.[43] While Aristagoras is clearly presented as manipulative and deceptive – especially in his presentation of Persia as easily conquerable – the idea that the promise of material gain could draw states into war is clearly considered plausible.

It would be a mistake, however, to conclude that material gain, in the form of slaves and other goods, was the only motivation for war. Thucydides' presentation of the motives for the Sicilian expedition is one of the most explicit accounts of the rationale for war, with material gain being presented alongside other motives such as the desire for power and prestige – for both individuals and states. For example, Thucydides famously presents Alcibiades, the chief proponent of the expedition, as driven by the desire for personal prestige as well as enrichment. He is also motivated by a personal rivalry with Nicias, an older and more conservative politician.

> Alcibiades, the son of Kleinias, pushed most eagerly for the expedition. He wished to oppose Nicias, with whom he disagreed about other policies and by whom he had been slandered. Most of all, he wanted to be given the command and hoped that Sicily and even Carthage would be conquered through his leadership. He also hoped to benefit privately both in material wealth and reputation, if successful.[44]

Similarly, Thucydides presents the motives of the mass of ordinary Athenians as complex. Although the prospect of material gain is prominent among their motives, Thucydides presents the Athenians as also driven by the desire to increase the power of their state.

> A lust (ἔρως) to sail on the expedition fell upon all alike. The older men thought that either they would succeed in conquering what they set out after or they would do no harm to their great power. The young men were filled with a desire to see foreign sights and to travel, confident that they would be safe. The mass of ordinary people and soldiers hoped to make some money in the present moment and to increase [Athenian] power, through which they would secure a never-ending source of income.[45]

According to Thucydides, then, the expectation of material profit was part of the Athenians' calculus in voting for the expedition. Even if Thucydides is keen to stress the irrationality of the Athenian decision, given the great

---

[43] Herodotus 5.97.1. [44] Thucydides 6.15.2. [45] Thucydides 6.24.3.

costs and risks of the expedition, it is striking that both Alcibiades and the Athenian masses are motivated by the prospect of material gain. Indeed, while considerations of power, prestige and – on an individual level – even adventure play a role, it is reasonable to conclude that the expectation of acquiring slaves along with other booty was a contributory motive for war among leaders and soldiers alike.

In sum, capture in warfare, along with capture in raids by pirates and bandits, were the most common ways of becoming a slave in ancient Greece. We will examine what the experience of capture and sale was like for individuals after surveying the remaining, somewhat less common, routes into slavery.

Birth into Slavery

A slave born into slavery was called "house-born" (οἰκογενής) as opposed to a "bought slave" (δοῦλος ὠνητός/ἀργυρωνητός) or a slave obtained through conquest or plunder (αἰχμαλώτος). For example, Plato, in his philosophical dialogue *Meno*, represents Socrates interrogating a slave who is identified as house-born.[46] Similarly, the records of auctions of confiscated property from 415 BCE list two slaves as house-born.[47] Indirectly, we can infer, from the evidence that female slaves sometimes served as wet nurses (see Chapter 3), that slave women were giving birth to house-born slaves, since lactation requires pregnancy and childbirth.

Such house-born slaves could be the offspring of two slaves or of a slave mother and a free member of the household, usually the master. The first scenario raises the question of the breeding of slaves as well as marriage-like unions among slaves and the existence of slave families. The second scenario relates to the more sinister topic of the sexual exploitation of slaves – a horrific practice that, as we shall see, is well attested in ancient Greece. Let's look at each of these scenarios in turn.

While previously considered only of minor significance, some scholars now judge slave breeding to have been quite widely practiced.[48] Ancient sources, however, are somewhat unclear as to whether masters engaged in

---

[46] Plato, *Meno* 82b. Other references to house-born slaves in Greek literature include Aristophanes, *Women of the Thesmophoria* 426, *Peace* 789; pseudo-Demosthenes 13.24; Sophocles, *Oedipus Tyrannus* 1123.
[47] *IG* i³.426.16, 427, 4. The total number of slaves on the list is forty-four. The inscriptions of grants of freedom to slaves from Delphi also describe many as house-born (see, e.g., *SDGI* 1684, 1692).
[48] Braund 2011, 125: "There is every likelihood that we underestimate the extent of slave breeding in Greek society."

breeding slaves as a deliberate strategy to increase labor supply or capital (wealth). Xenophon's treatise on household management, for example, is one of our best sources for the management of slaves, and seems to conceive of sexual relations among slaves as a means of control in the form of rewards and punishments rather than an obvious or reliable way of increasing available labor and capital.[49] In describing the layout of his household, for example, Xenophon's character Ischomachus observes that men's quarters are separated from women's quarters by a locked door, "so that slaves do not produce children without our consent."[50] He goes on to explain that "good slaves become better behaved after they have produced children whereas bad ones who mate become more badly behaved."[51] In so far as this passage acknowledges that sexual relations between slaves were permitted by masters, the emphasis seems to be on management concerns rather than on the potential of breeding to increase a master's wealth.

In this regard, it should be noted that there were costs and risks to slave breeding. First, slave children required clothing, shelter and food – not to mention care – all of which could be for naught if the child died before becoming old enough to be a productive member of the household or a valuable commodity for sale.[52] In addition, there was a significant risk that the slave mother might die in childbirth. For these reasons, some scholars have suggested that slave breeding was a realistic option only for wealthier slave-owners who could afford some losses.

An anecdote about a citizen of Acragas in Sicily in the second half of the fifth century does indeed suggest that breeding of slaves was a deliberate strategy among wealthy slave-owners. The story concerns one Gellias, who had many slaves and slave children in his home. When a visitor, who was a stricter slave-owner than Gellias, asked him why he did not put his slaves to work during the night, Gellias called forth the slave children and declared "these are the profits from the night work of my slaves!"[53]

In addition to deliberate slave breeding, we can assume that slaves formed casual sexual relationships and even informal partnerships, with or without the permission of their owner(s), and that children resulted. Indeed, our sources often take for granted sexual relations among slaves. For example, Euripides, in his play *Hecuba*, presents Hecuba's daughter Polyxena as anticipating with dread not only the domestic labor that she will be required to perform when she is sold into slavery but also the fact

---

[49] Schmitz 2012, 89–90. [50] Xenophon, *On Household Management* 9.5.
[51] Cf. also Aristotle, *On Household Management* 1.5, 1344b18ff. [52] Schmitz 2012, 75.
[53] Stobaeus 4.19.48; and discussed in Schmitz 2012, 75.

that she will share a bed with another slave.[54] The presence of slave children is also assumed. For example, several ancient sources mention situations in which citizen women might present the newborn children of their slaves as their own, if they were unable to conceive themselves. Most strikingly, in Sophocles' tragic play *Oedipus Tyrannus*, the ill-fated Oedipus assumes that his mother was a slave when he learns that he is not the child of the queen of Corinth, as he had previously thought.[55] Although the truth of Oedipus' birth is much more problematic than mere birth from a slave, the fact that Oedipus makes this assumption reveals that it was considered a plausible scenario at the time that this play was performed in the last third of the fifth century.

While there was no legal recognition of slave marriages in most Greek city-states (Gortyn in Crete seems to be the exception[56]), there is some evidence for family-like groupings of slaves including children in Sparta and Athens.[57] For example, recent archaeological work suggests that helots in Messenia may have lived in family groups.[58] Indeed, the Spartan poet Tyrtaeus observed in the seventh century that the helots "along with their wives" were required to mourn when their masters died.[59] In Athens, the lists of confiscated property from 415 feature a grouping of a Thracian slave man, woman and child who are sold together for a sum price – an indication that they were considered a unit of some sort.[60] More significantly, in the inscriptions recording grants of freedom from 330, there are thirty-three family-like groupings that contain male-female pairs of freed slaves, and sometimes up to three children.[61] These latter examples may be the success stories, however, in which slaves managed to form ties and pool resources in ways that were not typical. The rarity of the family groupings compared to isolated slaves on the property lists, however, and the fact that individual slaves are still in the majority on the lists of freed slaves, suggest that in Athens, at least, most slaves did not have the privilege of family life.

---

[54] Euripides, *Hecuba* 362–67.
[55] Sophocles, *Oedipus Tyrannus* 1062–63. Cf. Aristophanes, *Women of the Thesmophoria* 339–41, 407–8, 502–3, 564–65.
[56] Gagarin and Perlman 2016, 83.
[57] There is slightly more evidence for slave families in the Archaic period, although this may be attributed to the idealizing portrait of master-slave relations in the Homeric epics (Schmitz 2012, 74). Similarly, there is some evidence for slave marriages starting in the Hellenistic period, as attested in the plays of Menander (Cox 2013, 171–72) and in grants of freedom (Zelnick-Abramowitz 2005, 157, 163–70). See also Burstein 1984, 73; and Chapter 3 for discussion.
[58] See Chapter 4 for references and discussion.   [59] Tyrtaeus fr. 7 West. Cf. Hdt. 6.58.
[60] *IG* i³.422.193–99; with Schmitz 2012, 78.
[61] Schmitz 2012, 84–87. Similarly, the grants of freedom from Delphi contain some family groupings; for example, *SGDI* 1688 records a grant of freedom to a mother and son.

Nevertheless, casual and occasionally long-term pairings among slaves would have been one source of house-born slaves.

It is often impossible to tell whether slave children mentioned in our sources were the product of relations between slaves or between slaves and their masters. Most of the latter would have been a result of sexual violence, although it is possible that some of these relationships were consensual or a means for a slave to exert influence over her master. The story of Alcibiades' production of children with a woman enslaved after Athens' conquest of Melos in 415 BCE (discussed below) suggests violent domination. Indeed, Xenophon represents his character Ischomachus as distinguishing between the willingness of a wife to gratify her husband sexually and the forced sexual services of a slave.[62]

In some cases, a master might have become infatuated with his slave, possibly with active encouragement by the slave. In these cases, there might have been genuine attraction or affection, but in most cases, it is more likely the slave was motivated to try to gain influence over the master. The slave girl who is at the center of the dispute in a legal speech from the early fourth century, for example, is represented as vacillating in her affection between her two masters (she is jointly owned, according to the speaker) and seems to have been playing them off against one another for maximum advantage.[63] In any case, once again slave children could have resulted from one or both of these relationships.

Exposure, Debt Slavery and Enslavement as a Legal Penalty

There was an array of routes to becoming a slave that were less common compared to the modes of enslavement discussed so far. These can be discussed fairly quickly before turning to the more important question of what the experience of enslavement was like for the enslaved.

First of all, exposure (abandonment) of children, both free and slave, was practiced as a means of dealing with children born out of wedlock or of limiting family size.[64] This was done by setting out the infant in a remote location, sometimes in an earthenware vessel.[65] Such exposed children were sometimes rescued before dying, thereby providing a basis in reality for many a dramatic plot – most famously, Sophocles' *Oedipus Tyrannus*. Some exposed children, however, even if rescued from death, ended up in

---

[62] Xenophon, *On Household Management* 10.12.
[63] Lysias 4.8; cf. 17 with discussion in Chapter 5.
[64] Golden 1981; Patterson 1985.
[65] Aristophanes, *Wasps* 289 with scholion.

slavery. Since evidence for this latter scenario is naturally scarce, we can only make inferences from literary scenarios. In Menander's play *Men at Arbitration,* for example, a child of freeborn parents is exposed then rescued by slave-shepherds. In this story, the mother became pregnant after being raped at a festival.[66] While both the mother and father are free and indeed wealthy, the child is unwanted since it is not the product of a lawful marriage. The child is therefore set out to die in a remote place. The child is picked up by a slave-shepherd, who in turn hands it over to another slave who plans to bring it up as his own – that is, as a slave.[67] The play then follows a familiar story pattern – namely, the child is recognized as freeborn and reunited with his parents.

Despite the dramatic satisfactions of this literary plot, it is unlikely that in reality exposed children were ever reunited with their families. Most probably perished or became slaves of others. While it is likely that female babies were exposed more often than male ones, it is impossible to know the rates or absolute numbers of persons entering slavery this way. In all likelihood, however, it was of lesser importance than the modes of enslavement surveyed so far.

It is also worth mentioning debt slavery in this regard. As already noted, debt bondage was banned in Athens in the sixth century, but persisted in Crete and even sporadically in Athens in the classical period (Chapter 1). All indications are, however, that it was not a major path to slavery in classical Greece.[68]

Occasionally, enslavement appears as a penalty for certain offenses. For example, a mid-fifth-century law from Halicarnassus specifies that if any citizen tries to overturn a particular law, his property shall be confiscated and he himself is to go into exile. The law further specifies that if his property is below a certain amount, he himself is to be sold into slavery.[69] In Athens, non-citizen residents (metics) who were convicted of living in marriage with an Athenian citizen, or who did not have a citizen patron or pay a special tax, were sold into slavery.[70] Finally, those who attempted to be enrolled as a citizen but were found to be ineligible or illegally enrolled were also sold into slavery.[71] As in the case of debt bondage, however, sale into slavery as a result of a judicial penalty was not a common route into slavery.

---

[66] Menander, *Men at Arbitration,* 240ff. [67] Menander, *Men at Arbitration,* 469.
[68] Hunt 2018a, 33. [69] *ML* 32, though note Halicarnassus is of mixed Greek-Carian ethnicity.
[70] Pseudo-Demosthenes 59.16–17; Harpocration s.v. μετοίκιον.
[71] Aristotle, *Ath. Pol.* 42.1. The defendant in Demosthenes 57, for example, would have been sold into slavery if he lost the case for his citizenship. For further discussion, see Chapter 4.

The Experience of Enslavement

> O mother, who came from royalty and saw the day of slavery, just as you once prospered, so you now suffer.
>
> Euripides, *Hecuba* 55–57.

What was the experience of enslavement like? Apart from house-born slaves, who were born into slavery, most slaves underwent a process of enslavement that entailed the loss of almost everything that defined their previous existence, including family and social ties, not to mention their personal freedom. Although we have no first-hand accounts of the experience from those who were enslaved through capture by raiders or by conquest in war, we know enough about the process of enslavement to be able to imagine some of the physical and psychological trauma that it entailed. Moreover, as mentioned at the beginning of this chapter, we have some literary accounts of the experience of enslavement, and – even if these are written by free Greek males – they reveal how the ancient Greeks themselves (who were after all not unfamiliar with the experience, as we have seen) imagined the experience of enslavement. Let's begin with the process of enslavement before turning to the ways that the Greeks themselves portrayed the experience.

After conquest in war, the defeated would be rounded up in a central place for collective sale by the victorious state or its military representatives. Before this, as we have seen, some captives will have been seized by individual soldiers for private use or sale, and others may have taken their chances on escape and flight. Those who remained after these private seizures and defections would be held together under guard. Since the captors often hoped to sell the captives, they needed to maintain them in reasonable condition. As we saw, however, in the case of the captives held in the quarries at Syracuse, provisions could be minimal, and problems of crowding, sanitation and exposure to the elements could result in great suffering, illness and even death.

Beyond this physical distress, the fear and foreboding of what was to come must have been palpable. Captives will have wondered where they would be taken, who would buy them and whether they would be separated from friends and family members. While facing these uncertainties, moreover, most captives would still have been in shock from their capture and, not infrequently, from the sight of the total destruction of their homes, communities or army in the field. Some of them may have witnessed the slaughter of family members or comrades in arms, and would be experiencing – what we label today – posttraumatic stress. The sense of loss would be particularly stark in those cases of the capture of cities in which all the men had killed, and only the women and children remained. Cries of mourning and terror would have filled the air. It is probable that some of the captives chose suicide over the impending enslavement.

Transport

Most captives faced the prospect of transport to a market, if they could not be sold on the spot. Sometimes they were transported overland and sometimes by sea. Sometimes long marches from deep inland were followed by transport by sea. Slaves from Thrace, Scythia, Colchis and Anatolia, for example, would be marched overland to port cities in the Black Sea region or the Aegean where they would then be transported by boat to mainland Greece. Prominent port cities mentioned in our sources as entrepots for the slave trade include Abydus, Byzantium, Cyzicus, Perinthus on the Propontis and Chios, Ephesus and Clazomenae in the Aegean.[72] In the Hellenistic period, the Aegean island of Delos seems to have been a major market for the slave trade.[73]

In central Greece, prominent slave markets included Corinth and Athens, but also towns in Thessaly and Boeotia.[74] In the mythical scenario with which this chapter began, the captors of Demeter/Doso sailed from the island of Crete to the Greek mainland and disembarked at the village of Thorikos in the southern part of the Attic peninsula. The pirates may have intended to sell the goddess in the city of Athens itself or at Athens' port, Phaleron. Alternatively, their destination may have been Thorikos itself, or the nearby Sounion, both of which were close to the mines where there was a great demand for slave labor. In the West, we have seen that the native Sicilians from the city of Hykkara were transported by sea to the nearest major town, Catane, while those captured by the Syracusans, were transported by land to Syracuse and sold there (with the exception of the Athenians who were ransomed).

It is likely that captives being transported to market on land were forced to march in a line, chained together by the neck.[75] We have several representations of such coffles on ancient monuments, including one on the famous Behistun Inscription. This monument from the late sixth

---

[72] Aristophanes, fr. 556 K-A. On Perinthus, see Xenophon above.   [73] Strabo, *Geography* 14.5.2.
[74] Aristophanes, *Wealth* 521 mentions the many slave-dealers in Thessaly.   [75] Lewis 2016a.

century BCE commemorates the Persian King Darius' victories over rebellious subjects. The relief shows Darius receiving a group of nine captives chained at the neck. Darius stands facing the coffle and places his foot on top of a tenth captive in a clear gesture of domination. Even more explicitly connected to slavery is the funeral monument of a freedman slave-trader named Aulos Kapreilios Timotheos, dating to the first century CE (Fig. 1.3). This monument was found at Amphipolis, a Greek colony in the northern Aegean strategically located to exploit resources – including slaves – from Thrace. Amphipolis was presumably Aulos' base of operation for his slave-trading business. On the lowest register of the monument, a cloaked figure leads a group of ten slaves chained at the neck (Fig. 2.1). It is hard to determine the gender of the slaves, but it is clear that several children accompany the coffle. One of the children is female, and it also possible that the last adult figure in the coffle is also female.

Such coffles were capable of travelling up to twenty miles a day over rough terrain.[76] Sometimes they might be chained in pairs, and required to carry gear for the trip. In the anonymous comic biography of Aesop, the slaves march in pairs and carry a chest, reed mats, and bedding, as well as jars and baskets of food and drink.[77] While there is no mention of chains, this may simply be a result of the literary nature of the tale: the plot demands mention of the gear, but does not require mention of the chains. A description of a slave coffle in Virginia in 1843, however, shows that slaves

Fig. 2.1 Close-up of the lower register of the funeral monument of Aulos Kapreilios Timotheos, a slave-trader. (Drawing by Sophie Forsdyke Larsen.)

[76] Johnson 1999, 50. [77] *Life of Aesop* = Hansen 1998, 118.

not only were commonly chained in pairs but had to sleep in their chains at night in very rough conditions.

> [The slave drivers] had about three hundred slaves with them who had bivouacked the previous night in chains in the woods . . . The female slaves were, some of them, sitting on logs of wood, whilst others were standing, and a great many little black children were warming themselves at the fires of the bivouac. In front of them all, and prepared for the march, stood, in double files, about two hundred male slaves, manacled and chained to each other.[78]

The chains, of course, minimized flight risk and lowered the cost of transport since fewer supervisors were required.[79] For the slaves, however, these chains were a source of great discomfort, typically causing lacerations that could fester and leave lasting scars. A speaker in a lawsuit in Athens mentions the still visible scars on the calves of his opponent, who had wounds caused by the chains he wore as a slave.[80]

Sale

Once slaves arrived at a town with a market for slaves, they would have been prepared for sale. After a journey that was sometimes long and arduous, as we have seen, the seller might wish to fatten up and rest his slaves, so that they might appear stronger and healthier, and hence fetch a higher price.[81]

Slave-dealers, like many clever merchants, wanted to present their goods in the best light, so they often took pains to dress them in ways that accentuated their qualities and covered their faults.[82] The anonymous *Life of Aesop*, written in Greek but dating to the Roman period (perhaps second century CE), provides a description of the care which slave-dealers gave to the clothing of their slaves for sale. In this fictional account, a slave-dealer puts three slaves up for sale, including Aesop himself.

> [The slave-dealer] dressed the musician, who was good looking in a white robe, put light shoes on him, combed his hair, gave him a scarf for his shoulders, and put him on the selling block. But since the teacher had spindly legs, he put a long robe and high boots on him so that the length of

---

[78] Johnson 1999, 49. [79] Lewis 2016a, 322. [80] Demosthenes 53.8.
[81] See Johnson (1999, 119) with references for this practice of feeding up slaves after the long trip south for sale at New Orleans in the nineteenth century.
[82] See Johnson (1999, 119–21) for the grooming and clothing of slaves before sale in nineteenth-century New Orleans. Grey hair was plucked or "blackened" with dye, and slaves were dressed in clean and respectable, even fancy, clothing.

the robe and the protection of the boots would hide his ugly shanks, and then, when he had combed his hair and given him a scarf, he put him on the selling block. But he couldn't cover up or prettify Aesop, since he was a completely misshapen pot, and so he dressed him in a sackcloth robe, tied a strip of material around his middle, and stood him between the two handsome slaves.[83]

Although this is a fictional and ultimately comic account, it is probably based on historical marketing practices in which slave-dealers gave thought to the clothing and even poses which slaves would hold on the auction block. They even took pains to pair slaves in such a way as to present the best effect and thereby command the highest prices. A similar instance of attention to pose and pairing can be found in a fragmentary play by Menander, which opens with a scene in which an adult male slave and a four-year-old slave girl are placed together on the selling block, the girl perched on the man's arm, as he sits in a comfortable pose. Perhaps the pairing and pose were designed to suggest a stable and healthy father-child relationship, when in fact the young girl was freeborn and had been captured by pirates and sold into slavery along with her former slave caregiver.[84]

An indication of the marketing tricks and care of slave-dealers regarding the presentation of their slaves can be found in the evidence for laws of sale. These laws specify that a slave may be returned for full purchase price if the slave is discovered to have some physical defect or disease of which the buyer was not made aware in advance. For example, a speaker in a legal case at Athens cites such a law and makes explicit mention of the fact that slave-owners sometimes deceive buyers by hiding physical defects.

> [The law states that] whenever someone sells a slave he must declare in advance if the slave has some weakness. If he does not, the slave may be returned.[85]

In drafting legislation for his best possible state, Plato goes even further in specifying the types of defects that might be concealed and therefore might be grounds for return of the slave.

> If someone sells a slave who is sick with a wasting disease [such as tuberculosis or pneumonia] or a urinary tract disorder or epilepsy or with any other illness – physical or mental – that is not readily apparent to most people, although it is a serious and difficult to cure illness ... there is no right of return, not even if the seller declares the truth in advance. But if the seller is

---

[83] Hansen 1998, 119, trans. Hansen. [84] Menander, *Sicyonians* 5–10. [85] Hyperides 3.15.

a professional and he sells such a slave to a lay person, the buyer can return the slave within six months – except in the case of epilepsy. In that case, the buyer has twelve months to return the slave.[86]

At Athens, slaves were placed in circular pens or enclosures known as "The Circles."[87] Since our sources mention multiple "circles" we may imagine an area of the marketplace where several groups of slaves might be displayed and auctioned at once.[88] It is likely that slaves were grouped (and priced) by ethnicity, gender, age, size and/or skill level, although very young children would need to be kept by an adult, as we have seen in the case of the four-year-old slave girl.[89] Some evidence suggests that sales of slaves, along with livestock, were held on a monthly basis, and it is likely, in any case, that public sales (as opposed to private sales) were not held daily.[90] The presence of livestock alongside slaves in the market would have visually complemented the slaveholders' assimilation of slaves to nonhuman animals.

What was the experience of sale like for the slave?

Early on in Aristophanes' comic play *Wealth*, produced in 388, an Athenian master is waxing lyrical about how wealth is the source of everything good in men's lives and concludes that "everything is subject to wealth." His slave then quips: "Indeed I myself have become a slave because of a small bit of money, although I was free before!"[91] In the opening lines of the play, the same slave had lamented his fate of being a slave and therefore obliged to follow the commands of his master (who seemed to have lost his mind). He further observes that a slave is not the master of his own body, but rather the one who has bought him controls his body:

> Zeus and the gods, what a difficult thing it is to be a slave for a master who has lost his mind. For the slave attendant who happens to provide the best advice does not seem to do so to the one who has acquired him and consequently the slave is compelled to share in the bad results. For fortune does not allow the slave to have control over his own body, but rather gives control to the one who has bought it.[92]

---

[86] Plato, *Laws* 11.916. Cf. *SEG* 47.1026; *IC* IV 772, VII lines 10–15. See Hsychius s.v. ἐν λευκώμασι; Lycurgus, *Against Leocrates* 24; Xenophon, *Ways & Means* 4.24.
[87] Arnott 1996, 284: Alexis, fr. 104 K-A: "where are you taking me via the Circles?" ποῖ δή μ' ἄγεις διὰ τῶν κύκλων. Cf. Menander, fr.150 K-A, cited below; Pollux 7.11; and Harpocration s.v. κύκλοι.
[88] Lewis 2016a, 324.
[89] In nineteenth-century America, slave-dealers not only categorized slaves by these criteria but also gave them rankings such as "Prime, No.1, Second Rate and so on" (Johnson 1999, 118, 123, 138).
[90] Aristophanes, *Wasps* 169–71; Theophrastus, *Characters* 4.15; with Lewis 2016a, 324.
[91] Aristophanes, *Wealth* 147–48.   [92] Aristophanes, *Wealth* 1–7.

While this testimony comes from a comedy written by a free elite male for a mainly free and citizen audience, it purports to represent the perspective of the slave and certainly touches on some fundamental truths about slaves who are bought in the market – they lose control over their body to the person who pays "a small bit of money." Moreover, slaves are compelled to obey the commands of their new owner, even if these are ill-advised.

This loss of control over the body is vividly present even in the process of sale, as potential buyers feel free to poke and prod the slave to determine his health. Aristophanes alludes to such treatment of slaves in a scene in another play, the *Birds*. Here, the main character is explaining to a chorus of birds that they (the birds) used to be worshipped as gods by humans, but now they are treated as ignorant slaves – mere "Manes-es" (the plural of "Manes", a common slave name in drama).[93]

> So all men used to consider you to be great gods, but now they think of you as ignorant slaves, "Manes-es." And so they throw stones at you just as they do with crazy people, and even in holy places every bird catcher sets up snares, traps, limed-twigs and nets. Then after catching you they sell you all gathered together. And other men buy you, feeling and squeezing you all over.[94]

For a sense of what this "feeling and squeezing" might entail, we can compare this with the evidence for such examinations in the slave market of nineteenth-century New Orleans. Buyers, it seems, "ran their hands over the bodies of slaves, rubbing their muscles, fingering their joints, and kneading their flesh."[95] In addition, buyers "thumbed their way into slaves' mouths to look at their gums and teeth," just as they might do when buying a horse.[96] Both male and female slaves were often stripped so that buyers could have a closer look. Buyers "palpated breasts and abdomens" as they tried to judge the reproductive capacity of female slaves.[97]

To facilitate such physical examination, a slave might be stripped naked, as a fragment from a lost comedy attests. In the fragment, a slave imagines his future sale in the marketplace.

> By the gods, I already seem to see myself in the Circles, having been stripped [of my clothes], walking in a circle and being offered for sale.[98]

Once again, although this comedy is written by a free Greek male, the representation is realistic, as the mention of the "Circles" makes clear.

---

[93] For discussion of this name and slave names in general, see Chapter 4.
[94] Aristophanes, *Birds* 522–30.   [95] Johnson 1999, 141.   [96] Johnson 1999, 142
[97] Johnson 1999, 143.   [98] Menander, fr. 150 K-A.

In addition to physical handling, prospective buyers may have asked the slave questions. Through such questioning, the buyer may have sought to determine not only the slave's comprehension of Greek but also his ethnicity, skills, character and intelligence.[99] In the fictional *Life of Aesop*, for example, a buyer asks several slaves about their ethnicity, name and skills, before enquiring of the slave-dealer about the price.[100] While such direct questioning of the slave may not have been possible in cases in which the slave was newly imported to Greece (and hence not yet Greek-speaking), when it did take place, it was one part of the process of sale that actually acknowledged slaves' human capacities (speech, rationality) and hence their difference from livestock or inanimate objects that were also bought and sold.

Moreover, although slaves were mostly treated as inhuman objects in the process of sale, they did not necessarily passively accept the process. Indeed, slaves might even attempt to influence their sale either positively or negatively, depending on their assessment of the buyer.[101] Humorously, Aesop, in his fictive biography, talks back to a potential buyer, the philosopher Xanthos, and even ridicules his pretensions of wisdom. In their extensive conversation, Aesop even gives the buyer a lesson in slave management.

XANTHOS: I wish to buy you, but you won't try to run away will you?
AESOP: If I wish to do this, I will not make you my advisor in this enterprise, as you take me as your advisor. But who determines whether I run away? You or me?
XANTHOS: Clearly, you do.
AESOP: No, you do.
XANTHOS: Why do I?
AESOP: If you are a good master, no one, fleeing the good, goes to the bad, giving himself over to wandering and the expectation of hunger and fear. But if you are a bad master, I will not stay one hour with you, not even half an hour, not even a second.[102]

While this scene is an obvious comic reversal of actual real-life roles of masters and slaves (a common feature of ancient comedy), comparative evidence shows that the question of whether a slave was "in the habit of running away" was at the forefront of buyers' mind as they examined a slave and tried to discern their character.[103] More importantly, the scene

---

[99] For the questions of buyers in slave sales in nineteenth-century New Orleans, see Johnson (1999, 112) with references.
[100] Hansen 1998, 120–21.   [101] Johnson 1999, 162–88.   [102] Hansen 1998, 122.
[103] Johnson 1999, 146, 151, 175, etc.

acknowledges the fact that slaves – as human beings – had some agency of their own, and sometimes used it to negotiate the conditions of their enslavement (see Chapter 5). This agency could be exercised even in the process of sale, such that slaves might thwart the attempts of their sellers to present them in the best light, or they might proactively bargain with a potential buyer to attain a master who would give them the maximum autonomy or – at a minimum – the least brutal treatment.

Once again, evidence from better-documented slave societies demonstrates that some slaves were not shy about declaring their views of potential buyers and even went so far as to reject certain buyers openly. In the slave market of nineteenth-century New Orleans, a slave by the name of Moses Roper told a buyer "that I would, on no account, live with him if I could help it."[104] A slave buyer reported that she did not purchase a slave named Virginia "because she [the slave] had said that she would not come with her."[105] While some slaves took this direct route to deterring potential buyers whom they did not like, others did so indirectly by fabricating or exaggerating a sickness, behaving in a sullen or uncooperative way, or generally refusing to play the roles assigned to them by their sellers. Of course, slaves who behaved in these ways risked punishment from their sellers, but evidently some judged the risk worth taking in order to avoid a cruel master or gain a good-natured one. When all else failed, some took the first opportunity to run from their new owners right away. This was the case with one Mary, who "ran away before she could be carried away from New Orleans."[106]

Examples of slaves bargaining for better conditions – like Aesop – can also be found in the record of slave sales in nineteenth-century America. For example, slaves might entreat a buyer to purchase a family member along with themselves or appeal to slave-owners' own professions of paternalistic concern for their slaves.[107] While the effect of such negotiation should not be allowed to obscure the brutality of the process of sale, the potential of slaves to influence their own sale is a reminder of the human capacities of slaves and their potential for independent agency. We will have much more to say about slave agency in Chapter 5, where we examine the constant struggle between master and slave for control and freedom.

---

[104] Johnson 1999, 180. [105] Johnson 1999, 180. [106] Johnson 1999, 180.
[107] Johnson 1999, 181.

Separation of Families

A fascinating new piece of evidence for slave sales at Athens recently came to light in the form of a fragment from a legal speech by the fourth-century politician and speechwriter Hyperides. This text was discovered in 2005 barely visible underneath the print of a medieval prayer book. The parchment used to copy the prayer book had previously been used to copy Hyperides' orations, as well as some treatises by the famous third-century mathematician and scientist Archimedes. The text has a bearing on the question of whether slaves were usually sold individually or whether families were kept together.

The legal case concerns one Timandros, who is accused of mismanagement of the estate of four orphans of whom he had been appointed guardian. Foremost among his misdeeds, according to the speaker, was his separation of the young siblings – an act of cruelty that the speaker alleges was beyond what even slave-dealers were willing to do. The text is fragmentary in places but reads roughly as follows:

> When there were left these two brothers and sisters here, the girls being orphans without a mother or father and all of them small children ... this man Timandros brought up the younger sister in his own home, dragging her away and taking her to Lemnos when she was perhaps seven. And this is an act that no guardian nor any man of goodwill would do, not even those who hold war captives in their possession: even they sell them as far as possible as a family. Further, those slave-retailers and traffickers who do anything [shameless?] for profit, when they sell children, who are siblings or a mother with children ... take a loss and sell them for less, [this being] the right thing to do.[108]

The speaker claims that it was considered shameful even for slave-dealers to separate slave families. The question becomes whether this is a case of rhetorical exaggeration designed "to drive home an advocate's point" or reflects the actual practices of slave-dealers.[109]

In fact, the scant evidence we have for slave sales suggests that it was rare to respect family groupings. In the list of slaves to be auctioned at Athens in 415 BCE, for example, only one sale contains what appears to be a family – a Thracian slave woman and her two children.[110] Furthermore, while there is some evidence of family groups among slaves in classical Athens, it is difficult to tell in these cases whether the slaves were sold together or were simply born in the same household. For example, a legal speech by

---

[108] The translation follows Tchernetska et al. (2007) with the corrections of Jones (2008).
[109] Jones 2008, 20.   [110] *IG* i³.422, 193–99; with Schmitz 2011, 2012, 76–79.

Andocides mentions two slaves who are brothers and living in the same household.[111] Whether these brothers were sold as a pair or born into slavery is unknown. A fragment from a lost play by the comic poet Antiphanes, however, suggests that the Athenians were familiar with the joint sales of siblings, since the fragment concerns two sisters, transported from Syria to Athens and sold there as a pair. One of the sisters tells the story:

> I arrived here in Athens, with my sister, as we were brought by some trader. I am Syrian by birth. This guy, a loan shark, happened along when we were being auctioned, and bought us.[112]

This fictive example notwithstanding, the preponderance of the evidence suggests that family groupings of slaves were relatively rare, and that most slaves were sold as individuals, separately from their biological families.[113] We may conclude that the speaker's claim, in the speech above, about the scruples of slave-dealers is a convenient fiction rather than a reflection of social norms.

Comparative evidence strengthens this conclusion: "Of the two thirds of a million interstate sales ... in the decades before the Civil War, twenty-five percent involved the destruction of a first marriage and fifty percent destroyed a nuclear family – many of these separating children under the age of thirteen from their parents."[114] The much richer evidence from the American Old South, moreover, demonstrates not only the agony of slave families when they were separated by the trade, but also the maneuvers of slaveholders to avoid the difficulties – both ideological and practical – resulting from this practice. For example, slave holders constructed "a narrative of economic necessity" that – they alleged – overrode their reluctance to sell a slave and justified their brutal separation of families. Similarly, slaveholders arranged for family members to be absent when a slave was to be sold.[115]

There are exceptions, however, to the individualized sale of slaves. One example can be found in purchases of publicly owned slaves by the state. While most slaves in ancient Greece were privately owned (with the notable exception of the Spartan helots discussed in Chapter 1), Athens employed public slaves to perform all sorts of basic government functions,

---

[111] Andocides 1.12.   [112] Antiphanes fr. 166, trans. Olson (2007), adapted.
[113] Schmitz (2012) with catalogue of the evidence (pp. 99–101). The case of Midas in Hyperides 3 is a special case, since the buyer is erotically interested in his child and the seller is motivated to offload Midas' debts by exploiting the buyer's desire for the child (see Chapter 3).
[114] Johnson 1999, 19.   [115] Johnson 1999, 37–41.

including keeping records, minting and testing coins, and even providing basic policing of public spaces (see Chapter 3).[116] This latter function was filled by an ethnically homogeneous group of slaves known as the Scythian archers. With their distinctive patterned clothing and weaponry, these slaves stood out from ordinary citizens and hence could perform their duties without threatening the equality of citizens in a democracy. Since Scythians were required, the state occasionally made a purchase in bulk. For example, the Athenians purchased 300 Scythian archers in the middle of the fifth century.[117] These slaves – imported from the Black Sea region – may have gained some comfort at their collective sale, transport and ultimate occupation in Athens. Awareness of the possibility of the formation of a community among Scythian slaves in Athens does not, however, lessen the trauma of their separation from families and homeland, or the disorientation of their new situation in a Greek urban center (see below).

While the Scythian archers sold in bulk ultimately lived in a stable albeit alien lifestyle in Athens, another group of slaves, typically sold and bought in bulk, were not so fortunate. These were slaves intended for the mines. With the exception of certain skilled slaves who served as overseers or managers of mining operations, the majority of slaves who were sold to work in the mines were destined for a brutal and dangerous existence (see Chapter 3). As we have seen, the slaves who became workers in the mines in Attica would have been transported and sold at markets at Sounion or Thorikos – both close to the mining districts. These slaves typically numbered in the hundreds and might have shared an ethnic identity (see Chapter 4). Once again, while sale in bulk and collective assignment may have allowed for the formation of communities and mutual support among slaves, knowledge of the ultimate destination must have led many to despair.

Slave Prices

As we have seen, a slave in one of Aristophanes' comedies grouses that he has become a slave after being bought for "a tiny bit of money."[118] This is certainly a valid complaint from a slave's perspective, since even from a master's perspective slaves were relatively cheap in ancient Greece. Indeed, it is no paradox that the owner of the aforementioned slave in Aristophanes' play describes himself as poor. In Athens, ordinary citizens,

---

[116] Ismard 2015; and references in Chapter 3.   [117] Andocides 3.5; Aeschines 2.173.
[118] Aristophanes, *Wealth* 147–48.

even relatively poor ones, might own a slave or two (see Chapter 3).[119] It seems that low transport costs and a steady supply kept prices down.[120]

Judging from the lists of confiscated property that was put up for auction in Athens, the average price of a slave was between 150 and 200 drachmas, an amount equal to about 100–150 days of work for a skilled craftsman.[121] This price is only an average, of course, and much depended on the age, gender and skills of the slave. On the same list, a Carian child goes for as little as 72 drachmas and a Lydian woman goes for barely more (85 drachmas). At the other end of the scale, a Thracian woman is sold for 220 drachmas and a Syrian man for 301 drachmas.[122] These latter slaves presumably possessed valuable skills, judging from the evidence for prices of slave-craftsmen. The fourth-century Athenian politician Demosthenes claimed as part of his inheritance thirty-two knife-making slaves worth 5 or 6 minas (500 or 600 drachmas) each, and twenty couch-making slaves worth 2 minas (200 drachmas) each.[123] Very highly prized slaves could go for even more. The fifth-century Athenian politician Nicias is said to have paid a talent (6,000 drachmas) for one Sosias, a Thracian overseer who supervised mining operations on his behalf.[124] The high-class prostitute Neaira was worth 30 minas (3,000 drachmas).[125]

Once the sale was concluded, slaves would wonder in trepidation about the nature of the person who had acquired them. Even in cases in which a slave succeeded in influencing a sale, she might still worry about whether she had made the right judgment of her buyer? Would he be a brutal or a kind master? In the moments after the sale, the other slaves on sale – particularly those who had been waiting for a sale for some time and therefore might know some of the potential buyers – might offer moral support to the slave who was about to be removed to an unknown situation. This is the case in a scene from a comic play, in which a nearby slave tells a recently sold adult male and small child to "take courage" because the man who has purchased them is "a military commander, a good man and a wealthy one."[126]

---

[119] Aristophanes, *Wealth* 29. On slave ownership in Athens, the lawsuit claim of Lysias 24.6 is often taken as indicative, since, in this case, a crippled man with few resources, aspires to acquire a slave to take over his craft. For discussion, see Chapter 3.
[120] Lewis 2016a, 321–23.
[121] Braund 2011, 124. Lewis (2016a, 321) provides a slightly higher and wider range: 200–500 drachmas in the fourth century.
[122] *IG* i³.421, col. 1, lines 33 to 49.   [123] Demosthenes 27.9.
[124] Xenophon, *Memorabilia* 2.5.2, *Ways & Means* 4.14; Plutarch, *Life of Nicias* 4.2.
[125] Pseudo-Demosthenes 59.29. See Chapter 3 for further discussion of Neaira and slave-prostitutes in general.
[126] Menander, *Sicyonians* 11–15.

This anecdote raises the question of the slave's experience in the aftermath of a sale – not only the sense of foreboding about the character of a new master but also the experience of being transported to and integrated into a new home.

Cultural Dislocation

Whether kept as slaves of their captors or sold on to others, transport and cultural dislocation of greater or lesser proportions were inevitable.[127] Slaves captured and transported to Greece from Thrace, Scythia or beyond left behind small villages or a semi-nomadic life on the Eurasian steppes for Greek urban centers and surrounding farms. Language would have been only one of many differences that the new slave would have had to navigate. There were also new cults, lifestyles and individuals to which the slave would have had to adapt.

One of the more disorienting Greek customs that a newly acquired non-Greek slave would have encountered was the ritual of entry into the household.[128] On the day that he was purchased, the slave was brought into the household and placed by the hearth, the cultic center of the household. Next, the mistress would pour nuts and dried figs over the head of the slave. For the Greek members of the household, the casting of dried figs and nuts symbolized the hope that the slave would produce for the household lasting human and agricultural fertility, abundance and wealth.[129] For the master, the ritual marked the integration of the slave – a new productive force – into the community of the household under his authority and that of his wife. For the slave, however, the ritual signaled the end of his transition from his prior status (free or servile) and his assumption of a servile status in a new household. A moment of great hope and expectation for the master, therefore, was simultaneously a moment of utter loss and transformation for the slave. For a non-Greek slave who did not understand the significance of the ritual, it must have been a strange and even frightening experience.

Even more ominously, public slaves could meet with a brutal initiation into their new lives: they were branded with a mark signifying their status

---

[127] Although Hunt (2015, 131) suggests that the cultural dislocation of slaves in the ancient world was less than that endured by slaves brought from Africa to the New World.
[128] Aristophanes, *Wealth* 768–95 with scholia; Hesychius and Souda s.v. καταχύσματα; Pollux 3.76; pseudo-Demosthenes 45.74: "And he himself did not hesitate to marry his former owner, and to live with her who had poured the nuts and figs over him on the day he was purchased."
[129] Mactoux 1990, 60.

as publicly owned.[130] This branding was done to ensure that no one could claim a publicly owned slave as their private slave, or sell them or export them. For the slave, however, the application of a hot iron against their skin and the smell of burning flesh served as a violent and painful introduction to their new master: the state. Paradoxically, publicly owned slaves sometimes lived a relatively independent lifestyle and even sometimes accumulated considerable wealth. This fact, however, does little to mitigate the brutality and inhumanity of the process of branding, a procedure associated primarily with marking the possession of livestock.[131]

Greeks enslaved by fellow Greeks endured a smaller geographical and cultural dislocation, but their change in status must have been equally disorienting and shocking. A particularly vivid example of enslavement of a Greek by another Greek is described in a fourth-century legal speech preserved under the name of Andocides, but probably a rhetorical exercise composed by an unknown author at a later date. The speech refers to the aftermath of Athens' conquest of the Greek island of Melos in 415 BCE, when the Athenians killed the males and enslaved the women and children. The speaker describes how the fifth-century Athenian politician Alcibiades bought one of the Melian women and even had a child by her. While the main point of this speech is to illustrate Alcibiades' outrageous behavior, it is notable that it does so by representing, and implicitly calling on the sympathy of the Athenian jurors for, the suffering of an enslaved woman and her child.

> [Alcibiades'] offensive behavior goes beyond all bounds. After making a proposal for the enslavement of the Melians, he bought one of the female prisoners and had a son by her. That baby was born even more illicitly than Aegisthus: his parents are each other's greatest enemies, and he has relatives of whom some inflicted and others endured the utmost suffering. Let me make Alcibiades' audacity even plainer. He had a child by a woman whom he had made a slave instead of free, whose father and relatives he had killed, and whose city he had destroyed; thus he made his son a deadly enemy to himself and to Athens, so compelling are his motives for loathing them. But as for you, you think such deeds terrible when you see them in tragedies, but when you see them happening in Athens you don't care a scrap. Yet in the one case you don't really know whether they did happen in that way or have been invented by the poets; in the other case, when you know very well that these outrageous deeds have been done, you tolerate them easily.[132]

---

[130] Xenophon, *Ways & Means* 4.21.
[131] Although privately owned slaves who ran away were also often branded on recapture (see Chapter 5) and free Greeks who committed treason could also be branded as punishment (e.g., the Thebans at Thermopylae in 480 BCE).
[132] Pseudo-Andocides 4.22–23, trans. MacDowell.

While we do not know whether this is a fictional example, it is entirely plausible that an Athenian could have had a child by one of the captive women of Melos. Remarkably, the speaker invokes the jurors' outrage and empathy not only for the situation of a slave child, who was born from a liaison between a master and his slave, but also for the slave mother who lost her freedom and whose own relatives were slaughtered or sold into slavery by her master. Revealingly, the speaker chastises the Athenians for feeling empathy with victims of enslavement in tragic plays (see the quotation from Euripides' *Hecuba* above), but showing indifference to actual occurrences of enslavement in Athens.

While it suits the speaker's partisan interest in vilifying Alcibiades to take the perspective of the enslaved mother and child, this passage is still a remarkable window onto Greek views of the experience of enslavement. The author implies that the child and her mother are caught in a terrible dilemma, with the child particularly torn between its ties to its Athenian father and its Melian mother. Since a child born of a slave mother and a free father would become a slave, it is likely that the child would have identified with his mother, and been brought up to despise his father. On the other hand, a child born into slavery would have had less connection to his ancestral city on his mother's side, and – unless his mother managed to keep him in the same household and maintain some of her native polis culture (in this case, Dorian cults and dialect) in her new setting (see below) – the child may have become more assimilated into Athenian culture than to that of his mother's homeland.

Sometimes our Greek sources provide insight into the experience of enslavement through remarks made about Greeks who had been enslaved by non-Greeks. These sources illustrate both the shock of enslavement in a different culture and the ways that slaves had to adapt linguistically to their new masters. We can use these observations to understand the inverse experience – that is, non-Greeks being enslaved by Greeks.

The first example concerns a Greek woman who had been enslaved by the Macedonians when they conquered her native city of Olynthus in 348. In a legal speech aimed at discrediting his political rival, Demosthenes describes a banquet that was held shortly after the conquest in the home of a Macedonian citizen and attended by his rival. Demosthenes vividly describes the brutal and humiliating treatment of the Olynthian woman and particularly her distress and desperation as she tried to navigate the unknown mores of her new Macedonian masters.

> When they started drinking, [the host] brought in an Olynthian woman who was beautiful, but also free by birth and modest. At first, it seems, they compelled her gently to drink and to eat something … As the night wore on, however, and they grew heated with drink, they compelled her to lie on a couch and even to sing something. When the woman became distressed since she neither wanted [to sing] nor knew how, [the hosts] asserted that it was an outrage and not to be borne that she – who was a war captive … – put on airs. They said, "call a slave" and "bring a leather strap!" A slave came holding a whip, and – since they were drunk and easily provoked – when she said something and wept, the slave tore off her clothes and flogged her back repeatedly.[133]

The episode ended when the woman fell at the knees of one of the banqueters and begged for mercy. The banqueter took pity on her and she was saved. If this man had not intervened, we are told, the Olynthian woman would have been killed. Despite this narrow escape, the language is telling. The woman is publicly stripped of her clothing, a grave insult to a Greek woman.[134] She is then whipped with instruments used also on animals, thus reducing her to an inhuman status. The verb used to describe her flogging (ξαίνειν), moreover, means "to mangle or lacerate," and would have evoked an image of raw and bloody flesh. And all this brutal treatment was brought on by her inability to adapt quickly enough to the demands of her new masters. While this account is admittedly quite extreme – indeed, Demosthenes describes it in a way designed to evoke pity and shock in his Athenian audience – it captures not only the brutality but also some of the terror and confusion that a newly enslaved person might have experienced as they tried to navigate their new cultural context and status.

In the case of the Olynthian woman, as in the case of the Melian woman, language would not have been a major barrier to communication, since the Macedonians spoke a dialect of Greek or a closely related language. In other cases, however, language would have been a major part of the cultural disorientation of a slave. Again, we can get a sense of this non-Greek experience from its inverse – the experience of Greeks enslaved elsewhere. For example, an Athenian legal speech mentioned earlier in this chapter concerns a citizenship case in which the defendant was accused of being a foreigner on the grounds that his father spoke with an accent. As we saw, the defendant's explanation for his father's accent was that he was captured by the Spartans and their allies during the Peloponnesian War and spent many years in slavery.[135] In this case, as in the case of the Olynthian and

---

[133] Demosthenes 19.197.   [134] Herodotus 1.8.3.   [135] Demosthenes 57.18.

Melian women, the "accent" would have been simply a dialectical difference since the father was enslaved on the Greek island of Leucas, off the west coast of Greece. In any case, the anecdote is an indication of the ways that enslaved persons in Greece would have been exposed to new dialects and languages and would have had to adapt linguistically in their new environment.

A remarkable example of complete language adaptation – that is, learning a totally new language – by a slave in Athens is found in Xenophon's account of the expedition of some Greek mercenaries to aid the Persian prince Cyrus in his bid for the throne in 401 BCE. While the mission was ultimately unsuccessful, Xenophon, who participated in the expedition, reports a remarkable incident on the long march back to Greece. As the soldiers neared the southeast corner of the Black Sea, they found themselves confronted by a seemingly hostile local people as they tried to ford a river. Anxious that the Greeks had warlike intentions towards them, these people, whom we later learn were called Macronians, stood on the opposite bank of the river, shouting and throwing stones. At this point, one of the light-armed troops (peltasts) in the Greek army approached Xenophon (who was commanding) and made a startling revelation. The soldier reported that he had been a slave in Athens and that he recognized the language of the hostile tribe. In what must have been a very emotional moment for the soldier, he said, "I think this is my homeland." He then added, "If nothing prevents it, I would like to talk to them."[136]

Xenophon reports this incident only as a necessary detail of the plot of his account – namely, that the soldier's ability to communicate with the Macronians allowed the Greeks to explain that they were simply trying to return to Greece after fighting against the Persian king. Upon clarifying this point, the Greeks gained the assistance of the Macronians in crossing the difficult terrain and reaching the Black Sea. What is striking, however, is that this soldier's revelation suggests that he was captured many years ago in his homeland deep in the hinterlands of the Black Sea region and sold into slavery at Athens. Over the course of this man's life in Athens, he had apparently learned Greek and gained his freedom. And yet, he had no knowledge of his origins or native culture until this chance encounter.[137] This lack of knowledge suggests that he was captured at a relatively young age and transported to Athens. On the other hand, the fact that he could

---

[136] Xenophon, *Anabasis* 4.8.4.
[137] Braund and Tsetskhladze 1989, 120; Braund 2011, 130. The case of the miner Atotas (Braund 2011, 131; Hunt 2015; and Chapter 4) suggests some slaves maintained knowledge of their origins and pride in their ethnicity.

remember his native tongue when he first heard it, suggests that he was captured at an age at which he had language facility in his native tongue.

We can only imagine what the experience of this young child would have been as he found himself enslaved at Athens surrounded by people who spoke a different language, worshipped different gods and had a radically different way of life. While the outcome seems to have been relatively good – the man assimilated and even gained his freedom – we cannot underestimate the trauma caused by the experience of violence, separation from family and country, and the initial encounter with alien languages and behaviors. An indication of the initial difficulty of language acquisition for recently bought slaves is implied in the politician Demosthenes' critique of his rival Aeschines, whom he frequently claimed had slavish origins. Demosthenes alludes to Aeschines' slavish origins when he says that he engages in a lot of bluster and noise about lawsuits – "two or three simple words that even a slave bought yesterday could recite" – but doesn't have the rhetorical ability to see them through.[138] Language, however, was just one of the disorienting features of his new environment – the urban landscape, the population density and even the sounds of this bustling city must have been overwhelming to a child born in the thickly forested terrain of the Macronians.

Of course, a person born into slavery in Athens would have experienced less or no linguistic or cultural disruption. When Socrates wishes to interrogate a slave in Plato's philosophical dialogue *Meno*, his host provides him with a house-born slave, since such a slave "is Greek and speaks Greek."[139] Shockingly, but not surprisingly, a house-born slave is considered "Greek" by its owner, regardless of their mother's ethnicity. It was inevitable and even compulsory, of course, that the child learn the language and culture of its owners, and it is not surprising that from the perspective of the owners house-born slaves were simply "Greek" and "speakers of Greek." What is perhaps also unsurprising, however, is that some slaves made efforts to retain the language and customs of their homeland and teach them to their (enslaved, house-born) children. An anecdote recounted by the fifth-century historian Herodotus, for example, suggests that some slave mothers taught their children the language and customs of their homeland, in part, as a mode of resistance to their enslavers.

Herodotus tells the story as an explanation for the widespread Greek custom of referring to brutal acts as "Lemnian deeds." According to the Greek legend that Herodotus reports, when the original inhabitants of the

---

[138] Demosthenes 19.209.   [139] Plato, *Meno* 82b.

territory of Athens, the Pelasgians, were expelled and settled on the island of Lemnos, they sought revenge on the Athenians by capturing and enslaving some Athenian women. These women were held as concubines by their captors and soon produced children who – as they grew up – refused to associate with the Pelasgians' legitimate children and behaved as though they were superior to them. According to Herodotus, this behavior was a consequence of the fact that the Athenian women had taught their own children the Athenian language (the Pelasgians were not Greek speakers) as well as their customs. In response to the haughtiness of these children, the Pelasgians murdered their Athenian concubines along with their children – an act that gave the name of "Lemnian deed" to any act of unusual brutality committed thereafter.[140]

Interestingly, enslaved women might even teach their owners' children their language and culture, perhaps as a gesture of resistance or a desperate attempt to preserve their memories of their origins. Such a scenario is implicit in the *Homeric Hymn to Aphrodite*, where Aphrodite in disguise claims that she is a Phrygian princess, whose nurse, a slave from Troy, taught her the Trojan tongue.[141] This early exposure to the Trojan language by her slave-nurse provides a plausible explanation of why the disguised goddess is able to speak fluently to the Trojan Anchises. For us, the point is that these fictive stories suggest that while slaves were forced to adapt to the language and culture of their masters, some slaves may have made an effort to maintain their own language and culture. We will return to this subject when we consider slave identity (Chapter 4) and resistance (Chapter 5).

The Slave Population

Size

Turning now from the modes and experience of enslavement, we can attempt to sketch a general profile of the slave population in Greece. Of course, such a sketch will be very rough, because data is scarce, and what we have relates primarily to Athens and Sparta – just two out of the more than one thousand Greek city-states. This evidentiary pattern leaves us largely in the dark when it comes to slavery in Greece as a whole. Nevertheless, scattered testimony shows that slavery was widespread, from the little-known island of Leucas in western Greece, as we have just seen, to the

---

[140] Herodotus 6. 138. See Chapter 5 for further examples of cultural resistance to enslavement.
[141] *Homeric Hymn to Aphrodite* 113–16.

Greek cities of coastal Asia Minor. In fact, the island of Chios, off the coast of modern-day Turkey, was credited with originating the practice of chattel slavery in ancient Greece, and was considered to have one of the largest and best-managed slave population in the Greek world.[142] Moreover, the island of Aegina, off the coast of Attica, was known for its slave market and its allegedly enormous slave population. According to one ancient source, there were 470,000 slaves on this island of eighty-seven square kilometers![143] While this number, along with other exaggerated numbers in this source, is to be rejected, such numbers indicate that the Greeks themselves thought there were very many slaves on this island and in several other Greek city-states.

But how large? What was the proportion of slaves to free people? As already noted, absolute numbers and ratios elude us due to lack of evidence. We can, however, make rough guesses for a few places, chiefly Athens and Sparta.

Athenian sources often assume that every Athenian has at least one slave. For example, the fourth-century politician Demosthenes exhorts the ordinary citizens who manned the courts to "think to yourself about some slave you left at home ... some Syros or Manes or whatever name each has."[144] We have a good sense of the number of male citizens in Athens, which ranged from a maximum of 60,000 in the fifth century to about 30,000 in the fourth century.[145] If, as seems likely from the evidence of slave labor (Chapter 3), at least 50 percent of this population had a slave or two, we start with a minimum figure of c.30,000 to c.15,000 slaves in the fifth and fourth centuries respectively.[146] Of course, wealthy Athenians owned dozens, and, in a few rare cases, hundreds of slaves, so these figures are minimal numbers. To these minimum numbers, we can add the large number of publicly owned slaves – including the 300–1200 Scythian archers and the many scribes, heralds and coin testers who performed many of the state's basic functions (see Chapter 3). The most recent

---

[142] Thucydides 8.40.2; Theopompus *FGrHist* 115 F122 = Athenaeus 265d.
[143] Athenaeus 272b-d, citing a number of Hellenistic period Greek sources, as well as a census said to have been conducted by Demetrius of Phalerum in the last decade of the fourth century. See Fisher (1993, 34–35) on why these numbers are not to be trusted: they imply impossibly high population densities, and there is no evidence that the Greeks took censuses that included slaves.
[144] Demosthenes 45.86.   [145] Hansen 1999, 53–54.
[146] Contra Rihll (2011, 49) who infers from Aristotle's statements (namely, that democracy is the rule of the poor (*Politics* 1279b18–1280a6) and that the poor do not have slaves (*Politics* 1323a6–7)) that the majority of citizens in classical Athens did not have slaves. This interpretation, however, underestimates the ideological nature of Aristotle's definition of democracy as "rule of the poor," and ignores the substantial body of middling citizens (neither rich nor poor) that formed the majority of the Athenian citizen body. Such middling citizens would have owned one or two slaves.

estimate of numbers of publicly owned slaves in Athens is 1,000–2,000.[147] Next, we can add the very large number of slaves who worked the mines at Laurion in southern Attica. In the fourth century, Xenophon can imagine a scenario in which the state owns 10,000 slaves in the mines – a figure presumably based on the thousands of privately owned slaves working in the mines during his time. This is plausible given the fact that Nicias alone owned 1,000 slaves in the mines.[148] If we halve Xenophon's number, we come up with a low estimate of 5,000 for the number of slaves in the mines.

Adding up these figures, we can estimate a minimum total of 36,500 to 21,500 slaves in fifth and fourth-century Athens respectively. Less conservative estimates range from 50,000 to 120,000 during the classical period.[149] Numbers of this order of magnitude correspond well with several of the more plausible figures in our sources. First, Thucydides reports that "more than 20,000 slaves, the majority of whom were skilled workers, deserted" when the Spartans occupied the deme of Deceleia in Athenian territory in 413.[150] Second, the fourth-century politician Hyperides proposes in one of his speeches that in order to continue to resist the Macedonians after the defeat at Chaeronea in 338, the Athenians should enfranchise the slaves "in the countryside and in the mines" who number "more than 150,000."[151] While it is unlikely that either of these numbers is based on actual records, they must have been plausible to Athenians during the fifth and fourth centuries.[152] On these bases, we can estimate a total slave population ranging from 20,000 to 120,000, or somewhere between 8 percent and 50 percent of the total population of 250,000 (including women, children and free non-citizens). Taking the average, we might settle on 70,000 slaves or roughly 30 percent of the total population. While this is admittedly a very rough estimate, it gives us some sense of the total size of the slave population and the ratio of slaves to nonslaves. By any measure, there were a *lot* of slaves in classical Athens.

If Athens had a lot of slaves, Sparta had even more. Thucydides confidently asserts that the Spartans had the greatest number of slaves of any city-state in Greece, and that the island of Chios – considered the birthplace of chattel slavery in Greece, as mentioned already – had the second-largest slave population.[153] While Thucydides does not specify, this claim must refer to the size of the slave population in relation to the citizen or the

---

[147] Ismard 2015, 85. [148] Xenophon, *Ways & Means* 4.24. [149] Fisher 1993, 35. [150] 7.27.5.
[151] Hyperides fr. 29.
[152] Paul Cartledge, however, suggests to me that Thucydides' number may be based on Spartan records.
[153] 8.40.

total population of these states. Certainly, traditions about Sparta suggest that its large slave population was a constant threat to the stability of Sparta, and we know of at least one major helot revolt in Sparta following an earthquake in c.464 (see Chapter 5).[154] A sense of the size of the imbalance between Spartans and helots can be gleaned from Herodotus' account of the Battle of Plataea in 479, where he states that each Spartan soldier was accompanied by seven helots.[155] While this number may be exaggerated, it reflects the fact that the helots outnumbered the Spartans heavily. If the ratio between Athenian male citizens and their slaves was 1:2 (according to the rough calculation above), the ratio between Spartans and their slaves was even higher.

Ethnicity

As we saw in Chapter 1, the Spartan helots shared a common ethnicity since they were indigenous Greeks who were conquered and enslaved en masse by the Spartans by the end of the eighth century BCE. While there were several other such groups who were enslaved in situ, this was not the norm for most city-states. As we have seen, most slaves were brought from elsewhere through conquest or sale. While some of these slaves were fellow Greeks conquered in battle, they joined servile populations from diverse ethnicities in the communities to which they were taken. The question arises, what was the ethnic makeup of the slave population? What was the ratio between Greek and non-Greek slaves? Were any ethnic groups particularly prominent?

Before addressing this question, we might first ask, why does it matter? The ancients believed that – all else being equal – revolts were more likely to happen among slaves of the same ethnicity.[156] As we shall see in Chapter 5, however, the comparative study of slave revolts disproves this belief, and suggests on the contrary that heterogeneous slave populations imported from abroad are more likely to revolt. Yet the significance of ethnicity goes beyond resistance to the question of the experience of slavery itself. As we have seen, the cultural gap between the birth culture of a slave and the culture in which he is enslaved gives an indication of the trauma experienced by the slave. Indeed, the experience of slavery depended in part on the difficulty or ease of language acquisition and other aspects of cultural assimilation. Moreover, the numbers of slaves of the same ethnicity in a community also affected the experience of enslavement. It mattered

---

[154] 1.101.2.   [155] Herodotus 9.29.   [156] Plato, *Laws* 777d; Rihll 2011, 71–72; and Chapter 5.

a great deal if one was the only Egyptian slave in one's community or whether one was part of the large group of Thracian slaves who worshipped the Thracian god Bendis at Athens.[157] Age of enslavement, among other factors, also affects each of these points, of course, and therefore we will also try to sketch the age profile of the slave population.

As with the overall population, we also lack good data for determining the number and proportion of slaves of various ethnicities. Yet, for Athens, we can make rough guesses based on the patterns of ethnic names or other ethnic identifiers found in state-generated lists of slaves, such as of those sold in public auctions and of those who served as rowers in the Athenian navy. The proportions derived from these lists can be supplemented by a number of gravestones of slaves or ex-slaves, as well as a substantial body of dedications of freed slaves.[158] Yet, before we can make use of these documents, we must acknowledge that the data they present cannot be used as a direct proxy for percentages of various ethnicities in the slave population. This caveat is required because scholars have realized that ethnic names do not always correlate with actual foreign ethnicities and conversely that Greek names do not always correspond to Greek ethnicity.

While it has long been recognized that slave-buyers or slave-owners might give generic ethnic labels to slaves regardless of their actual ethnicity, one of the most striking breakthroughs of recent scholarship is the recognition that most slaves (53 percent of surviving slave names) have Greek names that are also borne by citizens.[159] Interestingly, fictional slave names such as those that appear in comedy and tragedy, reverse this pattern. That is, most fictional slave names bear ethnic or foreign names (57 percent). Finally, the vast majority of freed persons bear names that are also attested for citizens (70 percent). Whatever we make of these patterns, clearly we cannot simply equate names with ethnicity.

The pattern in literature seems to confirm the ideological tendency of free citizens to emphasize the gap between citizen and slave in order to justify slavery.[160] By representing slaves with non-Greek names on the stage, Greeks naturalized slavery in the same way Aristotle does when he – quoting Euripides – claimed that Greeks were natural rulers and that "barbarians" were natural slaves.[161] Yet, the evidence for historical slave

---

[157] Plato, *Republic* 327a; Garland 1987, 118–22; Hunt 2015, 134–35; and Chapter 4.
[158] Lewis 2018.
[159] Vlassopoulos 2010, 2015; Lewis 2018. For recent skepticism about the correlation between ethnic names and actual origins, see Tsetskhladze 2008.
[160] See Vlassopoulos (2015) for the points made in these paragraphs.
[161] Aristotle, *Politics* 1252b1–10.

names that are Greek and the same or similar to citizen names shows that, in real life, Greeks did not always try to "other" their slaves. In fact, Greeks may have conferred citizen-style names upon slaves to facilitate their ability to interact with citizens and hence enhance their performance of their duties. It is particularly striking, in this regard, that slaves who performed "white collar" jobs such as bankers and scribes seem to have Greek names that citizens also possess, while slaves in more menial positions have more clearly foreign or ethnic names.

It is also possible that the slaves themselves actively claimed Greek names for themselves and their children in order to promote their integration and success in Greek society, or even to escape detection as slaves (Chapter 4). This possibility is strengthened by the frequency of Greek names shared with citizens among historically attested freed persons. This latter pattern suggests that freed persons often adopted or retained names for themselves and their children that obscured differences between themselves and citizens. We must be cautious about the potential bias of our sources here, since records of freed persons represent a particular subset of the slave population – namely, those who were successful in escaping it through formal mechanisms. We cannot assume that most slaves were willing to abandon that part of their ethnic identity that was reflected in their names, and indeed some funeral monuments of foreigners who were probably slaves or former slaves reveal that at least some retained not only ethnic names but also a great deal of ethnic pride (Chapter 4). The occurrence of at least one historical slave with a foreign name (Skonus), yet also designated as "house-born," shows that even some slaves born in Greece took on ethnic names.[162]

With these methodological problems in mind, what can we say about slave ethnicity from the data we have? It seems best not to expect to be able to draw any fine-grained results about numbers or proportions of various ethnicities among the slave population at Athens. Instead, we must accept that we can draw only very limited conclusions about the ethnicity of slaves in Athens.

First, even if slave-traders or slave-owners gave generic ethnic names to their foreign slaves, these names probably still indicate the broadly defined regions from which the slaves were taken. If a slave is labelled "Thracian" or given an ethnic name like "Thraix" (male) or "Thratta" (female), then it is likely that the slave originated in the vast region that spreads from the northern coast of the Aegean to deep into the hinterlands of the areas west

---

[162] *IG* i³.422.71. Some freeborn Greeks, moreover, had ethnic names, such as Skythes ("Scythian").

and north of the Black Sea. While finer ethnic distinctions were sometimes made within this category – for example, Getas (from the Getai of the coastal areas of the northwestern Black Sea) – in most cases, it is not possible to be more precise. That said, we can divide the surviving slaves with ethnic identifiers into broadly defined regions and roughly estimate their proportion in this wide-brushstroke way. These broad regions include Anatolia, especially Phrygia and Caria, and the Levant, notably Syria and Phoenicia.

If we turn back to the evidence for slave names and ethnic identifiers, we can see that although "Thrace" seems to be the leading source of foreign slaves, the other regions are also very significant sources.[163] For example, a catalogue of grave monuments of foreigners, some of whom were slaves or ex-slaves, contains the following three ethnicities in the largest numbers: Thracians 25, Phoenicians 18, Phrygians 14. Since at least some of these are freed persons, we might ask whether these proportions reflect society at large, or reflect particularly successful ethnicities – like people of Indian or Korean descent in the contemporary USA. The large number of Phoenicians, for example, may reflect the success of this ethnic group in the banking field (Chapter 3). On a broad scale, however, it is significant that all three regions are represented in significant numbers in this sample, and our other data sets repeat this pattern. For example, in one of the lists of property confiscated from men convicted of sacrilege in 414 BCE, we encounter the following ethnicities and numerical proportions among slaves belonging to the metic Cephisodorus: of sixteen slaves in total, there are five Thracians, three Carians, two Syrians, two Illyrians, one Scythian, one Colchian, one Lydian and one from Melitene (perhaps).[164] On the lists of confiscated property as a whole, forty-one slaves are listed, and there are twelve Thracians, seven Carians, three Scythians, two Syrians, two Illyrians, and one each from Colchis, Phrygia, Lydia, Macedonia, Messenia (perhaps) and Cappadocia.[165] Finally, of the forty-six slaves with clearly foreign or ethnic names on the lists of crews of ships (triremes) from 423, fourteen are Thracian, nine are Phrygian, seven are Carian, six are Syrian, five are Lydian, two are Paphlagonian, two are Phoenician and one is Scythian.[166] Summing up these lists, we can conclude that there were diverse ethnicities represented in the slave population of Athens, with Thracians, Phrygians, Carians, Syrians and Phoenicians particularly prominent among them.

---

[163] Lewis 2016a.   [164] *IG* i³.421, col. 1, lines 33–49 (cited in Chapter 1).
[165] Tsetskhladze 2008, 313.   [166] *IG* i³.1032.

Determining the ratio of Greek to non-Greek ethnicity in the slave population is tricky because of the tendency, noted above, for slaves to have Greek names, even if they are otherwise known to be non-Greek. For example, in the lists of confiscated property, a slave identified as Scythian is named Dionysios, a common Greek name held by many citizens.[167] Given that non-Greek slaves were given Greek names, it is likely that the number of non-Greek slaves in the slave population is higher than the number of ethnic or foreign names on the lists would suggest. In other words, at least some proportion of non-Greek slaves is "hidden" from our view through the naming practices of masters, or perhaps the slaves themselves. Beyond this acknowledgement we cannot go much further.

In sum, we can conclude that there were many foreign slaves in Athens, and they came from a wide variety of locales in Thrace and the Eurasian steppe, Anatolia and the Levant. While there were also slaves of Greek ethnicity, as we have seen, it is difficult to judge how significant the number of these were, given the tendency to give non-Greek slaves Greek names. In a few cases, our lists specify the Greek ethnicity of slaves. For example, on the lists of confiscated property, there are slaves listed as "Polyxenus, Macedonian" and "Sosimenus, Cretan." We possibly even get an entry without a proper name but with a Greek ethnicity: "Messenian man." Similarly, on the naval lists several slaves have Greek ethnic names: Arcadion ("Arcadian"), Lacon ("Laconian") and Chionides ("Chian"). Proportionately, the number of slaves with Greek ethnicities as opposed to non-Greek on these lists is low (three out of thirty-four and three out of forty-five respectively), and this might be taken as evidence that non-Greeks predominate in the slave population. Yet we cannot be certain, since many slaves are listed without an ethnicity at all. For example, what are we to make of the following entry for a slave sold among the confiscated properties: "a man, Aristomachus"?[168] Aristomachus is a good Greek name, attested for many Greek citizens. Is this a slave of Greek ethnicity who is given an appropriately Greek name? Or is this a slave of non-Greek ethnicity whose ethnicity is obscured by the Greek name? We cannot tell.

Our difficulties in determining ethnicities of slaves listed in our sources are compounded by the nonuniform formulae used in our sources. For example, a slave child of Carian ethnicity might sometimes include a proper name ("a boy, Peisistratus, Carian") and sometimes just an ethnicity ("Carian child").[169] The following two entries from the lists of

---

[167] Vlassopoulos 2010. [168] *IG* i³.426, col. 2, line 44. [169] *IG* i³.421, col. 1, line 9 and line 46.

confiscated property further illustrate the wide range of identifiers used in our sources.

Entry #1

> From the property of those who committed impieties concerning the Mysteries ...
> ... slaves were sold.

Antigenes,
Thracian ethnicity
Strongulion,
Carian ethnicity
Simos,
Scythian ethnicity
Carion,
Carian ethnicity
Phanes,
Lydian ethnicity
Apollonides,
Thracian ethnicity.[170]

Entry #2

> From the property of Adeimantus son of Leucolophides of the deme of Skambonidai

Phrygian man
Apollophanes, man
Charias, blacksmith
Aristarchus, leather worker
Satyrus, leather worker
———on, houseborn.[171]

The first list is fairly systematic, providing proper names and then ethnicities. This list clearly shows how slaves of non-Greek ethnicity are given Greek names that are also held by citizens. For example, Antigenes is a common Greek citizen name, yet it belongs to a slave from Thrace in this case. Yet, also on this list there are slaves of non-Greek ethnicity who are given ethnic names ("Carion, of Carian ethnicity") or names that refer to bodily features (Strongulion, "round pot," Simos, "snub nose").

The second list provides a whole new array of identifying options: ethnicity, gender and a rough indication of age ("Phrygian man"), proper

[170] *IG* i³.427, col. 1, lines 1–13.　[171] *IG* i³.426, col. 1, lines 10–16.

name and rough indication of age ("Apollophanes, a man"), proper name and profession ("Charias, a blacksmith," "Aristarchus, a leather worker") or proper name and status as chattel slave or houseborn ("——on, houseborn"). Given this variety of presentation modes, we cannot assume that the failure to mention an ethnicity means that a slave is Greek, let alone that a Greek name implies Greek ethnicity.

Gender Ratio and Age Profile

What can we say about the gender ratio and age profile of the slave population? We might expect that adult male slaves were more in demand and hence prevalent among the slave population. Adult males, we might assume, were the best bet from the slave-owner's perspective, since they had survived the more vulnerable childhood years, and could perform the most demanding physical labor. Yet several bits of evidence contradict this assumption.

First, as we have seen, in a number of notable instances of conquest, it is the women and children who are enslaved, whereas the men are executed.[172] While adult men were certainly also enslaved in many cases, warfare provided a considerable supply of female and non-adult slaves as well. Second, there is evidence for women and children for sale, implying both a supply and a demand for such slaves. For example, in the fragment of a fourth-century comic play discussed above, a female character describes how she was sold in Athens as a young girl, after being brought from Syria by a trader, along with her sister.[173]

Although this source is a fictional play, it was presumably a plausible scenario for the audience and shows that both children and female slaves were bought and sold on the slave market in Athens. The lists of confiscated property show, moreover, that female slaves could be as expensive and hence as highly valued as male slaves. A Macedonian woman, for example, is auctioned off for 310 drachmas, well above the average price for a slave.[174] As the second most highly priced slave on the lists, it is likely that she had some highly valued skills. Comparison with the Carian goldsmithing slave recorded just above her on the list is revealing: he is the most expensive slave on the list at 360 drachmas and has a highly specialized skill. It is possible that the Macedonian woman was a highly valued prostitute, or textile worker. It is noteworthy, however, that the

---

[172] Many of the points made in this section draw on Hunt (forthcoming).
[173] Antiphanes, fr. 166 = Athenaeus, *Learned Banqueters* 3.108e–f.   [174] *IG* i³.422.79.

Macedonian woman is sold for far less than the most expensive prostitute we know of – namely, Neaira, who, as we saw above, was valued at 3,000 drachmas.

We can conclude that there was a demand for female slaves and that, therefore, there were significant numbers of female slaves, as well as child slaves. But can we go further and determine the ratio of male to female or adult to child slaves? We might extrapolate from the ratios in some of our evidence to the proportions in the larger population. Yet, as with our evidence for ethnicities, these do not map easily onto the wider population. In particular, much of the evidence is biased in favor of men. For example, the naval lists record only male slaves, since rowing in the fleet was a task given only to men. Similarly, the slaves recorded on tombstones and other types of inscriptions from the mining district of Laureion are all males. Even bodies of evidence that contain female slaves may also be skewed in favor of males. The lists of confiscated property, for example, contain thirty-one adult males and only seven females and three children. It is possible, that females do not appear on these lists because they often formed part of the wife's dowry and therefore were subtracted before the property was put up for auction.[175]

Yet, even on these lists, the estates of some individuals are apparently gender balanced. For example, the following entry records a slave-owner with two male and two female slaves:

> Slaves of Axiochus, the son of Alcibiades, of the deme Skambonidai:
>
> Arete, Thracian woman
> Grulion, Thracian man
> Habrosune, Thracian woman
> Dionysios, bronzesmith, Scythian.[176]

If, moreover, this count represents what remained after the wife's female slaves were removed, then perhaps there were even more female than male slaves in this household.

Another body of evidence comes closer perhaps to representing the ratio of male to female slaves. The dedications of silver bowls by freed persons from c.330 lists a total of 158 individuals, 63 of whom are women (40 percent).[177] But even in this case we must be careful. With few exceptions, male slaves had greater chances of being employed in professions in which they might accumulate resources with which to purchase and publicize their freedom (see Chapter 3). Indeed, of the women whose

---

[175] Hunt, forthcoming. [176] *IG* i³.422, col. 2, lines 195–99. [177] Rosivach 1989, 366.

profession is legible, 51 practice one apparently lucrative profession: wool working.[178] Moreover, when we consider the fact that some professions – for example, wet nursing – were performed exclusively by women, and mostly slave women, it seems likely that the figure of 40 percent undercounts the number of female slaves in the slave population.[179]

Conclusion

In this chapter, we have surveyed the principal ways that individuals became slaves and also attempted to reconstruct what the experience was like for the slaves themselves. Despite the fact that our sources were (for the most part) written by free Greek males, they nevertheless provide evidence for the traumas of enslavement, including capture, transport, sale and entry into an alien environment. Comparative evidence helped flesh out some of the ancient evidence and allowed us to understand the experience of slaves more vividly. The experience of birth into slavery revealed a different but comparable set of traumas, as the case of the child of the enslaved Melian woman and her owner Alcibiades poignantly illustrates. Even a child born from two slaves would be raised in a difficult and unstable situation since slave marriages were not legally recognized and families could be separated at the whim of their owners.

The chapter also addressed the demography of the slave population in ancient Greece. Here we encountered severe problems because of the lack of reliable quantifiable data. Beyond the general conclusion that slaves were ubiquitous in Greece and that numerous Greek city-states (e.g., Sparta, Chios, Athens, Aegina) had large slave populations, it is hard to provide exact quantities. Similar problems were encountered in assessing the ethnicities of slaves, principally because our chief evidence – slave names – is not a reliable indicator of ethnicity. Nevertheless, the evidence does suggest that there were large numbers of imported slaves in Athens and Chios, and that many slaves came from four regions: the Northern Aegean (Thrace), the Eurasian steppe (Scythia), Anatolia (Phrygia) and the Levant (Syria, Phoenicia). In addition, our sources make clear that there were also ethnically Greek slaves in Greece, not only the helots at Sparta, but also enslaved captives from various conflicts between Greek states. As we saw,

---

[178] Although female retailers are also present in the records (see Chapter 3).
[179] Some citizen women also served as wet nurses out of economic necessity: Demosthenes 57.45. On slave wet nurses, see Chapter 3.

home-born slaves stood in a middle ground between the Greek ethnicity of their owners and the ethnicity of their slave parent(s).

Finally, an attempt was made to assess the age and gender profile of the slave population. Despite any assumptions that we might have about a preference for adult male slaves, we identified clear evidence of the importation of women and children as slaves. Sale prices for female slaves, moreover, indicate that they could be highly valued for their skills, and the evidence of female slaves who gained their freedom shows that some women used their skills to accumulate resources that they controlled themselves (see Chapter 5). While the evidence for child slaves is scanty, it is clear that they were present in significant numbers not just as a result of birth into slavery, but even through purchase on the market. Despite the costs and risks associated with raising a slave child, they could be employed in menial roles or trained in a craft in ways that were ultimately profitable for their owners.

In the next chapter, we will survey the various roles of male, female and child slaves in ancient Greece. As in the case of the process of enslavement itself, we will attempt to recover the slaves' experiences of laboring. One of the most striking results will be to expose the variety of radically different laboring experiences of slaves in ancient Greece. While all slaves shared some basic features of slavery – ownership and control by another person or persons, as we saw in Chapter 1 – the lived experience of slavery could be quite varied for individual slaves, as we shall see.

CHAPTER 3

Being a Slave
Experiences of Slavery

What was it like to live as a slave in ancient Greece? This chapter begins to address this question by exploring how slaves spent the bulk of their days – that is toiling for their owners in various types of labor. Subsequent chapters will examine other aspects of the experience of slavery, especially the ideologies and institutions that shaped the lives of slaves, and the ways that slaves acted to minimize the restrictions on their autonomy.

While labor is not the only category through which the day-to-day experiences of slavery can be analyzed, it was certainly a central part of those experiences. Other possible analytical categories such as age, gender, ethnicity, level of independence and status as house-born or bought were, of course, important factors affecting the experience of slaves, and some of these have already been touched upon in the previous chapter. It is important to note, however, that these other factors were often interdependent with the type of labor that a slave performed. Female slaves, as we have seen, served as wet nurses. Banking, by contrast, was performed by male slaves. Similarly, there is evidence that certain ethnicities were favored for particular tasks – Thracian women in wet nursing and Phrygian men in mining, for example. While labor will be the key analytical frame, therefore, this chapter will also discuss the important role that these other factors played in the experiences of slavery in ancient Greece.

The title to this chapter uses the plural "experiences" not the singular "experience" of slavery. This is because there was no single experience but a variety of individual experiences which were correlated, as we have just seen, with a number of other factors including occupation, but also depended on the unique dispositions and characters of individual slaves. While it would be impossible to analyze the experience of slavery at the individual level, this chapter will aim to sketch some broad patterns among the wide range of experiences of slavery. We will begin with the four most prevalent slave occupations – agriculture, manufacturing, mining and domestic labor – before turning to less common but still prominent slave occupations such as banking, commerce and the state bureaucracy.

Finally, the presence of slaves in almost every aspect of life in ancient Greek city-states will lead us to assess whether the city-states were dependent on slavery: that is, whether the different societies of ancient Greece could not have functioned in the ways that they did without slavery.

Agriculture and Animal Husbandry

Literary sources assume that slaves were present on small farms and large. When slaves are absent, it is considered remarkable – as in Menander's play *The Bad-Tempered Man* about a man who farms an estate worth two talents (12,000 drachmas), yet has neither slave nor hired help.[1] Typically, the average small farmer had one or two slaves who labored alongside the free members of the family on the land and in the household.[2] Menander's play provides an example of this more customary arrangement in the character of Daos, a slave who farms alongside his master Gorgias. Daos is the only slave on the farm and divides his time between performing service for his mistress in the house and working in the field alongside his master. In one scene, Daos is depicted as somewhat resentful at being detained in the house by his owner's mother, and eager to get out to the field. In protest, he says: "I spent a lot of time here attending to you, while he [my master] is digging. I must go to him."[3] Daos' words suggest that such slaves often found themselves torn between service to their mistress(es) in the house and service to their master outdoors. Daos may well have been afraid of the punishment by the latter if he stayed too long inside. From the master's perspective, this lack of differentiation between domestic and agricultural labor was economically rational, since there was considerable variation in the amount of agricultural labor required at each time of the year and this way masters could get maximum benefit from their slave(s).[4]

Larger estates had more scope for specialization and slaves might find themselves working alongside a handful of other slaves under the supervision of an overseer. An example of this type of farm is found in Xenophon's treatise *On Household Management*, in which the operation of the estate of

---

[1] 328–31.
[2] De Ste. Croix 1981; Jameson 1977/78; Osborne 1995. The alternate view that slave ownership was not widespread (see, e.g., Westermann 1955, 5–12; Jones 1957, 3–20) has grown increasingly out of favor.
[3] Menander, *The Bad-Tempered Man* 206–8.
[4] For variations in the need for labor throughout the agricultural year, see Gallant 1991.

a wealthy Athenian citizen is described. While Xenophon's picture of the workings of this estate is certainly idealized, he clearly bases his depiction on the reality of large-estate ownership. One crucial aspect of this reality is the presence of dozens of slaves and their division of labor by gender: female slaves work in the house under the supervision of the mistress and/or a slave steward (ταμίας), while male slaves work in the fields and are supervised by a slave overseer (ἐπίτροπος) and sometimes the master himself. The presence of managerial slaves such as housekeepers and overseers attests not only to the size of the slave workforce on such estates, but also to the existence of a hierarchy among slaves and differential treatment. At the extreme ends of the spectrum of experiences, ordinary slave laborers might be chained at night to prevent them from running away, while managerial slaves might be rewarded with a share of the profits of the estate.[5]

For agricultural slaves, whether they were employed on a small or large estate, there were similar tasks to be performed. Outdoor labor included not only ploughing, sowing, planting, tending (such as vine dressing), harvesting, threshing and winnowing, but also the digging of drainage ditches, breaking up soil with hoes, weeding, manuring, and building or repairing of the terrace walls that were used to make the often rocky and steep terrain suitable for growing fruit-bearing trees.[6] Indoor work performed by female slaves included the storing and preservation of agricultural produce, the preparation of bread and other foodstuffs, and the production of clothing out of wool (see below under Domestic Labor).[7]

Much of this work was physically demanding, as a wealthy freeborn youth finds out in Menander's comedy when he tries to win over a girl's stern father by presenting himself as a hard worker on the farm: "But this mattock weighs a lot. It will kill me in advance!"[8] Later, the same youth appears on stage nursing an aching back and complaining about the burning sun.[9] While such physical exhaustion was an extraordinary and temporary feeling for this wealthy freeborn youth, it was the daily experience of many slave farm laborers (Fig. 3.1). In his comic biography, Aesop is depicted as a field slave digging with a mattock in a field alongside other slaves. Aesop and his fellow slaves are given two hours rest during the heat of the day, but otherwise are forced to

---

[5] Xenophon, *On Household Management* 3.4; 9.11–13. On punishment and rewards, see Chapter 5.
[6] Digging of ditches: Menander, *The Bad-Tempered Man* 207, 375; hoeing and weeding: Xen. *Oec.* 17.11–14, *Life of Aesop* 4–6; manuring: Menander, *The Bad-Tempered Man* 584; and building or repairing of terrace walls that were used to make the often rocky and steep terrain suitable for growing fruit-bearing trees: Menander, *The Bad-Tempered Man* 377.
[7] Xenophon, *On Household Management* 7.21, 25, 35–36.   [8] 390–91.   [9] 522–35.

Fig. 3.1 Agricultural scene showing ploughing and sowing grain. Note the figure to the left of the ploughman, who is using a mattock to break up the soil. While it is difficult to identify slaves definitively in vase painting (see Chapter 4), a plausible interpretation is that these are slaves supervised by their owner or a slave overseer. Attic black-figure cup, c.530 BCE. Paris, Musée du Louvre. Photograph by Hervé Lewandowski. © RMN Grand-Palais / Art Resource, NY.

work continuously under the watchful eye of an overseer who is not sparing in his use of the whip.[10] While Xenophon's idealized estate owner Ischomachus uses both rewards and punishments to induce his slaves to work productively (see Chapter 5), the reality for many slaves might have been quite different: basic subsistence for hard work, and physical punishment for anything less.

Here, it might be helpful to distinguish between the experience of slaves on large estates and those on smaller farms. The former might receive a reliable and sufficient supply of food and even occasional rewards of more or better food for good performance, as Xenophon suggests. The latter, by contrast, might have an irregular or insufficient supply of food. Such appears to be the case with Daos, the single slave on a small plot of land

---

[10] *Life of Aesop* 4–9.

whom we met above. In one scene in Menander's play, Daos exclaims "Evil Poverty! Why have we encountered you for so long? Why do you reside with us continuously and for so much time?"[11] It is important to stress that, in this case, unrewarding labor and insufficient food supply is not something experienced by the slave alone, since his master toils and eats alongside his slave. Indeed, Daos generalizes his complaints, remarking on the lamentable fate of the "Attic farmer" "who battles the rocks which produce nothing more than thyme and sage."[12] While there is undoubtedly some comic exaggeration in this statement, there is a grain of truth that would have been recognizable to Menander's audience: many farms achieved only bare subsistence and sometimes fell short of that. In such cases, while both owner and slave suffered, it was likely the slaves who felt food shortages first, as perhaps was the case with the slave girl whom we encountered in the last chapter who complained that her master brought nothing home to eat, not even thyme.[13] While this lament may again be a comic exaggeration, it probably touches on the reality of food shortages for some slaves.

Slaves on large estates might have several pairs of clothing, or have the opportunity to earn better clothing as a result of their good work. Ischomachus, in Xenophon's idealizing treatise, speaks of festival clothing as distinct from daily wear for the slaves of his household.[14] He also explains his strategy of rewarding better workers with better clothing: "I make sure that the clothing and shoes that I must supply for the workers are not the same ... I reward better workers with better clothing and give worse clothes to those who are not good workers."[15] Slaves on small farms might have only one set of poor-quality work clothes, such as the leather shirt put on by a freeborn youth who temporarily takes over the agricultural labor of a slave in Menander's comedy mentioned above.[16]

Some slaves with skills in particular agricultural tasks seem to have been able to live independently and even sometimes to accumulate sufficient resources to purchase their freedom. This is the implication of the appearance of two "vine-dressers" on the lists of those who dedicated a silver bowl in recognition of their attainment of freedom (330–320 BCE). Along with barley and olives, vines were an important crop in Attica, as the chorus of citizen-farmers in Aristophanes' comedy *Acharnians* attests when they

---

[11] 209–11. For poverty as characteristic of Greece in general, cf. Herodotus 7.102. For Herodotus, the infertility of the Greek landscape is key to understanding Greek values, including bravery in battle and the defense of freedom.
[12] 603–7.   [13] Antiphanes fr. 166.   [14] Xenophon, *On Household Management* 9.6.
[15] Xenophon, *On Household Management* 13.10.   [16] Menander, *The Bad-Tempered Man* 416.

Agriculture and Animal Husbandry

repeatedly complain that the Spartans have cut down their vines (Fig. 3.2).[17] The vine-dressers on the lists of freed slaves, along with eleven other individuals who are identified as "farmers" (γεωργοί) are recorded as resident in the city and hence probably living independently of their masters as did other skilled slaves (see below under "Manufacturing"). It is likely that the term "farmer" on these lists refers to slaves who worked on large estates as overseers or farm managers, or with some other specialized agricultural skill. As highly valued slaves, their owners may have rewarded them with independence and a share of the profit of the estate. It was with these resources that these individuals managed to purchase their freedom (Chapter 5).[18]

Through these examples, we can already begin to see the wide range of experiences of slavery in ancient Greece. Moreover, it is striking that this wide range of experiences exists within a single sphere of the economy (agriculture). The gap is substantial between the experience of the slave Getas, who farms a small plot of land with his master and simultaneously serves his mistress in the household, and the skilled slave "vine-dressers" and farm managers on large estates who lived independently and eventually bought their freedom. Likewise, we could point to the discrepant experiences of the unskilled agricultural slaves, who performed manual labor in groups under the supervision of an overseer and were chained at night to prevent flight, and the skilled slave steward (ταμίας) who stored and dispensed the goods produced on the farm and was duly rewarded with a share of honor and material possessions.

Animal husbandry was practiced alongside the cultivation of crops on both small and large farms, and manure of animals was often used to increase the fertility of the soil. The solitary farmer Knemon in Menander's play is depicted as seeking to move a pile of manure in one scene in the play, and we can assume that he had a few goats or sheep on his farm.[19] Larger estates might have flocks numbering fifty or more, as well as specialized herdsmen to tend to them.[20] Such appears to be the case with the speaker in a fourth-century lawsuit who claims that, as part of an ongoing legal dispute, his opponent unjustly seized fifty "soft-woolled sheep," along with the slave herdsman who was attending them, as well as another slave boy who happened to be present.[21] The speaker's farming operations evidently included agricultural as well as pastoral activity, since

---

[17] Aristophanes, *Acharnians* 986–87, 995 [18] Jameson 1977/8, 133–35.
[19] Menander, *The Bad-Tempered Man* 584.
[20] Xenophon, *On Household Management* 7.20, 18.5–9. [21] Pseudo-Demosthenes 47.52.

Fig. 3.2 Harvesting olives; four slaves (?) work together to gather olives. Two beat the tree with sticks to shake off loose olives, while one gathers olives from the ground and another picks olives from the branches above. Attic black-figure amphora, c.520 BCE. British Museum.

he mentions that he farms a plot of land and claims that his opponent entered his property and tried to seize his slaves who were working there. These slaves, like the female slaves in his house, managed to flee and narrowly evaded capture. For our purposes, the speech is important because it attests to the mixed farming regime (agricultural and pastoral) of wealthy Athenian citizens, as well as the presence of specialized slaves.

The estate in question consisted of numerous male and female slaves and operated according to a division of labor that included not only gendered indoor and outdoor work, but also a distinction between slave agriculturalists and pastoralists. This latter distinction has implications for assessing experiences of slavery, since slave herdsmen by necessity had more freedom of movement than agricultural slaves, as they constantly moved from one pasture to another with little or no supervision. For this reason, slaves assigned to animal husbandry not only would have had specialized skills, but would have been selected for trustworthiness, like slave managers and overseers. Odysseus' loyal swineherd Eumaeus in Homer's *Odyssey* is a literary idealized type of this sort of slave, and it is significant that he seems to have been honored by Odysseus and promised significant rewards (a wife, land) if his master should return. It is noteworthy, in this regard, that a person whose profession is listed as a tender of yokes of oxen (ζευγοτρόφος) appears among those who dedicated silver bowls in recognition of their achievement of freedom.[22] Evidently, this former slave's skills in animal husbandry resulted in financial rewards that earned him his freedom. That said, it is striking that in the legal speech just mentioned, pastoral slaves as well as agricultural and domestic slaves are equally liable to seizure and sale, if their owners found themselves in legal trouble. We will have more to say about this aspect of the experience of slavery in the next chapter.

A special category of agricultural slaves existed at Sparta and a few other regions of Greece (Crete, Thessaly). As we saw in Chapter 1, almost all of the helots of Sparta farmed the land of Laconia and Messenia and were required to hand over one half of their crop to their Spartan owners. Freed from agricultural labor, the Spartans were able to focus full time on their political and especially their military duties. As such, the experience of helots was different from that of most agricultural slaves in Athens or Chios. Not only did they work without the help of their masters, they also had control of one half of the fruits of their labor. Moreover, as far as the Messenian helots are concerned, they worked and lived quite independently of their Spartan owners, being separated from them by a mountain range. This latter situation, as we shall see (Chapter 5), contributed to the propensity of the helots to revolt – a risky and unusual strategy among slaves.

[22] *IG* ii².1576.73–75.

Skilled Trades and Manufacturing

Slaves laboring in various skilled trades worked either alongside their masters, just as in agriculture, or in workshops with sometimes dozens of other slaves. These trades included metalworking, carpentry and leatherworking, among many other occupations. Such slaves were active even in the production of ceramics (Fig. 1.2), which are some of the most visible remains from ancient Greece.[23] While evidence is scarce for slaves working alongside their masters in small household operations, one piece of indirect evidence is suggestive. In a law-court, speech written in defense of a man who was accused of accepting a public subsidy while allegedly having sufficient resources to support himself, the defendant gives proof of his poverty partially on the basis of the fact that he practices a craft by himself and has not yet been able to acquire someone (presumably a slave) to take it over.[24] The inference that may be drawn is that only the poorest of citizens would not be able to acquire a slave to help them with their trade.

That many Athenians practiced a trade themselves, with or without a slave, is clear despite evident disdain in many of our elite sources for such "slavish labor."[25] It has recently been estimated that over 50 percent of the Athenian population was engaged in various artisanal and commercial enterprises. Moreover, only 12 of the over 170 different occupations documented in Athens are associated with agriculture.[26] Even our elite sources occasionally acknowledge that free citizens practice such crafts, as when Xenophon represents Socrates as observing that the assembly where the citizens gather to discuss and vote on public affairs is made up of not just farmers and traders, but also blacksmiths, leatherworkers, carpenters and those who process raw wool to prepare it for weaving.[27] We must imagine that most Athenians had a slave or two working alongside them in these crafts, just as ordinary citizen-farmers worked alongside their slaves.

One trade for which we have good evidence of slaves working alongside citizens and resident non-citizens (metics) is stone-masonry. In the many public works programs of the fifth century, records of expenditures were inscribed on stone, thus preserving the payments made to various workers. Remarkably, these inscriptions also preserve the legal status of the workers

---

[23] A number of potters and painters with ethnic names (e.g., Skythes, Kolkhos, Lydos, Amasis) may be slaves. See Braund and Tsetskhladze 1989, 122; Braund 2011, 130.
[24] Lysias 24.6.
[25] Aristocratic disdain: Aristotle, *Politics* 1278a; Xenophon, *On Household Management* 4.1–4, 6.6–10. For the reality, see Demosthenes 57.45.
[26] Bresson 2007, 150; Harris 2002; Andreau and Descat 2006, 11.
[27] Xenophon, *Memorabilia* 3.7.6; Vlassopoulos 2007.

and so we can see not only that citizen, metic and slave often performed the same skilled labor side-by-side, but also that they were paid the same amount for their labor. For example, consider the following entries in the records of the building accounts for the Erechtheum:

> For fluting of columns at the east, by the altar; the one by the altar of Dione, Laossos of Alopeke, 20 dr.; Philon of Erchia, 20 dr.; Parmenon [slave] of Laossos, 20 dr.; Karion [slave] of Laossos, 20 dr.; Ikaros, 20 dr.;
>
> The one next to it in order, Phalakros of Paiania, 20 dr.; Philostratos of Paiania, 20 dr.; Thargelios [slave] of Phalakros, 20 dr.; Philorgos [slave] of Phalakros, 20 dr. . . .
>
> The one next to it in order: Simias living in Alopeke, 14 dr. 2 ob.; Kerdon, 14 dr. 2 ob.; Sindron [slave] of Simias, 14 dr. 2 ob.; Sokles [slave] of Axiopeithes, 14 dr. 2 ob.; Sannion [slave] of Simias, 14 dr. 2 ob.; Epieikes [slave] of Simias, 14 dr. 1 ob.; Sosandros 14 dr. 1 ob.[28]

In the first entry, we find a citizen, Laossos, working alongside two of his slaves. We know Laossos is a citizen because he is identified by his political district (deme), Alopeke. In the second case, we find another citizen, Phalakros, again identified by his deme (Paiania), working alongside two of his slaves. In the third entry, we find Simias, who is identified as a non-citizen foreigner (metic) by his residence, working alongside three of his slaves as well as the slave of a third person. The implication of this data is that masters and slaves worked together as teams of skilled workers, replicating in the public sphere the small workshops that they also worked in privately. In addition, the presence of a slave owned by someone else in the last group suggests that some masters "rented out" their slaves to the public work project. This inference is confirmed by the presence of such rented-out slaves on another building project, the sanctuary of Demeter and Kore at Eleusis.[29] Of course, the slave's earnings on these public projects would belong in principle to his owner, and it would be a matter of the owner's discretion as to whether he allowed the slave to make use of his pay himself, in whole or in part. Similarly, on the day-to-day work in a small workshop, the master had the power to decide whether to share any of the profits with the slave.

In contrast to the small workshops where free and slave-craftsmen worked together, there were also larger workshops owned by wealthy Athenians where anywhere from 10 to over 100 slaves might work under

---

[28] *IG* i³.476.221–42, trans. Lambert and Osborne, "Erechtheion building accounts, 408/7 BC," Attic Inscriptions Online, updated April 11, 2020, https://www.atticinscriptions.com/inscription/IGI3/476.

[29] Clinton 2008, 184. Cf. Demosthenes 53.20–21; and Isaeus 8.35.

the supervision of a slave manager. For example, the estate of an Athenian named Komon consisted of two houses, and two workshops manned by slaves. The slaves in the first workshop were weavers of sack cloth (σακχυφάνται). Those in the second workshop were grinders of colors for dyes (φαρμακοτρίβαι).[30] Among the color grinders, one slave named Moschion was particularly trusted, and is claimed to be knowledgeable about all of Komon's business affairs. We may surmise that Moschion served as a slave manager and business agent for his master in addition to his specialized craft.[31] While the total number of slaves in each workshop is not provided in our source, the mention of Moschion, the trusted manager, suggests that they were sizeable enough to require supervision over and above what the master could provide. It turns out, however, that Moschion was not as trustworthy as Komon thought: he later confessed to stealing more than 8,000 drachmas from his master! Whether we consider this act as theft or simply a just redistribution of the fruits of the labor of Moschion and the other slaves is something that we will consider in Chapter 5.

More specific numbers of slaves in small workshops are provided in two famous examples. The fourth-century politician Demosthenes reveals that his father bequeathed him two workshops, one composed of thirty-two or thirty-three slaves skilled in knife making and another consisting of twenty slaves who manufactured couches.[32] Both these enterprises were very profitable for their owner, bringing in, according to Demosthenes, 3,000 and 1,200 drachmas respectively in income per year. While Demosthenes had some incentive to inflate his figures (he is suing his three guardians on the grounds that they did not hand over his full inheritance), it is unlikely that he is off by an order of magnitude. Once again, we hear of a slave manager, Milyas, who oversaw the knife factory. The presence of an overseer shows that a workshop with more than thirty slaves required specialized supervision. In this case, moreover, we know that Milyas was rewarded for his management of the workshop by a grant of freedom in Demosthenes' father's will.[33]

The largest workshop recorded in our sources belonged to the resident non-citizen (metic) Lysias and his brother Polemarchus. As many as one hundred and twenty slaves may have worked in their workshop manufacturing shields.[34] On the other end of the scale, one Timarchus is said to

---

[30] Pseudo-Demosthenes 48.12.   [31] Pseudo-Demosthenes 48.14–15.   [32] Demosthenes 27.9
[33] Demosthenes 27.19, 29.5, 29, 59. On grants of freedom, see Chapter 5.
[34] Lysias 12.8, 19. It is not certain that all of these slaves made shields. A shield factory is also mentioned in Demosthenes 36.4.

have inherited, in addition to a house and two pieces of land, "nine or ten slaves, leather workers (or shoemakers), who paid him a commission of two obols a day each, as well as a manager of the workshop who paid him a commission of three obols a day." In addition to these slaves, Timarchus inherited "a woman who was skilled in making fine linen and sold her wares in the market and a man skilled in embroidery."[35] Timarchus' slave operations are interesting, since they are the first concrete examples we have encountered of artisanal slaves who apparently live independently of their master and pay him a commission (ἀποφορά) out of their profits.[36] While the text is not explicit that the woman skilled in making linen and the male embroiderer enjoy this privilege, it is likely that they do since the woman is said to sell her wares in the market herself.

What was it like to labor in these workshops? As usual, we have little or no direct evidence and must infer what conditions were like from indirect comments in our sources. One telling source is Xenophon who represents Socrates as critical of the effects of practicing a craft on one's body.

> You speak well, Critoboulos, for the so-called manufacturing occupations are infamous and rightly held in low regard in cities. For they ruin the bodies of those who practice them and those who supervise them, forcing them to sit and to remain indoors. Some even spend the whole day by the fire. When their bodies become effeminate, even their souls become much weaker. In addition, the so-called manufacturing occupations leave men no leisure to care for either their friends or their city. As a result, such men seem to be bad both in regard to their treatment of friends and in their ability to defend their country.[37]

While Xenophon's point in this passage is to argue that craftsmen are unsuitable for citizenship, it is significant that he bases his claim on the detrimental physical effects of practicing a craft on a person's body as well as the constant toil required. These points are likely derived from his observations of the lives of actual craftsmen in Athens. Aristotle echoes Xenophon's comment on the negative effects of practicing a craft on the body, as well as the unsuitability of craftsmen for citizenship, when he writes that the body of the ideal citizen is "erect and unsuited to such occupations."[38]

---

[35] Aeschines 1.97.
[36] On slaves who lived apart and rendered a portion of their income to their owners (χωρὶς οἰκοῦντες), see Fisher 2008; Kamen 2011; and Chapter 4.
[37] Xenophon, *On Household Management* 4.2–3; cf. 6.5–10.
[38] Aristotle, *Politics* 1.2.14 (1254b30).

As we have already seen, however, many citizens did in fact, labor alongside slaves at such occupations. But more important for us than this contradiction between elite ideals of citizenship and the lived reality of ordinary citizens is the way that Xenophon and Aristotle justify their idealized distinction between citizen and slave labor: slave labor ruins men's bodies (and souls) and deprives them of the leisure needed to fulfill their duties towards friends and state. We may infer that many slaves (and free men) who worked in manufacturing found themselves toiling for long hours in poor conditions. By being forced to stay seated, crouched over in indoor spaces and potentially exposed to extreme temperatures and toxic fumes, slaves in workshops often endured poor working conditions. This observation might be particularly true of those working in iron-working workshops or ceramic production where slaves worked at forges and hot kilns (Figs. 3.3 and 3.4). Fulling shops where wool was processed used urine and sulfur to clean the wool and were smelly and unhygienic as a result. The same was true of dyeing and tanning workshops.[39] Other crafts, such as weaving or spinning might have "ruined men's bodies" by requiring constant physical effort at repetitive tasks for hours on end.

The unique piece of direct evidence with which this book began is relevant, again here since it concerns a slave, Lesis, who is working in a foundry, or metal-casting factory (as in Figs. 3.3 and 3.4). It consists of a letter written or dictated by Lesis requesting transfer to a different workplace on the grounds that his current condition is intolerable.

> Lesis sends [this letter] to Xenocles and his mother, [asking] that they not overlook at all the fact that he is perishing in a foundry, but that they go to his masters and find a better situation for him. For I have been handed over to a thoroughly wicked man, and I am perishing from being whipped. I am tied up. I am treated like dirt ... more and more![40]

Whether Lesis' suffering is caused primarily by the cruelty of the overseer of the workshop, or by the conditions and nature of the work, this letter provides a unique window onto a slave's experience in a workshop from his own point of view. The constant whipping and degradation are an aspect of this experience of slaves – not just those working in workshops – that is most vividly represented in the letter. Unfortunately, this is an almost unique piece of first-person written evidence concerning slavery in ancient Greece. Nevertheless, it reminds us of what might fill the silences that we so

---

[39] Burford 1972, 77–78.   [40] Trans. E. Harris 2004 (with slight modifications).

Fig. 3.3 Slaves (?) working in a blacksmithing shop specializing in bronze sculptures (Side A). Red-figure vase, c.490–480, found at Vulci, Italy. Photograph by Johannes Laurentius. © Antikensammlung, Staatliche Museen Zu Berlin, Preussischer Kulturbesitz, F2294.

often encounter when trying to understand the experiences of slaves in ancient Greece.

Of course, probably not all slave-craftsmen's experiences were so dire. We have already encountered the small shoemaking workshop owned by Timarchus where the slaves worked and lived independently, rendering a portion of their income back to their owner. Timarchus' linen-weaving and embroidery-specialist slaves may have similarly enjoyed autonomy as one-person operations, as might the slave "goldsmith" who was sold among the confiscated property of a citizen in the late fifth century.[41] Even a slave who makes charcoal (ἀνθρακεύς) seems to operate independently of his master, living on his own with a wife, and rendering a commission to his master.[42] Such slaves not only enjoyed relative autonomy, but like managerial slaves, they seem to have had greater potential to gain their freedom,

[41] *IG* i³.422.77–78.   [42] Menander, *Men at Arbitration* 258–59, 376–80, 408, 465.

Fig. 3.4 Slaves (?) working in a blacksmithing shop specializing in bronze sculptures (Side B). Red-figure vase, c.490–480, found at Vulci, Italy. Photograph by Johannes Laurentius. © Antikensammlung, Staatliche Museen Zu Berlin, Preussischer Kulturbesitz, F2294.

either through a grant from their master (as in the case of Milyas, mentioned above) or by saving the portion of their profits that they were permitted to keep in order to buy their freedom, as in the case of the former slaves who made dedications of silver bowls on the occasion of their attainment of freedom (see above). Indeed, it is notable that two "goldsmiths" appear among those who marked their freedom in this way (see Chapter 5).

Practitioners of numerous other crafts appear among the dedicators of silver bowls, including nine leatherworkers, two sandal makers, one tanner of hides, one cobbler, one seamstress, one gem engraver, one jar maker, one furniture maker and one glue maker.[43] It is likely that such slave-craftsmen rose to positions of management of workshops or operated independently of their masters. Such slaves rendered only a portion of their earnings to their masters, and thus were able to accumulate enough resources to buy

[43] *IG* ii².1553–78.

their freedom. One category of craftsmanship stands out among the dedicatees for the sheer number of practitioners, and that is "wool-workers" (ταλασιουργοί). No fewer than fifty-one of these women dedicate silver bowls to mark their attainment of freedom. The remarkable number of women who seem to have been successful enough at this trade to buy their freedom has raised questions. Are these really wool-workers or was this merely a polite way of avoiding mentioning the real source of their income: prostitution?[44]

Indeed, some have doubted whether wool working was profitable enough to allow a slave to buy their freedom. Others doubt whether there could have been that many professional wool-workers in Athens. Both these objections, however, seem to be countered by a passage from Xenophon's *Memorabilia* where Socrates is represented as drawing on the example of the owners of several clothes-manufacturing workshops, to show how such establishments can be highly profitable for their owners.

> **Socrates**: Do you not know that from one of these occupations, the milling of barley, Nausikudes feeds not only himself and his household but also many pigs and cattle in addition to these and makes such a surplus of cash that he has often financed many public activities. And similarly, Kurebos supports his whole household and lives lavishly from bread making. And Demeas of the deme of Kollytus does the same from cloak making, and Menon from making women's frocks, and most of the people of Megara from making tunics?
>
> **Aristarchus**: Yes, by Zeus, for these men own slaves, having bought them, and force them to make what is convenient.[45]

These examples are not of individual wool-workers, but of larger workshops, but they demonstrate the demand for such goods and the profitability of such enterprises.[46] Moreover, several pieces of evidence attest to the presence of individual wool-workers, or wool-workers operating independently of their masters and giving a commission to their masters, as in the case of Timarchus' weaver of linen and embroiderer.[47] A speaker in another lawsuit mentions that many citizen women have been forced into

---

[44] Wrenhaven 2009. Rosivach (1989) suggests that this was a designation for housewives, and in fact, these women were not professionals at all but the wives of men who were claiming their wives' freedom along with their own. As Wrenhaven (2009, 370) points out, however, only a small fraction of the women (five) appears to be part of family groupings.
[45] Xenophon, *Memorabilia* 2.7.
[46] Compare the "sackcloth" weaving workshop of Demosthenes 47, which no doubt supplied sails and other nautical equipment for the fleet.
[47] Aeschines 1.97.

spinning or weaving wool due to financial need.[48] Finally, tombstones of five apparently professional wool-workers survive, attesting to a level of wealth from this profession – judging by their ability to pay for a substantial tombstone.[49] It is certainly possible, therefore, that women designated as "wool-workers" in the dedications were professional wool spinners or weavers; that is, women who sold wool or woolen products that they themselves manufactured. That said, it is also possible that at least some of these women earned money (also) through prostitution, given the depiction of wool working equipment in some vase paintings that also appear to represent prostitutes.[50]

Regardless of our interpretation of the "wool-workers," it is clear that these women, as well as the practitioners of the other crafts who dedicated silver bowls, were able to keep enough of their earnings to buy their freedom.[51] Presumably, such slaves lived independently of their masters, enjoyed considerable autonomy in their day-to-day life and had some property of their own. The late fifth-century author known as the "Old Oligarch" seems to be referring to such slaves in his critique of the license of slaves in democratic Athens. While there is certainly ideologically motivated exaggeration in his argument, his account reflects the reality that such slaves enjoyed considerable autonomy and prosperity, and were sometimes able to purchase their freedom.

> The lack of restraint of slaves is greatest at Athens, and there [in Athens] neither is it permitted to beat a slave nor will a slave make way for you. I will tell you why this is the local practice. If it were the custom for a slave or a metic or a partially free person to be struck by a free person then many times he would strike an Athenian, thinking him to be a slave. For the people there [in Athens] are dressed no better than the slaves and the metics, and they are no better in appearance. If someone is amazed at this also – namely, that they permit slaves to indulge in luxury and some even live extravagantly – they appear to allow even this by intelligent design. For wherever power is based on the fleet, it is necessary to be a slave to the slaves, in order that we may receive the commission (ἀποφορά) from the slave's labor. We even let slaves go free for this reason. And wherever there are rich slaves, it is no longer profitable for my slave to fear you. In Sparta, my slave would fear you [but not in Athens]. But if your slave fears me, he will run the risk of handing over money [to buy] himself so that he does not run a risk concerning his personal safety.[52]

[48] Demosthenes 57.45.   [49] Kosmopoulou 2001.   [50] Wrenhaven 2009.
[51] The bowls themselves cost 100 drachmas, separate from the cost of inscribing, and represented a kind of tax on slaves to register their freedom publicly. These costs were in addition to whatever the slave paid his or her former owner to purchase his or her freedom (see Chapter 4).
[52] Pseudo-Xenophon, *Constitution of the Athenians* 1.10–11.

This ideologically colored slave-owner's representation of the life of slaves in Athens corresponds in part with what we know of a certain class of slaves in Athens: managerial or skilled slaves who earned money for their work and rendered a portion of it back to their master. The claim that slaves in Athens are rich, indulge in luxury and even live extravagantly – although ideologically convenient for the snobbish author's argument – may also touch on an element of the reality for some slaves, as we shall see shortly in regard to slaves in commerce, banking and public service. It is not out of the question that certain highly skilled craftsmen and women also became prosperous enough to provoke the ire of conservative citizens like the Old Oligarch.

Mining and Quarrying

Mining and quarrying constituted some of the most physically demanding labor performed in ancient Greece. The labor in quarries was performed by mixed teams of free and slave labor, not unlike the teams of masons working on building sites such as the Erechtheum that we have already encountered.[53] Transporting the stone from the quarries to the building site was done by ox team, and required little labor, except an ox driver, who might be slave or free.[54] It is significant, in this regard, that a "keeper of yoke of oxen" is listed among the dedicators of silver bowls recognizing grants of freedom.[55] While this man could have earned his freedom by accumulating resources from working his team of oxen in agriculture (see above), he could also have made money from transporting stone.[56] There was certainly money to be made in the latter work, as transport costs were high relative to the cost of quarrying and fitting the stone in place at a building site.[57]

While there is some evidence for free labor in mining, it seems that the bulk of the work was performed by slaves.[58] Plausible estimates of the numbers of slaves working in the mining district of southern Attica at any one time range from 10,000 to 30,000 during the fifth and fourth centuries.[59] These slaves were typically leased out to mine operators by their owners, as in the case most famously of Nicias who had 1,000 slaves

---

[53] Osborne 1985, 103–10; Thompson 2003, 134–35.   [54] Burford 1972; Thompson 2003, 134.
[55] *IG* ii².1576.68–71.
[56] See Clinton (2008, 184–244) for the prominence of transportation costs in the Eleusinian building records.
[57] Osborne 1985, 108.   [58] See Lauffer (1979, 8–13) for the evidence for free workers.
[59] Osborne 1985, 111; Thompson 2003, 148.

working in mining operations. Xenophon lists a number of other wealthy Athenians with slaves in mining, including Hipponicus who had 600 and Philemonides who had 300.[60] Other Athenians owned workshops in the mining districts where the ore was processed into refined metal.[61] One such workshop became the subject of a legal dispute and from the speech of the prosecution we learn that it consisted of thirty slaves along with processing facilities for grinding, washing and smelting the ore.[62] This size was probably typical for such workshops.

The archaeological evidence for ore-processing workshops suggests the presence of slaves. Indeed, at several locations in the mining districts of southern Attica, archaeologists have uncovered walled complexes that include not only areas for grinding, washing and smelting ore, but also living spaces. Groups of small rectangular rooms may be identified as sleeping quarters for slave-workers.[63] Burials nearby suggest that at least some slaves may have lived in family groupings, and evidence from the Roman period suggests that women as well as men may have worked in the ore-processing workshops.[64] Some complexes include a private dining room (ἀνδρών), possibly an indication of the presence of free workers who labored alongside slave-workers, or of privileged slaves who enjoyed better living conditions.[65] The tasks performed in these workshops involved both unskilled or semiskilled manual labor (grinding, sorting and washing ore) and skilled labor (smelting and resmelting at very high temperatures to separate high-value metals such as gold and silver from base metals like lead and copper). It is likely that slaves performed much of the unskilled or semiskilled labor and even a large portion of the more skilled labor, given the numbers of slaves employed in mining as well as the evidence for slaves who worked their way up to more skilled positions (see below).[66] Working conditions in these facilities, as in other workshops, could be unhealthy. In addition to the physical labor and the high temperatures of the furnaces, the process of smelting produced noxious fumes such as sulphur dioxide.[67]

A sixth-century ceramic plaque from Pendeskouphia, a hill near Corinth, depicts men excavating in an underground pit or cavern (Fig. 3.5). Recent interpretations suggest that the material being extracted is clay

---

[60] Xenophon, *Ways & Means* 4.14–15.
[61] Demosthenes 21.167. Wood was needed to fuel the furnaces used for smelting the ore, and we know of at least one Athenian who generated a substantial income from delivering six donkey loads of wood a day, probably to an ore-processing facility: pseudo-Demosthenes 42.7.
[62] Demosthenes 37.4.   [63] Thompson 2003, 149; Mussche 1998.
[64] Lauffer 1979, 61–62; Diod.Sic. 3.13.2.   [65] Rihll 2010.   [66] Rihll 2010.
[67] Thompson 2003, 149.

Fig. 3.5 Slaves (?) in a clay pit or mine. Corinthian ceramic plaque. Photograph by Johannes Laurentius. © Antikensammlung, Staatliche Museen Zu Berlin, Preussischer Kulturbesitz, F871.

for use in pottery manufacture, a Corinthian specialty.[68] Others, however, interpret the scene as a mining operation, and, whether the material is clay or metal, the working conditions are likely to be broadly similar.[69] One worker in the scene wields a pickaxe or hammer that is not dissimilar to the miner's tools that have been found in various mining locations in Greece.[70] The three other workers are collecting the mined material in baskets and transporting it out of the pit. At least two of the figures are smaller in stature and may be children or adolescents who were able to maneuver through narrow tunnels and cramped spaces.[71] As often remains the case today, mining was a dangerous business and potentially hazardous or even fatal to the lives of the miners due to poor ventilation and the constant

---

[68] Palmieri 2016, 189–90.   [69] Thompson 2003, 148.
[70] Thompson 2003, 152–53; Lauffer 1979, 20–21.
[71] Thompson 2003, 152; Chatzidimitriou 2005, 139–40; Fischer 2012, 118–19. For children in mines, see Diodorus Siculus 3.13.1. Cf. n.73.

threat of shaft collapse. Whether he is referring to these dangers or the risk of financial failure, Plutarch is not wrong when he notes that the Athenian general Nicias had acquired much property in the mining district that provided great revenues but also were "not without danger in their operation."[72]

A later account of the mines in Spain during the Roman period gives a vivid portrait of the hard labor demanded of slaves in the mines and the extreme toll it took on the well-being of such slaves. While the Spanish mines were richer and more extensive than the mines in Attica (though not perhaps than the highly productive mines of the Pangaeum district of northern Greece), the conditions of workers are likely to be similar.

> The slaves working in the mines produce an abundance of revenue for their masters, but they themselves wear out their bodies night and day in pits under the ground. Many die through the excess of suffering. For there is no relief or pause in the work for them, but they are forced by the blows of their overseers to endure the terrible evils and to surrender their unfortunate lives. Some hold out for a long time against the suffering through strength of body and spirit. Indeed, death is more desirable than living for them on account of the enormity of their hardships.[73]

Lest we think this report is exaggerated, a detail in the terms for leases of slaves to mine operators confirms that there was a high mortality rate for mining slaves. The terms for Nicias' lease of his slaves, for example, contained a clause specifying that – in addition to rendering Nicias one obol per slave per day – the contractor was obliged to maintain the number of slaves as equal to the number originally leased.[74] This clause has the ominous implication that at the outset it was likely that a significant number of slaves would die during their work in the mine. By adding this clause, Nicias required the mine operator to assume the cost of replacing any slaves who died while under contract in the mine. In this way, Nicias protected his capital, while also reaping the rewards of the revenue generated by his slaves.

Another significant detail in the description above is the presence of overseers, who are represented as driving the workers on with whips. We may recall the plea of Lesis, the foundry slave, who said he was "perishing from being whipped." Besides the inherent dangers of mining (lack of

---

[72] Plutarch, *Life of Nicias* 4.2.
[73] Diodorus, Siculus 5.38.1. For conditions in ancient mines and ore-processing facilities (this time gold mines in Egypt in the second century BCE), see also Diodorus Siculus 3.12–14.
[74] Xenophon, *Ways & Means* 4.14.

ventilation, noxious fumes, structural collapse), slave-miners were evidently sometimes driven hard at the hands of overseers and it is likely that some died of exhaustion.

As in the case of agricultural managers, these overseers were often slaves themselves, but were valued more highly by their owners than less skilled slaves. A Thracian slave named Sosias, for example, oversaw the mining operations of Nicias. Sosias must have been an extraordinarily skilled manager (ἐπιστάτης) since Nicias is said to have paid a talent (6000 drachmas) – some thirty times the normal price – to purchase him.[75] Sosias' Thracian background may partly explain his high value. As a native of this mineral-rich area of northern Greece, Sosias may have had a great deal of mining experience. Perhaps he began as a manual laborer in a mine and worked his way up to supervisor. Whatever his exact trajectory, Sosias' talents were such that he was eventually freed by Nicias and operated his own mine in Attica, even leasing slaves from Nicias himself.[76] In a law-court speech, we hear of another managerial slave who oversaw a mining operation, this time an ore-processing workshop.[77] While there is no indication that the slave in this case was granted his freedom, nevertheless the fact that he was trusted with large sums of money and placed in charge of a workshop where valuable metals were produced is indicative of his relatively privileged position as a slave.[78]

The story of another miner confirms that not all slave-miners lived in dire straits. Remarkably, an elaborately decorated tombstone from the fourth century BCE, found in the mining region of southern Attica, features an inscription in grand poetic style commemorating a slave who worked as a miner. Although we cannot be certain that this individual was a slave (at least originally), there are several indications that this status is likely. First, he bears a non-Greek name, Atotas, and identifies himself as a native of Paphlagonia, a region south of the Black Sea. Second, the inscription laments his death "far from his homeland" – a hint perhaps that he was removed unwillingly from his homeland. Despite this probable status as a slave or former slave, however, Atotas boasts of his skill as a miner and aggrandizes his foreign origins in a way that evokes Greek heroic traditions.

---

[75] Xenophon, *Memorabilia* 2.5.2. [76] Xenophon, *Ways & Means* 4.14. [77] Demosthenes 37.25.
[78] Demosthenes 37.20.

Atotas, a miner

> From the Black Sea, a great-hearted Paphlagonian, Atotas,
> Far from his homeland he released his body from toil.
> No one rivalled me in skill. I am from the stock of Palaimenes,
> Who died subdued by the hand of Achilles.[79]

It is clear that Atotas is proud of his profession and his skill as a miner. Even more significant, however, are the implications of this grand monument with its Greek inscription in heroic style. First, Atotas or his relatives clearly had enough spare money to afford a large and beautiful burial monument. Second, Atotas knew enough of Greek culture to draw on Homeric epic in order to champion his own non-Greek origins. For example, the phrase "great-hearted Paphlagonian" and the allusion to the fate of Palaimenes are both drawn from the *Iliad*, although in that poem Palaimenes is killed by Menelaus rather than Achilles. By identifying as a descendant of Palaimenes, moreover, Atotas aligns himself with the Trojans, since Palaimenes was a Trojan ally. This sophisticated appropriation may suggest both integration with and resistance to Greek culture in equal proportions (see Chapter 4). Whatever we make of this remarkable grave marker, it is not the monument of a wholly oppressed slave. Perhaps Atotas rose to be a managerial slave, and, like Sosias, even won his freedom.[80]

This record of a proud and independent possibly ex-slave should not, however, cause us to disregard the fact that most slaves who worked in mining endured back-breaking work with little hope of relief. A stark reminder of this reality is provided by the evidence for flight and even rebellion of slaves working in the mines. Thucydides reports that more than 20,000 slaves fled after the Spartans established a garrison in the district (deme) of Deceleia in Athenian territory in 413 BCE.[81] He further notes that the slaves were skilled manual workers (χειροτέχναι), a vague designation that could include skilled slaves in the mining districts, as well as agricultural slaves (e.g., vine-dressers) and artisanal slaves.[82] If we accept that the larger part of these slaves were probably mining slaves, then it seems that many of these preferred to take their chances on flight rather than endure their slavery in mining operations.[83] More direct evidence that slaves in mining found their conditions intolerable is to be

---

[79] *IG* ii².10051 = Bäbler 1998, #35.
[80] Lauffer 1979, 198–204; Bäbler 1998, #95–97; Hunt 2015, 136–38. [81] Thucydides 7.27.
[82] Hanson 1992; Osborne 1995; Hornblower 2008, 591–92.
[83] A fourth-century source reports, however, that many of those that sought refuge with the Spartans were sold as slaves to the Thebans and other Boeotians (*Hell. Oxy.* 12.5).

seen in the occurrence of an actual slave revolt there in a slightly later time period (c.100 BCE).

> Tens of thousands of Attic slaves worked in chains in mining operations ... [They] revolted and murdered those who were guarding the mines. Then they captured the acropolis at Sunium and plundered Attica for some time.[84]

Presumably, the revolt – which may have been influenced by similar occurrences in contemporary Sicily – was put down eventually, as was the fate of most slave revolts in history. For our current purposes, however, it is important to stress that slave rebellions are rare in history, since they are so risky for the slaves (see Chapter 5). Slaves who undertook such revolts, therefore, were usually those who did not have much to lose. This must have been the case with the slaves who revolted c.100 BCE. The flight of the slaves in and after 413 BCE – if indeed the preponderance were mining slaves – is another indication that such slaves were willing to take considerable risks to escape their conditions. While it is difficult to generalize about the experience of slaves (and we have just encountered several privileged and even liberated former slaves in the mining industry), nevertheless it is not an exaggeration to say that many mining slaves endured extreme hardships and even died as a result of the abuse that they suffered.

Domestic Labor

A final major area of slave labor in ancient Greece was in the household. Such work consisted of a wide variety of household tasks including preparing and serving food, childcare, clothes production (weaving) and cleaning. Moreover, except in the wealthiest households where there might be half a dozen or more slaves, most domestic slaves were jacks of all trades, expected to serve their masters not only in routine domestic tasks but also outside the house in agricultural work, shopping in the market and even attending their owners on military campaigns. While it is impossible to survey every service a domestic slave might perform, the account below focuses on some of the most common tasks, as well as those bits of evidence that most illuminate the experience of domestic slaves.

Food preparation ran the gamut from grinding grain to cooking feasts. While there were some commercial mills (see below), the existence of small grindstones or representations of them (Fig. 3.6) shows that such work was often done in individual homes. A work song sung by a woman as she sat at

---

[84] Athenaeus 6.272e–f = Poseidonius *FGrH* 87 F59.

Fig. 3.6 Woman grinding grain. Terracotta, c.450 BCE, from Kameiros, Rhodes. British Museum.

her grindstone similarly suggests a domestic context since she works alone. Significantly, her song also suggests that this labor was usually performed by lower-status individuals in so far as she remarks on the paradox that Pittacus, who once ruled Mytilene, used to grind his own grain.

> Grind, mill, grind.
> For even Pittacus used to grind
> When he was ruler of great Mytilene.[85]

Even, if is likely, "grind" has sexual connotations and is intended to mock the political leader, it still reveals the normative assumption that low-status females not powerful male citizens performed this type of labor.[86] We cannot be certain that the woman who sang this song was a slave, but it is likely that grinding grain was a task usually performed by household slaves, as was the baking of bread.[87] The song may, moreover, hint at a critique of slave-owners or elites in general in so far as it invokes the idea of role

---

[85] Plutarch, *Moralia* 157e = Carmina popularia, *PMG* 869.
[86] For the possible sexual connotations of this song, see Forsdyke 2012, 101.
[87] For baking as a task performed by a slave, cf. Xenophon, *On Household Management* 10.10. See further, the section "Milling, Baking and Cooking" below.

reversal (here between master and slave), a common theme of popular culture.[88]

Male domestic slaves also engaged in food preparation. For example, in a scene from a late fourth-century comedy, a male slave, who serves as a kitchen hand to a cook, complains about the effort of preparing a sacrificial meal for his owners at a rural shrine to Pan.

> What new evil? Do you think I have sixty hands, man? I have lit the charcoal, I receive, I carry, I wash, I cut up the entrails – I do everything at once. I knead, I carry around the pots, by this deity [Pan] here, becoming blind from the smoke. I seem to be the donkey who makes this party for these folks.[89]

In this scene, we get a sense of the many demands put on domestic slaves, particularly, in the preparation of festival meals. A kitchen hand, like other domestic slaves, was a dogsbody who was at the beck and call of his superiors – in this case, the cook. In another comedy, a slave named Cephisophon plays the role of doorman and general errand boy, as he fetches various items from around the house at the request of his master, Euripides.[90] Slaves were even called on to participate in cultic activities of the household, as in the scene from a comedy in which a household slave named Xanthias ("Blondy") is made to carry the model phallus in the procession in celebration of a rural festival of Dionysus (Fig. 3.7).[91]

Household slaves also often attended their masters and mistresses when they left the house to go to the market, for example, or to a festival or on military campaign.[92] As such, they served as porters, carrying purchases, festival equipment or other belongings for their owners. In a law-court speech, for example, a slave woman is described as regularly going to the market with her master.[93] In a comedy, a man who wants to participate in a women's festival pretends to have a female slave attendant as part of his disguise, indicating that such attendants were the norm for women at festivals.[94] In another legal speech, a defendant is depicted as arrogant because he always has no fewer than three slaves following him as he goes about the

---

[88] Forsdyke 2012, 96, 101; Karanika 2014, 144–46; and Chapter 5.
[89] Menander, *The Bad-Tempered Man* 546–51.   [90] Aristophanes, *Acharnians* 400–480.
[91] Aristophanes, *Acharnians* 243, 259–60. For slaves' participation in the domestic cult, see further Chapter 4.
[92] Hunter 1994, 87. Walking in street or marketplace: Antiphon 2.1; Demosthenes 21.158, 36.45, 54.27–30; travelling: Aeschines 2.126–28; Antiphon 5.24; Demosthenes 50.48; Lycurgus 1.55; performing military service: Demosthenes 54.4. Other activities that a slave might attend with his master include a legal proceeding (Demosthenes 45.61), a choral practice (Antiphon 6.22–23) or a drinking party (Xenophon, *Symposium* 1.11).
[93] Lysias 1.8, 16, 18.   [94] Aristophanes, *Women at the Thesmophoria* 279–80.

Fig. 3.7 Phallus procession in honor of Dionysus. In the household version of this rite, a single slave might carry a model phallus. Attic black-figured cup, c.550 BCE. Florence 3897. Courtesy of the Soprintendenza per i Beni Archeologici. Su concessione del Museo Archeologico Nazionale di Firenze (Direzione Regionale Musei della Toscana).

town.[95] The appearance of a slave carrying loads for his master was apparently so common on the streets of Athens that it became a standard scene in comic plays. Menander, for example, depicts the slave Getas cursing his mistress for the enormous load of pots, pans, rugs, cushions and mattresses that he has to carry to a rural shrine of Pan for a sacrifice.[96] Aristophanes even made a metatheatrical parody of such scenes in his play *Frogs*, of 405 BCE.

XANTHIAS (a slave): Shall I say one of the customary things, master, at which the audience always laughs?
DIONYSUS (master of Xanthias): By Zeus, say whatever you want, but not "What a weight!" – I am wholly sick of that by now.
XANTHIAS: Then some other witty comment?
DIONYSUS: But not "It's really chafing my shoulder!"
XANTHIAS: What then – shall I say that really funny one?
DIONYSUS: By Zeus, of course. But as long as you don't say that one . . .
XANTHIAS: Which one?
DIONYSUS: The one where you shift your burden to your other shoulder and say that you want to take a shit.
XANTHIAS: And not the one where I say that I'm carrying such a load that if someone doesn't relieve me, then I will explode with farts!

[95] Demosthenes 36.45. [96] Menander, *The Bad-Tempered Man*, 403–6.

DIONYSUS: Not that, I beg you, except when I am about to puke anyway!
XANTHIAS: Why, then, did I carry this stuff, if I am not going to do anything of those things that [the comic poets] Phrynichus, Lycis and even Ameipsias have their slave characters do?[97]

While this scene was clearly intended to raise a laugh, a less funny reality lies behind it – namely, that slaves were at the beck and call of their masters and often loaded up with heavy burdens to cart back and forth. Perhaps some of them even cursed their masters as they toiled along under these heavy loads.

On the other side of this equation, however, domestic servants were sometimes entrusted with errands outside the house or asked to deliver a message without the direct supervision of their owners.[98] While on such errands, they might enjoy some freedom of movement, perhaps paying visits to other slaves or spending time in the marketplace. Even when in the company of their masters, they may have found time to socialize with other slaves. For example, in the comic scenario mentioned above, the man disguised as a woman at the festival of Demeter dismisses his slave attendant when the proceedings begin since only citizens can participate.[99] At such times, slave attendants would be unsupervised and we can well imagine that they would make good use of their autonomy. The relatively close proximity of domestic slaves to their masters, therefore, must be balanced with the freedom that resulted from the relationship of trust that sometimes developed between them.

One of our most vivid descriptions of the life of a domestic slave comes from a fourth-century legal speech that concerns a murder resulting from an adulterous affair. In the speech, we learn that a female domestic slave not only took care of the master's newborn baby but also – allegedly – facilitated meetings between her mistress and her lover.[100] According to the speaker, this female slave (we are never told her name) induced the baby to cry in order to signal to her mistress to come down to her lover whenever he was in the house. When the master learned of the affair, his first action was to interrogate the female slave. Under threat of punishment, the master induced the female slave to tell him about the affair, and even to arrange for him to catch her lover in the act. The slave did so, and the husband then killed his wife's lover *in flagrante delicto*. The trial took place sometime later

---

[97] Aristophanes, *Frogs* 1–10, trans. Sommerstein (1996), adapted. [98] Hunter 1994.
[99] Aristophanes, *Women at the Thesmophoria* 294–95. [100] Lysias 1.8–12.

and concerned the question of whether the husband's act was a justified homicide.

While the female domestic slave is only an accessory to the case, we learn a fair amount about her life in the incidental details of the story. Firstly, we learn that she lived in women's quarters in the house, and that these quarters were separated from the men's quarters, which were located on the second floor.[101] This is a pattern that is replicated in other houses; for example, in the ideal household described by Xenophon (above).[102] Secondly, we learn that the female slave is permitted to leave the house to go to the market and do shopping for the family.[103] Indeed, it is in the marketplace that the wife's future lover makes contact with the slave woman and induces her to help him seduce her mistress. Thirdly, as we have seen, we learn that the female slave is charged with looking after the baby, although she does not breastfeed the baby herself – as some domestic slaves did (see below). Finally, we also learn that this female slave was subject to sexual assault by the master, a horrific fact that is casually reported in the speech as the mock-comic excuse given by the wife for shutting her husband in his room while she goes to see her lover. According to the speaker, the wife jokes that her husband is sending her to tend to the baby "in order that you can make an attempt on the slave girl. For another time when you were drunk you assaulted her."[104] Distressingly – for modern audiences, at least – the speaker reports that he laughed at his wife's joke, especially when she playfully locked the door on him.

This legal speech also demonstrates how a domestic slave could be caught between the commands of her mistress and those of her master. While the slave woman may have willingly helped her mistress conduct her affair in secret in the hopes of a special reward for the trust placed in her, this service put her in direct conflict with her master. Indeed, when the master learned of the affair and confronted the slave woman, he threatened her with severe punishment if she was unwilling to betray her mistress and reveal the details of the affair to him. Specifically, he threatens to send her to a mill, where she will be "constantly whipped and never cease to be oppressed by such toil."[105] Hard labor in a mill was clearly a more brutal form of slave labor, perhaps not unlike toiling in the mines, where, as we saw above, slaves were often driven on by whips (see also below).

---

[101] Lysias 1.9. [102] Xenophon, *On Household Management* 9.5.
[103] Lysias 1. 8, 16, 18; with Hunter 1994. [104] Lysias 1.12.
[105] Lysias 1.18. On slave punishments, see Chapter 5.

At first, the slave held out against this threat, refusing to betray her mistress, but she later gave in and told her master all. While, in this way, the female slave may have avoided punishment, it is important to stress that such a painless outcome was not always the case. Some slaves found themselves in possession of key information for the legal affairs of their masters and, as a result, were under threat of being tortured as a necessary step of the legal process for supplying usable witness testimony (see Chapter 4). The important point for the moment is that domestic slaves often found themselves caught between the demands of their master and mistress or between those of their master and another citizen. Such situations were difficult to navigate and probably often resulted in physical punishment by their master or judicial torture by the state – not to mention psychological distress. Household slaves and managerial slaves seem to have been particularly liable to such treatment, since they often had knowledge of their owners' affairs, including not just their financial affairs but also their personal affairs (see Chapter 4). On the flip side, slaves might make use of such knowledge to blackmail the owner into granting privileges or even freedom (see Chapter 5).[106]

Domestic slaves were sometimes tasked with breastfeeding the master's children as part of their childcare duties. This intimate service often resulted in strong bonds between the slave wet nurse and the master's children. A fourth-century legal speech provides a vivid portrait of such a relationship and the potential benefits and risks for both master and slave. The legal case is complicated, but the part of the speech that concerns us is a description of how the speaker's opponent trespassed upon his property and seized his belongings as compensation for a fine that was owed to him. The speaker claims that his opponent barged into his house and encountered his wife and his old wet nurse (τίτθη) who were dining in the courtyard with his children. He goes on to tell the story of his wet nurse as follows:

> She is a benevolent and trusted woman, who had been liberated by my father. She lived with her husband when she was liberated. But when he [her husband] died and she was an old woman and she had no child to take care of her, she returned to live with me. For I was obliged not to overlook the need of either the woman who had been my wet nurse or the man who had attended me when I was a boy. Besides, I was also about to sail as captain of a ship, so that this way I was leaving with my wife . . . a housekeeper of this fine sort.[107]

---

[106] For the role of domestic slaves in "policing" their masters, see Hunter 1994.
[107] Pseudo-Demosthenes 47.55–56.

This brief vignette illustrates not only the affectionate relationship between a slave and the free members of the family but, significantly, that such loyal slaves could be granted freedom as a reward. Interestingly, the male slave who attended the master when he was a boy had also been granted his freedom. The oversight of male children from boyhood to adolescence was frequently assigned to a male household slave, known as a *paidagogos* (παιδαγωγός), literally, the "child-raiser."[108] These slaves were also responsible for escorting their charges as they went about town, especially to the gymnasia for athletic training.[109] It is not surprising, then, that slave-nurses and attendants developed such close relationships with the children of the household that they ultimately were granted their freedom. Even more striking, however, in the passage above is the fact that the former master (the speaker) affirms his obligation to care for both his slave-nurse and his slave attendant in their old age.

The next part of the story, however, shows how the nurse's loyalty ultimately led to her death at the hands of the speaker's opponents. This example illustrates once again how a master's legal troubles can have terrible consequences for his slaves. According to the speaker, in the skirmish with the speaker's opponent, his nurse tried to hide a small cup in her bosom to save it from his opponent's grasping hands. As a result, his opponent viciously beat her as he wrenched the cup away. Although the speaker brought in a doctor to treat her, the nurse died some days later from the wounds.[110]

This example shows that such slave wet nurses often served families well beyond the infancy of their charges, and combined general child-rearing services with a variety of other housekeeping roles. The often lifelong relationship between these nurses and their masters' families are well attested in a remarkable series of grave monuments commemorating wet nurses that have survived from Athens.[111] While the erection of funeral monuments alone suggests an unusual degree of honor and respect towards these slaves, several of them are quite elaborate and include not only fine sculptural relief but also inscriptions attesting to the love felt by their owners towards them. One fourth-century monument shows a nurse, Melitta, and her young mistress, Hippostrata, below which is written:

[In memory of] Melitta . . .

> In this place, the earth covers up the good nurse of Hippostrata. Even now she is longing for you. And just as I used to love you when you were living,

---

[108] Demosthenes 18.258.   [109] Aeschines 1.10.   [110] Pseudo-Demosthenes 47.67.
[111] Kosmopoulou 2001.

nurse, so now I honor you even though you are beneath the earth and I will honor you as long as I live. I know that if there is respect for good people below the earth, honor will be first to you in the house of Persephone and Hades.[112]

While it is difficult to determine the exact status of Melitta, it is likely that she is a slave or former slave.[113] While there is some evidence indicating that free women sometimes worked as wet nurses out of economic necessity, most evidence suggests that this was considered a servile profession.[114]

A final central task of female domestic slaves was wool production and weaving. As we have seen, while some slaves spun and wove wool for sale in the marketplace, most domestic wool production was aimed at supplying clothes for members of the family, including free and slave. While in smaller households female slaves would work alongside their mistress at this task, in larger houses the mistress would supervise the slaves engaged in spinning and weaving (Fig. 3.8). This latter situation appears to be the case in Xenophon's ideal household, where the wife is exhorted "not to be sitting around always like a slave but to stand before the loom as a mistress of the household should, and teach slaves whatever she knows better than anyone else."[115] In the same source, the wife is said to arrive at her husband's house knowing only "how to take wool and make a cloak out of it" and "how the tasks of wool working are assigned to the slaves."[116] Similarly, among the tasks that the ideal wife undertakes is to see that clothes are produced from the wool that is brought in to her after shearing.[117]

* * *

So far we have surveyed the experiences of slaves in the most common types of labor. Now we turn to the less common slave occupations, including civic administration, banking and prostitution. Although slaves in these occupations were less numerous, many of them were prominent in the civic landscape because of their importance for the political and economic functioning of the state. Others – for example, prostitutes – were part of the street life of the ancient city, and remarkably some among these moved in high social circles and lived quite prosperously. That said, these

---

[112] *IG* ii².12814. Cf. Kosmopoulou 2001.
[113] The inscription mentions that her father enjoys the privilege of equal taxation with citizens and therefore shows that he is a privileged non-citizen, even perhaps a former slave (see Chapter 4). This designation makes it likely that Melitta is also a non-citizen and most likely a slave or former slave.
[114] Demosthenes 57.35, 45.   [115] Xenophon, *On Household Management* 10.10. Cf. 7.21, 41.
[116] Xenophon, *On Household Management* 7.6.
[117] Xenophon, *On Household Management* 7.35–36.

Fig. 3.8 Slaves (?) spinning and weaving wool. Black-figure oil flask (lekythos), 550–530 BCE. The Metropolitan Museum of Art, New York.

categories display a wide range of experiences, just as in the major slave occupations.

Publicly Owned Slaves

One prominent group of slaves in Greek city-states was publicly owned slaves (δημόσιοι).[118] As opposed to the vast majority of privately owned slaves, these slaves performed various functions for the state ranging from

---

[118] Ismard (2015) provides an account of public slaves in Athens that highlights their expertise. He argues that the Athenian democracy relied on slaves to perform certain specialized public functions in order to prevent citizens from translating expertise into power. An older but still useful account is Jacob (1928).

menial tasks related to the upkeep of public buildings and streets to skilled labor such as testing state-minted coins and keeping public records.

In Athens, there may have been as many as 2,000 publicly owned slaves at any one time. A large proportion of these would have been engaged in routine policing activities, including keeping the public order and assisting a group of public officials known as the Eleven in overseeing the jail. For the former task (as noted in Chapter 2), the Athenian state had purchased 300 Scythian archers in the fifth century, a number that may have risen to 1,200 by the fourth century.[119] These slaves were housed collectively in the center of the city and could be called on by presiding magistrates to help them keep order in the Assembly or Council, and at other public gatherings.[120] They even carried whips and small swords, as well as their bows, which they could use to enforce order among citizens.[121] While the task of policing citizens may seem inappropriate for a slave, it is important to stress that these slaves were under the command of a citizen magistrate at all times. They were simply enforcers and had no authority of their own.[122]

Some of these slaves assisted magistrates as they made arrests, confiscated property and oversaw citizens held in prison.[123] A scene from a comedy performed in 411 gives a sense of the work of these slave assistants. In this scene, a magistrate is accompanied by a single Scythian archer, whom he instructs to arrest a citizen malefactor. The slave follows the magistrate's orders, including the command to prepare the citizen for execution through exposure on a plank.

> Magistrate: This is the criminal whom Cleisthenes told us about! . . . Lead him away, Archer, and fix him to the plank! Once you've positioned him there, guard him and don't allow anyone to approach him. If someone comes near, holding your whip, beat him![124]

That publicly owned slaves played a role in executions is confirmed by the most famous execution of Greek history – that of Socrates.[125] According to Socrates' student Plato, a public slave not only took care of Socrates while he was in jail, but also prepared and administered the deadly hemlock potion that Socrates was required to drink. Apart from the similarity of tasks performed by the public slave in each of these accounts, however, the

---

[119] Aeschines 2.173; Andocides 3.5–7; Ismard 2015, 76–77.
[120] Aristophanes, *Acharnians* 53–54, 61, 94, 824, 864; *Knights* 665; *Women of the Assembly* 143, 258–59; Plato, *Protagoras* 319c; *Theatetus* 930–34; *Lysis* 433–62; Pollux 8.104, 131–32. Housed together: Souda s.v. τοξόται.
[121] Aristophanes, *Women of the Thesmophoria* 930–35 (whip), 1127 (knife or short sword), 1197 (quiver).
[122] Hunter 1994, 146. [123] Xenophon, *History of Greece* 2.3.54–55.
[124] Aristophanes, *Women of the Thesmophoria* 930–35. [125] Plato, *Phaedo* 116c–118a.

slaves themselves are characterized quite differently. In Plato, the public slave who attends Socrates speaks perfect Greek, admires Socrates' fortitude in the face of death and even develops a friendship with Socrates. In the comedy, by contrast, the Scythian slave is portrayed not only as foreign but also as a buffoon, who – although he obeys the magistrate's orders – is ultimately lured offstage by a young prostitute, thereby allowing the citizen to escape execution.[126] Furthermore, the Scythian archer is depicted as only barely acculturated to Greek society, and speaks a "garbled pidgin Greek."[127] While much of this characterization can be dismissed as comic exaggeration, it does raise the question of the level of integration of such public slaves in Greek society. In all likelihood, there was a range of ethnicities and levels of integration among public slaves, just as there was among privately owned slaves. Besides the public slave who attended Socrates in prison, two further examples of particularly well-acculturated public slaves are well attested in our sources (see below). Indeed, these slaves raise the question of whether public slaves could sometimes pass as citizens (see below and Chapter 4).

Another area in which public slaves performed routine physical labor under the supervision of magistrates was in keeping public spaces clean and clear of obstructions. Ominously, a group of city magistrates used public slaves "to remove the corpses of those who died in the streets."[128]

Publicly owned slaves were also assigned to various skilled tasks relating to the coining of silver and the verification of the authenticity of coins in the marketplace. This labor required not only some metallurgic competence but also trustworthiness, since valuable metals were involved and, even more importantly, the validity of transactions in the marketplace depended on the reliable verification of coinage. A remarkable law from Athens dated to 375/4 BCE provides some details of the working conditions of the public slaves who served as approvers of silver coinage and, indirectly, also of mint workers. The first part of the law demonstrates the great trust granted such slaves, who had authority over the currency in both private and public transactions.

> Attic silver shall be accepted when it is found to be silver and has the public stamp. The public slave who is the approver shall sit between the [bankers'] tables [in the marketplace] and approve on these terms every day except

---

[126] Cf. Aristophanes (*Lysistrata* 561–64, 433–36, 452–64), where some women who have occupied the acropolis successfully defend themselves against the Scythian archers who have been sent to drive them away. See also Bäbler 2005.
[127] Austin and Olson 2004, 308–9.   [128] [Aristotle] *Constitution of the Athenians* 50.2.

> when there is a deposit of money [to the public treasury] when he will sit in the Council house. If anyone brings forward foreign silver having the same stamp as the Attic —, he shall give it back to the man who brought it forward; but if it has a bronze core or a lead core or is counterfeit, he shall cut through it immediately ... If anyone does not accept the silver which the approver approves, he shall be deprived of whatever he is selling that day.[129]

In this part of the law, we see that a public slave was entrusted with the task of approving coins used in the marketplace and in payments to the public treasury. The slave who performed this task would need knowledge and experience in distinguishing valid from counterfeit coins by examining their appearance and weight. Moreover, the law shows that the decisions made by this slave were authoritative, since penalties were set out for those who did not accept the coins that he approved. The last part of the law reinforces the impression that the public slave who was entrusted with the task of approving coinage enjoyed a privileged status befitting the responsibility that was invested in him. This privileged status is also clear from the fact that the law makes provisions for the payment of a salary to the coin approver, including a second one who is to approve coinage in the port of Athens, as well as the mint workers.

> So that there shall also be in the [port of] Piraeus an approver for the ship owners and the import traders and all others, the Council shall appoint from the public slaves if available or shall buy one ...
>
> The salary payment for the approver in the import market shall start from whenever he is appointed ... and the treasurers shall allocate as much [in salary] as for the approver in the city, and, for the future, the salary payment shall be from the same source as for the mint workers.[130]

The provision of a salary shows that these publicly owned slaves were able to keep their earnings since they had no private owners who might claim all or part of it. Such slaves, therefore, may have lived independently and accumulated resources, including slaves of their own. Slave-ownership by public slaves is confirmed by the appearance of a publicly owned slave among those who granted freedom to their slaves.[131] While it may seem paradoxical for a public slave to grant freedom to his slaves rather than seeking freedom for himself first, it, in fact, makes perfect sense in the context of privileged public slaves. Such slaves had a salary and considerable independence. Freedom might enhance their independence, but would make them ineligible to serve as a public slave and hence eliminate

---

[129] RO 25. [130] RO 25, translation slightly adapted.
[131] *IG* ii².1570, lines 78–79; cf. *IG* ii².1566, lines 33–35; Fisher 2008, 133.

their salary. Some may have been able to find employment in the private sector, but the guaranteed work and salary of at least some of the more privileged public slaves were not to be thrown away lightly. This analysis underscores the relatively comfortable lifestyle of certain slaves, including one Pittalacus, as we shall see shortly.

One part of the law on silver coinage, however, shows that these skilled public slaves, however privileged, did not escape the standard violence that accompanied much slave labor in classical Athens.

> If the approver does not sit, or does not approve in accordance with the law, he shall be beaten by the convenors of the people with fifty lashes with the whip.[132]

This provision illustrates that the public slave who performed this duty was subject to the same kind of corporal punishment that was reserved for slaves in Greek law.[133] Furthermore, as mentioned in Chapter 2, public slaves were branded with a public mark, a brutal practice that stood as a lasting symbol of the enslavement and dehumanization of these slaves. One politician, for example, denigrates his opponent by claiming that his father was a branded public slave who worked in the mint.[134] Similarly, Xenophon remarks that no one is likely to steal a public slave since he is branded with a public mark.[135] Besides the physical pain endured, such brands would mark them out in daily life as publicly owned slaves and would have remained with them even if they gained their freedom.

Another group of publicly owned slaves worked as scribes, archivists and accountants in the civic administration.[136] For example, a public slave was in charge of preserving and keeping order in public records such as decrees of the assembly or records of payments made to the public treasury. By the end of the fifth century, these records were kept in a public archive known as the Metroön, or "Sanctuary of the Mother of the Gods," over which a public slave was appointed, as the fourth-century politician Demosthenes observes: "The matter ... is in your public records in the Metroön, of which the public slave has charge."[137] Regarding financial records, pseudo-Aristotle provides a vignette of the routine archival work of the public slaves as they bring documents to magistrates from the public archive and return them again after they have been used or updated.

---

[132] RO 25. [133] Hunter 2000; see also Chapter 4.
[134] Andocides fr. 5. = Scholia to Aristophanes, *Wasps* 1007. [135] Xenophon, *Ways & Means* 4.21.
[136] Sickinger 1999, 140–57; Ismard 2015, 67–70. [137] Demosthenes 19.129.

> The documents, written out according to the times of payment, are brought into the Council and kept by the public slave. When there is a payment of money, he [the public slave] hands these same documents to the receivers, taking down from the racks those relating to the men who have to pay money ... The receivers take over the documents and delete the sums paid, in the presence of the Council, and give back the documents to the public slave again.[138]

In some cases, public slaves were charged with making the records themselves, as is shown by a third-century decree in which some magistrates are instructed to "choose a public slave to make a record" of what they had done.[139] Similarly, public slaves served as clerks to financial officers who accompanied the Athenian army on campaign.[140] Some evidence suggests that public slaves could serve as auditors of financial records, thereby providing financial oversight of citizens who served as magistrates or paid taxes.[141] In this sense, public slaves served as a kind of neutral professional bureaucracy that prevented partisan manipulation of the state apparatus for personal advantage.[142] For our purposes, it is significant that these tasks were entrusted to slaves who were not only highly literate and numerate, but also granted considerable trust. As such, these slaves would have enjoyed a privileged status, probably entailing the receipt of a salary, and the ability to live independently and accumulate wealth.

Public slaves also assisted magistrates in the routine administration of the law courts, including the process of selecting citizen-jurors by lot and their assignment to various courts.[143] Although citizen-jurors were assigned to oversee administrative tasks during the trial – such as keeping time for the litigant's speeches and tallying the vote – it is likely that they were assisted by slaves assigned to the court.[144] Another group of slaves assisted the Council, and evidently their role was considered so important that they were honored alongside the Councilors themselves for their work each year.[145] Another indication of the relatively high status of these public slaves is the fact that they enjoyed privileged seating in the theater, judging by an inscription reserving certain seats for "the public slaves of the Council."[146]

---

[138] [Aristotle] *Constitution of the Athenians* 47.5–48.1.   [139] *IG* ii³.1.1154, lines 42–43.
[140] Demosthenes 8.47.   [141] Demosthenes 22.70–71.   [142] Ismard 2015, 70–71; Hunter 1994.
[143] [Aristotle] *Constitution of the Athenians* 63.5, 64.1, 64.3, 65.4.
[144] [Aristotle] *Constitution of the Athenians* 69.1, 66.4, 66.4.
[145] Agora 15.37 lines 4, 62, col. V lines 10–18, Agora 72, col. I line 5, col. II lines 67, 211, col. III lines 83, 266. See also Oliver 2009; and Ismard 2015, 67.
[146] *IG* i³.1390; Pickard-Cambridge 1968, 20; Ismard 2015, 67.

Another remarkable source of evidence – the building records for the sanctuary of Demeter and Kore at Eleusis – reveals the important role that public slaves played on such public works. In addition to the privately owned slaves who were paid a daily wage for their labor, there were publicly owned slaves who performed various tasks on the construction site. One of these publicly owned slaves is identified as overseer of the other publicly owned slaves, and another is in charge of keeping records of expenses.[147] Interestingly, these two slaves were paid a salary in addition to the food allowance that was allocated to the other public slaves (whose work is unspecified). Strikingly, all the public slaves were provided with a sacrificial victim and wine for the celebration of the festival of the Choës ("Wine-Jugs"), in honor of Dionysus.[148] This latter detail suggests a level of recognition and even integration in the ritual life of the community that is rarely attested for slaves (see Chapter 4).

The idea that among the publicly owned slaves there were certain privileged ones who were honored and rewarded for their skills, gains further illustration in the curious story of a man named Pittalacus. According to the law-court speech in which his story appears, Pittalacus was a public slave whose love affair with a young Athenian citizen got him into legal trouble. In the course of the speech, we learn that Pittalacus had his own house and was in fact, very well-off financially. In addition, he regularly socialized with freeborn citizens, including members of prominent political families, at gambling houses where cockfighting and dice games took place. Pittalacus may even have used his own house as a gambling establishment, since he is said to have both fighting cocks and dicing equipment at his home. It was at one of these gambling events that Pittalacus first gained and then later lost the affections of the freeborn youth, Timarchus. In the struggle over this young man with a citizen named Hegesandrus, Pittalacus was savagely beaten with whips. When Pittalacus brought a legal action against Hegesandrus for assault, the latter tried to claim him as his privately owned slave, presumably to prevent him from bringing suit. In response, Pittalacus found another citizen to vouch for his freedom, and continued to press charges against Hegesandrus. Eventually, however, Pittalacus dropped the charges, realizing that the arbitrator who was appointed to settle the case was a friend of Hegesandrus.[149]

---

[147] *IG* ii².1672, lines 5–6, 12, 44, 181, 205, 362–64. See Clinton 2008, 184; and Loomis 1998, 113–14.
[148] *IG* ii².1672, lines 266–67. See Clinton 2008, 184. [149] Aeschines 1.54–59.

One of the most striking features of this account is the indeterminacy of Pittalacus' status.[150] The speaker asserts several times that he was a public slave, yet he is both claimed as a private slave by a citizen and later redeemed as a free person by another citizen. Moreover, Pittalacus appears to enjoy legal rights, since he lodges a suit for assault against Hegesandrus. The simplest way to resolve these contradictions is to infer that Pittalacus began life in Athens as a publicly owned slave, prospered enough to live independently and – at some point – buy his freedom, after which he lived as a free non-citizen resident (metic).[151] If this reconstruction is correct, Pittalacus represents a success story. Although we never learn what task he performed as a public slave, he certainly prospered and achieved the ultimate goal of many slaves: freedom. Nevertheless, the fact that Pittalacus' enemy Hegesandros both beat him with a whip and tried to claim him as a slave shows that even such successful and privileged slaves or ex-slaves might be subjected to treatment as a slave and find their freedom in jeopardy.

Commerce/Business/Banking

The precarious yet potentially privileged status of some slaves is also evident in the areas of commerce, business and banking.[152] Such slaves worked as retailers in the business enterprises of their owners and as business agents of their masters in their domestic and overseas commercial operations. They also managed banks for their owners, and sometimes even rose to become owners of banks – after gaining their freedom and (rarely) even citizenship. A few examples will help flesh out the range of experiences of such slaves.

The first example concerns a slave named Midas who managed a perfume shop for his owner, Athenogenes, a free, but non-citizen, resident (metic) of Athens. Midas had two children who were also owned by Athenogenes. Unfortunately for Midas, a citizen named Epicrates became erotically interested in one of his sons, and Athenogenes agreed to sell the family to Epicrates for 4,000 drachmas. This sale, it turned out, was part of an elaborate scheme by Athenogenes to rid himself of some debts that Midas had contracted while running the perfume shop. Epicrates then brought suit against Athenogenes, arguing that the sale was invalid since the full extent of the debts had not been

---

[150] Fisher 2008. [151] Todd 1993, 192–94; Zelnick-Abramowitz 2005, 298; Fisher 2008, 135.
[152] See Cohen (1992) and (2000) for detailed and foundational studies of slaves in these sectors.

disclosed. From the speech of the plaintiff at this trial, we learn some details about Midas' experiences as a manager of a shop.

Firstly, Midas had children. Although we learn nothing about the mother of his children, it is likely that he was able to enjoy family-like relations and form a stable family unit. This certainly seems to be the implication of the fact that Midas was sold together with his children. The fact of their sale, on the other hand, underscores Midas' status as a piece of property and his lack of control over his circumstances.

Secondly, it appears that Midas exercised considerable autonomy in managing the perfume shop. Indeed, he is able to borrow large sums of money (5 talents = 30,000 drachmas), apparently without consulting his owner, in order to purchase supplies for the shop. While his owner remains legally liable for the debts, Midas himself appears to be the one who actively contracted the debts.[153] According to the speaker, Midas presented his accounts to Athenagoras only once a month.[154] Even more strikingly, the speaker alludes to his opponent's claim that Athenagoras had no knowledge whatsoever of the debts that Midas had contracted. While the speaker dismisses this claim as ludicrous, it is revealing that such a claim could be considered to be plausible enough to present to the jurors. Either way, the trust and responsibility in which Midas was held – both by his owner and his creditors – are remarkable.

The trust placed in slaves who were business agents for their masters is also evident in the story of a slave named Antigenes, who belonged to an Athenian citizen named Nicobulus. Once again, our information about Antigenes' activities comes from a legal case in which his master was involved.[155] The case is complicated, but the essential facts are that Nicobulus and a partner leased out a mining workshop to another citizen named Pantaenetus. According to Nicobulus, who left town on a trading enterprise shortly after the lease was contracted, Pantaenetus defaulted on his monthly payment to him and his partner. Pantaenetus, by contrast, argued that Nicobulus' slave Antigenes had received the payment and, in fact, Antigenes had appropriated a payment that Pantaenetus' own slave had been conveying to the state treasury to pay rent for a mine. It is unclear from the speech whether Panaenetus' slave had confused the two payments and mistakenly handed over the payment due to the state to Nicobulus' slave, or whether Antigenes had taken the initiative to collect the money due to his master in any way possible. Either way, the agency displayed by

---

[153] Whitehead 2000, 293. Cf. Hyperides 3.22.   [154] Hyperides 3.19.   [155] Demosthenes 37.

both slaves and their responsibility over large sums of money are quite remarkable.

It was Antigenes' intimate involvement with his master's business affairs, however, that also exposed him to the threat of judicial torture and reveals his vulnerable status as a slave. Indeed, according to Nicobulus, Pantaenetus challenged him to allow Antigenes to be tortured to extract the truth about each side's claims. As we shall see in more detail in Chapter 4, slave testimony was valid only if extracted under torture according to terms prearranged by the slave's owner and his opponent. The details of the proposal for judicial torture reveal the brutality of the process: if Antigenes supported his master's case, the parties agreed that Antigenes' value would be assessed in order that Nicobulus could be financially compensated for any damage done to his slave.[156] We may assume that these damages included physical maiming, potentially culminating in Antigenes' death. In a cold act of calculation, Nicobulus would have agreed to the level of financial compensation that he would accept for Antigenes' death. As it happens, Nicobulus claims that the judicial torture was not ultimately performed, since Pantaenetus changed the terms of his challenge and then rejected even the second proposal. Pantaenetus' alleged behavior in rejecting the challenge – even if exaggerated by his opponent – illustrates the additional extra-judicial abuse that slaves might endure as a consequence of their knowledge of their master's business affairs. According to Nicobulus, Pantaenetus "grabbed hold of Antigenes and treated him roughly, subjecting him to all kinds of outrageous treatment."[157]

An even more striking example of the paradoxical position and incongruent experiences of slaves who served as business agents for their masters can be found in another law-court speech involving a slave named Lampis.[158] Lampis, we are told, was the slave of a man named Dion, and served as his business agent in the port of the kingdom of Bosporus (now Crimea on the Black Sea).[159] Lampis was also a ship-captain (ναύκληρος) who brought cargoes from Athens to the Black Sea and back again. On the trading voyage from which the legal case arose, Lampis was both captaining the ship and one of the investors in its enterprise. Indeed, we are told that Lampis lent 1,000 drachmas to the defendant in the case, a metic named Phormion, who was a grain trader. Such loans were risky but also very lucrative if successful. The fact that Lampis was able to make such

---

[156] Demosthenes 37.40. [157] Demosthenes 37.42. [158] Demosthenes 34.
[159] Demosthenes 34.5.

a substantial loan, therefore, suggests that he was well-off financially and could afford to take risks.

Lampis was not Phormion's only creditor. Chrysippus, another metic, had also lent Phormion money. The legal dispute arose because Phormion claimed that, after he and Lampis arrived in the Bosporus, they were unable to sell the cargo right away. Phormion said that he had nevertheless given a large sum of money to Lampis, in accordance with the contract, with instructions to Lampis to bring it back to Athens to pay off Chrysippus.[160] According to Phormion, the ship had sunk when barely out of the port and the money was lost (although Lampis himself was rescued). Since trading contracts stipulated that if a ship was lost at sea there was no obligation to repay creditors (hence the riskiness of such investments), Phormion claimed that he no longer owed money to Chrysippus. Chrysippus argued, by contrast, that Phormion had never given the money to Lampis and was cheating him of his money. The important point for us is that Phormion either entrusted Lampis with a large sum of money (120 gold Cyzicene staters, the equivalent of 3,920 drachmas) or expected the Athenian jury in the case to believe that he had. Moreover, the fact that it had apparently been written in the contract that Phormion should repay the loan to Lampis confirms that it was considered normal business practice for slaves to handle financial transactions involving large sums of money.

Interestingly, Chrysippus himself also deployed a slave agent in the Bosporus and gave him considerable responsibility in overseeing his trading interests there. Chrysippus claims that he had given Phormion letters for this slave agent with detailed instructions for the oversight of his trading deal with Phormion. From his brief account, we get a sense of how much Chrysippus relied on this unnamed slave to ensure that the contract was fulfilled according to his wishes.

> Now [Phormion] went to the Bosporus with letters which I gave to him to bring to my slave who was spending the winter there and who is my business partner. I wrote in the letter the amount of money I had lent and the security, and I instructed him to inspect and keep track of the goods as soon as they were unloaded.[161]

According to Chrysippus, however, these efforts to instruct his slave were in vain, since Phormion never delivered the letters to his slave. Regardless of the truth of this claim, the trust and responsibility that Chrysippus invested in his slave are striking and parallel to the trust allegedly placed by

---

[160] Terms of the contract: Demosthenes 34.32, 35.   [161] Demosthenes 34.8. Cf. 34.28–29.

Phormion in Lampis. It is unclear, however, whether Phormion's confidence in Lampis was warranted, since Chrysippus claims that Lampis gave contradictory accounts of whether Phormion had given him the money. According to Chrysippus, at first Lampis denied that he had received the money and then agreed that he had.

Whether Lampis behaved dishonestly or not, he nevertheless had a reputation for trustworthiness in so far as both sides had agreed to have it written in the original contract that Phormion would hand over the money to Lampis. The contract was written in Athens, moreover, where Lampis, we learn, lived with his wife and children.[162] Since slaves did not enjoy legally recognized marriages (see Chapter 4), it is striking that the speaker uses the term "wife." Moreover, we get the impression that Lampis circulated about the city freely and was well known in business circles. When Chrysippus initially tried to track down Phormion to claim repayment, his strategy was to contact Lampis first since he assumed (correctly) that Lampis would know where to find Phormion. Indeed, Lampis escorted him directly to Phormion, who was found in the area of the marketplace where perfumes were sold.[163] In sum, Lampis appears to have been a wealthy, trusted slave who lived independently with his family in Athens and enjoyed considerable autonomy both in the city and abroad.

While Lampis was still a slave despite his financial success, other slaves involved in overseas trading enterprises apparently used their resources to claim their freedom. No fewer than seven long-distance traders (ἔμποροι, φορτηγοί) are listed among those who dedicated silver bowls to mark their attainment of freedom. Even more impressive is the eight retail merchants (κάπηλοι) and the twelve more specialized merchants who also dedicated bowls. Among the latter we find one bread-seller (ἀρτοπώλης), one wool-seller (ἐριοπώλης), two fishmongers (ἰχθυοπῶλαι), three incense-sellers (λιβανοπῶλαι), one honey-merchant (μελιτοπώλης), one pulse-seller (ὀσπριοπώλης), one sesame-seller (σεσαμοπώλης), one flax-seller (στυπειοπώλης) and one dealer in salt fish (ταραχιπώλης). Yet once again, we must reconcile such apparent success stories with evidence that reveals the differential treatment and hence vulnerability of slave merchants compared to their free counterparts in the same profession. For example, the law on approvers of silver coinage discussed above states that any free merchant who does not accept coinage that has been approved will have his or her merchandise confiscated for the day. A slave merchant, by

---

[162] Demosthenes 34.37.   [163] Demosthenes 34.12–13.

contrast, "shall be beaten with fifty lashes with the whip by the magistrates."[164]

Perhaps the most remarkably contradictory experiences of slavery can be found among slave-bankers. Banking, like long-distance trading, was a risky enterprise, but one that could also bring great profits. Legal speeches mention a number of bankers who went bankrupt, but also tell the story of several who became very successful.[165] These latter men not only became wealthy, but were granted their freedom and became owners of the banks in which they once served as slave-accountants. Even more remarkably, some of these men married the widows of their former owners and also gained citizenship, a gift granted by the Athenian people in gratitude for their many donations to the community.[166] Let's look at a few examples to gain a sense of the texture of these slaves' lives.

Let's start with Pasion, perhaps the most extraordinary of the banking slaves whose lives can be sketched in rough outline.[167] Although Pasion rose to become a wealthy citizen, it is important to stress that he started off as a slave-accountant in a bank owned by two men, Antisthenes and Archestratus, who were probably Athenian citizens.[168] Pasion's origins are unknown, but it is likely that he was non-Greek, perhaps Phoenician or Syrian by birth.[169] The bank was located in the market of the port of Athens, Piraeus, and consisted of a simple table at which Pasion, along with other slaves, provided their services. These services would have consisted primarily of currency exchanges, but also keeping records of deposits and withdrawals. Bankers also kept copies of business contracts, particularly loans made on trading voyages.[170] Evidently Pasion was very skilled and rose up to become "chief cashier and manager" of the bank.[171] Whatever his native tongue, he apparently overcame any linguistic and cultural barriers quickly and made a lot of money for his owners. At some point, his owners rewarded him with freedom, and at some time after that he became owner of the bank. It is likely that he first leased the bank from his former owners and then bought it once he had accumulated sufficient resources.[172]

Two other facts about Pasion's life are significant for assessing the range of experiences of slaves who worked in banking. First, after gaining his

---

[164] RO 25, lines 16–18 and 30–32. On distinctions in legal penalties between free and slave, see further Chapter 4.
[165] Bankruptcies: Demosthenes 36.50–51. Successes: see below. [166] Demosthenes 36.47.
[167] Modern accounts: Trevett 1992, 1–49; Cohen 1992; Davies *APF* 11672.
[168] Demosthenes 36.43. [169] Davies, *APF* 11672, 2; Trevett 1992, 1, 17–18.
[170] Demosthenes 34.6.
[171] See Trevett (1992, 5) for this description of the duties of the senior slave in a bank.
[172] Trevett 1992, 2.

freedom, and thus becoming a free non-citizen resident (metic), Pasion married a woman named Archippe, who was probably also a metic.[173] With Archippe, Pasion had two sons, Apollodorus and Pasicles, who inherited his great wealth (70 talents = 420,000 drachmas) upon his death.[174] Second, Pasion and his children were granted Athenian citizenship "on account of his good works on behalf of the city."[175] From another law-court speech, we learn that these good works consisted of some generous financial contributions, and possibly service as trierarch (captain of a warship) on several occasions.[176] The prominence of the family is evident from the fact that his elder son, Apollodorus, became a well-known politician, who moved in the highest social circles and became embroiled in numerous legal cases. It is thanks to Apollodorus' legal troubles that we know so much about his family.

As owner of the bank, Pasion became the master of the slaves who worked in the bank and performed the tasks that he used to execute. We know a bit about the lives of two of the slave-managers of his bank, both of whom also gained their freedom and one of whom also became a citizen like Pasion. The first slave-manager was named Cittus. We learn about Cittus' activities from a legal case in which Pasion was accused of refusing to return money that had been deposited in his bank. Pasion's accuser in the case challenges Pasion to have Cittus subjected to judicial torture so that they can learn the truth about the deposit, since Cittus "knew all about it."[177] According to his accuser, Pasion first tried to avoid having Cittus give testimony under torture by claiming that Cittus was not a slave, but a free man and hence not subject to judicial torture.[178] Later, Pasion allegedly consented to the subjection of Cittus to questioning, but not to physical torture.[179] While the speaker suggests that Pasion's reluctance to have Cittus tortured (whipping and the rack are mentioned) was because he was afraid that Cittus would reveal the truth, one might conjecture that Pasion's reluctance might rather be due to his own former status as a slave who similarly would have been subject to judicial torture.[180] Interestingly, Cittus is later sent by Pasion as his business agent to the Bosporus where, according to the speaker, he declared himself free and a Milesian by birth.[181] If this is an accurate account of Cittus' trajectory, then he, like Pasion, achieved freedom, although he continued to work as business agent

---

[173] Trevett 1992, 2.   [174] Trevett 1992, 4.   [175] Demosthenes 59.2; cf. 45.35.
[176] Demosthenes 45.85. There is some debate about whether metics could serve as trierarchs; however, see Trevett 1992, 22.
[177] Isocrates 17.11, 53.   [178] Isocrates 17.13–14, 27, 49, 53.   [179] Isocrates 17.16–17, 55.
[180] Mirhady 2000, 85–86.   [181] Isocrates 17.51.

or partner with Pasion after his liberation. The next manager of Pasion's bank was Phormion, whose story is almost as remarkable as Pasion's. Indeed, Phormion's story, along with those of several other bankers who achieved freedom and citizenship, shows that Pasion's trajectory was not a complete anomaly.[182] Phormion, like Pasion, was of non-Greek origin. He had been purchased by Pasion and trained to work in his bank.[183] Several sources mention that Phormion never learned to speak fluent Greek, but this cultural deficit does not seem to have interfered with his ability to run the bank and may well have been exaggerated by his legal adversaries.[184] Regardless, Phormion became Pasion's trusted slave, who managed the bank and became "very useful in Pasion's business affairs."[185] As his own masters had done for him, Pasion granted Phormion his freedom and allowed him to lease his bank and a shield factory from him.[186] These were very profitable enterprises generating 10,000 and 6,000 drachmas per year respectively.[187] Phormion, like Pasion before him, became a very wealthy man.[188] While Phormion's wealth was certainly derived primarily from banking, he evidently diversified his operations at some point, since, in addition to the management of the shield factory, he also owned trading ships in the Bosporus.[189]

Apollodorus, Pasion's eldest son, records how Pasion taught Phormion the requisite skills of the banking trade that made his meteoric rise in status possible. Apollodorus' comments also reveal the great trust that Pasion placed in his slave.

> Since my father – the one who bought [Phormion] – was a banker, and since he taught him to read and write and trained him in the business and put him in control of vast sums of money, Phormion has prospered.[190]

The great trust placed in Phormion by Pasion is especially evident from the fact that, when Pasion died, he both betrothed his wife, Archippe, to Phormion in his will and made him guardian of his younger son, Pasicles.[191] Remarkably, we learn from a lawsuit that Apollodorus lodged against Phormion, that it was not uncommon for bank owners to betroth their wives to their former slaves.

---

[182] We know the names of four other bankers who rose from slave to wealthy citizen: Epigenes, Konon, Aristolochus and Timodemos (Dinarchus 1.43; and Demosthenes 45.63 and 36.29, 50; with Trevett 1992, 161).
[183] Demosthenes 45.71–72, 80–82.   [184] Demosthenes 45.30, 73, 81, 36.1
[185] Demosthenes 36.44, 45.33.   [186] Demosthenes 36.4, 45.29–33.   [187] Demosthenes 36.11, 37.
[188] Demosthenes 45.66, 71–73.   [189] Demosthenes 45.64.
[190] Demosthenes 45.72, trans. A. Scafuro.   [191] Demosthenes 36.7–8, 45.3, 28.

Socrates, the well-known banker, after being released by his masters just as Apollodorus' father had been, gave his own wife in marriage to Satyrus, who had once been his slave. Socles was another banker who gave his own wife in marriage to his former slave Timodemus, who is still alive to this day. This is the practice of men engaged in that business, not only here, men of Athens, but in Aegina, where Strymodorus gave his wife to his slave Hermaeus and after her death he went on to give him his daughter. Many such instances could be mentioned.[192]

While this selective sample from a tendentious law-court speech cannot be taken to show that this practice was typical, it at least demonstrates that it was not unique to Pasion. The aim, it would seem, was to co-opt the great financial skills of these former slaves and keep the business in the family.[193] While the speaker was clearly responding to prejudice against ex-slaves marrying the widows of their former owners (see Chapter 4), apparently the social stigma could be overcome when financial interests were at stake. Moreover, it is worth stressing that these marriages are not examples of freeborn citizens marrying former slaves but rather in most cases probably former slaves marrying other former slaves. In the case of Phormion, for example, Archippe was probably a slave earlier in her life, just as Pasion himself had been. This caveat notwithstanding, it is testimony to the remarkable potential mobility of banking slaves that some of them not only gained freedom and became owners of the bank in which they formerly worked as a slave, but also married the widows of their former owners.

The final significant event in Phormion's life was his receipt of citizenship, like Pasion before him.[194] The grant of citizenship was likely in return for financial and other contributions to the city.[195] Moreover, it is apparent that, at this point in his life, Phormion moved in the highest circles among the wealthiest and most influential citizens.[196] For example, the politician Demosthenes wrote a speech in his defense when he was prosecuted by Apollodorus, and probably spoke at his trial.[197] Phormion, therefore, like Pasion, exemplifies the extraordinary potential of slaves who worked in this sector of the economy to achieve not only wealth but freedom, citizenship and elite social status. While the stories of these two slaves are relatively well documented, we know only the names of four others who also rose from banking slaves to well-respected citizens.[198] Although these remarkable individuals are certainly not typical, they at least demonstrate the

---

[192] Demosthenes 36.28–29, trans. D. MacDowell.   [193] Cohen 1992, 61–110.
[194] Demosthenes 46.13.   [195] Demosthenes 36.56–58.   [196] Demosthenes 46.1.
[197] Dinarchus 1.111.   [198] See n.166 above.

possibilities for skilled and ambitious slaves who happened to be put to work in this field.

Prostitution

While the field of banking was populated by male slaves, prostitution was dominated by female slaves and ex-slaves. Remarkably, moreover, some female slaves working in prostitution experienced a degree of social mobility that was almost as dramatic as that experienced by male slaves working in banking. Indeed, we know the names and at least part of the life stories of a few remarkable women who began as slaves working in brothels and became wealthy and free. Moreover, even if these women did not achieve citizenship as did their male counterparts in banking, they at least socialized with leading citizens. That said, the lives of these women were very hard and their status precarious even after they achieved considerable autonomy. In sketching the story of the most well known of these women, it should be stressed that most slaves in prostitution probably remained slaves and continued to be exploited throughout their lives.[199]

The best-known example of a slave-prostitute is a woman named Neaira, who began life as a brothel slave in Corinth.[200] We know of her story because she was involved with a prominent citizen, Stephanus, who became embroiled in a lawsuit lodged by his political opponent Apollodorus (the son of Pasion, mentioned above). In the lawsuit, Apollodorus charged Neaira with the crime of living in marriage with a citizen, although she herself was not a citizen. In his speech for the prosecution, Apollodorus goes much further, however, than simply proving that Neaira was not a citizen. Rather, he presents an account of Neaira's life that emphasizes her work as a prostitute from childhood onward. The speech clearly aims to discredit Neaira – and more importantly his rival Stephanus – and therefore may exaggerate or even invent some sordid events in her life. Nevertheless, the broad outlines of Apollodorus' account are plausible and provide a vivid illustration of both the hardships and opportunities for slaves engaged in this occupation.

In early childhood, Neaira and six other girls were acquired by a freedwoman, Nicarete, and trained to work as prostitutes in Corinth. We do not know how Nicarete gained ownership of these girls, but she

---

[199] Glazebrook and Henry 2011b.
[200] Other women who rose up from slavery through prostitution include: Rhodopis, Leaina, Phryne, Pythionike, Alke (Isaeus 6.19–20 and below). On exposure at birth leading to slavery, see Chapter 2.

may have received them as unwanted children either directly from their parents or indirectly through exposure. Nicarete was apparently an expert at detecting the potential of young girls for prostitution and training them so that they brought in a good living for her. According to Apollodorus, Nicarete passed them off as her daughters, thereby enabling her to charge higher prices on the pretext that they were free. Indeed, it appears that Neaira and the other girls served elite customers, including the wealthy Athenian metic Lysias, and prominent aristocrats and citizens from throughout the Greek world. Nicarete even travelled with her girls outside of Corinth to meet with clients.

At a certain point, two clients offered to buy Neaira for their personal use. They offered the extraordinary payment of 3,000 drachmas for Neaira – a sum of money that attests to Neaira's skill in her trade and profitability for Nicarete. Nicarete accepted the offer, nevertheless, perhaps because Neaira was past her prime. Indeed, Apollodorus describes Nicarete's mercenary exploitation of the girls in this way: "When she had profited from the youth of each of them, she sold all seven of them outright."[201] The two men who had bought Neaira shared her and made use of her sexually for some time before they decided to get married. At this point, the men could have sold her back to a brothel, as some men did when they no longer have a use for their slave-prostitutes.[202] Instead, the men agreed to free her if she could come up with two-thirds of her purchase price. While Apollodorus presents this offer as initiated by the two men, it is possible that Neaira played an active role in lobbying them to help her take this step towards her own freedom.

Neaira's active role in seeking her freedom is certainly evident in the next phase of Apollodorus' account, where Neaira is said to have gathered together "the money that she had collected from her other lovers as contributions towards her freedom, together with money that she put aside from her earnings."[203] Apparently, Neaira had been saving to buy her freedom, and was also able to call on a circle of former lovers to raise more cash. However, even after successfully negotiating to bring down her purchase price, she was still somewhat short of the full price and ultimately made an appeal to another former lover, an Athenian named Phrynion, who paid the remainder of the price for her freedom. Despite this successful negotiation, however, Neaira's status was precarious, since Phrynion apparently felt entitled to abuse her sexually as compensation for having paid the final installment for her "freedom." Indeed, we next hear of Neaira

---

[201] Pseudo-Demosthenes 59.19. [202] Antiphon 1.14. [203] Pseudo-Demosthenes 59.31.

living with Phrynion in Athens, where, according to Apollodorus, she was compelled to have sex with Phrynion and other men. Therefore, while Neaira had a comfortable lifestyle by this point and had material possessions and even slaves of her own, she evidently was not fully free. Perhaps for this reason, she took the initiative again and fled to neighboring Megara. There she worked as a prostitute for two years before returning to Athens to live with the prominent Athenian Stephanus.

A key episode upon her return underscores Neaira's precarious position. When Phrynion learned that Neaira was again in Athens, he came to claim her, presumably as his slave, since he had paid the final installment of her "freedom" price. In response, Stephanus asserted her freedom in a legal procedure which required him to provide guarantees that she would appear in court. The case never came to trial, however, and was settled through arbitration. The settlement, moreover, put Neaira in a somewhat ambiguous position between free and slave. On the one hand, the arbitrators granted her freedom and control over her own affairs. On the other hand, they required her to live with each of the men on alternate days or according to whatever arrangement the two men reached between themselves.

According to Apollodorus, Neaira continued to work as a prostitute while living in marriage with Stephanus. She was also accused of trying to pass off her daughter as the legitimate child of Stephanus, and hence a citizen. Whatever the truth of these charges, it is clear from Apollodorus' account of Neaira's life that she was both a victim of brutal sexual exploitation from a very young age and also a clever strategist who made use of her skills to earn money and influence from powerful men in the hope of gaining freedom for herself and her children. Arguably, she achieved as much freedom as a woman was allowed in classical Athens, given the legal constraints on free-citizen married women: arbitrators confirmed her personal freedom and authority over her own affairs, yet she was still subject to the (sexual) will of two men and was not able to live independently. If we are to believe Apollodorus, even her quest to gain freedom and citizenship for her children was only partially successful: her daughter was briefly married to two citizens in succession and, although her grandson was acknowledged as legitimate by his citizen father, his citizenship was denied by his father's kinship groups (phratry and genos) – the two social groups that served as witnesses to citizenship status (see Chapter 4).

As ambiguous as Neaira's final status was, therefore, it represents one of the better scenarios for a woman who started her working life as a prostitute. While we do not know the outcome of Apollodorus' suit against her, up to that point she was apparently living as a free woman in Athens, possessing wealth and slaves of her own, and socializing with leading citizens of Athens. We know of a number of other women who worked as prostitutes and rose from slave to wealthy free women. Herodotus, for example, tells the story of a Thracian woman named Rhodopis who was the slave of a Greek man from the island of Samos, sometime in the early sixth century BCE.[204] At some point, she was sold to another Greek man from Samos, who brought her to the Greek trading port of Naucratis in Egypt where she worked as a prostitute. Like Neaira, Rhodopis found a man (in fact, a brother of the poet Sappho) to buy her freedom for a very high price, and, also like Neaira, she apparently continued to practice prostitution as a free woman. Rhodopis became wealthy enough to make a dedication of ox-size iron spits at Delphi that were still on display there in the late fifth century. Fragments from fifth- and fourth-century comic plays preserve the names of a number of other wealthy and independent prostitutes (*hetairai*) and Socrates is depicted as conversing with one named Theodote in a dialogue by Xenophon.[205] Another of these women, by the name of Phryne, seems to have risen from destitution to great wealth and even had a golden statue of herself dedicated at Delphi.[206]

Not all slave-prostitutes achieved such successes, and indeed our sources tend to mention the exceptions rather than the norm. Some ex-slave-prostitutes became managers of brothels after gaining their freedom. For example, a law-court speech mentions a woman named Alke who, after gaining her freedom, seems to have become manager of the brothel in which she had once worked.[207] The same may be true of Nicarete, the woman who acquired and trained Neaira. Like Neaira, moreover, Alke seems to have lived with an Athenian citizen and even, allegedly, had her child by another man accepted as citizen. In spite of these many stories of slave-prostitutes who achieved freedom, wealth and even fame, a more typical experience was to remain in the brothel or to end up in a brothel after being discarded by a citizen.

Facilities in brothels ranged from small rooms to elaborate entertainment facilities. A building in Athens has been identified as a brothel, and several of the artifacts reveal aspects of the slaves' experience there.[208]

---

[204] Herodotus 2.134–35.
[205] Athenaeus, *The Learned Banqueters* 13.568ff; Xenophon, *Memorabilia* 3.11.
[206] Athenaeus, *The Learned Banqueters* 13.591b. Cf. Keesling 2006.
[207] Isaeus 6.19–20. Cf. Glazebrook 2011, 51–52.   [208] Knigge 2001; Glazebrook 2011, 39–41.

Firstly, the presence of loom-weights suggest that these women engaged in textile production alongside prostitution.[209] Secondly, various objects associated with the worship of Astarte and Cybele suggest a non-Greek origin for the residents. In all likelihood, the women had been brought as slaves from the eastern Mediterranean.[210] A comic fragment celebrating the wide availability of prostitutes in brothels inadvertently allows us to visualize the experience of the typical brothel slave, although not her own reactions to it.

> You can look in broad daylight at them
> lined up one after the other in a column – half-naked,
> standing there in fine, sheer fabric, the type
> of girls the sacred waters of the Eridanus make grow –
> and purchase your pleasure for a small sum.[211]

Some brothel slaves who were trained as flute players and dancers, were rented out by their owners to entertain at male drinking parties (symposia).[212] At such events, they provided sexual as well as musical entertainment. This double duty is crudely referenced in a portrait of an uncultured man who boasts to his dinner guests that, "the delight of the guests has been arranged ... My slave is sending her now from the pimp so that we may all be piped by her into happiness."[213] In Athens, city magistrates had among their duties the obligation to ensure that female musicians were not paid extravagantly, presumably by men too inebriated to make good financial decisions.[214] Of course, any money such slaves earned was their owner's property, unless a portion was granted to them as a favor or an incentive (see Chapter 5).

As well as female prostitutes there were, of course, male prostitutes, and it is likely that many of these were slaves. One law-court speech from Athens concerns a dispute over a rent boy who may have been a slave.[215] Another speech concerns a freeborn youth who allegedly prostituted himself, and the speaker evinces such disgust at such behavior by a free citizen that we can infer that male prostitution, like female, was generally associated with slaves.[216] Indeed, the speaker cites laws that prohibit citizens from practicing prostitution and prescribe penalties for doing so.

---

[209] Glazebrook 2011, 39–41, 43–45. [210] Cohen 2006; Glazebrook 2011, 50.
[211] Eubulus, *Nannion* fr. 67 = Athenaeus, *The Learned Banqueters* 13.568f.
[212] Athenaeus, *The Learned Banqueters* 13.607d. [213] Theophrastus, *Characters* 20.10.
[214] [Aristotle] *Constitution of the Athenians* 50.2. [215] Lysias 3; with Dover 1978, 32.
[216] Aeschines, *Against Timarchus*; with Fisher 2001.

Milling, Baking and Cooking

Our sources mention that being sent to labor in a mill was a punishment meted out to disobedient slaves.[217] From this evidence, we can infer that the grinding of grain was primarily performed by slaves. Moreover, the fact that such labor was considered a punishment suggests that toiling in a mill was one of the most physically demanding and undesirable of slave jobs. It was perhaps akin to working in a mine which, as we have seen, was characterized by extreme toil in unhealthy and even deadly conditions. As one slave-owner says in threatening to send a female household slave to a mill: once she is thrown into the mill, she will "never have respite from suffering."[218] Moreover, in addition to the physical suffering, this sort of labor would have been especially psychologically degrading since it reduced human beings to the level of animals – namely, the beasts of burden (cattle, oxen) that were also used to turn mills to grind grain. We can imagine slaves being worked to death in these conditions, driven on constantly by the whip.

Bread making was also a task performed by slaves. Although we hear of several citizen bread makers, our sources make clear that they employed slaves in their operations. A character in Xenophon's *Memorabilia*, for example, points out that a citizen bread maker has become rich by "buying foreign slaves" and "forcing them to toil."[219] A set of terracotta figurines from Thebes in Boeotia, moreover, depicts a row of five female workers kneading dough as another figure sets the pace (Fig. 3.9). It is likely that the female kneaders are slaves.

Bread selling was also a trade practiced by slaves, if we are to judge from the appearance of a bread seller on the list of donors of silver bowls in recognition of gaining freedom.[220] Another dedication from the Athenian acropolis, moreover, lists a female bread seller whose name (Phrygia – "Phrygian woman") suggests that she may be or once have been a slave.[221] It seems that slaves as well as citizens could become prosperous from bread making and selling, and these last two examples show that some slaves in this trade were able to keep some of the profits of their labor, and perhaps lived independently of their owners.

---

[217] Lysias 1.18; Demosthenes 45.33; Menander, *The Shield* 245; and Chapter 5.   [218] Lysias 1.18.
[219] Xenophon, *Memorabilia* 2.7.6. Another citizen baker is mentioned by Plato, *Gorgias* 518b; Aristophanes, fr. 1; and Antiphanes, fr. 176 Kock.
[220] *IG* ii².1556.30–32.   [221] *IG* i³.546.

Fig. 3.9 Slaves (?) kneading dough with a slave (?) flute player setting the pace. Terracotta model from Thebes, Boeotia, 525–475 BCE. CA804. Photo: Gérard Blot. Louvre. © RMN Grand-Palais / Art Resource, NY.

In addition to milling and baking, some slaves specialized in cooking and were rented out by their owners to prepare meals for dinner parties, weddings and also for festival celebrations. Like slave bread sellers, slave-cooks may have lived and worked independently from their owners, rendering a portion of their fees back to the owners and keeping the rest. Indeed, they appear frequently as characters in comic plays, where they contract their own deals in the marketplace.[222] Some cooks evidently earned enough to pay for their freedom, since three such individuals are listed among the donors of silver bowls marking their attainment of freedom.[223]

Child Labor

It is important to acknowledge that slave children labored in almost all of the tasks discussed above.[224] Of course, free children from poor families might also be put to work tending animals or performing menial tasks, so child labor was not confined to slave children. Yet slave children performed many more types of labor, and some types of work, such as prostitution

---

[222] See, for example, Menander, *The Shield* 216–32.   [223] *IG* ii².1555.21–22, 1570.36–38, 92–94.
[224] For an overview, see Fischer 2012, 115–21. On children and childhood generally, see Golden 1990.

and work in the mines, were performed exclusively by slaves. The case of Neaira shows that some slave girls were made to start working in prostitution at a very young age: Neaira is one of seven "small" children bought by the brothel owner Nicarete, who raises them and trains them in the arts of prostitution.[225] As mentioned above, slave children may have been used in mines because of their ability to work in small spaces.

Vase painting shows what appear to be slave children working in the full range of occupations (the diminutive size of these figures clearly suggests that they are children and cannot be attributed to a convention of depicting slaves as smaller in stature (see Chapter 4)). Indeed, vase paintings depict slave children attending their free owners in all sorts of tasks, including personal hygiene, dressing, carrying belongings, serving food and drink at dinner parties. Slave girls are also depicted performing domestic labor, including weaving and child-minding. Slave children might even be rented out to workshops, as the case of Lesis in the foundry suggests (see above).

Warfare

One final area of the slave experience must be mentioned – namely, warfare. It has long been recognized that Greek soldiers were often accompanied on campaign by their slaves, who carried their equipment, prepared meals and served as valets for their owners.[226] More recently, however, it has been recognized that slaves also sometimes served as combatants, either as light-armed soldiers who reinforced the heavily armed citizen-soldiers (hoplites) in the phalanx, or even as hoplites themselves.[227] Among naval powers such as Athens and Chios, moreover, slaves were often deployed as rowers in the fleet.[228] This conclusion seems paradoxical, since relying on slaves whose loyalty could be doubtful was risky and, in any case, arming slaves could risk a slave uprising. There are, however, plenty of parallels for this practice in other slave-owning societies, and indeed it makes some sense to make use of the manpower of slaves for this purpose.[229] Moreover, slaves were sometimes incentivized to fight loyally with their owners by the promise of a grant of freedom (see Chapter 5).

One of the reasons that the role of slaves in Greek land and naval warfare was not fully recognized is that our sources mention it only occasionally in

---

[225] Pseudo-Demosthenes 59.18.   [226] Pritchett 1974, 50. Cf. van Wees 2004, 70–71.
[227] Hunt 1998.   [228] Graham 1992, 1998; Jordan 2000, 2003; Hunt 1998, 83–101.
[229] For the historical parallels, see Brown and Morgan 2006.

passing and put emphasis on the connection between citizenship and military service, as Greek civic ideology demanded.[230] Even though free non-citizen resident foreigners were required to perform military service in some states such as Athens (see Chapter 4), they tended to serve in separate regiments, and pride of place was given to the citizen soldier in both practice and in representations of Greek warfare. Nevertheless, there are striking indications of the role of slaves in our sources, beginning in the Persian Wars and intensifying over the course of the fifth century.

For example, slaves served as light-armed soldiers fighting alongside their owners at two major land battles in the Persian Wars, Marathon (490) and Plataea (479). At Marathon, a separate funeral mound for the slaves killed in battle was still visible in the Roman era alongside that of the Athenian citizen dead.[231] In addition to this remarkable privilege of a war monument, the slaves who fought were offered freedom by the Athenians in return.[232] At Plataea, moreover, seven helots accompanied each Spartan hoplite and a good case has been made that they served as light-armed troops alongside their Spartan masters.[233] By the time of the great conflict between Athens and Sparta in the last third of the fifth century (the Peloponnesian War), it appears that helots sometimes served as heavily-armed hoplites as well. For example, the Athenian historian Thucydides is very explicit that the 700 helots who accompanied the Spartans' crack-commander Brasidas on campaign in Thrace in 424 served "as hoplites."[234] Moreover, Thucydides also records that the Spartans voted to grant freedom to these helots and the right to live wherever they chose.[235] These helots therefore became "newly-enrolled members of the people" (νεοδαμώδεις), the usual Spartan term for helots who had been granted their freedom (see Chapter 1).

While the land power Sparta deployed slaves as infantry, naval powers such as Corcyra, Chios and Athens deployed slaves as rowers. Thucydides reveals this detail when he describes the differential treatment of slaves compared to their citizen owners when ships were captured by their enemies. For example, when the Corinthians captured some Corcyrean ships with over one thousand rowers aboard in 433, they sold eight hundred of the men who were slaves and kept captive some two hundred and fifty men who were Corcyrean citizens.[236] Similarly, in 411 the Athenians treated the rowers aboard some captive Chian ships differently according to their status: they freed the slaves and imprisoned the citizens.[237]

---

[230] This is the principal insight of Hunt 1998. [231] Pausanias 1.32.3. [232] Pausanias 7.15.7.
[233] Hunt 1998, 31–39. [234] Thucydides 4.80.5. [235] Thucydides 5.34. [236] Thucydides 1.55.
[237] Thucydides 8.15.

The evidence for the Athenians' use of slaves as rowers in their fleet is both direct and indirect. Most significantly, a long honorary inscription lists the men who served in the Athenian fleet between 410 and 390.[238] For each ship, the crew includes both citizen rowers, free non-citizen rowers and slave-rowers, besides the commander and hoplite marines on board. From these lists, it appears that between 20 and 40 percent of the crew of each ship was composed of slaves.[239] More indirectly, the fact that two special ships used for religious and diplomatic missions were "manned exclusively by free Athenian citizens" suggests that this was not true of other ships in the Athenian fleet.[240] Moreover, while it appears that the Athenians did not normally offer slaves freedom for service in the fleet, slave-rowers could be so rewarded in times of exceptional need. The evidence for this claim is the Battle of Arginusae in 406 when the Athenians appear to have rewarded slave rowers not only with freedom but also with citizenship for their role in this important victory during the final difficult years of the Peloponnesian War.[241]

What was it like for a slave to be called upon or compelled to fight with his owner in a conflict that he had no role in initiating? On the one hand, we might imagine that a slave would resent being forced to put his life on the line for a cause that was not his own, and seek an opportunity to flee. This, apparently, was the choice of one helot, who, after leading his Spartan owner (who was suffering from an eye infection) into battle at Thermopylae in 479, fled from sight.[242] Similarly, slaves in the Athenian navy at Syracuse deserted in great numbers as the Athenian situation deteriorated in 413.[243] On the other hand, some slaves may have identified with the cause of their masters, or judged that compliance was the best option or have been motivated by the potential reward of freedom. In any case, once committed to fighting, we must imagine that the circumstances of extreme danger and the need to depend on each other would have at least temporarily broken down distinctions of status and created some degree of an emotional bond between slave and owner.

Conclusion

This chapter has surveyed the principal areas of slave labor and has attempted to reconstruct the experiences of slaves. It should be stressed

---

[238] *IG* i³.1032. [239] Graham 1998. [240] Thucydides 8.73.5.
[241] Aristophanes, *Frogs* 33, 190–91, 693–94, 700–702; Hellanicus *FGrH* 323a F25; with Hunt 2001.
[242] Herodotus 7.229. [243] Thucydides 7.13.

that this survey is not comprehensive, and that slaves performed so many tasks that it is not possible to mention them all. Nevertheless, the survey demonstrates that slaves were active in almost every area of the social, political and economic life of the Greek state. This is not to say that there were not differences between city-states in the roles of slaves. In Sparta, for example, helots were primarily active in agriculture, although, as we have just seen, they also sometimes served as soldiers in the Spartan army, and the Laconian helots performed some domestic labor for their owners in addition to agricultural labor. In Athens, by contrast, slaves were present in these and all other spheres of life, including skilled crafts and manufacturing, commerce and banking, as well as civic administration and the navy. Most other Greek states fell somewhere between these two extremes in their deployment of slaves.

While this chapter – and indeed this book – is focused on slave experiences and slave perspectives, after surveying the evidence for slave labor, it is worth briefly addressing a key question that has often been asked about slavery in ancient Greece: was Greek civilization dependent (in the sense spelled out at the beginning of this chapter) on slavery? This is not a simple question, and a proper answer would require better data than is available for ancient Greece. In the absence of data such as numbers of slaves and productivity, we are reduced to more qualitative judgments concerning the centrality of slavery. By this measure, the answer must be a resounding yes, although some distinctions should be made between different states with their various institutional arrangements and economic bases. For example, the Spartan way of life, with its focus on military training, would not have been possible without the agricultural labor of helots. The Athenians, on the other hand, often worked alongside their slaves on the land or in the workshop. Nevertheless, without slave labor, it is unlikely that the Athenians would have enjoyed the quality of life – the material prosperity and the opportunities for civic engagement – that they clearly did during the classical period. This is a point to which we will return in the final chapter.

A further question, however, follows on from this judgment of the dependence of Greeks on the domination and exploitation of slaves: what leverage, if any, did this dependence provide for the slaves? It is this question that the next two chapters will address.

CHAPTER 4

Slaves and Status

> Our forefathers ... forbade slaves from doing things which they thought to be fitting for free men to do. The law says that a slave is not to exercise in the gymnasium nor to rub himself down with oil in wrestling grounds. For when they observed the fine things that are derived from exercise in the gymnasia, they barred slaves from partaking of them.
>
> Aeschines, *Against Timarchus* 138

> There is very great license among the slaves and resident non-citizens (metics) in Athens. Indeed, it is not possible to strike them in Athens, nor will a slave get out of the way for you. I will tell you why this is the custom. If there were a law that a slave, or metic or freedman could be struck by a free citizen, often someone would strike a citizen, thinking he was a slave. For the mass of citizens is no better dressed there than the slaves or metics.
>
> Pseudo-Xenophon (or the "Old Oligarch"), *Constitution of the Athenians* 1.10–12

The law cited in the first quotation above implies that the Athenians were acutely aware of status distinctions between slave and citizen and strenuously reinforced these distinctions through legislation. The second quotation, however, suggests that in everyday encounters between citizens and slaves on the streets of Athens, status distinctions were invisible. Indeed, according to the author of this observation, it was impossible to tell by dress or by behavior who was slave and who was citizen.

These quotations raise the question of the distinctions that were made between slaves and citizens in ancient Greece. The importance of this question is reinforced by some of the facts that we have established in the previous two chapters – namely, that slaves came from populations that were not physically distinct (e.g., in skin color) from their masters and often worked in many of the same professions as their free and citizen owners. Moreover, as we have seen, some slaves were relatively independent of their masters, and even well-off financially. As such, slaves may have been indistinguishable from their masters in appearance, profession and lifestyle. How did one tell who was a slave and who was not?

In order to answer this question, this chapter will explore the ways that the Greeks drew ideological distinctions between free and slave and reinforced them through their differential treatment in the laws and through institutional structures.[1] Conversely, the chapter will show that these efforts were sometimes futile, as the reality of a common humanity, as well as the centrality of slaves to all aspects of life, continually undermined these distinctions. Moreover, in line with a central theme of this book, we will examine how slaves themselves actively challenged attempts to impose artificial distinctions. For example, might the law cited above be a response (rather than a preemptive injunction) to the fact that some slaves were usurping the privileges and behaviors through which free citizens performed their identity?[2] That is to say, were some slaves – perhaps the relatively independent and even prosperous ones discussed in the last chapter – exercising in the gymnasia and rubbing themselves down with oil? If so, did they intend their actions to be understood as an explicit challenge to status distinctions between slave and free?

Ideological Distinctions

We have already seen how Aristotle developed a theory of natural slavery that attempted to establish differences between slave and free that were grounded in nature (Chapter 1). We also saw how this theory ran afoul of the obvious objective truths – namely, that there were no consistent, natural differences in physical and mental characteristics between slave and free, and, moreover, that many individuals became slaves merely through conquest.

Despite these evident facts and the consequent failure (at least to most modern sensibilities and even to some ancient critics) of Aristotle's quasi-racialized theory of slavery, it is necessary to acknowledge that ideas of natural slavery and even arguments based on race or ethnicity underwrote widely held Greek justifications of slavery. Indeed, although the Greeks tended to emphasize the environmental and cultural – rather than racial – factors that they believed led to "slavish" characteristics, these claims easily

---

[1] Prior excellent treatments include Hunter and Edmondson (2000) and Cartledge (2002, 133–66).
[2] Lewis 2018, 123.

slid into statements about the propriety or "naturalness" of the enslavement of certain racial or ethnic groups. In other words, even though the Greeks routinely enslaved other Greeks, they tended to assimilate all slaves to non-Greeks, whom they viewed as having a slavish nature as a result of either their natural or their cultural environment.

To see how this slippage worked, let's examine a medical text, the Hippocratic *Airs, Waters, Places*. This text is preserved among the writings attributed to the doctor Hippocrates of Cos, who lived in the fifth century BCE, but may have been composed by a member of his school, rather than Hippocrates himself.[3] For our purposes, the important point is that the author's explanations are scientific versions of more widespread beliefs about connections between the environment – including the climate, wind exposure, water quality and even mode of government and lifestyle – and the physical, mental and moral qualities of a people.[4] In some cases, these connections are explicitly said to make certain groups of people more suitable for slavery.

In the first part of the treatise, the author concerns himself with the physical effects of the environment on its inhabitants. For example, he writes that the inhabitants of a city that is exposed to hot winds have humid and flabby bodies, while those whose city is exposed to cold winds have firm and slender bodies.[5] As the analysis progresses, however, mental and moral qualities are added to the catalogue of environmental effects. For example, those who live in moderate climates not only are physically healthier, according to the author, but also have better tempers and are more intelligent than those who live in colder climates.[6] By the middle of the treatise, moreover, the author is ready to draw sweeping distinctions between those who live in "Europe" and those who live in "Asia," based on environmental conditions. Interestingly, not all distinctions reflect badly on non-Europeans. For example, the mild climate of Asia produces both beautiful and abundant plants, as well as a gentle and affectionate people.[7]

Yet, it is precisely this mildness of character that is correlated with certain qualities that make "Asians" more susceptible to slavery than Europeans. Whereas the rough and infertile landscape of Europeans makes them spirited and courageous, the temperate climate of the Asians makes them prone to indolence and passivity. Moreover, the prevailing

---

[3] For Hippocrates and his school, see Jouanna 1999.
[4] For racism as entailing the use of imagined physical, mental and moral traits to justify the superiority of one group over the other, see Isaac 2004. Cf. Lape 2010.
[5] Hippocrates, *Airs, Waters, Places* 3–4. [6] Hippocrates, *Airs, Waters, Places* 5.
[7] Hippocrates, *Airs, Waters, Places* 12.

political conditions also contribute to the character of Asians, as monarchic rule conditions men to avoid risks since any effort results in benefits for the king rather than themselves.[8] The Europeans, by contrast, are free and therefore undertake risks on their own account.[9] While the direction of causality is sometimes vague and contradictory in the course of the treatise, it is clear that the author associates certain environmental and political conditions with character traits that result in free or slavish dispositions. It is a short step, then, to equate the character of Europeans with a suitability for freedom and that of Asians with a suitability for slavery.

Aristotle makes this connection explicit when he writes,

> The people of Asia are intelligent and skilled with respect to their temperament, but lacking in spirit and for this reason are continually subject to rule and live as slaves. By contrast, the Greeks both live in a middle position geographically and have a share of both intelligence and spirit. For this reason, they are continually free and have the best constitutions and are capable of ruling all men.[10]

Aristotelian philosophical texts and the Hippocratic "scientific" treatise have clear correspondences with more widespread ideas about the relation between slavery and race or ethnicity, as expressed, for example, in Euripides' tragic play *Iphigeneia in Aulis* where the character Iphigeneia defends her decision to die for the sake of the good of Greece by saying,

> It is fitting ... that the Greeks rule the Barbarians, but not that the Barbarians rule the Greeks. For the one is slavish, but the other is free.[11]

Aristotle, in fact, quotes the first sentence of these lines in his more philosophical justification of slavery, as an illustration of his claim that "[t]he barbarian/non-Greek and the slave are the same thing by nature."[12]

It is important to point out that there were some critics of these blatantly racist views of non-Greeks as natural slaves. Indeed, Aristotle was explicitly arguing against those who argued that all slavery, because it was based on violence, was morally wrong. The Greek historian Herodotus, moreover, provides a nuanced portrait of non-Greeks in his many ethnographic digressions, and often challenges Greek ethnocentric views.[13] In addition, some of the theories of the evolution of human society promulgated by

---

[8] Hippocrates, *Airs, Waters, Places* 12, 23.
[9] This idea is adapted to a Greek political context to justify democratic over tyrannical rule by Herodotus (5.78). For discussion, see Forsdyke 2001 and 2006.
[10] Aristotle, *Politics* 1327b27–33.   [11] Euripides, *Iphigeneia in Aulis* 1399–401.
[12] Aristotle, *Politics* 1252b9.
[13] For discussion, see, for example, Pelling 1997; Isaac 2004; and Gruen 2011.

a group of late fifth-century intellectuals known as sophists posited some uniquely human characteristics – such as a sense of justice – that allow all men to form political communities and distinguish them from animals.[14] As we saw in Chapter 1, even Aristotle draws some distinctions between humans and animals (such as the capacity for speech and moral reasoning) that are in tension with his attempt to assimilate slaves to beasts. More pointedly, one of the late fifth-century sophists, Antiphon, challenges the Greek-Barbarian dichotomy precisely on the grounds of the common humanity of all mankind. While the context is a discussion of natural law and human conventions rather than slavery per se, his declaration of the essential commonality of Greeks and Barbarians is striking.

> It is possible to examine what is necessary of the things that exist by nature for all humans and what is provided to them in conformity with the same properties. In regard to these same things, none of us is defined as either Barbarian or Greek. For we all breathe into the air through our mouth and nose. And we laugh when we are happy in our mind or we cry when we are pained. And we take in sounds through our hearing. And by means of light, we see through vision. And we work with our hands and we walk with our feet.[15]

Admittedly, this text is somewhat difficult to understand and exists only on a papyrus fragment whose gaps have been filled with scholarly conjectures. Nevertheless, it represents a challenge to easy dichotomies between Greeks and non-Greeks, including implicitly the free-slave distinction.

More explicit, however, is the statement of an otherwise unknown philosopher, Alcidamas, from Elaea in the region of Aeolis – on the coast of modern-day Turkey. Alcidamas is reported to have written that "the divinity left everyone free, nature made no one a slave."[16] Even though this statement was probably made in the context of the liberation of the Messenian helots after the Battle of Leuctra in 371, it is clearly framed as a more general condemnation of the idea of natural slavery.[17] As such, it is probably as close as we can get to the anonymous opponents of slavery mentioned by Aristotle in the *Politics*.

Needless to say, these sophistic explorations were marginal to mainstream Greek beliefs about the necessity and propriety of slavery, especially

---

[14] Plato, *Protagoras* 322a–d. For an earlier articulation of this idea, see Hesiod, *Works and Days* 274–81.
[15] Antiphon D38b. For the sake of simplicity, I have translated the text without marking scholarly conjectures about the text.
[16] Alcidamas, scholiast to Aristotle, *Rhetoric* 1373b18.
[17] Garnsey 1996, 75–76. For the view that Alcidamas' statement refers to the more limited case of the Messenian helots, see Cambiano 1987, 24.

of non-Greeks. As we have seen, this belief rested on imagined physical, mental and moral traits that distinguished slave from free. In fact, Aristotle tied himself in knots trying to explain why the bodies of slaves were sometimes indistinguishable from those of the free, despite his claim that physical traits such as a stooped posture differentiated slave from free.[18] We might ask, however, whether these imagined distinctions between slave and free were replicated in Greek visual media as well as textual sources? While it is true that it may have been difficult to depict mental or moral characteristics (e.g., intelligence) in Greek art, we might well imagine that slaves would be portrayed as physically different from free persons. Moreover, figures could be designated as slaves or non-Greeks through clothing, hairstyle or other attributes such as bodily modifications (e.g., tattoos or branding marks).

Interestingly, visual representations of slaves rarely depict them as physically different from free persons, and indeed scholars have struggled to find clear criteria for distinguishing slave from free in Greek vase painting and sculpture.[19] One might wonder whether this lack of discrimination reflects the reality that slaves were not physically distinct from free. Or one might even posit that the lack of distinction reflects the fact that slaves themselves played a role in the production of Greek vase paintings and sculpture (see Chapter 3) and resisted the imposition of imagined differences between slave and free. On the other hand, these objects were produced primarily for free consumers, who may have wished to see status differences displayed, even if based on imaginary differences.

In light of this last observation, it is worth noting that distinctions were sometimes made in Greek art. Perhaps the most frequent method of designating slave status in Greek art is size: slaves are sometimes depicted as smaller in stature than their free counterparts. For example, figures who attend to other figures in typical servile roles (carrying baggage, serving food or helping a woman dress) are sometimes depicted as half the size of those whom they are serving (Fig. 4.1). Sometimes these figures have physical characteristics like snub noses and thick lips that seem to mark them as different. Other such figures are depicted as old, bent over or otherwise physically misshapen.[20] The slave Aesop, for example, is depicted in art and in literary sources as hunchbacked and "turnip-like." Moreover, some scholars have posited that women with short-cropped hair are slaves, or

---

[18] Aristotle, *Politics* 1254b25; cf. Xenophon, *On Household Management* 4.2–3.
[19] Osborne 2011, 138; Wrenhaven 2012, 77.
[20] On physical deformities and disabilities in the Greco-Roman world generally, see Garland 2010.

Fig. 4.1 Sostratus, an Athenian citizen, and his slave, who is holding an oil flask for his master to scrape himself down after exercise in the gymnasium. Grave marker of Sostratus, Athens, c.375. The Metropolitan Museum of Art, New York.

that certain states of dress or undress are markers of slaves. However, as in the case of size and other physical features, these criteria are not consistently applied. Indeed, it must be emphasized that most slaves are depicted in Greek art as indistinguishable from their masters in appearance.

A potential area of status distinction between slaves and nonslaves in life and in art is body modification such as tattooing or branding. Certain non-Greek populations from which the Greeks obtained slaves, such as Thracians and Scythians, practiced decorative tattooing.[21] Moreover, we know that the Greeks branded slaves for particular offenses, especially running away.[22] While far from all slaves were tattooed or branded, textual

---

[21] Jones 1987, 145–46. Jones (1987, 141, 144–45) also points out that Egyptians and Syrians also practiced religious tattooing.
[22] Branding of delinquent or runaway slaves: Aristophanes, *Birds* 760–61; *Frogs* 1508–14; *Wasps* 1296; Eupolis, fr. 259; Diphilus, fr. 67 K-A; Menander, *Samia* 321–24; 654–57; Herodas 5.65–67, 77–79. See also Chapter 5.

evidence suggests that tattoos and brands became associated with slave status. For example, many Athenian politicians were accused by their opponents of being slaves, and one way to do this was to suggest that they had brand or tattoo marks. For example, the late fifth-century Athenian politician Hyperbolus was derided in a comic play as a slave by suggesting he bore such marks.[23] Similarly, some figures on Greek vases display tattoos which mark them as non-Greek (especially Thracian), and possibly as slaves.

Finally, it is perhaps worth considering a few physical features that are not evident in our written and visual sources but may have characterized slave bodies in reality, regardless of the Old Oligarch's claims about their indistinguishability at Athens. Besides a stooped posture that might be a product of continuous hard labor, slaves' bodies must often have been marked by bruises, gashes and scars as a result of whipping or other corporal punishment (Fig. 4.2). These marks may not always have been visible beneath clothing, however. What may have been more visible were signs of malnutrition, at least among slaves who were not relatively privileged. As we saw in Chapter 3, however, even relatively privileged slaves were subject to violence, and whipping was the standard punishment for both private and public slaves.

Language and Ethnicity

If we now turn from physical and bodily markers of slave status to cultural ones, we might ask whether slaves were marked out in daily life or in the Greek imagination as different in terms of language and other cultural practices associated with particular ethnicities? Did slaves speak non-Greek languages or speak Greek with a foreign accent? What about slave names? Did slave names reveal particular origins or ethnic identities? Did masters (re)name their slaves and, if so, did their naming practices distinguish slave from free?

Let us begin with language. Since most slaves, even Greek ones, were brought from other regions and either were not native speakers of Greek, or spoke a different dialect of Greek, it was an easy ideological move to slip inferentially from incorrect/different Greek to non-native origins to slave status. Just as not all slaves were branded, yet brands became associated with slave status, so in the case of language: not all slaves spoke Greek badly, but an inability to speak Greek correctly, or in the correct dialect,

[23] Plato, Comicus fr. 203 K-A.

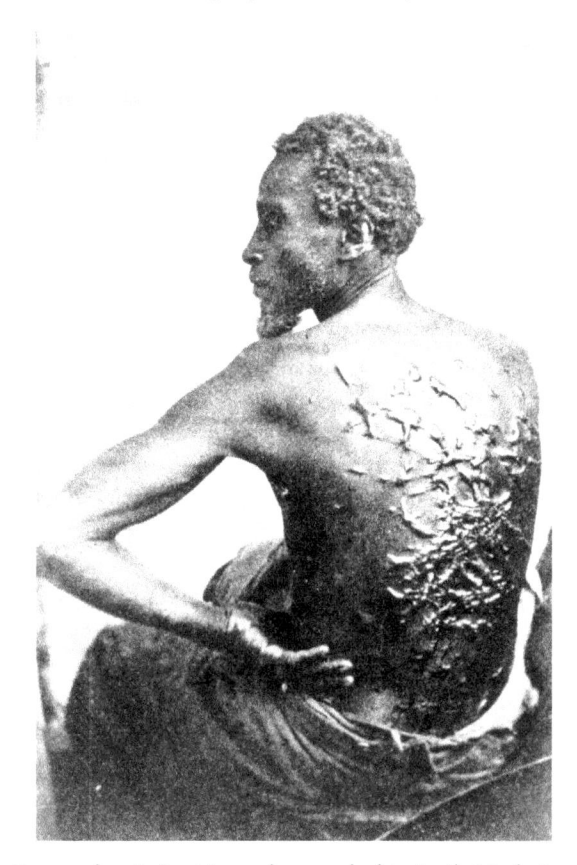

Fig. 4.2 Peter, a slave in Louisiana, photographed in April 1863 during the Civil War. Smith Collection / Gado / Getty Images.

became a marker of slave status. For example, as we saw in Chapter 2, the speaker in a law-court case over the issue of citizenship has to defend himself in part by rejecting the claim that his father's foreign accent connotes non-Greek and even slavish origins.[24] Interestingly, the speaker does not deny that his father was a slave, but explains that he was captured in battle and sold into slavery on the island of Leucas, off the coast of Acarnania, a region in which the dialect of Doric Greek, as opposed to Attic Greek, was spoken. After his ransom and return to Attica many years later, his enemies attacked him for speaking with a "foreign" accent and

[24] Demosthenes 57.18–19.

therefore not being a citizen. This anecdote is significant in that it suggests that slaves did develop fluency in the native languages or dialects of their place of enslavement, but also, paradoxically, that speaking with a foreign accent was thought of as a marker of slave status. This association between slavery and inability to speak Greek or the proper dialect of Greek goes all the way back to the sixth century BCE when the Athenian reformer Solon decried the fact that Athenians were being sold into slavery abroad and, upon return, no longer spoke Attic Greek.[25] As we saw in Chapter 3, in a law-court speech from the fourth century, a former slave (Phormion) was criticized for not speaking Greek correctly. Similarly, in a fifth-century comedy, an Athenian politician was tarnished with associations of slavery on the grounds that he did not speak the Attic dialect of Greek properly.[26]

The paradox that slaves did learn Greek in order to perform their duties, yet were also marked out ideologically as imperfect speakers of Greek, is reflected in comic representations of slaves. That is to say that in comedy, although most slave characters speak in exactly the same proper Greek as their masters, there are a few examples where slaves are portrayed as speaking non-Greek languages or garbled Greek.[27] The Scythian archers (who were public slaves), for example, speak garbled Greek in Aristophanes' comedy *Women of the Thesmophoria*.[28] The fact that most comic slaves are indistinguishable from their masters linguistically may of course, be simply a theatrical convenience for the sake of comprehensibility. But it probably also reflects the reality that most slaves spoke perfectly good Greek, despite stereotypes to the contrary.

Indeed, even imported slaves must have had to learn Greek in order to take commands and be useful to their masters (see Chapter 2). Xenophon notes the importance of the ability of a slave net-keeper to know Greek as he assists on the hunt, and even Aristotle allows that slaves can understand rational commands from their Greek-speaking masters even if slaves are not fully rational themselves.[29] Some slaves, moreover, worked in professions such as banking or public administration that demanded high

---

[25] Solon, fr. 36.11–12.
[26] Demosthenes 36; Plato, Comicus 183 K-A. For discussion of comic ridicule of Hyperbolus' alleged servile birth, see Lape 2010, 64–71.
[27] Similarly, the Persian ambassadors in Aristophanes' *Acharnians* (100, 104) and the Triballian in Aristophanes' *Birds* (1615, 1628–29 and 1678–79) speak either garbled Greek or some non-Greek Near Eastern language. See Long 1986.
[28] Aristophanes, *Women of the Thesmophoria* 1001–225. Pulleyn (1997) notes that slaves in comedy tend to make requests simply in the optative rather than through carefully formulated prayers such as free characters do (cf. Aristophanes, *Knights* 3). I thank Carl Anderson for this point.
[29] Xenophon, *On Hunting* 2.3; Aristotle, *Politics* 1254b23–4.

literacy. Others would have been born slaves and spoken the correct form of Greek from birth. Plato, for example, assumes that house-born slaves speak Greek.[30] As we shall discuss in the next chapter, the Greek language competency of slaves has important implications for their capacity to form a collective identity, despite diverse origins, and resist their domination. Another relevant question is whether slaves retained their native languages and dialects, while also speaking Greek in their day-to-day working lives. We will return to this question shortly, since it bears on the larger inquiry into whether slaves were culturally distinct from their masters.

It is worth examining slave names to determine whether they served to mark slave status in everyday life.[31] As we have seen in Chapter 2, there is a revealing discrepancy in name types depending on the source of evidence. In literary sources, fictional slave characters tend to have names that suggest non-Greek origins. In comedy, for example, slaves have names such as Carion ("from Caria"), Syros ("Syrian"), Manes (associated with the Phrygian divinity Men), Daos ("from the Daoi," a tribe near the Danube) or Xanthias ("Blondy"). By contrast, the names of slaves preserved in inscriptions show that although *some* historical slaves had ethnic names such as Thratta ("Thracian woman"), most had names that were indistinguishable from citizen names. For example, slaves and citizens alike bore names such as Apollodorus, Callias, Nicias and Philocrates.[32] The divergence in naming patterns between literary and historical sources reveals a gap between ideology ("all slaves are foreign") and reality ("slaves are frequently indistinguishable from Greeks"). The pattern can perhaps be explained through recognition of the variety of circumstances through which individuals became enslaved, but also the ways that master's interests in naming may have sometimes diverged but sometimes also converged with slaves' own interest in choosing their names. Let's briefly unpack each of these points.

First, some slaves were themselves Greek and presumably would have retained their original Greek names upon enslavement, unless their master or mistress willfully decided to change them. Secondly, there is no reason to doubt that masters, as part of their rights of ownership, had the power to rename slaves who came to them from other parts of Greece or from non-Greek locations. Plato, for example (in an otherwise thematically unrelated philosophical discussion of the "correctness" of the words), assumes that masters change the names of individuals who become their

---

[30] Plato, *Meno* 82b.　[31] This discussion draws heavily on Vlassopoulos (2010, 2015).
[32] Vlassopoulos 2010, 2015; Lewis forthcoming shows that the pattern is valid across the Greek world.

slaves.³³ This power to name would presumably extend also to slaves born within the household, unless the master gave permission – as a privilege – to the slave parent(s) to name their child. It is likely that the evidence for historical slaves with generic slave names such as Manes or Daos or Thratta is the result of the choices of the masters themselves since it is hard to imagine slaves choosing such homogenizing and degrading names for themselves. But how are we to explain the many instances of slaves with Greek names? It is unlikely that all of these can be explained by the presence of ethnically Greek individuals in the slave population.

Here we might note that the bestowal of a Greek name on a slave (or allowing a slave to choose such a name) might be of practical value in increasing the utility of the slave to his or her master.³⁴ In so far as slaves working in high-skill occupations such as banking and government administration seem to bear names that are indistinguishable from citizen names more frequently than those working in low-skill occupations such as mining or wet nursing, it is likely that the utility and value of slaves were signaled in part through their names. A master, therefore, might well grant a citizen name to a slave. On the other hand, we might also note that slaves might themselves be eager to adopt Greek names in order to obscure their identity as slaves (at least in interactions beyond their households) and hence pass as free.³⁵ The fact that slaves who had been freed, as well as their children, tend to have citizen-attested names strengthens this hypothesis.³⁶

The accusations of servile birth that elite politicians flung at one another provide further evidence. For example, the politician Demosthenes claims that his opponent Aeschines deployed precisely this strategy of renaming his parents with Greek names to hide the fact that they were slaves.

> I am at a loss as to what to mention first! Shall I mention that your father Tromes was a slave in the house of Elpias? ... Indeed, it was only yesterday and the day before he became both Athenian and a public speaker and by putting two syllables together he renamed his father Atrometus instead of Tromes. Similarly, he gave his mother the high-sounding name Glaukotheia, although everyone knew her as Empousa.³⁷

Of course, Demosthenes has no proof of Aeschines' servile birth, and he is simply imputing this name-changing behavior to Aeschines as part of his assault on his character. Yet the strategy had to be plausible to the Athenians in order to discredit Aeschines, and, indeed, the use of such

---

[33] Plato, *Cratylus* 384d5. [34] Vlassopoulos 2015, 112–13. [35] Vlassopoulos 2015, 116–19.
[36] Vlassopoulos 2015, 119.
[37] Demosthenes 18.129–30. For this and further examples, see Vlassopoulos 2015.

a strategy is attributed to several other fictive and historical individuals. For example, Theophrastus recounts an allegation that an individual changed his name from the name Sosias (which is exclusively associated with slaves) to Sosistratus and then Sosidemos (which are characteristic of citizen names).[38] Similarly, the former slave Neaira is said in a law-court speech to have renamed her daughter Phano, dispensing with her former name, Strybele, which was likely associated with prostitution and slavery.[39]

That said, not all slaves would have wished to lose their individual and ethnic identity in this way, and some may even have resisted. Indeed, we have some examples of individuals who were either slaves or ex-slaves who proudly proclaimed their non-Greek names and ethnic origins on their tombstones.[40] Interestingly, these figures evince a hybrid identity, evoking both non-Greek and Greek associations in their funeral monuments. This double identity suggests that these individuals sought a middle ground between their two cultures and hence that neither "resistance" nor "accommodation" fully captures the sentiment behind their monuments.

A prime example is the fourth-century funeral monument of the probable slave or ex-slave Atotas from the region of Paphlagonia, just south of the Black Sea. As we saw in Chapter 3, Atotas seems to have been very successful at his profession (mining) and reasonably prosperous. More significant for our current purposes is the fact that he highlights his Paphlagonian ethnicity in his epitaph, yet uses the Greek language and Greek cultural references to do so.

Atotas, a miner

The great-hearted Paphlagonian Atotas, from the Black Sea,
Released his body from toil far from his homeland.
No one rivalled me in skill. I am from the stock of Pylaimenes,
Who died subdued by the hand of Achilles.[41]

The name Atotas, which is repeated twice in the inscription, is not a Greek name and is in fact attested frequently in inscriptions from Paphlagonia.[42] This emphasis on his non-Greek origins continues with the explicit reference to his Paphlagonian ethnicity and homeland in the region of the Black (Euxine) Sea.

Despite these features evoking Atotas' non-Greek identity, however, it is striking that the epitaph is written in Greek and in high-epic style with numerous allusions to the *Iliad*, the great Greek epic poem by Homer. The

---

[38] Theophrastus, *Characters* 28.2–3. [39] Pseudo-Demosthenes 59.121. Cf. Kapparis 1999, 266.
[40] Bäbler 1998; Hunt 2015. [41] *IG* ii².10051; Bäbler #35, pp. 94–97. [42] Bäbler 1998, 95.

adjective "great-hearted" is applied to many heroes in Homeric epic, and the phrase "great-hearted Paphlagonians" occurs twice in the *Iliad*.[43] Moreover, the inscription alludes to the death of Pylaimenes, the leader of the Paphlagonians – who were allied with the Trojans in the Trojan War. As mentioned in Chapter 3, there is a small discrepancy between the epitaph and the Homeric poem since, in the former, Pylaimenes is killed by none other than Achilles, the greatest of the Greek fighters, while in the latter, he is killed by Menelaus, a mediocre fighter at best. Perhaps this discrepancy is an error, showing imperfect knowledge of the Greek epic, or perhaps it reflects a strategy to elevate his ancestor by matching him with the greatest Greek warrior. The latter scenario is perhaps more likely given the overall self-congratulatory tone of the epitaph. In whatever way we interpret this inscription, however, it should be stressed that Atotas is laying claim both to non-Greek origins as well as deep familiarity with Greek cultural traditions.

Yet, what is perhaps the most striking feature of the inscription is Atotas' emphatic stress on his occupation and skill as a miner. Indeed, his profession as a miner is prominently placed in the first large-letter line of the inscription, alongside his name. Whereas a citizen epitaph typically lists the father's name (patronymic) and political district (deme), Atotas states only his profession. Furthermore, Atotas evinces a marked self-confidence and pride in his expertise. For example, he boasts that "no one rivalled me in skill."

The mention of occupation is in fact a common way – alongside mention of owners' names – of identifying slaves and ex-slaves in Greek public inscriptions.[44] For example, some of the slaves listed in the records of confiscated property in 414 are identified by their names followed by their professions. Hence, among the confiscated slaves is Sconus, a table-maker, Alexitimus, a mule-driver and Poteinus, a goldsmith.[45] Perhaps even more significantly, the ex-slaves who recorded their grant of freedom in Athens c.330 list their professions as leatherworking, sandal-making, hide-tanning, furniture-making and so on.[46] By contrast, citizens are never identified by occupation on public inscriptions, but rather by patronymic or political district (deme).

---

[43] Homer, *Iliad* 2.864–66, 5.576–77.
[44] For the mention of owner's names, see, for example, the slaves listed on the building accounts for the Erechtheum on the acropolis at Athens: *IG* i³.476.221–42, translated in Chapter 3 in the section "Skilled Trades and Manufacturing."
[45] *IG* i³.422.70–80. [46] *IG* ii².1553–78.

Indeed, for this reason and several others, it is likely that Atotas is a slave or an ex-slave. The fact that mining operations were mostly performed by slaves strengthens this identification, as does the existence of a number of ex-slaves with managerial or supervisory roles (see Chapter 3). The fact that Atotas was able to afford an expensive and well-crafted funerary monument suggests that he was a relatively privileged slave, at the very least, who was able to keep a share of his earnings. What is notable then is that Atotas does not mention his legal status as slave or freedman, yet also does not distance himself either from his profession with its associations with slavery or from the practice of naming slaves on inscriptions through reference to their profession. If Atotas was a slave, it is significant that the name of his master is absent – perhaps a deliberate omission. If he was a freedman, we might expect him to lay claim to this enhanced – yet still tarnished-by-association-with-slavery – status. He does neither, as we have seen, and instead emphasizes three aspects of his identity: his Paphlagonian origins, his facility with Greek culture and his occupational prowess. In doing so, he forges his own unique identity and status.

In this regard, we might use the modern concept of intersectionality to describe Atotas' identity, since he advertises multiple intersecting identities. For example, he presents himself as an (unwilling?) immigrant to Athens of Paphlagonian origins, yet also as Greek-speaking and an acculturated resident of Athens. Furthermore, his self-presentation identifies him both as a relatively low-status slave or former slave and yet also as a successful professional with personal pride in his expertise. Indeed, Atotas' self-presentation suggests the complex "processes of multicultural adjustment" that slavery imposed on its victims.[47] In the straitened circumstances in which slaves often found themselves, slaves created a middle ground between "resistance" to the loss of their original identities and "accommodation" to the new conditions of their existence. Indeed, it was often a matter of their survival to find this compromise position between former and present selves. More will be said about this in the next chapter.

A second example will illustrate the importance of occupational identities in cutting across other status categories, but also may point to ethnic enclaves of slaves or former slaves who maintained a hybrid identity between their native origins and their status in Greek society. They did

---

[47] For the phrase, see Webster 2001 (on the cultural interactions between Romans and the peoples of the Roman provinces). There is a large literature on the creation of hybrid cultures and identities, and various terms including creolization and intersectionality have been coined to describe the process. On intersectionality, see Crenshaw 1991. Useful approaches in regard to ancient Greece and Rome include Gruen 2011; Mattingly 2011; Hall 2002, 104–11.

so, it seems, by clustering in certain neighborhoods (by force or by choice) and by maintaining certain practices of their native culture such as religious cults.[48]

This second example concerns the monument of a Phrygian woodcutter and dates to the third quarter of the fifth-century BCE. His tombstone reads:

> The best of the Phrygians in spacious Athens was
> Mannes Orumaios, whose fine monument this is.
> And, by Zeus, I never saw a better woodcutter than myself!
> He died in battle.[49]

Once again this monument combines assertions of non-Greek identity with references to Greek culture. Mannes' Phrygian heritage is highlighted explicitly in the opening words of the inscription, yet it simultaneously references the Homeric epic formulation "the best of the Achaeans" used to designate the great Greek hero Achilles. Significantly, "Phrygians" is substituted for "Achaeans" [Greeks], and implicitly Mannes thereby equates himself with Achilles. In the second line, we get Mannes' personal name, followed perhaps by a patronymic (Orumaios) imitating citizen naming practices.[50] Yet Mannes is a typical slave name with ethnic associations since it is derived from the Phrygian god Men.

Like Atotas, Mannes is proud of his skill, and uses a typical Greek exclamation ("by Zeus") to underline his superiority. Interestingly, he claims that he is the "best" of the Phrygians in "spacious Athens," using an adjective to modify a place name in characteristic Greek epic style. What is even more significant for our purposes is that Mannes seems to reference a community of Phrygians in Athens. The question of whether this community took the shape of a particular location in Athenian territory where Phrygians lived or associated with one another is raised by the fact that Thucydides mentions a cavalry battle that took place during the Peloponnesian War "in Phrygia," and several ancient sources identify Phrygia with a region in Attica.[51] Some scholars locate this place to the north of the city, where charcoal was produced and hence woodcutting was in high demand. Others locate it in the mining district of Laurium to the south, where large quantities of wood were also needed for smelting ore.[52]

---

[48] This section, as the former section, draws heavily on Hunt 2015. [49] *IG* i³.1361; Bäbler #69.
[50] Another possibility is that Orumaios is a geographic reference: Hunt 2015, 140; with further discussion in Bäbler 1998, 159–63.
[51] Thucydides 2.22 with scholia and Alexis, fr. 167 K-A.
[52] Hornblower 1991, 276–77 (deme of Athmonon); Lauffer 1979 (Laurium). The find spot of the inscription discussed above is listed simply as "Athens" and so is not revealing. It is now located in the Louvre.

Either way, we possibly here have a reference to an ethnic enclave, a "Little Phrygia" within the community of Athens.

Before we expand on this observation, two further points should be noted about Mannes' epitaph. First, despite his likely status as a slave or freedman, Mannes makes no mention of his legal status. Like Atotas, he emphasizes his non-Greek ethnic identity, while also displaying his virtuosity within Greek cultural conventions and boasting of his occupational prowess. As in the case of Atotas, Mannes' use of his occupational identity affiliates him with a marker of slave, as opposed to citizen, identity. Yet, like Atotas and the ex-slaves who claimed their freedom in 330, Mannes lays claim to his occupation as a badge of honor. Secondly, we should note that Mannes died in battle. Like all free non-citizen residents of Athens (metics), freed slaves were required to perform military service (see below). In addition, slaves were often conscripted in informal ways to fight alongside their masters (see Chapter 3). It is not unlikely, then, that Mannes died fighting alongside the Athenians, perhaps against the Spartans in the skirmish mentioned by Thucydides.

The prospect of a "Little Phrygia" in Attica raises the question of whether slaves were distinguished by their residence in or frequenting of certain ethnic enclaves, and the broader question of whether they had cultural practices – cults and festivals – that were distinctive.[53]

The first thing to note is that, whether slave or free, there were large numbers of non-Athenians – that is, resident foreigners or metics – living in Athens. Even if a slave could not find slaves of the same ethnic and cultural background to associate with, there was still a possibility of finding associates among the metic population, some of whom will have been former slaves themselves. Many of these metics were involved in commercial enterprises, since (with a few exceptions) land ownership and farming were not an option for them by law. As a consequence, most metics resided in the chief commercial hub of the city, the harbor area known as the Piraeus.

Secondly, it is striking that we have evidence of cults of foreign gods in the Piraeus and elsewhere that suggest a vigorous cultic life among some groups of foreigners at Athens. Indeed, some of these cults were so strong that they even became popular among the citizen population. For example, Plato famously depicts Socrates' enthusiasm for the festivities associated with the worship of the Thracian goddess Bendis in the Piraeus.[54] These

---

[53] Hunt (2015) is foundational here, and I draw heavily on his insightful work.
[54] Plato, *Republic* 327a.

included a torch race on horseback and an "all-night rite." An inscription, moreover, reveals that the cult was officially recognized and granted land on which to build a shrine.[55] A further sign of its official status is that a procession was authorized from the Prytaneum, the symbolic center of the city, to the shrine of Bendis. By 430 BCE, the cult had enough funds to be one of the many temples from which the state contracted loans.[56] By the early fourth century, moreover, the shrine of Bendis was a familiar landmark in the Piraeus.[57]

Significantly, for our purposes, this cult seems to have arisen from an association of slaves or ex-slaves, judging from the names listed on decrees regulating the cult.[58] Strikingly, a dedication to the goddess Bendis in thanks for victory in the torch race is made by a man with a characteristic slave name: Daos (see above).[59] Moreover, although there were many Thracians who were metics – mercenaries, for example, are well attested – they seem to be particularly prominent as slaves or ex-slaves.[60] As we saw in Chapter 3, Xenophon mentions a Thracian mine operator by the name of Sosias, who was probably a slave before rising to this position.[61] In addition, the twenty-five surviving funeral monuments of Thracian men and women are also likely for slaves or ex-slaves. Some of them, for example, bear the adjective "useful" or "worthy" (χρηστός) often used to designate slaves, while others perform occupations often associated with slavery such as wet nursing.[62]

If Thracian slaves joined together in the Piraeus to worship, it is possible that Phrygians similarly gathered in the mining area of Laurium. There we find two dedications to the Phrygian god Men, likely made by slaves working in the mines.[63] In addition, fourteen grave monuments of Phrygians survive, again many with names typical of slaves including numerous "Manes"-es – a name that Demosthenes uses in a speech to indicate a generic slave.[64] While the provenance of many of these gravestones is unfortunately unknown, the number of monuments suggest a considerable population of Phrygian slaves and ex-slaves in Athens. Furthermore, the appearance of cults to several other Phrygian divinities suggests a collective identity that, like the cult of the Thracian Bendis, had

---

[55] *IG* ii².1283. [56] *IG* i³.383. [57] Xenophon, *History of Greece* 2.4.11.
[58] *IG* ii².1283; Parker 1996, 170. [59] *SEG* 39.210.
[60] Mercenaries: Thucydides 7.27–30; *IG* ii².1956. Thucydides even mentions that the son of the Thracian king Sitalkes was granted Athenian citizenship in 431: Thucydides 2.29.5; cf. Aristophanes, *Acharnians* 138–50.
[61] Xenophon, *Ways & Means* 4.14. [62] Bäbler 1998, 268–82.
[63] Lauffer 1979, 179–80; Garland 1987, 128; Hunt 2015, 135. [64] Demosthenes 45.86.

some influence on Greek culture. Inscriptions and other evidence attest to the worship at Athens of the Phrygian "mother of all," a goddess whose worship took on features of Gaia and even Demeter in its Greek context.[65] Furthermore, literary sources make mention of the rites of the Phrygian god Sabazius, an ecstatic cult similar in some ways to the cult of Dionysus.[66] A comic reference to this god by two slaves suggests that slaves were particularly invested in this cult.[67]

Interestingly, just as the worship of foreign deities influenced Greek culture, so Greek culture shaped certain aspects of the cultic associations of non-Greeks. For example, these groups used the Greek language and terminology to describe their association, and erected dedications and decrees regulating their cult just as did citizen cultic associations. Indeed, groups of slaves and ex-slaves sometimes made collective dedications to Greek gods in ways that were exactly parallel to citizen dedications. A striking example is a dedication to Pan dating to the fourth century.[68] The monument is similar to other votives to Pan in decoration and dedicatory inscription, yet the list of names of dedicators suggests that they are likely slaves and former slaves.[69] Fourth-century dedications to the Nymphs and other gods and heroes (e.g., Heracles) by cultic associations seem to include slaves, ex-slaves and citizens.[70] Indeed, it is notable that distinctions of legal status are absent from these dedications, and scholars have resorted to inferring status from the names alone (an imperfect guide as we have seen). However, the presence on these lists of characteristic slave names, such as Daos, Lydos and Syros, suggests at least some of the dedicators were slaves or freed slaves. Remarkably, it appears that citizenship and freedom were not considered significant enough to be marked in this context.[71]

Besides cultic associations, moreover, slaves and ex-slaves also joined together for mutual aid to help pay for a funeral monument, for example, or the freedom of one of their members.[72] Interestingly, such clubs borrowed the structure of similar Greek associations, and referred to their club using the Greek terminology (κοινὸν ἐρανιστῶν "an association of joint-contributors").

In regard to the Thracians and Phrygians who gathered together to celebrate their native gods, it is likely that they also maintained some other features of their indigenous cultures, in particular, their language. This

---

[65] Parker 1996, 188–92.   [66] Aristophanes, *Horai* fr. 578; with Parker 1996, 194.
[67] Aristophanes, *Wasps* 9–10.   [68] *SEG* 54.318.   [69] Taylor 2015, 35, 45.
[70] *SEG* 24.223, 54.236; *IG* ii².2354, 2934, 2938, 2940; with discussion by Taylor 2015.
[71] Taylor 2015, 43–44.   [72] Taylor 2015 with *IG* ii².1553.

possibility is suggested by the concentration of certain ethnicities in certain professions and neighborhoods. In addition to the Thracians in the Piraeus and the Phrygians and Paphlagonians in the mining region of Laurium, it seems that Phoenicians were especially well represented in banking and commerce – enterprises associated with the port of Piraeus. Indeed, eighteen funeral monuments of Phoenicians have been discovered (the second highest number of monuments to foreigners after the Thracians), and of those whose find spot is known, six were found in the Piraeus.[73] As we saw in Chapter 3, Pasion, the most famous ex-slave banker in Athens, was possibly of Phoenician origin. Pasion's own slave, Phormion, apparently never learned to speak Greek properly, suggesting that he learned Greek relatively late and probably spoke his mother tongue (Phoenician?) throughout his life in Athens.[74]

A perhaps even more striking example, when considering the retention of native culture among slave and ex-slave foreigners at Athens, is the funeral monument of a Phoenician trader from the fourth century.[75] While not necessarily of slave or ex-slave status, his monument illustrates the possibility of maintaining native language and culture in a Greek setting, while still conforming to some conventions of Greek culture. Indeed, this monument contains the Greek name of the deceased in the Greek language followed by the Phoenician name in Phoenician language and script. Moreover, the dual names are followed by an epigram in (slightly ungrammatical) Greek and the whole monument is decorated with a relief with Semitic religious symbolism.[76] In other words, the blending of Greek and Phoenician elements is quite astounding and illustrates the delicate balance that foreigners – including slaves and ex-slaves – strove to obtain between their native cultures and their residence in Greece.

Also revealing in this regard is the stunning story of the ex-slave mercenary soldier whom we encountered in Chapter 2.[77] While travelling with an army of Greek mercenaries near the eastern end of the Black Sea, this man encountered a people whose language he understood. Delighted, he begged his Greek commander to be allowed to speak to these people since he thought he might have found his native land. The brief story ends there, unfortunately, leaving many unanswered questions and possibilities. A few conjectures may be proposed nevertheless. As suggested in Chapter 2, we might assume that the man had been enslaved at a young age and

---

[73] Bäbler 1998, 240–50.   [74] Demosthenes 45.30; Trevett 1992, 125.
[75] *IG* ii².8388; Bäbler 1998 #51, 240–41.   [76] Bäbler 1998, 131–42.
[77] Xenophon, *Anabasis* 4.8.4; with Hunt 2015; and Chapter 2.

brought to Athens, given that he appears surprised by the discovery of his homeland. Yet, the fact that he could understand the language of his native people when he encountered them would seem to indicate that he was old enough to be a fluent speaker before he was removed. It is unlikely that there was a community of Macronians at Athens that maintained the language and other Macronian cultural practices (hence his ignorance of his ethnic identity until this chance encounter). Most likely, he spoke fluent Attic Greek at the time of the incident in question.

In sum, we might note that the degree to which slaves were able to maintain their native language and culture after being brought to Greece would depend on various factors such as age of enslavement and the existence of other members of one's culture in the community to which one was transferred. It would also depend on the type of labor to which one was assigned, and the chances for upward mobility to positions of privilege or even freedom. A slave working in relative isolation on a small farm in rural Attica might have fewer chances to find communities of shared ethnicity than a slave working among thousands of other slaves, some of the same ethnicity, in the mining region of Laurium. Slaves in urban households who had opportunities to frequent the marketplace, and slaves who worked in banking or commerce in the port of Piraeus perhaps had the best chances of maintaining their culture and identity.

It is important to stress, however, that slaves and ex-slaves may have had as much interest in assimilating to Greek cultural norms as in resisting them. The complex negotiation between their native and Greek identities means that distinctions were often apparent in some contexts, blurred in others and simultaneously marked and elided in others (e.g., funerary monuments).

Household and Civic Religion

In discussing cultural markers of difference between slave and free we have noted that slaves sometimes worshipped non-Greek divinities, sometimes alongside free Greek citizens, and also sometimes worshipped Greek gods and heroes, along with free and citizen worshippers. As a result, differences between slave and free are sometimes marked, but often unmarked. That is to say, that in the ritual spheres discussed so far, there does not seem to be a great concern to enforce distinctions between slave and free.[78]

---

[78] Taylor 2015.

But what about household cults of the Greeks? Were household slaves included in domestic cult and, if included, did they have distinct roles? And what about the major civic festivals of the Olympian gods? Again, were slaves included and, if so, was their participation differentiated in any way?

Beginning with household cults, it is important to emphasize that slaves were a constituent part of the household (οἶκος), the fundamental building block of Greek society. As we saw in Chapter 1, for Aristotle, the household consists of a series of paired relationships comprising husband-wife, parent-child and master-slave. Although subordinate and the receiver of commands, the slave was nevertheless an integral part of the household and vital to its operation. It is noteworthy in this regard that newly acquired slaves were ritually introduced to the household in a ceremony that was parallel to the introduction of wives to their husbands' households.[79] As we have seen in Chapter 2, in this ceremony, slaves, like wives, were led to the hearth, the symbolic center of the house, and showered with figs and nuts.[80] This ritual marked the acceptance of the new slave into the household unit and signalled the hoped-for prosperity that would continue and even increase as a result of the new addition. It was perhaps at this time that slaves received their new names, if a new name was deemed necessary by the master.

In terms of the day-to-day ritual life of the household, it seems that slaves participated, and not just in menial roles that echoed their service for their master in other spheres of daily life.[81] For example, as we saw in Chapter 3, slaves participated in the ritual procession from the house to the altar at the celebration of the rural festival in honor of Dionysus.[82] They carry the phallus pole in the procession just as the master and the master's daughter carry other ritual objects (Fig. 3.7). Another ritual in honor of Dionysus that probably included slaves was the drinking competition known as the Choës on the second day of the Anthesteria. This at least is the inference from the fact that in the accounts of the temple of Eleusis there is an entry for the cost of providing public slaves with a sacrificial victim, wine and even the specialized wine jugs for the festival.[83] In the case of privately owned slaves, it is likely that they feasted and drank alongside their masters in their homes.[84] Another common household ritual that included slaves involved sacrifices to Zeus Ktesios or Zeus, the protector of

---

[79] Mactoux 1990; Parker 2005, 13.   [80] Demosthenes 45.74; Aristophanes, *Wealth* 768.
[81] Parker 2005, 169.   [82] Aristophanes, *Acharnians* 250–79.   [83] *IG* ii².1672.204.
[84] Parker 2005, 294.

household wealth. This again is the inference from the fact that a speaker in a law-court case implies that one head of household was unusual in excluding slaves from participation.[85]

A central household festival that definitely included slaves was the Kronia, an annual festival celebrating the mythical era of the pre-Olympian god Kronos. According to myth, the age of Kronos was a time when the earth gave up its bounty without the toil of men.[86] As a celebration of plenty, the festival took place at the time of the harvest, and masters and slaves feasted together on the bounty of the harvest.[87] According to some of our sources, masters even served their slaves in a reversal of the social order that is characteristic of numerous festivals from ancient to modern times.[88] According to some interpretations of these rituals, they served to temporarily release social tensions caused by the hierarchical social order. According to other interpretations, they provided models and opportunity for real protest by peasants and slaves and thereby played an important role in negotiating the limits of domination and exploitation in these hierarchical societies.[89] We will return to these issues in the next chapter. For current purposes, however, the important point is that the Kronia was a festival that included slaves and celebrated the results of their (often joint) labor with their masters. In this ritual context, distinctions between slave and free were eliminated or even reversed. Elsewhere in Greece, festivals of Hermes and of Apollo (e.g., at the Hyacinthia at Sparta) feature similar inclusions of slaves in feasting alongside their masters and also, sometimes, reversals.[90]

Finally, we must consider rituals associated with death since the proper burial of the dead and the tending to tombs were an important duty of households. Were slaves treated differently in death? A law cited in an inheritance case at Athens suggests that masters were responsible for ensuring that their deceased slaves, just as the deceased free members of their household, were duly buried in order to avoid pollution.[91] But besides the minimum requirement of burial, most slaves were probably not given elaborate funeral rites, let alone the expensive tombstones that served as focal points for ongoing funerary ritual by the free members of the

---

[85] Isaeus 8.16.
[86] See, for example, Hesiod, *Works and Days* 109–20; and discussion in Forsdyke 2012, 53–59.
[87] Macr.*Sat*.1.10.22 = Philochorus *FGrH* 328 F97. According to Osborne (1987, 15), figs, almonds and chickpeas were harvested at the time of the festival of Kronos (July-August). See also Foxhall 2007, 127.
[88] See, for example, Accius fr. 3; and discussion in Forsdyke (2012, 124–33).
[89] For these interpretations, see Forsdyke (2005 and 2012, 117–43).
[90] Evidence discussed in Forsdyke 2012, 125–26.   [91] Demosthenes 43.57.

household. Certainly, as we saw in Chapter 2, there were some favored slaves, such as nurses and childminders, who were treated as family, and some tombstones for beloved nurses do survive. Yet, the vast majority of slaves – household and other – were probably buried in unmarked graves or graves marked only with temporary perishable materials. That said, it is important to note that far from all free Greeks received fancy tombstones, and the Athenian law mentioned above provides penalties for kinsmen who fail to bury their free relatives, suggesting that it was not just slaves but also sometimes poor or neglected citizens who failed to receive burial rites.

The (at least minimally) inclusive picture that emerges from the household cult contrasts fairly sharply with the evidence from the civic cult where strong distinctions between free and slave are made. Indeed, at Athens speakers in law courts stir up great outrage by alleging violations of restrictions on participation in civic cult. For example, a speaker denounces the audacity of a woman named Acte, who, although formerly a slave and a prostitute, dared to join a procession and sacrifice in honor of Demeter and Persephone.[92] The speaker even refers to a law that apparently prohibited such a woman from entering the sacred precinct and participating in the rites of the Thesmophoria. Even more pointed is another speaker's hyperbolic outrage at another former slave and prostitute who passed herself off as a citizen and not only married a citizen but performed sacred rites on behalf of the entire community when her husband was chosen by lot to serve as chief magistrate of the city.[93]

These outcries against violations of the ban on slave participation in civic cult are complemented by evidence for a ban on participation by slaves in the athletic competitions in honor of the gods in both civic and panhellenic cults. For example, slaves and foreigners were barred from competing in one of the most prestigious sports in the Panathenaic Games – the competition in mounting and dismounting a moving chariot.[94] Similarly, slaves were barred from participating in the athletic competitions in honor of Zeus at Olympia.[95] These prohibitions recall the law cited at the beginning of this chapter banning slaves from the gymnasia. It seems that athletics and the festivals in which athletic prowess was displayed were key arenas for the policing and promulgation of distinctions between free and slave.[96]

---

[92] Isaeus 6.49. [93] Pseudo-Demosthenes 59.72–87.
[94] Pseudo-Demosthenes 61.23 with Golden 1998, 3.
[95] Philostratus, *Gym.* 25; Dionysius of Halicarnassus, *Ars Rhet.* 7.6.55–59. [96] Golden 1998, 4–5.

That said, it is important to acknowledge that slaves would have been present in the civic cult at least in so far as they performed some of the key menial tasks required for celebrating the gods.[97] At the great panhellenic festivals, for example, slaves would have prepared the equipment for sacrifices and maintained the facilities, including temples, altars, baths, wrestling grounds and tracks.[98] In regard to the athletic competitions themselves, slaves may even have served as jockeys and charioteers in equestrian competitions.[99] As in the case of other slaves performing services at cult sites, however, slaves who participated in horse races were part of the "equipment" and the acts of worship in which they were involved, including victories, were credited to their free owners. More striking, however, is the admission by one law-court speaker that slave women and foreign women can observe and offer supplications at civic festivals, even if, it is implied, they cannot participate directly.[100] Furthermore, slaves could be initiated by their masters into the Mysteries in honor of Demeter at Eleusis. Indeed, such initiation was required for the slaves who actually worked in the sanctuary at Eleusis since the uninitiated were forbidden to witness the proceedings. Yet occasionally, the privilege of initiation was granted to favored slaves who were not needed for the performance of the rites.[101] The fourth-century speechwriter and metic Lysias, for example, had a slave prostitute named Metaneira initiated in the Mysteries as a personal favor to her. As our source explains, he did this as a benefaction to her that was distinct from the money that he paid to her owner for her services.[102]

In sum, the evidence for household and civic cult at Athens presents a mixed picture. While slaves and ex-slaves seem to have engaged in private worship of both non-Greek and Greek divinities, and even to have been included in most household cultic activity, they were explicitly barred from active participation in major civic cults to Athena, Demeter and Dionysus, as well as the principal panhellenic festivals. If we glance at other city-states such as Sparta, the situation is similar: slaves were included in household cult but excluded from major civic festivals which were the prerogative of free citizens. In the case of Sparta, moreover, the participation of the Spartan slave-like helots in their own private cults is exemplified in several cases. First, as we shall see in Chapter 5, helots sometimes sought refuge from their owners at the sanctuary of Poseidon at Tainaron in southern

---

[97] Parker 2005, 169.   [98] Golden 1998, 54.   [99] Golden 1998, 3, 82.
[100] Pseudo-Demosthenes 59.85.
[101] *IG* ii².1672.207, 1673.24; Theophilus fr. 1; with Parker 2005, 169–70.
[102] Pseudo-Demosthenes 59.21.

Laconia.¹⁰³ Such behavior suggests that cults of Poseidon may have been particularly important to them. Even more striking is the case of the helots who resided in the region of Messenia. As mentioned in Chapter 1, in contrast to Laconian helots, Messenian helots lived independently from their masters (as was natural given their geographical distance from Laconia) and formed their own communities and households. As such, Messenian helots (as well as those in Laconia) practiced their own religion, even if, as Greeks themselves, their cults were Greek and centered on the Olympian gods just as the Spartans' cults were.¹⁰⁴

A key question, in the case of the Messenian helots, but also in the case of slave religion in general, is whether slaves experienced religion differently from their masters and the free? Whether worshipping Greek gods or non-Greek gods, whether alongside their masters or within slave or ex-slave communities, what meanings did slaves draw from cultic worship and how was it similar to or different from those of citizens and the freeborn? Comparatively speaking, we might note that slaves in the American South repurposed Christianity to meet their need not only to endure their slavery, but also to resist it.¹⁰⁵ Should we expect something similar in ancient Greece?¹⁰⁶

While evidence is mostly lacking for the perspectives of slaves, a few conjectures may be made. For example, as we saw in Chapter 2, a new slave's introduction into the household was accompanied by a rite that aimed to promote the human and agricultural fertility of the household. Newly imported non-Greek slaves might be confused and frightened by the rite, while culturally Greek slaves would have understood the significance yet felt a similar profound sense of loss of independence and identity as they became a subordinate member and piece of property in the household of another. Celebration of the household cult throughout the year would continually evoke this initial loss, yet we might imagine that slave members of the household reacted to household ritual in a range of ways, from identification with the prayers of their owners, to heartfelt opposition to their masters.

---

[103] For evidence and discussion see the section "Slave Rebellion" in Chapter 5.
[104] Luraghi 2008, 202; Deshours 2006.
[105] Du Bois (1904) 1994, 115–25; Genovese 1974, 161–284; Levine 1977.
[106] The view of Bömer (1957–63) that slaves had no religion separate from their masters, was the orthodoxy in slave studies until recently (see, e.g., Garlan (1988, 198–99)). Hodkinson and Geary (2012, 8) note that recently scholars have argued that slaves developed an autonomous sphere of religion.

Similarly, we might ask what Lysias' slave mistress, Metaneira, made of her initiation into the mystery cult at Eleusis? Since she had been raised in a brothel in the Greek city of Corinth, we can assume that she was familiar with the basic practices of Greek religion, including mystery cults.[107] Indeed, Metaneira seems to have actively desired initiation, in so far as Lysias pays for it "as a favor" to her. Therefore, she would have been familiar with the goals of this cult – namely, to ensure a better afterlife for worshippers. Yet, we might ask whether a slave initiate would conceptualize what was desirable in the afterlife differently from a free worshipper? For example, might a slave view death as an emancipation from the control of others? Did slaves even imagine their fate in the afterlife as different from that of their owners who (they might hope) would suffer? Or did some slaves identify more fully with their masters and join together in celebrating the Mysteries without thoughts of opposition or resistance? Whatever meaning Metaneira derived from her initiation into the Mysteries, it is significant nonetheless that she was able to get a freeborn Greek metic (Lysias) to pay for it. Such financial outlay – while undoubtedly a minor expense to the rich Lysias – is an indication of the (albeit small) measure of influence that she wielded over those who paid for her services.

Mystery cults raise an interesting issue since they were widespread in the ancient Mediterranean and even non-Greek slaves may have been familiar with them prior to encountering them in Greece. More generally, the fact that the Greek culture and the cultures from whom the Greeks imported slaves were alike polytheistic means that slaves could more easily accept the worship of Greek gods alongside their own, and vice versa.[108] Indeed, in addition to the participation of slaves in the cults of Pan and the Mysteries at Eleusis, we have evidence that slaves consulted Greek oracles just as did citizens and the freeborn.[109] At the oracle of Zeus at Dodona, for example, both slave men and slave women sought advice from the oracle and their questions reveal that their concerns were quite distinct from those of the free. Specifically, some of them inquire about their freedom or the question of whether they should flee their masters or not.[110] Oracular consultation,

---

[107] We might note that prostitutes were devotees of Aphrodite, as might be expected. See Kurke (1996) for discussion.
[108] Compare Hodkinson and Geary (2012, 12–22), who critique orthodox scholarly understanding of slaves in Brazil as completely detached from African religions. They acknowledge that, though slaves in Brazil came from diverse tribes and spoke different languages, they had enough similarities in basic religious concepts, worldview and language to be mutually intelligible.
[109] Eidinow 2007, 100–104.   [110] Eidinow 2007, 131.

therefore, demonstrates very clearly that slaves made use of Greek religious institutions for their own distinct purposes.

Another example of slaves making distinctive use of Greek religious practices can be seen in the foundation of a hero cult to a runaway slave named Drimakos on the island of Chios. Chios was famous in antiquity for its importation of large numbers of slaves, and we can be fairly certain that the majority were non-Greek. It is remarkable, therefore, that slaves on Chios made use of the Greek institution of hero cult to celebrate the leader of a band of runaway slaves upon his death. Moreover, this cult was not only a focal point for the slave community, but also served as a symbol of a social contract of sorts between masters and slaves.[111] According to the foundation myth of the cult, Drimakos successfully negotiated a truce between masters and slaves by only accepting into his colony of runaways those slaves who had been mistreated by their masters, and only stealing as much food from the masters' crops as was needed to sustain the colony.[112] In recognition of this modus vivendi between the slaves and their masters, the cult to Drimakos was founded after his death and both sides made offerings to the dead slave: the slaves dedicated a share of whatever they stole from their masters, and the masters made sacrifices in Drimakos' honor in thanks for the warnings of uprisings of their slaves that they received from him in their dreams.

In sum, slaves in ancient Greece made use of Greek religious practices to articulate their identity, reinforce their sense of community, negotiate the terms of their slavery or even to seek freedom altogether. In the next chapter, we will see that slaves also made use of the widespread Greek practice of offering asylum at shrines in order to seek protection from abusive masters, gain transfer to new masters and possibly to obtain freedom itself.

Political and Legal Distinctions

The attempt by Greek city-states to draw strong distinctions between slave and free is most clearly visible in the sphere of politics and law.[113] Slaves were marked off from both citizens and the free non-citizen population in numerous ways. As non-citizens, slaves could not participate in the

---

[111] Forsdyke 2012, 37–89. [112] Athenaeus, *The Learned Banqueters* 265d–266e.
[113] For an excellent overview of status distinctions in Classical Athens, see Kamen (2013). Kamen along with many recent studies such as Jones (1999), Cohen (2000), Vlassopoulos (2007) and Taylor and Vlassopoulos (2015) emphasize the contrast between ideological distinctions regarding status categories and the blurring of status categories in everyday life.

political assembly where the decisions by which the city-state was ordered were made. Nor, obviously, could they hold any of the public offices through which citizens took turns administering the state. In Athens, these offices included serving as a member of the Council or as one of the hundreds of magistrates who ran the machinery of the state. That said, as we have seen in Chapter 3, many of these magistrates were assisted by publicly owned slaves, who served as bureaucrats in the civic administration and played a surprisingly crucial function in many ways. Public slaves made records of decrees and laws, managed the public archives, kept financial records and even minted and validated the coinage. In other words, slaves were ubiquitous in the political, legal and financial apparatus of the state. Yet it is important to stress that these slaves were conceptualized (at least by the citizens) as precisely part of the "apparatus," in contrast to the magistrates themselves who were viewed as autonomous politically empowered citizens.

Acknowledgment, therefore, of the strong distinctions made between citizen and slave in politics and law must be tempered by the ever presence and indeed central function of slaves in these spheres of civic life. We might well ask how public slaves perceived their role in the state? Did public slaves and their fellow privately owned slaves use their evident capabilities to counter (at least ideologically among themselves) their political and legal disenfranchisement? One might conjecture that these skilled slaves felt pride in their skills, upon which the citizens were dependent. A close look at the Athenian citizenship law reveals the clear distinctions made between citizens and slaves, but also possibly hints at slave resistance to these distinctions.

In the middle of the fifth century BCE, the Athenians adopted a new law on citizenship that required citizens to have citizen parents on both sides. What is significant for our purposes, however, is the fact that the law also required applicants for citizenship to prove that they were free – that is, not slaves seeking to enter the citizen rolls surreptitiously. Here is how the Aristotelian treatise the *Constitution of the Athenians* describes the procedure for determining the parentage and free status of would-be citizens:

> Men who are born from two citizen parents and have obtained the age of eighteen are enrolled as citizens. And when they are enrolled, the men of the deme [local district] vote on them, having sworn an oath about them first as to whether they are the age required by law. And if they do not seem to be, they go back to the class of children. Secondly, the men of the deme take an oath that the person is free and was born according to the laws. And if they vote against him on the grounds that he is not free, he makes an appeal to

a court, and the men of the deme choose five men from among themselves as prosecutors. And if he seems not to be enrolled justly, the city sells him into slavery. But if he wins his suit, it is necessary for the men of the deme to enroll him as a citizen.[114]

The citizenship law and the procedures that it specifies clearly enforce the distinction between citizen and slave. Citizens must have (free) citizen parents, have obtained the age of eighteen, and have their free birth attested on oath by the citizens of their district. The distinctions between citizen and slave therefore were forcefully articulated every time this law was referred to in political assemblies of the state or local district. Moreover, the distinction would be reenforced every time a potential citizen came up for a vote in his local district. Indeed, cases in which an applicant was denied citizenship and sold into slavery would be particularly vivid illustrations of the distinct and privileged status of citizens.

Yet, despite the evident force of this law in maintaining political distinctions, it is worth asking why the law spells out in such precise detail the procedure for resolving cases in which the citizens of a district vote against a candidate on the grounds that he is not free. Are these procedural details a product of an exaggerated fear that slaves might infiltrate the citizen rolls, or a reasonable response to the reality that some slaves did in fact try to pass as citizens? While we cannot answer this question definitively, there are several bits of evidence that suggest that slaves did sometimes seek to pass as citizens.

First, we might observe that the Athenians deemed it necessary to review the citizen rolls on three occasions (510, 445/4 and 346 BCE), and a speaker in a lawsuit claims that many were expelled from the rolls on the last occasion on the grounds of not being citizens.[115] Moreover, several lawsuits survive that concern individuals who, it is alleged, were slaves or former slaves who attempted to pass as citizens.[116] Before examining some of these cases, a few preliminary observations are needed.

First, it is important to note that successful passing leaves no trace, so we cannot be certain how often it happened.[117] It is reasonable to assume, however, that not all slaves would have the opportunity to generate the support among citizens that a formal application for citizenship required. Moreover, not all slaves would have the legal and political knowledge to present themselves for citizenship and defend themselves in the trial that

---

[114] [Aristotle] *Constitution of the Athenians* 42.   [115] Demosthenes 57.2.
[116] Lysias 23, pseudo-Demosthenes 59. See Forsdyke (2019) for discussion.
[117] For excellent discussions of passing in the American South, see Gross 2008; and Sharfstein 2011.

would follow if their application was challenged. We must therefore assume that only particularly privileged slaves – such as household slaves who had the opportunity to move about the civic spaces of the city, skilled slaves who lived apart from their masters and public slaves who became familiar with the legal and political culture of the state – would seek formal recognition as citizens. That some did in fact attempt or even succeed in breaching the divide between citizen and slave is probable, and several sources provide hints about how slaves or former slaves might persuade or compel citizens to support their citizenship or the citizenship of their offspring, falsely.

For example, a speaker in a lawsuit describes how a citizen, Euktemon, became intimate with a freedwoman and was persuaded by her to introduce her eldest child into his "brotherhood" (phratry), which was the key basis of support for the citizenship of its members and their relatives.[118] When Euktemon's son objected and the men of the phratry refused to admit him, Euktemon countered with a threat to remarry and produce new heirs. Euktemon's son then relented and the child of the freedwoman was admitted to the phratry. In this case, it appears that the freedwoman used ties of affection to influence a citizen to have a non-citizen enrolled as a citizen. In other cases, it appears that the same result could be achieved through bribery. For example, the speaker in another lawsuit responds to the accusation that he had bribed men into presenting themselves as relatives and testifying at his enrollment as a citizen although he had slavish origins.[119] Even if the speaker denies this claim, it must be assumed that his opponent thought that this charge was at least a plausible scenario to the jurors who were to judge the case. Indeed, the adjudication of cases in which bribery is used to attain citizenship falsely was among the duties of the chief judicial magistrates at Athens.[120]

Again, it should be noted that bribery was a possibility only for a certain privileged subset of slaves; namely, well-off slaves – such as skilled slaves who lived independently of their masters and public slaves – who had de facto control of at least a portion of their earnings. Nevertheless, these examples suggest that some slaves did attempt to become or indeed succeed in becoming citizens, thereby challenging or undermining the distinctions between citizen and slave. In what is undoubtedly comic exaggeration, in a line from a lost comedy dating to the fourth century, it is claimed that many who are slaves today will be citizens tomorrow by enrolling as

---

[118] Isaeus 6.21–22. [119] Demosthenes 57.24–25, 52–55.
[120] [Aristotle] *Constitution of the Athenians* 59.3.

citizens in the district of Sounion: "many are currently not free, but tomorrow they will be demesmen of Sounion."[121] While the number of slaves who presented themselves for citizenship was probably not as large as this line suggests, the joke is probably based on a kernel of truth that some slaves did so.

If we turn to another important legal status in the Greek city-state – the status of resident foreigner or metic (from *metoikos* "one who has changed his residence") – we can see the same pattern of distinctions made in politics and law, as well as challenges by slaves to the imposition of these distinctions by the Greek city-state. In the case of metic status, moreover, the crossing of boundaries was made easier by the fact that some metics came from the same places that slaves were imported from, and therefore shared culture and language with slaves. Those lucky slaves who were granted freedom, joined the metic population rather than becoming citizens (as was the case at Rome), and therefore many metics were former slaves.[122] How did the state enforce the distinction between metic and slave given the strong overlap between these populations?

Perhaps the most striking features of metic status were the requirements that metics have a citizen representative or patron (προστάτης) in Athens, and that they pay an annual "metic tax" to a special magistrate – the polemarch – who oversaw their affairs. In the case of a metic who was a former slave, the former master took the role of patron.[123] A free migrant by contrast, would choose his patron independently. As non-citizens, metics had no political rights and therefore were similar to slaves in their exclusion from the political assembly and ineligibility for public office. On the other hand, metics, like citizens, had legal rights, and could prosecute and defend themselves in court, either through their patron or in their own person.[124] However, cases involving metics were overseen by the polemarch as opposed to the various magistrates who oversaw cases of citizens. Moreover, metics could not own land, unless by special grant from the Athenian people. As a result, metics tended to be employed in the crafts and trades, rather than agriculture. Ex-slaves who became metics probably worked in the same professions that they had practiced as slaves, potentially

---

[121] Anaxandridas, fr. 4 K-A.
[122] Akrigg (2015) argues that most metics were in fact former slaves, rather than free persons who migrated to Athens for economic reasons. Kamen (2013), by contrast, suggests that the Athenians made distinctions between these two groups, although both were classified as metics.
[123] Kamen 2013, 43–61.
[124] Scholars debate whether metics were required to be represented by their patron or not: Kamen 2013, 47–48.

further blurring the lines between metics and slaves in everyday life. Was it always well known who was a slave working independently from his master and who was a metic working the same profession?

One surviving law-court case from Athens is revealing in this regard.[125] It concerns a young man named Pancleon whose legal status came under scrutiny when he got into a dispute with a citizen. In his speech, the citizen explains how he decided to prosecute Pancleon because he was continually wronging him. Assuming that Pancleon was a metic, he went to the fulling shop where Pancleon worked and summoned him to appear before the polemarch to hear the charges against him. Pancleon responded by claiming that he was a citizen, and more specifically that he was one of the Plataeans who had been granted Athenian citizenship when the Thebans destroyed their city in 426 BCE. However, according to the speaker, when enquiries were made among the enfranchised citizens among whom Pancleon said he belonged, no one had any knowledge of him.

The plot thickened, according to the speaker, when one of these new citizens said that although he knew of no *citizen* by the name of Pancleon, he did know of *a slave* of that name, age and profession. Later in the same speech we learn that two other individuals both laid claim to Pancleon as their slave. We never learn which of these two, if either, succeeded in asserting their ownership of Pancleon, but it is clear in any case that Pancleon's status as citizen, metic or slave was in dispute: Pancleon claimed he was a citizen, the speaker thought he was a metic, and at least three other people thought he was a slave. Significantly, Pancleon's trade as a fuller is ambiguous as to his status. The speaker assumes he is a metic, while the anonymous informant indicates he is a slave. Perhaps he was at different times both of these statuses? In other words, he perhaps worked initially as a slave in a fulling shop, earned his freedom and continued working as a metic in the same shop.

Another potential area of status blurring between metics and slaves was in military service. Metics were required to perform military service, and were regularly employed both as hoplites and as rowers in the fleet, just as were slaves, as we have seen in Chapter 3. A key difference, of course, is that the service of metics was officially recognized, whereas that of slaves was generally kept obscure so as not to disturb the official ideology of the citizen as defender of the city-state.[126] As a consequence of this ideological need, moreover, the service of metics was distinguished from that of citizens by enrolling them in separate units.[127] The primary aim of this

---

[125] Lysias 23.   [126] Hunt 1998; and Chapter 3.   [127] Whitehead 1977, 83–84.

compromise was to make use of metic manpower without collapsing distinctions between citizen and metic. Yet, a secondary effect may have been to collapse distinctions between metic and slave and even citizen, since it would not always have been clear, in the heat of battle, who held which status.

A similar pattern can be seen in the field of civic religion where metics were official participants alongside citizens, yet their roles were different from those of citizens. For example, in the Panathenaic festival, male and female metics were permitted to carry particular ritual objects in the procession to the altar, and stood out from citizens due to their red clothing.[128] As we have seen, slaves were excluded from official participation in most civic cults, yet were ubiquitous as attendants and assistants in the ritual acts. Once again, then, while the city-state was most concerned to draw distinctions between citizens and metics, the official participation of metics also marked them off from slaves. Yet once again, the reality on the ground would have been that citizens, metics and slaves were all active (albeit in different roles) in the performance of the civic cult. As mentioned above, foreign cults such as that of the Thracian goddess Bendis would have served as focal points for Thracians in Athens, whether they were metics or slaves. In the performance of a private cult, however, status differences were less marked, and we see citizens, metics and slaves all worshipping together.

If we turn now to the legal sphere, the most fundamental difference must be stated. Whereas citizens and metics had legal rights, slaves had no legal rights. They had no legal personhood and their "marriages" and "families" were not legally recognized. Moreover, with but few and debatable exceptions, slaves could not defend themselves in court or prosecute those who wronged them.[129] Neither could they appear as witnesses in courts, and certainly they (like metics) could not serve as one of the

---

[128] Whitehead 1977, 86–89; Maurizio 1998; Parker 2005, 170–71; Wimja 2014.

[129] As noted in Chapter 1, there are a few examples from Athens of privileged slaves who seem to exercise some legal rights. The principal evidence involves a slave named Lampis who was a business agent for his owner (see Chapter 3) and appears to have provided testimony in his own person, and possibly was a party to the legal case against Phormion (Demosthenes 34.5, 18, 36). Cf. Harrison 1968, 167 n.6. The status of Lampis, however, is somewhat unclear. Lampis is called an οἰκέτης, one of the common terms for a household slave (Demosthenes 34.5), yet scholars have questioned his status both because of the legal capacities he seems to have enjoyed and because he is said to reside in Athens and have a wife and children there (Demosthenes 34.37). Yet, if we consider legal rights, including marriage, to be one of the privileges enjoyed by a certain class of slave, then this evidence is admissible. In another case, the speaker claims that his slave Callarus has been indicted by his opponent twice (Demosthenes 55.31–34). The speaker, however, seems to reject the legitimacy of the indictment on the grounds that a slave would not have performed the action at issue (walling off property in such a way that water from storms damaged the property of his neighbor) without the explicit instructions of his master. In other words, the speaker argues that if damages have been

hundreds of jurors who adjudicated cases on a daily basis. This latter right was reserved for citizens and was considered one of the key rights of citizenship alongside the right to hold public office.[130] Yet, while the differences between citizens, metics and slaves were marked in these and other ways, we shall see in Chapter 5 that slaves sometimes found ways to overcome their legal disabilities and leverage the law to their advantage. But before we get to this paradox, it is important to observe the ways that the Greek city-state reinforced distinctions between slaves, metics and citizens in the legal sphere.

Perhaps the most striking example of the marking of difference is the requirement that slave testimony be extracted through torture and that any testimony so obtained be read out in court by a clerk rather than spoken in person, as citizens and metics were permitted to do. The legal requirement for extraction of slave testimony through torture arises from the ideological need of the state to draw distinctions between slave and free combined with the recognition that slaves were often key witnesses to the affairs of the citizens, whether in their homes or the public spaces of the city.[131] The state struck a compromise therefore that allowed litigants to make use of vital slave testimony, yet denied slaves legal personhood by having their testimony read out in court by others after it had been extracted through torture.

In law-court speeches, we hear of litigants offering their slaves for torture as a sign of their own innocence, or, conversely, accusing their opponents of refusing to have their slaves tortured as proof of guilt.[132] It appears that at least some citizens were reluctant to let their fate rest on the testimony of slaves, since the speeches frequently mention challenges to have slaves tortured that were not granted and none that were granted. Nevertheless, significantly, litigants were not averse to making rhetorical use of the rejection of a challenge in a subsequent trial.[133] The repeated reference to this procedure in law-court cases that were judged by hundreds of citizens (and witnessed by many more onlookers) would have served as a constant reminder of the difference between a slave and free citizen or metic according to civic ideology.[134]

---

sustained, he, the master, rather than his slave should be liable. Nevertheless, this case represents incontrovertible evidence that slaves could in fact be prosecuted directly.

[130] Aristotle, *Politics* 1275a22–4.   [131] Hunter 1994, 70–95.
[132] For example, Andocides 1.22; Demosthenes 29.11, 17; Lycurgus, *Against Leocrates* 28–35; Isaeus 8.17.
[133] Indeed, some scholars have suggested that such challenges were mere rhetorical devices and that such torture never actually took place: for example, Gagarin 1996; contra: Mirhady 1996, 2000.
[134] Hunter 2000.

When such torture took place, it often happened in a public space of the city, such as the sanctuary of Hephaestus in the central market place.[135] In such places, it would have been witnessed not only by the litigants themselves and their witnesses, but also by any others who happened to be in that part of the center of the city. It is worth stressing the gruesome nature of such torture of slaves, and the visual spectacle that it provided of the treatment of slaves.[136] Whipping and stretching on the rack were typical means of torture, and we can imagine with horror the sufferings of such slaves and the sounds of agony that emanated from the scene.[137] Moreover, such torture could even result in the death of a slave, since in one case, we are told that litigants agree on the value of the slave prior to performing the torture so that the owner can be compensated if he wins the case but his slave dies.[138]

Another area of the law in which distinctions of status are made is in punishments. While citizens typically paid fines in compensation for their misdeeds, slaves were held physically liable. Indeed, the Athenian Demosthenes claims – with some rhetorical exaggeration – that the greatest difference between slave and free is this difference between monetary and physical punishment.

> And, in fact, if you wish to examine the difference between a slave and a free person, you would find the following to be the greatest thing: the bodies of slaves are accountable for all their crimes whereas the bodies of free persons are spared, even if they are extremely unfortunate. For it is fitting for the free to be punished through fines of their property.[139]

While Demosthenes' statement is a simplification of a more complex reality, it captures one strand of Greek penal logic that is concerned to make distinctions between slaves and citizens.[140] One of the most striking examples of this feature is the Athenian law on silver coinage, discussed already in Chapter 3.[141] As we saw, this law specifies penalties not only for

---

[135] Isocrates 17.15
[136] Antiphon (5.29–32 and passim) provides one of our most detailed accounts of judicial torture of slaves. Demosthenes (37.40–46) attests to the brutality of the process: the slave was tortured until the parties agreed that he spoke the truth, or until the slave died – whichever came first. In Antiphon (5.33 and passim), the slave dies as a result of torture. If the slave died, the master would be reimbursed by his opponent for the value of the slave, or in the case of Antiphon (5.47), the slave was purchased in advance in anticipation of his death. On the other hand, if the slave testified satisfactorily to his owner, he could be offered his freedom (Antiphon 5. 31).
[137] Isocrates 17.15; Antiphon 5.32.   [138] Demosthenes 37.40.   [139] Demosthenes 22.55.
[140] Hunter 2000, 1–29; 1994, 154–84.
[141] The law code of Gortyn on Crete is another excellent example of penalties being exacted according to status; see Hunter 2000, 3–4.

the public slave who was in tasked to verify coinage, but also to both free and slave merchants who refused to accept verified coinage. Regarding the public slave who serves as approver, the law reads,

> The public slave who is approver shall sit in between the tables [in the marketplace] and approve on these terms ... If the approver does not sit or does not approve [coinage] in accordance with the law, let the magistrates of the people beat him with fifty lashes of the whip.[142]

Later in the same law, penalties are spelled out for merchants who refuse to accept verified coinage. After specifying that merchants who do not accept genuine coinage shall have their merchandise confiscated, the law further specifies the penalties for slave merchants: "If the seller is a slave-man or slave-woman, let him submit to be beaten with fifty lashes of the whip by the magistrates to whom each matter is assigned."[143] In this last provision, we see very clearly the difference between the financial penalty of free merchants and the physical punishment of slave merchants.

It is important to stress that this distinction in penalties is *not* due to the fact that slaves lacked the financial resources with which to pay fines. As we will see in Chapter 5, masters were liable for offenses committed by their slaves and routinely paid compensation for damages inflicted by their slaves. Moreover, public slaves such as the coin approver were among a group of privileged slaves who were able to keep a portion of the fruits of their labor (Chapter 3). Indeed, the last part of the law on silver coinage makes provisions for the payment from the public treasury of a salary for the public slave who serves as approver.[144] Therefore, public slaves such as the approver, and slaves in general, could have been made to pay a fine, if the state desired to extract one. It seems that in imposing punishments the state was more concerned with reinforcing status distinctions than in generating additional revenue through fines. Moreover, the display of the law itself in the highly trafficked space of the marketplace, as well as the enforcement of these differentiated penalties, would have been daily illustrations of the weight that the state placed on differences of status.

The distinctions between slave and free in the legal procedure were, of course, echoed in the private sphere as owners were free to whip, torture and even kill their own slaves with impunity, whereas free persons could not be so treated.[145] As we saw in Chapter 1, the Athenian law on

---

[142] RO 25.13–16.   [143] RO 25.30–32.   [144] RO 25.49–54.
[145] Citizens could not be tortured, according to the decree of Scamandrius, mentioned by Andocides 1.43. Citizens could, however, be held in the stocks (Andocides 1.93) for theft, for example (Demosthenes 24.114).

outrageous treatment, or *hubris*, did little to mitigate the routine brutality towards slaves in public and private life. Nevertheless, as also sketched briefly in Chapter 1 and discussed in more detail in the next chapter, the attempts of Greek law to relegate slaves to legal non-personhood and their assimilation to inanimate pieces of property were sometimes frustrated by the reality of the humanity of slaves. As discussed in the next chapter, slaves obviously had human capacities for agency independent of the will of their masters. It must be acknowledged, therefore, that the mechanisms by which the Greek state reinforced status distinctions through law are only part of the story.

Conclusion

In sum, we have seen how the Greeks constructed imagined mental, moral and physical traits that supposedly distinguished slave from free. We have also seen that the Greeks made strenuous efforts to enforce these distinctions in law, politics and religion. Yet, this chapter has demonstrated that these efforts were constantly destabilized by the reality that there was often little difference between slave and free in everyday life. Slaves often performed the same labor as citizens – especially farming and skilled crafts – and were also often indistinguishable from metic traders and retailers in their working lives. Even in the sphere of politics and the law, slaves were central to the apparatus of the state even if they did not have political or legal rights. Moreover, slave bodies were largely indistinguishable from those of the free, both in physical features and dress. Furthermore, slaves mostly spoke Greek (although sometimes with an accent), and often bore the same Greek names that citizens held. In this regard, it was observed that slaves and ex-slaves may have had as much interest in assimilating to Greek cultural norms as resisting them.

That said, we have seen that some non-Greek slaves made efforts to preserve elements of their birth culture, including language, cults and ethnic identity. Indeed, the cases of Atotas the Paphlagonian and Mannes the Phrygian demonstrate strikingly not only the potential for slaves or ex-slaves to lay claim to their ethnic heritage but also their willingness to assert their command of Greek culture as well as their skills in a particular profession. The presence of cultic associations devoted to foreign deities attests to the formation of communities of slaves and ex-slaves and even possibly the existence of ethnic enclaves in the Greek state. Moreover, slaves seem to have participated in cults to some Greek gods and heroes, despite their prohibition from direct participation in major civic cults. While the participation of free non-citizens (metics) in civic festivals was marked off from that of citizens in various ways, the presence of slaves (who often shared ethnicity with metics) in various functions at civic festivals further undermined the distinctions between slave and free in the field of religion.

Finally, we observed that slaves participated in private cult as members of citizen households, and even made use of Greek religion (hero cults, oracles) for their own distinct purposes. Most strikingly, the Athenian citizenship law reveals that slaves sometimes sought to enter surreptitiously into the ranks of citizens. The next chapter will follow up on these observations to examine examples of slaves using their intimate knowledge of Greek institutions and culture either to improve their conditions in slavery or to escape slavery altogether.

CHAPTER 5

Resourceful Slaves and Controlling Masters

> It is clear that a slave is a difficult piece of property to own, since a human being is a troublesome creature and does not wish to conform to the necessary distinction between slave and free person and master.
>
> Plato, *Laws* 777b4–8

A central tension runs through all slave-owning societies. On the one hand, slave-owners are compelled to deny the humanity of their slaves in order to justify the subjection of their fellow human beings. On the other hand, slave-owners simultaneously desire to exploit the human capabilities of their slaves so as to maximize their utility and profitability. In the quotation above, Plato both asserts the necessity and acknowledges the difficulties of classifying some humans as slaves and pieces of property. In response to this difficulty, the Greeks sometimes fantasized about automata that could perform labor for them without the pesky features of human slaves who could equally thwart as well as follow their owner's commands.[1]

It is this central tension between denial and recognition of the humanity of slaves that provided an opening for slaves to advance their interests within the system of slavery and sometimes to resist or escape the system of slavery altogether. In other words, it was the human capabilities of slaves that gave them the ability both to conceptualize themselves as more than mere automata and to leverage their human talents to carve out a livable space for themselves. Slave-owners, on the other hand, struggled to find a balance between exploiting the human capacities of their slaves and avoiding the threat to the system that acknowledgement of the humanity of slaves could present.

---

[1] See, for example, the comic fantasies of a world in which the earth produces food without human labor, and cooking pots prepare food by themselves and clean themselves afterwards (preserved in Athenaeus, *The Learned Banqueters* 267–69); cf. Aristotle, *Politics* 1253b29–1254a1. For discussion, see Forsdyke 2012, 55–58. On robots and automata in the ancient world generally, see Mayor 2018.

In this chapter we will examine this delicate dance between slaves and their owners. In the process, we will see that accommodation in various degrees to the system of slavery was often the best way for slaves to survive and advance their interests. This fact is clear from the general absence of slave revolts in Greece in the fifth and fourth centuries BCE. One exception is the helot revolts at Sparta, where, as we will see, particular conditions existed that were conducive to such extreme action. In most cases, however, slaves avoided overt or violent resistance to slavery or their personal enslavement. Instead, slaves resorted to a variety of strategies, ranging from cooperation with their masters in order to gain rewards (including the ultimate reward of emancipation) to various forms of under-the-radar resistance such as working slowly, playing sick or engaging in verbal games that on the surface presented themselves as docile, but that often sent coded messages of resistance to fellow slaves.

One strategy that lies between conformity and low-level resistance was, of course, desertion or flight from one's master. Indeed, flight represents perhaps the most common form of overt resistance to slavery in ancient Greece. Yet, as we shall see, even flight could be risky, since slave-owners pursued runaways and often offered rewards for their apprehension. Moreover, a slave had to weigh the uncertainties of travelling to one's homeland or finding refuge in a new community against the certainties (not always dire) of her present condition. Some slaves avoided these difficulties by forming colonies of runaways that could defend them against attacks by their owners and provide their collective livelihood. One of the best-known accounts of a slave revolt that survives from ancient Greece – the story of the runaway slave Drimakos, mentioned already in Chapter 4 and discussed further in this chapter – illustrates the potential success of this strategy.

In sum, this chapter will emphasize the resourcefulness of slaves both in living within the system of slavery and in escaping from it. In the process, we shall see that slaves found ways to communicate among each other, build networks of support even among the free population and make use of features of Greek culture – the legal system and beliefs about the gods, for example – to optimize their personal advantages. In particular, this chapter will highlight two examples of the ingenious ways that slaves used Greek culture against itself to improve their conditions in slavery. In these examples, we shall see that slaves sometimes maneuvered to be transferred to new, presumably better owners, rather than to escape slavery altogether. The chapter will also examine the ways in which owners attempted to control their slaves, including both punishments for "misbehavior" and rewards for loyal service. The final part of the chapter focuses on grants of freedom, and shows how these were an effective tool that incentivized certain slaves to work hard in their owner's interest. It is also demonstrated that the reward of freedom was realized by relatively few slaves overall.

Accommodation

The majority of slaves accommodated to their situation of enslavement. Some were born into slavery and knew no other life. Others became enslaved at some point in their lives and found the risks of attempting to resist too overwhelming. Slaves of both types may have found it more profitable to accept their condition and work within the system to pursue their goals, whether these were a basic level of well-being and personal security or wealth and freedom. Slaves whose circumstances were relatively comfortable – household slaves with kind masters, for instance – seem often to have accommodated to their situation. Conversely, however, slaves who lived under constant compulsion in brutal circumstances – slave-miners, for instance – had little choice but to accept their situation since they were constantly monitored, often chained in barracks at night and subject to vicious whipping for the slightest infractions. Such slaves may have become resigned to their situation and aimed at survival alone – getting enough food and avoiding punishment as much as possible.

Privileged slaves – such as skilled slaves living independently of their masters and some categories of public slaves – would also have relatively good incentives to accommodate to their enslavement. As we have seen (Chapter 3), such slaves were able to keep a portion of their earnings or draw a salary from the public treasury. Although these slaves lacked the benefit of political or legal rights, they seem to have enjoyed de facto control of their earnings. Some of them even became prosperous, as in the case of the public slave Pittalacus or the slave-banker Pasion (see Chapter 3). Indeed, Pasion's is a striking (if exceptional) case that illustrates the potential rewards for skilled slaves who played the system well: he was rewarded for his good service with freedom, ownership of the bank and ultimately citizenship for himself and his family members. While Pasion's case is truly exceptional, since very few slaves gained citizenship, the award of freedom was presumably the ultimate dream of most slaves who tried to work within the system of slavery (see below).

The fact of accommodation, however, does not mean that slaves accepted their enslavement psychologically, or refrained from resisting – even in covert ways. As we shall see, there were many ways in which slaves could resist their masters without being detected. Even Pasion, whose biography suggests that he suppressed any opposition that he felt to his enslavement for the purpose of advancement, may have harbored objections to slavery in private. Indeed, one detail in a law-court speech suggests that Pasion, after gaining his freedom and ownership of the bank, objected to the examination of his slave under torture to obtain testimony in a court case.[2] It is unlikely that Pasion developed such qualms only later in life. Pasion's son Apollodorus, by contrast, seems to have embraced the privileges of freedom and citizenship with great exuberance, if we are to believe our sources (which include some of his own speeches), since his treatment of his father's former slave Phormion shows that he was as eager as any native-born citizen to police the boundaries of status once he himself had obtained citizenship.[3]

Let us now survey the ways that even accommodating slaves may have covertly resisted slavery, before turning to more overt forms such as flight and rebellion.

Weapons of the Weak

In Xenophon's treatise on the management of estates, he argues that the difference between productive and unproductive estates depends on whether the owner is concerned to ensure that his slaves are working effectively. He then proceeds to enumerate the ways in which slaves can work ineffectively, essentially providing a catalogue of low-level strategies of slave resistance – namely, starting work late or leaving work early, taking breaks during working hours or working slowly.

> In farming large estates with many slaves, it makes a big difference in regard to profitability or unprofitability if the overseer is mindful or not of whether the slaves are working during working hours or not. For it is easy for one man in ten to make a difference by working during the proper time, while another man will make a difference by leaving early ... Therefore, in work, there is a great difference in achievement between those who work at what they are assigned and those who do not, but find excuses for not working or are allowed to work slowly.[4]

Xenophon's advice to large landowners is based on experience, and therefore likely reflects the actual strategies used by slaves. Such resistance, moreover, might go unnoticed, which is why Xenophon is concerned to

---

[2] Isocrates 17.16–17, 55; with Mirhady 2000, 85–86; and discussion above in Chapter 3.
[3] Demosthenes 36.48 and passim.   [4] Xenophon, *On Household Management* 20.16–20.

highlight to his readership the importance of having a vigilant overseer. For slaves, however, finding covert ways to decrease productivity was a key way of resisting their domination and thwarting the will of their owners. Stopping work or working slowly, moreover, might be facilitated by other techniques such as playing sick or breaking tools, both of which are well attested in both slave-owning and peasant societies in which the fruits of the labor go to elite landowners rather than the workers themselves.[5] We might well wonder whether some of the "sick" slaves whose care Xenophon entrusts to the estate owner's wife, really were sick?[6]

A further technique of covert resistance was the deliberate misunderstanding of instructions by slaves. In other words, slaves played dumb in order to thwart their masters' will. The anonymous comic biography of Aesop provides a brilliant parody of this technique and is the principal surviving evidence of this strategy among slaves in ancient Greece. For example, when Aesop's master commands him to "pick up the oil flask and towels" for a visit to the public baths, Aesop gets the oil flask but neglects to fill it with oil. When his flustered master complains, Aesop reminds him of his earlier instruction not to harm him "by doing anything more or less" than he is told:

> You told me to "take the oil flask and the towels" but you didn't mention oil. I wasn't supposed to do anything more than I was told. If I slipped up on my instructions, I was going to be answerable at the cost of a beating.[7]

A series of further "misunderstandings" ensues until Aesop teaches his master a lesson in slave management: "If you had not been so strict in setting down the rules, I would have served you much better." One way of interpreting this conclusion is to observe that the fictional Aesop uses the strategy of playing dumb to force his master into granting him more leeway in following his orders. In other words, Aesop forces his master to acknowledge that he is not a mere tool, but a human being with the capacity for using his initiative to serve his master better.[8]

This comic fantasy aside, in real life the slave strategy of playing dumb was used by slave-owners as evidence that slaves were lazy, unintelligent or unskilled.[9] This superficial interpretation of slaves' deliberate acts of subversion was, of course, far from the truth. Nevertheless, this view was

---

[5] Genovese 1974, 295–324; Scott 1985. [6] Xenophon, *On Household Management* 7.37.
[7] *Vita G*, trans. Hansen (1998). [8] Forsdyke 2012, 84.
[9] McKeown (2011, 167) citing Xenophon, *On Household Management* 9.11–15, 10.10; *Memorabilia* 2.4.2–5 and 2.10.3.

convenient for slave-owners, since it contributed to their sense of superiority and helped them to justify the institution of slavery.[10]

A final important technique of covert resistance was to "steal" from one's owner. Of course, from the perspective of slaves, such acts were not theft but justified reappropriation of the fruits of their own labor. That such acts of repossession were common is indicated by their frequent depiction in comic literature. For example, in a comic oxymoron, a master tells his slave that he is both "his most trusted slave and his most thievish slave."[11] The comic biography of Aesop, moreover, depicts theft of food by slaves, in this case a basket of ripe figs.[12] When Aesop's fellow slaves accuse him of eating the figs that they had in fact consumed, Aesop outwits them by sticking his fingers down his throat and vomiting to prove to their master that he did not in fact eat them. This comic scene reflects undoubtedly one of the most common objects of slave theft: food. Whether taking food directly from the field or plundering the storerooms, slaves would have secretly accessed this vital sustenance out of necessity or a sense of rightful ownership, or both.

Theft of foodstuffs by slaves was apparently such a rampant problem that Plato felt it necessary to specify the punishment in his regulations for his thought experiment of founding a colony: "If a slave takes anything of this sort [i.e., fruit] without the consent of the owner of the land, he shall be whipped with as many strokes as the number of grapes or figs that he has taken."[13] Even slave managers or overseers might avail themselves of the master's property, since Xenophon names among the criteria of a good overseer "keeping clear of the master's property and not stealing."[14]

In contrast to such petty theft, some slaves were bold enough to appropriate assets on a grand scale. As mentioned in Chapter 3, a slave named Moschion stole more than 8,000 drachmas from his master. Although Moschion worked in a drug-making shop owned by his master, he also served as household slave. It was this latter position that seems to have given him the opportunity to appropriate such a large amount of money.

> Komon had a slave named Moschion whom he considered very trustworthy. This household slave knew almost all of the affairs of Komon and especially where his money was – that is, the money that was stored in his house. Komon, being rather old and trusting his slave, did not notice that his household slave was secretly taking the money. First, Moschion stole one

[10] Cf. Genovese 1974, 285–324. [11] Aristophanes, *Wealth* 26–27. [12] *Vita G.*
[13] Plato, *Laws* 845a. [14] Xenophon, *On Household Management* 14.2.

> thousand drachmas which was stored separately from the rest of the money, then he stole the remaining seven thousand drachmas. And Komon did not notice his slave doing these things. And the household slave himself kept the entire amount.[15]

Even though Moschion acquired an enormous sum, he correctly judged that his thefts would go unnoticed by his elderly and trusting master. While Moschion's "theft" later became known when the heirs of Komon's estate became suspicious, we might wonder how many other trusted slaves managed to pull off such acts unnoticed? It is noteworthy that Moschion proceeded with caution: first he appropriated a smaller sum, and then – when the first act went unnoticed – a much larger sum. By stealing in two stages, he was able to monitor the level of risk before engaging in his major appropriation. He might have judged that, if the first act failed, the penalty would be lower. And, of course, Moschion might also have expected to be able to deny the charge. Indeed, several sources indicate that slaves routinely defended themselves before their masters against accusations of wrongdoing. For example, Xenophon says that he practices public speaking by cross-examining his slaves "when they are making an accusation or defending themselves."[16]

Two passages in Aristotle's *Rhetoric* confirm the impression that slaves were not passive in their own defense when accused (rightly or wrongly). In the first passage, Aristotle is describing the causes of anger, and mentions, as an example, the anger of owners against slaves who deny their wrongdoing.

> And [one becomes angry] more at those of no account, if they belittle [one] in some way; for anger resulting from being belittled is . . . against those who have no right to do it, and inferiors have no right to belittle. A sign [of how belittlement causes anger] is seen in the punishment of slaves; for we punish all the more those who argue and deny, but we cease our wrath towards those who confess themselves justly punished.[17]

In a second passage, Aristotle makes a comparison between the slave who avoids answering his master directly and the introductions to law-court speeches in which the speaker brings up extraneous matters in order to distract the jurors from the facts of the case.

> The introductions (προοίμια) to judicial speeches address things outside the real argument . . . [they] address a hearer who is morally weak . . . since if he

---

[15] Pseudo-Demosthenes 48.14–15. [16] Xenophon, *On Household Management* 11.23.
[17] Aristotle, *Rhetoric* 1379b.

were not such a person, there would be no need of an introduction, except for setting out the headings of the speech ... Those who do this ... have or seem to have a bad case in which it is better to spend words on anything other than the subject. That is why slaves do not answer questions but go around in a circle and proem-ize.[18]

In these passages we have evidence of slaves actively defending themselves against accusations of wrongdoing. Yet these same passages also show that some slaves chose the opposite strategy – namely, deference to their owners and acceptance of guilt and punishment. Specifically, Aristotle follows up on the first passage above with the statement that some slaves show respect for their owners by humbling themselves before their masters and not contradicting them. In doing so, they "admit to being inferiors" and therefore are no threat to the dignity of their owners. If we consider this strategy from the point of view of slaves, we can recognize the efficacy of defusing an owner's anger through an outward display of deference. In fact, this strategy is well attested among subordinate groups, and is one aspect of a larger sphere of verbal obfuscation that is sometimes referred to as the "hidden transcript." While the owner views the slave's confession as submission, the slave (and her fellow slaves) understand it as a strategy to deflect or minimize punishment. In other words, expressions that appear deferential to the owner have quite a different meaning to slaves.

Hidden Transcripts

The idea that slaves embedded coded messages of resistance in speech that was outwardly submissive or innocuous is well accepted in the study of slavery across time.[19] In particular, scholars have recognized that slaves even developed genres of oral performance – for instance, the trickster tales of Brer Rabbit in the American South – that appeared to be harmless tales to masters but often contained messages of resistance for the slaves who told them. As Lawrence Levine writes, such tales were "the vehicle through which slaves rehearsed their tactics, laughed at the foibles of their masters ... and taught their young the means that they would have to adopt in order to survive."[20] Several types of such slave tales have survived from ancient Greece, and the animal fables attributed to the slave Aesop are a prime example. Yet we can also excavate from Greek literature some other forms of oral tales that are likely to have originated among slaves but have been appropriated by elite writers without endorsing (or even recognizing)

---

[18] Aristotle, *Rhetoric* 1415b. [19] Scott 1990. [20] Levine 1977, 125.

their subversive messages.[21] It is also possible that some of these tales were acted out in popular forms of performance art such as mimes. Let's look at examples of each of these types.[22]

Aesop's fable about the Eagle and the Dung beetle is referred to in several comedies dating to the fifth and fourth centuries.[23] In the fable, a lowly dung beetle gets revenge on a mighty eagle who had wronged him. The beetle avenged himself by finding the eagle's nest and rolling the eggs out so that they fell to the ground and were smashed. When the eagle sought refuge in the lap of Zeus (with whom the eagle was associated in Greek culture), the dung beetle flew up to Zeus and dropped a pellet of dung in his lap. Zeus jumped up to shake off the dung pellet and caused the eggs to fall, smashing them to the ground once again.

This fable makes comic use of the skill of the dung beetle – rolling dung pellets (Fig. 5.1) – to tell a story about the revenge of the low on the high.

Fig. 5.1 A dung beetle rolling a pellet of dung. Paul Souders / Getty Images.

---

[21] Forsdyke 2012.
[22] These and other slave tales are discussed in much more detail in Forsdyke 2012.
[23] Aristophanes, *Peace* 129–130; *Wasps* 1446–48.

When recited among slaves, we might surmise, slaves understood the lowly dung beetle to stand for themselves, and the mighty eagle to refer to their powerful owners. When the same fable was performed among citizens – such as the audience of a comic play – it was presumably merely a humorous tale, an animal story without threatening implications for the system of slavery.

Another genre of slave tale is the extended oral narrative recounting the story of a heroic slave. One example of such a narrative is the comic biography of Aesop himself – a source that we have referred to on several occasions already. For present purposes, it is important to observe that, as this fictional biography survives for us today, it contains themes relevant primarily to free citizens. For example, some of the episodes poke fun at the pretensions of philosophers, and others provide advice to slave-owners about the correct management of slaves. Yet a case can be made that elements of an original slave tale that celebrated the clever slave Aesop are embedded in a text written for free Greek audiences. For example, Aesop constantly outwits his master, the philosopher Xanthos, and proves that his master is utterly dependent on his slave rather than the other way around. In one episode, for example, when Xanthos is called upon by the citizenry to interpret a portent, he is in despair until Aesop agrees to provide an interpretation. When the citizenry complains that a mere slave is offering an interpretation of a matter of such importance, Aesop manipulates his master into freeing him. Although Aesop ultimately dies unjustly through an act of treachery, his wrongful death is avenged by Zeus and both Greeks and foreigners are forced to recognize Aesop's greatness.

Another narrative that is likely a product of a slave tradition is the account of the slave Drimakos mentioned in the previous chapter. In this narrative, Drimakos deserts his master and forms a colony of runaways in the mountains of the island of Chios. What is remarkable about Drimakos is that he is a skilled commander of men and he and his fellow rebels are represented as defeating their owners repeatedly in battle. Moreover, Drimakos negotiates a contract of sorts with the owners, securing a guaranteed supply of food for his "maroon" colony in return for sending back any runaways who had not been mistreated by their owners. When Drimakos dies, finally, as an old man, a hero cult is founded in his honor and both slaves and slave-owners celebrate the greatness of the slave.

As in the biography of Aesop, the central focus of the story of Drimakos is on the feats of a slave, his repeated victories over the masters, his depiction as just and his final heroization. It is not hard to see that these are themes that would particularly resonate with slaves. These features, then, are suggestive of an original oral tale circulating among slaves. On the other hand, the tale survives as a small episode in a very extensive written text that was directed at the concerns of the free Greek population. Specifically, the larger text addresses the problems of slave ownership, and particularly the management of large numbers of slaves that was characteristic of slavery in Roman times when the text was written. Within this narrative framework, the tale of Drimakos serves as an historical example from ancient Greece of the problems of managing slaves. As the story survives today, therefore, embedded as it is in a literary text written for free citizens, the story is made to fit a theme relevant for contemporary slave-owners – namely, how to manage your slaves. In particular, the literary version aims to inculcate a central lesson for slave-owners: "treat your slaves well or they will rebel." In the original slave tale, performed before an audience of slaves, however, it might be hypothesized that the feats of a heroic slave were the central focus and that the theme of skillful and successful resistance was the dominant message.

An anecdote in another Roman-era account of a slave rebellion provides a hint of a third performative genre in which slaves may have acted out their fantasies of revenge on their masters. In Diodorus Siculus' account of a slave war which took place in the native Sicilian city of Enna in the first century BCE, he mentions that during the revolt, the slave leader Eunus and his fellow slaves put on dramatic mime performances that depicted the slave rebellion for the citizens of Enna. According to Diodorus, the slaves themselves acted out the skits and depicted the events of their very own rebellion against their masters. Furthermore, Diodorus writes, "the slaves poured contempt on the arrogance and outrageous insolence that had led to the slave-owners' self-destruction."[24] Once again this anecdote is embedded in a longer written text, and one of the main themes of this larger text is the instruction of slave-owners on the management of their slaves. Nevertheless, the anecdote is suggestive of a performance culture among slaves in which dreams of revenge were enacted. As a form of drama, and a lowly one at that, the contents could be dismissed as mere absurdist fantasy. For slaves, however, such performances may have been a community-building expression of their perspectives and even a medium for rehearsing real protest.[25]

---

[24] Diodorus Siculus 24.46, trans. Shaw (2001, 92–93).
[25] See Richlin (2017) for the idea that slaves engaged in a rich performative culture that survives for us today only as reflected in the comedies of Plautus.

Flight

If we turn now from indirect forms of resistance to more overt ones, flight from one's owner comes to the fore as one of the most common responses to slavery. Literary sources mention runaways in passing as incidental to the events that they narrate, and give an impression not only that slaves often ran away, but that masters spent time hunting them down. For example, a character in a dialogue by Plato explains his absence from the city by the fact that he had gone to Oenoe, a town on the border of Athenian territory, in pursuit of his slave Satyrus, who had run away.[26] Similarly, a speaker in a law-court speech mentions that his co-prosecutor, a citizen named Apollodorus, had been falsely accused of murder after he had gone to Aphidna, another town near the border, in pursuit of a runaway slave.[27] The fact that both these sources mention towns in northern Attica suggests that slaves in Athenian territory often fled on foot and took the most direct land route to escape.

Some masters offered rewards for the capture and return of runaway slaves. Xenophon attests to this practice, for example, in his record of a conversation between Socrates and another Athenian named Diodorus.

> "Tell me, Diodorus," [Socrates] said, "If one of your slaves runs away, do you take steps to recover him?"
> "Of course, by Zeus," he said, "and I summon others to help by proclaiming a reward for the recovery of the slave."[28]

Presumably such proclamations would be spread both by word of mouth and through written notices – on wood or papyrus – posted in public places. Since these materials are perishable, they have not survived from ancient Greece. Such records have survived, however, in the dry sands of Egypt from the Hellenistic and Roman periods, and are well attested in later slave societies (Fig. 5.2). These later documents can give us some idea of what such announcements might have looked like, and particularly the characteristics that owners considered useful for identifying runaways. One example from Egypt, dating to the second century BCE, reads:

> A slave belonging to Aristogenes, son of Chrysippos, ambassador from Alabanda, has run off to Alexandria.
> Name, Hermon, also known as Neilos; Syrian by birth, from the city of Bambyke, age about eighteen; medium height, no beard, well-formed legs,

---

[26] Plato, *Protagoras* 310c3–4.   [27] Pseudo-Demosthenes 59.9.
[28] Xenophon, *Memorabilia* 2.10.1–2.

> **100 DOLLARS REWARD!**
>
> Ranaway from the subscriber on the 27th of July, my Black Woman, named
>
> **EMILY,**
>
> Seventeen years of age, well grown, black color, has a whining voice. She took with her one dark calico and one blue and white dress, a red corded gingham bonnet; a white striped shawl and slippers. I will pay the above reward if taken near the Ohio river on the Kentucky side, or **THREE HUNDRED DOLLARS**, if taken in the State of Ohio, and delivered to me near Lewisburg, Mason County, Ky. **THO'S. H. WILLIAMS.**
> August 4, 1853.

Fig. 5.2 Advertisement for a reward for the recapture of a runaway slave, 1853. Smith Collection / Gado / Getty Images.

cleft in his chin, mark near the left side of his nose, scar above the left corner of his mouth, right wrist tattooed with barbarian letters.

Took with him when he fled: a belt containing three gold coins weighing three minae and ten pearls; an iron ring on which were an oil flask and some body scrapers; clothing on his body – a short riding cloak and a loincloth.

The one who returns him shall receive two (later raised to three) talents of bronze.[29]

These examples demonstrate that slaves were identified by gender, age, physical features including both natural features (height, nose shape etc.) and acquired features (scars, tattoos). In addition, they might be identified through the clothing they wore or the objects that they took with them. We might conjecture that slaves who were given some freedom of movement (such as household slaves and skilled slaves working in crafts, business or trade) had more opportunities to flee than slaves who were

[29] P. Paris 10, trans. Shaw (2001, 56).

constrained to remain in barracks at night (such as agricultural slaves working on large estates and slaves working in mining or milling).

While many slaves undoubtedly escaped successfully, some did not. Such slaves were branded on the forehead. Presumably such treatment was designed both as a punishment and also a visible marker of their status as slaves in case they should try to flee again. Once again, we know of this practice only through an incidental reference: a character in comedy is accused of growing his hair long to cover up the brand on his forehead that marks him as a runaway slave.[30] Citizens were encouraged to seize runaways and return them to their masters, and some states required public heralds to issue warnings not to help runaways escape.[31] Plato reflects such public concern about apprehending runaways in his legislation for the imaginary ideal state of Magnesia: he allows for both the apprehension and punishment of runaways by their own masters, and by third parties who might "acting for another, lay hold of a runaway slave for safe keeping."[32]

In addition to these incidental comments on single runaways, we also know of instances when large numbers of slaves fled at the same time. Typically, such incidents occurred during times of crisis, such as external or internal war, when conditions were unstable.[33] The most remarkable instance of such mass desertion happened in and after 413 BCE, when the Spartans established a successful base in Athenian territory during the long war between these two rival states. Because of this occupation, Thucydides tells us, the Athenians were forced to retreat within their walls and suffered great harm.

> For they had been deprived of the whole countryside, and more than 20,000 slaves had run away and a large number of those were skilled laborers, and all the livestock and beasts of burden had been lost.[34]

A few years later, the Athenians were the beneficiaries of a similar mass desertion of slaves on the island of Chios, which had rebelled against the Athenian empire. When the Athenians established a stronghold on Chian territory, "straightaway, the majority [of the slaves of the Chians] deserted to the Athenians and these slaves did the most damage [to the Chians] since they knew the landscape."[35]

Invading enemies and rival factions in civil wars might even encourage desertion by slaves by offering freedom to deserters, as happened during

---

[30] Diphilus, *The Busybody* fr. 67 K-A = Athenaeus, *The Learned Banqueters* 6.225b.
[31] Diodorus Siculus 15.52.   [32] Plato, *Laws* 914e.   [33] Cartledge 1985.   [34] Thucydides 7.27.3–5.
[35] Thucydides 8.40.

a brutal conflict between oligarchs and democrats on the island of Corcyra in 427 BCE. When both sides had gained control of different parts of the city, they each "sent messengers into the countryside inviting the slaves to join them and promising them freedom. The majority of the slaves became allies of the democrats, but the oligarchs obtained eight hundred mercenaries from the countryside."[36]

In these examples, we see slaves taking advantage of unstable conditions to flee their masters, escape enslavement and sometimes even gain a grant of freedom. The fact that they did so en masse is testimony not only to the incentives offered by rival factions, but also to the channels of communication between slaves, as information about conditions and opportunities for desertion spread through the slave population. This point needs to be emphasized, since scholars have long dismissed the evidence for communication and coordination among slaves in ancient Greece. Indeed, it has often been thought that slaves in Greece had no sense of common identity or ability to organize collective resistance due to their "heterogenous character" and lack of a "common language or culture."[37] As we have seen, there *is* evidence for common culture among slaves if one looks hard enough (Chapters 3 and 4). Moreover, the examples just discussed serve as concrete evidence of the fact of coordination. It is no coincidence that 20,000 (or some large number) of slaves in Athens fled to the Spartans in 413 BCE, or that the majority of slaves on Corcyra fled to the side of the democrats in the civil war of 427 BCE. In both cases, it is likely that the slave population shared information about the opportunity for desertion and the incentives offered by each side.

An example of how knowledge of an opportunity for flight and escape from slavery could spread among a slave population can be found in a remarkable episode in American history. As a more recent, better-documented episode in history, it provides comparative historical evidence suggestive of the possibilities for communication between slaves across a wide geographical space. One morning in 1861, in the early days of the Civil War, three young slaves rowed across the James River in Virginia and asked for asylum in a citadel, named Fort Monroe, belonging to the Union. These slaves had been leased out to the Confederate Army to construct defenses at a strategic point across the river from Fort Monroe. Although Virginia had seceded from the Union earlier that year, the Union had retained control of Fort Monroe. The commander at Fort Monroe was one Benjamin Butler, a lawyer by training and an opponent of slavery. Butler

[36] Thucydides 3.73.   [37] De Ste. Croix 1981, 146.

declared the fugitives "contraband of war," shrewdly arguing that, if Virginia considered itself to be a foreign power by seceding from the Union, then he was under no obligation to return the fugitives, as would otherwise be required by the Fugitive Slave Act of 1850.

Almost immediately after this decision, a massive flood of slaves began streaming towards Fort Monroe. According to one account of this incident, "within weeks ... slaves were reported flocking to the Union lines just about anywhere there *were* Union lines."[38] A soldier who was present at Fort Monroe wrote to his family in wonderment at what he called the "mysterious spiritual telegraph which runs through the slave population." The soldier wrote that it was enough to "proclaim an edict of emancipation in the hearing of a single slave on the Potomac, and in a few days it will be known by his brethren on the gulf."

It is likely that a similar "mysterious spiritual telegraph" existed among slaves in ancient Greece, despite differences in native language and ethnicity. Like slaves in the American South, slaves developed facility in the language of their masters and formed communities (Chapters 3 and 4). The ability of slaves to communicate regarding opportunities for flight is exemplified by two more remarkable examples of coordinated action by slaves in ancient Greece. First, is the famous example of the revolt of the Spartan helots in around 464 BCE.[39] The revolt began among the helots in Laconia (the region of Sparta itself) and soon spread to helots of Messenia (the territory held by the Spartans but separated from Laconia by a mountain range). In Messenia, the helots established a stronghold on Mount Ithome from which they held out against their masters possibly for as many as ten years before being resubjugated. A second example of slave communication and coordination is the revolt of slaves on Chios sometime in the third century BCE that is probably the historical incident upon which the heroic slave tale of Drimakos, mentioned above, was based. In this episode, once again a large group of slaves fled from their masters and established a stronghold in the mountains from which they resisted their owners for many years.

In both of these cases, the slaves did not flee the state entirely but sought independence and freedom within the territory of the state that had formerly held them as slaves. Such a strategy is well attested in other slave-owning societies such as Rome, Brazil and the Caribbean, where the territory was favorable to the quick establishment of a stronghold by

---

[38] Goodheart 2011, 59. [39] Thucydides 1.101.

fugitive slaves.[40] What is remarkable about these incidents, however, is the ability of slaves to coordinate their action. Granted the Spartan helots were all of the same ethnicity and language (Greek), in the other examples, notably Chios, the slaves were of heterogenous origins. Indeed, Chios was famous in antiquity for being the first state to import large numbers of bought (chattel) slaves rather than enslaving the indigenous inhabitants of their lands, as did the Spartans. As such, slaves on Chios would have come from a variety of places and spoken a variety of languages.[41]

Slave Rebellion

While several of the cases discussed above could be classified as slave rebellions rather than instances of flight, it is generally the case that there were few instances of full-scale slave rebellion in classical Greece.[42] The case of the Spartan helots in 464 is one generally accepted instance, and the particular conditions in Sparta, as we shall see, help explain why this is one of very few examples. In general, however, it seems that slaves in Greece avoided the risks of full-scale rebellion in favor of less dangerous and more covert methods. Therefore, in this section we will identify the factors that rendered revolt risky in ancient Greece, and conversely explain why Sparta was an exception to this general rule. In the next section, moreover, we will examine several strategies by which slaves sought to improve their conditions *in slavery* rather than escape slavery altogether, let alone take the precarious step of risking a violent uprising.

The study of slave rebellions in comparative perspective has revealed that certain conditions have been conducive to slave rebellion throughout history and that such conditions explain its prevalence in some regions rather than others.[43] In particular, the conditions which prevailed in the Caribbean were more favorable to slaves organizing a rebellion than those in the American South. Foremost among these conditions are the following:

1. A depersonalized relationship between master and slave.
2. The existence of economic distress and famine.
3. Large slave-holding units.

---

[40] Rome: Shaw 2001, 61–68; Brazil and Caribbean: Genovese 1979, 51–81.
[41] Theopompus *FGrH* 115 F122 = Athenaeus, *The Learned Banqueters* 265b–c.
[42] In the Hellenistic period, we do hear of a revolt of the tens of thousands of slaves who worked in the mines at Laurium in Attica: Poseidonius *FGrH* 87 F35 = Athenaeus, *The Learned Banqueters* 272e–f (cited above, Chapter 3).
[43] Genovese (1979) upon which Cartledge (1985) draws. This section draws heavily on the work of both these scholars.

4. The existence of conflict within the slave-owning population due to external or internal war.
5. A high ratio of slave to free in the population.
6. A high ratio of imported slaves to home-born slaves in the population.
7. The emergence of a leadership class among slaves.
8. Geographical factors such as easily defensible mountains or islands.

We have already had cause to mention a few of these conditions in the examples already discussed. The earthquake in Sparta in 464 BCE caused great disruption and probably economic distress which the helots duly exploited to rebel from their Spartan masters. Later in the fifth century, the conflict between Athens and Sparta provided many opportunities for slaves on both sides to flee to the enemy side. In addition to the examples already discussed, our sources preserve several examples of Athenian support of rebellion of helots at Sparta. For example, the Athenians sheltered and resettled runaway helots after the Spartans suppressed their revolt in about 454.[44] Moreover, in 425, during the first phase of the Peloponnesian War, the Athenians established a base in Spartan territory at Pylos, to which many helots deserted.[45] The Spartans, in turn, tried to preempt helot revolt by sending some seven hundred of them to northern Greece to fight as heavy-armed infantry (hoplites) in the Spartan army under their crack commander, Brasidas.

> The Spartans were glad for a pretext to send some of their helots away, since they were worried that the [Athenian] occupation of Pylos might encourage the helots to start a rebellion. Indeed, in their fear of the intransigence and numerical strength of the helots (for at all times most of the Spartans' relations with the helots were based mainly on security) ... they eagerly sent seven hundred helots out as hoplites with Brasidas as their commander.[46]

The conditions of war between Sparta and Athens therefore favored slave rebellions in both societies. Moreover, the geography of both states – particularly the presence of easily defensible mountains – was another factor that enabled slave rebellion, as it did on Chios. Why then, did helots revolt at Sparta but slaves at Athens did not? Consideration of the remaining conditions provides at least a partial answer, since several favorable conditions existed at Sparta but not at Athens. Foremost among these conditions were a depersonalized master-slave relationship and a high ratio of slave to free in the population.

---

[44] Thucydides 1.103. [45] Thucydides 4.41. [46] Thucydides 4.80.

Fig. 5.3 Topographical map of Greece. Bridgeman Images.

Starting with the first factor, we might observe that the revolt in 464 was centered on the Messenian helots who lived quite far from the center of the Spartan state and were separated by a high mountain range (Figs. 5.3 and 5.4).

Given the geographical separation of the Messenian helots from their Spartan masters, it is likely that they had little or no personal acquaintance with one another. Indeed, Messenian helots were obliged to hand over half of the produce of their fields to their Spartan masters, but otherwise seem to have lived quite independently. Archaeological evidence suggests that helots lived in family and village units and had their own cults and other communal activities (see Chapter 4).[47] While these latter factors may have made the life of the Messenian helots less harsh than that of many other servile populations, the basic fact of depersonalized relations is a significant condition favoring revolt. Moreover, it presents a stark contrast to Athens, where slaves often lived and worked side-by-side with their masters, and knew them intimately.

If we consider treatment of helots by the Spartan state, we find further evidence for depersonalized relations. First, there was the annual declaration of war against the helots by the Spartan officials known as

---

[47] Luraghi and Alcock 2003; Luraghi 2008; and Chapter 4 above.

Fig. 5.4 View of Mt. Taygetus. DeAgostini / Getty Images.

Ephors.[48] By treating the helots as the "enemy within," the Spartans not only reinforced a hostile relationship but also legitimized the killing of helots by Spartans without penalty or religious pollution for the killer. Indeed, it was part of the training of Spartan youths to be sent out at night to kill helots whom they found on the road.[49] Finally, the Spartans made periodic efforts to kill off helots who stood out for their strength and spirit, thereby not only terrorizing the helots but also removing any potential leaders of rebellion.[50] While the latter result helped eliminate one potential favoring condition for rebellion (#7 the emergence of a leadership class

---

[48] Plutarch, *Life of Lycurgus* 28, citing Aristotle. [49] Plutarch, *Life of Lycurgus* 28.
[50] Thucydides 4.80.

among slaves), the overall brutal treatment of helots would have done much to destroy any potential personal sentiments between helots and their masters. It is important, however, to keep in mind a possible distinction between the treatment of Laconian as opposed to Messenian helots. The latter may have been less terrorized due to their distance from their Spartan masters.

A second crucial factor favoring slave rebellion at Sparta was the ratio of slaves to free in the population. In his classic study of slave rebellions in comparative perspective, Eugene Genovese observed that slaves heavily outnumbered the free on the sugar plantations in the Caribbean where rebellions were relatively frequent.[51] In Jamaica, for example, the ratio was 10 slaves for every free person. By contrast, in the American South, where revolts were less frequent, slaves outnumbered free in only two states (South Carolina and Mississippi) and then only by a small margin (55%). In most states, slaves constituted 20–40% of the population, a number that compares well with that of classical Athens where, as we have seen (Chapter 2), slaves comprised 25–33% of the population.

While precision is impossible in assessing the size of the helot population, it is likely that the helots outnumbered the Spartans by at least 2:1. Indeed, as noted in Chapter 2, the historian Herodotus records that each Spartan was accompanied by seven helots at the Battle of Plataea in 479, suggesting a much higher ratio.[52] Even more striking is the ratio suggested in an anecdote about an (ultimately unsuccessful) conspiracy against the Spartan state that took place sometime around 399. According to Xenophon, the leader of the conspiracy was one Kinadon – a Spartan who had failed to become a full Spartan citizen, namely, one of the "Equals." Kinadon gained support for his rebellion by counting how many Spartans were in the marketplace on a given day and comparing this number to the number of non-Spartans. The result was a ratio of 1:100. Granted this latter number included not just helots, but also those Spartans who had failed to gain full Spartan citizenship, and the Spartan equivalent of the metics at Athens – the "dwellers-around" or *perioikoi*. Nevertheless, the anecdote assumes that the full Spartan citizens were heavily outnumbered. More specifically, Kinadon is said to have pointed to the estates of the Spartans and observed that there was one on each estate who was the enemy (the master) but many (helots) who would be allies to the revolt. Colorfully, Kinadon claimed that each of these latter would "gladly eat the Spartans even raw!"[53]

---

[51] Genovese 1979. [52] Herodotus 9.10, 29. [53] Xenophon, *History of Greece* 3.5–11.

We might imagine that Plato was thinking of the situation of the Spartans when he imagined the fear that a slave-owner might feel if he were to be whisked away by a god from his fellow citizens and put down with his many slaves in a deserted place: "Can you imagine the terrible fear he would feel for himself, his children and his wife – fear that they would all be killed by his slaves?"[54] Indeed, the preponderance of helots in comparison to free citizens provides the context for Thucydides' statement cited above that the Spartans were always fearful of the "numerical strength of the helots." It also explains the extreme measures the Spartans took to terrorize the helots into submission. The revolt of 464 and the conspiracy of Kinadon show that the Spartans were only partially successful in this effort to subdue the helots and that the helots were constantly ready to rise up when conditions were favorable.

Indeed, when Spartan power was checked decisively by the Thebans after the Battle of Leuctra in 371 and the Thebans led a huge invasion of Sparta's home territory, the Messenian helots revolted en masse and were able to establish the free state of Messene in 369. It is often said that the only successful slave rebellion in history was that led by Toussaint L'Ouverture, that resulted in the creation of the free state of Haiti in 1804 (Fig. 5.5). However, the long struggle of the Messenian helots that culminated in their collective achievement of freedom arguably deserves a place alongside that of the slaves who fought successfully to found Haiti.

If we consider the remaining conditions favoring revolt, we see that they were absent at Sparta and largely also in other Greek states. In contrast to the large sugar plantations of the Caribbean, slaves in ancient Greece were dispersed in the homes, farms and small manufacturing operations of their masters. While the tens of thousands of slaves in the mines at Laurium in southern Attica are one exception, there are few examples of slave-owners in Athens possessing more than a few dozen slaves. Moreover, the helots of Sparta were a homegrown slave population rather than a heterogenous imported one, a factor unfavorable to revolt (contrary to what Plato thought[55]). By contrast, we might expect the imported slaves of Athens or Chios to be more likely to revolt. The existence of other factors disfavoring revolt at Athens (e.g., personal relations between slaves and masters; a lower ratio of slaves to free) explains the relative absence of revolt compared to Chios.

In sum, the general absence of slave rebellion in classical Greece, and indeed in history generally, can be explained by the conditions which

---

[54] Plato, *Republic* 578e.   [55] Plato, *Laws* 777c.

Fig. 5.5 Toussaint L'Ouverture, the leader of a successful slave rebellion that led to the establishment of the modern state of Haiti in 1804. Stock Montage / Getty Images.

tended to make violent uprising dangerous. While the Spartan helots and the slaves of the Caribbean are exceptions, this result prompts us to look harder for other ways that slaves dealt with the system of slavery that helped them cope or even improve their living conditions. In particular, the next section examines slave strategies that form a middle ground between the low-level and common forms of resistance discussed above and full-scale rebellion. These examples are revealing, because they illustrate the ingenious ways that slaves maneuvered to create a living space for themselves, and particularly how they leveraged prominent features of Greek culture – the legal system and religious beliefs – to improve their living conditions.

Transfer to a New Master or Creating a "Living Space"

It was observed at the beginning of this chapter that a central tension running through all slave-owning societies is the need to both deny and accept the humanity of slaves. Moreover, as we saw in Chapter 1, this tension is especially apparent in the sphere of the law where the attempt to classify slaves as pieces of property that were completely subject to the will of their owners was undermined by the need of masters to deny liability for acts committed by slaves without their consent. Closer examination of several laws on legal liability regarding slaves reveals some of the ways that slaves exploited the law to improve their conditions. In particular, these laws show how slaves took advantage of the provision for the surrender of the slave to the victim in order to arrange for their transfer to a new and hopefully better master. Strikingly, moreover, the evidence of these laws shows that slaves themselves were active agents in this legal maneuver, suggesting not only that some slaves had considerable legal knowledge but also that they were able to recruit members of the citizen population to support their efforts to improve their conditions.[56]

Our evidence for Greek laws on the surrender of slaves to victims (often referred to as "noxal surrender," or surrender of the offending object – "noxa" – to the victim, according to later Roman usage) comes from two laws, both of which appear in Plato's treatise the *Laws*. The legislation in Plato's *Laws* is, of course, not a direct record of historical legislation, but rather a creative reworking of contemporary legislation in service of Plato's vision of a well-ordered society.[57] We must be cautious, therefore, in assuming that any Platonic law reflects directly or precisely historical legislation. In the case of Plato's laws on slavery, however, it has been convincingly demonstrated that they have many parallels with existing historical legislation.[58] Specifically, the two laws discussed below have verbal and substantive parallels with Athenian laws, suggesting a close relation.[59]

The laws in question concern procedures for dealing with damage or wounding caused by slaves. The first part of each law specifies that owners are responsible for damage, and requires them to make amends.

---

[56] For the exploitation of the law by slaves – despite their lack of legal rights – in slave-owning societies of Latin America and the antebellum American South, see, for example, de la Fuente 2004; Gross 2000; Twitty 2016; Jones 2018.
[57] Schofield (2016, 3) writes that "Plato's ... legal code is much of it a reworking of contemporary Athenian law."
[58] Morrow 1939. Cf. Morrow 1960.
[59] See Forsdyke (forthcoming) for detailed discussion of the parallels.

> If a male or female slave does damage to someone else's property [and] if the person who was harmed is not himself also to blame due to lack of experience or some other use that is not prudent, let the master of the slave who did the damage make full amends for the damage or let him hand over the slave who did the damage.[60]
>
> If a slave wounds a free man in anger, let the owner hand over the slave to the wounded man to treat as he sees fit. If the owner does not hand the slave over, let the owner himself make full amends for the damage.[61]

The first part of each law lays out remedies for damages or wounding caused by the slave of one citizen to the property or person of a second citizen. In such cases, the master of the slave is responsible for making amends for the damages or he must hand over the slave to the victim. In this part of the laws, then, provision is made for compensating a citizen for damages caused by the slave of another citizen, either through direct transfer of money or by handing over the slave as the equivalent of a certain monetary value. This part of the law, therefore, corresponds closely to the provision in Athenian law that masters were responsible for compensating victims of crimes committed by their slaves.[62] The law on wounding, moreover, suggests that the slave – besides serving as monetary compensation – might also be physically punished by the victim of the crime ("the victim may treat the slave as he sees fit").

It is the provision for handing over a slave to an injured party that gives rise to the second part of each law. In this part of the laws, the lawgiver seems to envision a scenario in which a slave actively conspires with the victim in order to get transferred to a new owner.

> But if the master who is accused asserts that the slave is to blame through a joint intrigue of the slave doing the damage and the one who was harmed for the purpose of depriving him of his slave, let him make a suit for evil scheming against the one who says that he was harmed. If he wins, let him receive twice the value of the slave that the court assesses. If he loses, let him repair the damage and let him hand over the slave.[63]
>
> If anyone contends that the affair is a scheme resulting from an agreement between the slave and the wounded party, let him bring a suit. And if he does not win the case, let him pay three times the damages. And if he wins the case, let him prosecute the one who colluded with the slave on a charge of kidnapping.[64]

---

[60] Plato, *Laws* 936c–e.　[61] Plato, *Laws* 879a–b.
[62] See Chapter 1 under the section "Ancient Greek Laws and Legal Conceptions of Slavery."
[63] Plato, *Laws* 936c–e.　[64] Plato, *Laws* 879a–b.

The second part of each law therefore provides remedies for the master whose slave has conspired to get transferred to a new master. Indeed, the laws suggest that slaves themselves, and citizens who coveted slaves belonging to others, sometimes contrived together to take advantage of the provisions in the first part of each law in order to remove a slave from the ownership of his master. In fact, it is likely that the second part of each law is an addition to the original law, and aimed to prevent the previously unforeseen strategic exploitation of the first part of the law by imposing a new legal procedure and stiff penalties to deter or punish such cases of collusion. The second part of the law on damage caused by a slave, for example, provides for a new suit against the alleged victim for "evil scheming", and grants the master twice the value of his slave if he is able to win the case. In the law on wounding, moreover, the reward for a successful prosecution in a new suit for "kidnapping" is not specified, but we can imagine it to be comparably harsh. Interestingly, the law on wounding *does* specify a penalty for the master if he loses his suit for alleged kidnapping. In this case, the victim wins three times the damages.

There are several possible scenarios that might have given rise to the second part of the law. One scenario is that a citizen schemed to deprive another citizen of his slave by colluding with the slave to make a claim for damages or wounding. In such cases, the first citizen would hope that the master would rather settle the case by handing over his slave than by paying for damages, so that in that way he would gain possession of the slave. In such cases, the citizen presumably would have to make a claim for damages worth at least the value of the slave, if he expected to have a chance of gaining possession of the slave. A second possible scenario is that it was the slaves themselves who arranged with a third-party citizen to make a claim for damages in the hope that they would be "handed over" to a new master who they expected would be a more lenient owner, or even one who was willing to grant them their freedom. Again, the claim would have to be fairly high if the slave expected his master to be willing to hand him over to a new owner in compensation.

Several details of the laws suggest that the slave was an active collaborator, and possibly the prime mover, in these schemes. The law on damage, for example, specifies that the slave himself and the third-party citizen engage in a "joint intrigue." In the law on wounding, moreover, the ruse is described as a "scheme" resulting from "an agreement between the slave and the wounded party." Even more striking is the fact that the law on damage appears to envision that the slave is to blame when it states "If the master who is accused says that the slave is to blame."

It is important to stress, however, that – even if the third-party citizen was contriving to gain a new slave – it would seem that the citizen would have to offer the slave something in order to gain his or her cooperation. If the slave were initiating the ruse, she too would have to offer her new master something in return – loyal service or continued good service after emancipation. The important point is that, either way, the slave would expect to improve her situation and thus must be recognized as an active player in this legal game.

That said, it is crucial to remember that slaves did not have legal rights and therefore could not initiate a legal claim themselves.[65] Rather, slaves wishing to exploit the law on damage needed to conscript a citizen to make the legal claim. Without the cooperation of a citizen, a slave could not initiate this ruse. This fact shows that slaves would have had to have developed close relationships with free persons who were not their masters and negotiated skillfully with them to entice them to act in their interests, or at least for their own mutual benefit. As we saw in the case of attempts by slaves to enroll as citizens (Chapter 4), and as we will see in the case of appeals for asylum (below), slaves needed to build networks of support among citizens to engage in some of the tactics that they deployed to improve their situations. This was particularly true when these tactics involved the political and legal institutions of the state, to which slaves were officially denied access.

One plausible situation in which such a sort of collaboration between a slave and a citizen might occur is in the case of a romantic or sexual relation between the third-party citizen and the slave. In such cases, it is possible that a slave granted sexual favors in order to gain the cooperation of the free citizen in the legal ruse. In this regard, it is noteworthy that the law on damages explicitly envisions either male or female slaves as participants in this legal dodge. This fact strengthens the likelihood that romantic or sexual relations could be a motivating factor for the perpetration of such ruses.

But how did slaves gain knowledge of the potential to manipulate the law in this way? They might have been instructed by self-interested citizens, of course, but it is equally likely that they learned the law as they performed their duties as slaves. As we have seen, slaves were essential to the machinery of the Greek state, just as they were essential to the operation of many Greek households and businesses. In particular, publicly owned slaves assisted magistrates as they went about their duties and

---

[65] Kamen 2013; and discussion above in Chapter 4.

worked as scribes, archivists and accountants in the civic administration. Even privately owned household slaves frequented the market place and might have stopped by the court or the Council house to observe the proceedings.[66] In short, slaves were ubiquitous in the civic spaces of the Greek state and had ample opportunity to learn the workings of the law. Moreover, as we saw above in the case of opportunities for flight, information could spread very rapidly through the slave population, and the opportunity to exploit laws of noxal surrender would be no exception. Indeed, the fact that the laws on damage and wounding were *both* supplemented with an extra provision to deal with cases of collusion suggests that such exploitation was frequent enough an occurrence to necessitate legislation.

Consideration of a second example illustrates how slaves made use of Greek religious customs, particularly the right of asylum at sanctuaries, to maneuver for better living conditions. As briefly mentioned in Chapter 1, Greek sanctuaries offered refuge to slaves, thereby recognizing the personhood of slaves alongside that of free persons. A close look at several examples, however, reveals how slaves might use the right of asylum to escape a brutal master and negotiate transfer to a new master. These examples again demonstrate that slaves, whether Greek or non-Greek, had deep knowledge of Greek culture and exploited this familiarity to their own advantage. Before illustrating this claim, some background is needed.

It was a long-established Greek custom that suppliants at religious sanctuaries could be granted asylum and thereby protected from any reprisals that might threaten them.[67] In many cases, the right of asylum would have been invoked by free persons. For example, Thucydides recounts the story of Cylon, the would-be Athenian tyrant, whose partisans fled to the sanctuary of the Reverent Goddesses (*Semnai Theai*) when their coup failed c.630 BCE.[68] Similarly, Thucydides relates the story of the Spartan regent, Pausanias, who sought refuge in the "Brazen House," a temple of Athena, when he was detected in seditious activity in Sparta c.470.[69] In both these cases, famously, the right of asylum was violated, and the suppliants were dragged from the sanctuaries and killed.[70] Indeed, our

---

[66] For court watching by emancipated slaves in the American South, see Booth forthcoming.
[67] For discussion of this phenomenon, see Sinn 1990, 1993; and Chaniotis 1996. For supplication in the ancient world, including temple supplication, see Naiden 2006.
[68] Thucydides 1.126.   [69] Thucydides 1.134.
[70] The violation of the right of asylum by slave-owners is also dramatized in several plays, including Menander's *Girl from Perinthos* and Plautus' *Rudens*. I thank Peter Hunt for these references.

sources usually report incidents only when the right of asylum was violated.⁷¹

Slaves were also protected by this right of asylum, and particular shrines were known to give refuge to slaves. The shrine of Poseidon at Tainaron in Laconia and the sanctuary of Theseus at Athens are two well-known examples.⁷² Thucydides mentions that the Spartans expelled a group of helots who were presenting themselves as suppliants at the shrine of Poseidon at Tainaron in the 460s.⁷³ The Spartans then executed the helots and Thucydides reports that "even the Spartans believe that the great earthquake [of 464] was a result of this impiety."⁷⁴ Aristophanes alludes to the function of the sanctuary of Theseus as a place of refuge in his comic play *Knights* of 424, and an ancient commentator on the play explains that slaves who fled to the precinct of Theseus gained asylum.⁷⁵ In the fourth century, Aeschines mentions the sanctuary of Theseus as the place where magistracies were allotted, and an ancient commentator adds a reference to a law regarding slaves who fled to the shrine: "There was a law that those who fled to the precinct of Theseus should be inviolate."⁷⁶ A long lexicographic tradition echoes and confirms this function of the sanctuary of Theseus in classical Athens.⁷⁷

On the basis of the surviving literary and epigraphic evidence, one scholar has summarized the process of requesting asylum as follows:

> If someone ... wished to avail himself of the protection of a sanctuary, he had to appear openly and set forth the reasons for his coming. After such a presentation, the sanctuary was in turn obliged to work towards a solution of the problem, as a rule by undertaking the role of a go-between.⁷⁸

While this description of the process concerns all types of suppliants including free persons fleeing violence at the hands of their political

---

⁷¹ Sinn 1993, 93.
⁷² See Christensen (1984) for a complete list with sources; see also Kudlien 1988, 243–45; Gottesman 2014. Besides the Athenian Theseion (references cited below) and the temple of Poseidon at Tainaron in Laconia (Thuc. 1.128), attested slave refuges include the sanctuary of Herakles at Canopus (Hdt. 2.113), a sanctuary at Messene (*IG* v¹.1390) and a sanctuary in Gortyn (Law Code of Gortyn 1.38–45). The Athenians apparently made some efforts to keep runaway slaves from the sanctuaries on the acropolis, as attested in an inscription concerning a wall to keep them out (*IG* i³.45; Chaniotis 1996, 72).
⁷³ Thucydides 1.128. Kennell (2010, 87) claims that the sanctuary that Thucydides describes in this last example is in fact a precinct near the city; thus the refugees were probably helots from Spartan households (i.e., domestic slaves) rather than rural helots from Spartan estates.
⁷⁴ Thucydides 1.128.   ⁷⁵ Aristophanes, *Knights* 1311–12 with scholion to line 1312.
⁷⁶ Aeschines 3.13 with scholion: "νόμος δ' ἦν τοὺς ἀποφυγόντας τῶν ἱκετῶν εἰς τὸ τοῦ Θησέως τέμενος ἀτιμωρήτους εἶναι."
⁷⁷ Etymologicum Magnum, Hesychius and Photius s.v. Θησεῖον.   ⁷⁸ Sinn 1993, 91.

opponents, as well as criminals, it also holds for slave suppliants. But what reasons might a slave set forth for fleeing his master? On the basis of the scant surviving evidence, it seems that a slave needed to accuse his or her master of unjust treatment. For example, in Achilles Tatius' novel, *Leukippe and Kleitophon* (second century CE), we learn that female slaves who fled to the temple of Artemis at Ephesus made formal accusations of wrongdoing against their masters.[79] A fragment of Eupolis' late fifth-century BCE comic play *Cities*, moreover, features a female slave who prefaces her reasons for fleeing to the sanctuary of Theseus by saying that she is suffering the evil things of the sort that she will now enumerate.[80] Unfortunately, the fragment breaks off before the specific offenses are listed!

As observed already in Chapter 1, at Athens slaves were covered by the law on hubris, which forbade outrageous treatment of one human being by another. Acts of hubris, therefore, were possibly cited by slaves to justify a claim to asylum at the shrine of Theseus.[81] While it is difficult to discern what exactly constituted hubris towards slaves at Athens, it is likely, however, that intolerable physical abuse by the slave's master – beating or starving a slave to the point of death – was the basis of a slave's request for asylum.[82] Plutarch's *Life of Theseus* comments on the general humanity exhibited at the shrine of Theseus towards the vulnerable, including slaves. The shrine of Theseus, Plutarch writes, was "a place of refuge for slaves and all the weak who fear the stronger, since Theseus himself was an advocate and helper and he received humanely the appeals of the lowly."[83]

Cases of asylum were decided by the priests of the sanctuary themselves, or by other magistrates in the polis.[84] An inscription from Andania in Messenia dating to 92 BCE, for example, indicates that the sanctuary is to serve as a refuge for slaves and specifies that priests are to adjudicate the cases of slaves.[85] On Samos in the third century BCE, temple officials

---

[79] 7.13; with Chaniotis 1996, 81.   [80] Eupolis, *Cities* fr. 229 K-A, quoted below.
[81] Christensen 1984; with earlier scholarship cited therein. It is important to emphasize that slaves, who had no legal rights at Athens, depended on their master or another citizen to prosecute a case of hubris. If the master himself was the alleged perpetrator, then the slave would have had no legal recourse except flight to the sanctuary of Theseus where even slaves could be heard (see below). On the law of hubris in relation to slaves, see Fisher 2005; Canevaro 2018.
[82] There were laws concerning cases in which a master killed his own slave, and they are referenced in several Athenian sources. For example, see Antiphon 6.4, where it is noted that a slave who is killed by his own master goes unavenged, although the master still purifies himself and avoids polluting shrines. Lycurgus (*Leoc.* 65) suggests that, in the old days, the penalty for killing a slave and free man was the same (death), implying that it was different in the fourth century.
[83] Plutarch, *Life of Theseus* 36.4.   [84] Chaniotis 1996, 79.
[85] *LSCG* 65 lines 80–84; cited in Chaniotis 1996, 80 n.56.

preside over the court responsible for interrogating the master and his slave.[86] In Achilles Tatius' novel (second century CE), "magistrates" arbitrate between the slave and her master.[87]

There were three possible outcomes of the process. If the master won the case, then the suppliant slave was to be handed back to him. If the slave won, then either the slave was dedicated to the god and became a slave of the god or the slave was sold to a new master.[88] Herodotus reports that, even up to his own time, any slave who fled to the sanctuary of Heracles at the mouth of the Nile became inviolate if he permitted himself to be branded with sacred marks and gave himself over to the god.[89] Herodotus seems to suggest that the slave became a servant at the shrine, and this seems plausible given that both branding and temple servants are well attested for ancient Egypt.[90]

A similar outcome may have resulted for helots who fled to the temple of Poseidon at Tainaron. A remarkable set of six inscriptions dating to the fourth century BCE records the dedication of individuals to the god.[91] While there is some question whether these individuals are Spartan helots or slaves belonging to the free non-citizen inhabitants of Laconia (the *perioikoi*), it is nevertheless clear that these inscriptions involve dedications of slaves. A further question, however, is whether, by entrusting themselves to the god, helots became temple slaves or free persons? This question arises because in later periods consecration at a temple became a standard mode of liberating a slave (see below).[92]

In regard to the temple at Tainaron, it has been argued that there is no need to consider dedication and liberation as exclusive options. By dedicating the slave to the god, the slave gained the god as his new master, and the god protected the slave from being seized by his former master. The slave is therefore free with regard to his former master, but is bound to perform certain services for the god. This paradoxical condition is

---

[86] Habicht 1957, 226–31.   [87] Achilles Tatius 7.13.
[88] Chaniotis (1996, 83), who states that "supplication did not change their legal condition but only their owner. There is no evidence that they were manumitted." Cf. Kudlien 1988, 243–45.
[89] Herodotus 2.113.2.
[90] Asheri et al. 2007, 323, with references. For temple slavery in ancient Greece, see Euripides *Ion*, 309–10. There, slaves are said to be either dedicated or sold to the temple (ἀνάθημα πόλεως ἤ τινος πραθεὶς ὕπο).
[91] *IG* v¹.1228–33; Ducat 1990. That said, the fact that only six survive is a puzzle. What happened to the many more helots/slaves who must have fled there over the centuries? Why are there only six dedications if this was the regular procedure? What makes these special? The loss of epigraphical record cannot be the only answer.
[92] Sokolowski (1954) proposed that sacral manumission originated in the right of asylum at sanctuaries, following Latte (1920, 105–108). Contra: Bömer 1960, 14.

exemplified in an inscription from Cos (third century BCE) in which a slave, Libys, and his descendants are dedicated to a sanctuary of Heracles and declared free, if they perform certain services.[93] In several other inscriptions, moreover, specific services, such as assistance with sacrifices, are enumerated.[94] For our purposes, what is clear is that this sort of partially free status was an amelioration of the slave's former condition.[95]

Such an improvement of one's condition was also probably the effect of the third possible outcome of a slave's flight to a sanctuary – namely, sale to a new master. This outcome seems to have been the expectation of slaves who fled to the shrine of Theseus at Athens. The second century CE lexicographer Pollux cites two fragments from lost comedies that attest to the fact that slave fugitives at this sanctuary were given the opportunity to seek a new master. They did this by formally "requesting a sale."[96]

> What people now say is that slaves "request" a sale, but in Aristophanes' [comedy] *Horai* they "find" a sale:
>
> "It is best for me to flee to the shrine of Theseus
> and there to remain, until I find a sale."
>
> Conversely, in Eupolis' [comedy] *Cities*, [a character says]
>
> "Such evils
> I suffer and so should I not request a sale?"

This comic evidence suggests that slaves took the initiative to flee to sanctuaries in order to seek sale to a new master. Yet one might reasonably wonder who would buy "a slave who had caused his master trouble by alleging ill-treatment and seeking sanctuary?"[97] One possible answer to this question is that "only slaveholders whose operations were based on brute violence and physical constraint, such as mill or mine operators," would be

---

[93] *LSCG* 177; with Ducat 1990. [94] Ducat 1990, 192–93.
[95] For other examples of such partially free status, see Zelnick-Abramowitz 2005; Sosin 2015.
[96] Christensen (1984, 24) citing Pollux (7.13), who cites in turn lines from Aristophanes' lost play *Horai* and Eupolis' lost play *Cities* (translated above): ὃ δ' οἱ νῦν φασὶ τοὺς οἰκέτας πρᾶσιν αἰτεῖν, ἔστιν εὑρεῖν ἐν Ἀριστοφάνους Ὥραις· ἐμοὶ κράτιστόν ἐστιν εἰς τὸ Θησεῖον δραμεῖν, ἐκεῖ δ', ἕως ἂν πρᾶσιν εὕρωμεν, μένειν = 577 K-A; ἄντικρυς δ'ἐν ταῖς Εὐπόλιδος Πόλεσι· κακὰ τοιάδε πάσχουσα μηδὲ πρᾶσιν αἰτῶ = 229 K-A. Cf. Plutarch, *Moralia* 166d.
[97] Hunt 2016, 153. Hunt notes (personal correspondence) that, according to Watson (1987, 121), in Roman law it was "standard practice in buying a slave to demand a guarantee that he had not fled to the statue [of the emperor and thus be afforded protection]." A tablet from Roman London concerns the sale of a female slave and provides evidence for an attestation that the slave in question was not "liable to wander off or run away." See Tomlin 2003. I thank Greg Woolf for drawing my attention to this example.

willing to buy such slaves.[98] But this answer fails to satisfy, since we might equally pose a different question, looking from the perspective of the slave: what slave would flee to a sanctuary, if he were bound to be sold to a master whose operations were based on brute violence and physical constraint, including the two most brutal and dangerous slave occupations of milling and mining? In other words, what was in it for slaves, if their conditions were bound to be bad and probably worse than those they had escaped? We might further observe, along with the character Aesop in his comic biography, that "no one, fleeing the good, goes to the bad."[99]

The answer to this puzzle is to acknowledge a slave's capacity for negotiation with a potential new owner in such a way as to ensure that *both* parties' interests were met. In fact, there is comparative evidence for just such negotiations between a potential owner and slave in the process of sale. In his study of slave markets in the antebellum American South, Walter Johnson demonstrates how slaves – despite their weaker position – were able to influence the outcome of sales in significant ways. Indeed, Johnson writes that "many slave sales had to be negotiated twice through – once with the buyer and once with the merchandise."[100] One example from Johnson's book will help illustrate how this worked, and may shed light on the sort of negotiations that might have taken place between a slave who had taken refuge in a sanctuary in ancient Greece and a potential new master.

Johnson relates the story of a slave named Edward Hicks, who "used flight to renegotiate the terms of his own sale." When Hicks learned that he had been sold to a slave-trader, he ran away. Hiding out in the woods, Hicks remained in contact with his "friends and brothers" in town "who told him that he had been advertised as a runaway" and "advised him to go to an old house where the cotton was kept and there to stay until the advertisement was over." Hicks followed these instructions and hid out in the house until "the slave-trader gave up and set off for New Orleans without him." When the slave-trader returned for another season of buying the next spring, somehow there was a white man in the town who wanted to buy Hicks. The trader then sold to this white man "the chance of Hicks' capture in the woods" – a common practice at the time. The price for Hicks was set at 800 dollars and, once the deal was made, the white man sent out some of his boys to tell Hicks, and a few days later Hicks presented himself to his new owner.[101]

---

[98] Hunt 2016, 154.   [99] *Vita G*, 26.   [100] Johnson 1999, 30.   [101] Johnson 1999, 32–33.

By hiding out, yet remaining in contact with his fellow slaves – and apparently also with potential buyers – Hicks avoided being sold away from his community and even exerted some control over the terms of his purchase. As Johnson writes,

> The connection between Hicks and the man who eventually bought the chance of his capture is obscure ... What is clear is that he had plenty of help from neighboring slaves in escaping, hiding and deciding when to come out. With the help of the very community from which he was to be separated by the trade, Hicks stayed away until he was satisfied with the terms of his own sale.[102]

For Hicks, the key condition for allowing himself to be captured would likely have been a prohibition on future sale. In return, Hicks would have promised his new master loyal service.[103]

Mutatis mutandis, this scenario sheds light on how slaves might negotiate their sale to a new master by seeking refuge in a sanctuary. It is noteworthy, moreover, that one might reasonably ask in the modern example, as of the ancient example, "who would buy a runaway"? The modern example emphatically shows that there were buyers even for runaways and, more importantly, that such sales were a product of negotiations between potential buyers and the slaves themselves.[104]

A fifth-century law from Gortyn may have implications for this reconstruction of negotiations between suppliant slaves and potential buyers. The law forbids the sale of suppliant slaves for a year after they have fled to the sanctuary.[105] Some scholars think that this delay was intended to allow time for extensive negotiation between the master and his slave before a sale was allowed.[106] Looking at the law from the slave-owner's perspective, some scholars suggest that the interval of up to a year was intended to allow the slave's master time to persuade the slave to return to his service. They suggest that if this persuasion was unsuccessful, then the slave would be

---

[102] Johnson 1999, 33.
[103] Another modern example can be found in the ways that runaway slaves managed to negotiate down the terms of their enslavement after the passage of the Northwest Ordinance in 1787. After the passage of the law, slaves in the Detroit area "ran away more frequently and refused to return unless they could negotiate better circumstances" (Miles 2017, 152). One tactic was to agree to return only as an indentured slave (voluntary slavery was not prohibited by the Northwest Ordinance), thereby establishing a time limit on servitude. Miles recounts the story of a slave named John Reed, whose tactic of flight and negotiation with a bounty hunter has striking parallels with Hicks' actions. Like Hicks, Reed negotiated favorable terms for his return: time-limited indenture rather than slavery.
[104] Johnson (1999, 45–46) reproduces a list of twenty-two slave sales recorded by a slave-trader. One entry concerns a slave who is noted to be a runaway, and although he is sold at a loss (bought at $750 and sold at $540), he is nevertheless sold.
[105] Gagarin and Perlman 2016 G41.4; cf. G72.1.39–49.   [106] Chaniotis 1996, 82.

sold.[107] But if we look at the law from the slave's point of view, it is equally true that such an extensive waiting period allowed a slave suppliant plenty of time to identify a potential new buyer and conduct the necessary negotiations regarding future treatment. Aristophanes' coinage of a term for one who hangs out in the shrine of Theseus, a "shrine-of-Theseus-loiterer," similarly suggests a long period of waiting and hence ample time for such negotiations.[108]

Summing up, one might conclude from this discussion that slaves in ancient Greece exploited Greek beliefs about the sanctity of temples and the right of divine protection in order to improve their conditions of enslavement. It is obvious that slaves would not have fled to sanctuaries if their conditions were bound only to get worse. Knowledge of the outcomes for slaves who fled to sanctuaries would have spread quickly among the slave community and the practice would have ended if it regularly resulted in worse outcomes for slaves than their previous conditions. That the practice did not end, and indeed was a common feature of life in fifth-century Athens, is again suggested by Aristophanes' coinage mentioned above – the "shrine-of-Theseus-loiterer." The most likely outcome of such situations, one might suggest, is that slaves would have been sold to new masters who entered into a bargain to swap humane treatment for loyalty.

Once again, we see in this example how slaves may have exploited Greek laws – this time religious laws – to improve their conditions in slavery. The example illustrates slaves' knowledge of Greek law and customs, as well as their ability to negotiate successfully with potential new masters. A big question that remains, however, is how frequently slaves actively manipulated sacred and secular law in order to improve their conditions. If the examples discussed above are simply rare cases, then there is reason to conclude that, in most cases, slaves were unable to exercise control over their fate. Moreover, it should be acknowledged that slaves in ancient Greece were variously situated and may not all have had the opportunity to exploit these tactics. A slave chained in the mines or imprisoned in a mill is unlikely to have had the opportunity to flee to a sanctuary, let alone engage in the type of legal ruse mentioned in the laws on damage and wounding. On the other hand, many slaves were embedded in the everyday life of the state and would have had ample opportunity not only to gain knowledge of the laws and customs of their owners but also to develop

---

[107] Gagarin and Perlman 2016, 298.
[108] Etymologicum Magnum s.v. θησειότριψ; with Gottesman 2014, 178.

social ties with citizens as well as other slaves (networks).[109] Some slaves, of course, were fellow Greeks in which case they would have been familiar with Greek customs concerning asylum and might even have had similar laws in their own states to Athenian laws on damage and wounding.[110]

Furthermore, the evidence we do have suggests that these actions by slaves were not rare. The existence of laws responding to the problem of collusion between slaves and third parties in suits for damage and wounding indicate that the problem was common enough to require legislation. The ubiquity of slave refuges in the Greek world, moreover, and the plentiful evidence for its importance at Athens and Sparta, suggest that slaves not infrequently resorted to this option. In short, while it would be rash to say all or even most slaves engaged in these tactics of resistance, there is enough evidence to show that they were a significant venue for slaves' maneuvers in their efforts to improve their conditions in slavery.

Controlling Masters: The Stick and the Carrot

Corresponding to the various modes of resistance by slaves surveyed above was a system of control that attempted to render slaves docile and obedient. While authors like Plato and Xenophon foreground the ways that masters could induce obedience through rewards and humane treatment, these same authors also reveal a much more brutal side of slave management involving chains, whipping and deprivation of food – among other cruel practices. In one of his works, Xenophon, for example, represents Socrates as exhorting his companion to

> consider how masters treat slaves ... they bring their lustfulness under control through starvation; they prevent them from stealing by locking up the places from which they could take anything; they stop them running away by chaining them; they drive out their laziness by blows.[111]

Similarly, Plato observes that some slave-owners treat slaves "like animals, using goads and whips, making the souls of their slaves slavish not once but many times over."[112]

Despite such stark portraits of the management of slaves, in his treatise on estate management, Xenophon is at pains to advocate a system of

---

[109] On the ways that citizens and slaves interacted in daily life, despite rigid legal categories, see Jones 1999; Cohen 2000; Vlassopoulos 2007; Taylor and Vlassopoulos 2015; and Chapters 3 and 4 above.
[110] See, for example, the laws concerning the liability of slaves at Gortyn, as discussed by Lewis (forthcoming).
[111] Xenophon, *Memorabilia* 2.1.16.   [112] Plato, *Laws* 777a4–6.

rewards rather than punishment as a better way of incentivizing slaves. Indeed, he begins his discussion of slave management by having his character Ischomachus, a wealthy Athenian citizen, observe the paradox that

> [i]n some households the slaves are all chained yet run away frequently; whereas elsewhere they are unchained and wish to work and to remain.[113]

The implication of this observation is that brutal physical constraint is often insufficient to create obedience, and that positive incentives are a better management tool. Indeed, Xenophon's character Ischomachus stresses that slaves – especially managerial slaves such as the household manager or steward (ταμίας) and the male overseer (ἐπίτροπος) – need positive inducements, e.g., praise or a share of the profits, just like free men, if they are to be productive and loyal.[114] Similarly, Plato in the *Laws* advocates treating one's slaves justly, rather than degrading their souls so they become less virtuous and more slavish. In these passages, both authors recognize the potential of slaves to act virtuously and in doing so come dangerously close to acknowledging the basic humanity and equality of slaves with the free. Plato even observes that some slaves have been superior to their free owners in terms of human goodness.[115]

Nevertheless, both Xenophon and Plato acknowledge that physical punishment is also a useful tool and that distinctions between slave and free should not be undermined by treating them as equals.[116] In particular, Xenophon emphasizes the similarity between training animals and slaves – a parallel that evokes the essential equation made by the Greeks between domesticated animals and slaves (see Chapter 1). Xenophon's character Ischomachus bluntly states, "The method of training that seems best for wild animals is also useful for teaching obedience to slaves."[117] In another work, moreover, Xenophon attributes this practice to the Persian king, who allegedly fed his slaves from his own table on the grounds that this practice would "implant in them a certain amount of goodwill, *just as it does in dogs* [emphasis mine]."[118] While Xenophon emphasizes the method of rewarding of both animals and slaves with food, we should not ignore the more brutal implications of the equation between slaves and animals: slaves, like animals, could be physically punished with goads, whips and other cruel methods of constraint and compulsion. Moreover, while

---

[113] Xenophon, *On Household Management* 3.4.
[114] Xenophon, *On Household Management* 14.9.   [115] Plato, *Laws* 776d–e.
[116] Plato, *Laws* 777e; Xenophon *On Household Management* 13.19, 14.3–8.
[117] Xenophon, *On Household Management* 13.9.   [118] Xenophon, *The Education of Cyrus* 8.2.4.

Xenophon emphasizes the technique of granting better food and clothing to well-behaved slaves, his stress on rewards obscures the opposite end of these management tools: starvation and deprivation of adequate clothing and shelter.

Another cruel tool of control is implied by Xenophon's character Ischomachus in an episode in which he takes his young wife on a tour of the slave quarters on his estate. He points out that the female slaves are separated from the male ones "so that they not produce children without his permission."[119] He then justifies the reward of well-behaved slaves with the opportunity to reproduce by arguing that good slaves become more loyal when they have children, whereas bad slaves become more troublesome. In other words, a slave-owner's control over his slaves was enhanced through the granting or withholding of reproductive rights – a practice that made some slaves more loyal presumably out of fear of the consequences of "misbehavior" for their families. This sort of psychological manipulation could undoubtedly be as cruel and traumatizing for slaves as more overt physical torture.

Masters also controlled their slaves through the threat of sale. In order to be effective, such a threat must have implied that the change would entail a move from a better to a worse condition of slavery, or equally would result in a rupture of whatever informal familial or other bonds of affection that a slave had formed. As we saw in Chapter 2, slave-owners typically showed no concern for the affective bonds of slaves when making a sale. Moreover, the threat that one Athenian slave-owner made to a female household slave, as we saw in Chapter 3, makes clear the implications of the sale for the well-being of the slave. According to the speaker in this lawcourt case, the owner threatened that, if the slave woman did not tell him all that she knew about his wife's adulterous affair, "she would be whipped and thrown in a grain mill with no respite from suffering."[120] A comic character, moreover, confirms that sale to a mill was a punishment for slaves who misbehaved, since "the mills are full of us Thracian slaves, since we are real men [i.e., unwilling to submit]."[121] As we have seen in Chapter 3, grain mills, like mines, were physically punishing and often dangerous places to labor. As the threat above implies, slaves who were sent to such places were required to toil continuously, driven on by the whip, suffering both exhaustion and physical pain. While we have no evidence for the

---

[119] Xenophon, *On Household Management* 9.5. [120] Lysias 1.18. Cf. Demosthenes 45.33.
[121] Menander, *Aspis* 245.

ultimate fate of such slaves, it is likely that they, like many slaves in the mines, were literally worked to death and quite quickly too.

Just as slaves could be rendered obedient through punishment, they could also be incentivized to work hard through rewards. On a small scale, these rewards could be better food or clothing, as we have seen, and even words of praise from the master. On a more significant scale, masters could reward their slaves with greater responsibilities; for instance, with managerial roles on a farm, or in a workshop or bank. Such slaves were often granted greater personal autonomy, such as the right to reproduce, form a family or live independently from their masters.[122] One of the most significant perks for such slaves, moreover, was the privilege of keeping a share of the profits of their labor. It is important to stress that a slave's earnings were granted as a reward that could be retracted at any time. In other words, a slave's income was not legally secure but subject to the continued goodwill of his owner. Nevertheless, the de facto control of a portion of their earnings was a huge incentive to slaves to work loyally and profitably for their masters. The effectiveness of this tool derived not only from its capitalization on the slave's desire for some financial autonomy but also from the slave's goal of freedom itself. Indeed, if the master was willing, the slave could save up her earnings and purchase herself (or a family member) from her master.

Grants of Freedom

The ultimate carrot that a master could offer for the hard work of his slave was a grant of freedom. Indeed, the effectiveness of this incentive was recognized not just by private owners but also by the state, which sometimes offered freedom to slaves in return for military service or information about subversive plots in times of crisis (see below). Unfortunately, however, the evidence suggests that most slaves were never offered this reward, and only those slaves who managed to obtain their master's goodwill and were very enterprising in gathering resources to purchase their freedom were able to obtain this reward. Moreover, of those who were freed, many were granted this privilege only on the death of their masters, or even after a period of continued service to the family following the death of their masters. A few examples will illustrate these points.

---

[122] On skilled slaves who lived independently of their masters, see Chapter 3 above; Fisher 2008; Kazakévich 2008; and Kamen 2011. Kamen, however, suggests that these are freed ex-slaves, not slaves.

One extraordinary example of a slave who managed to purchase her freedom was the prostitute Neaira, whom we have already encountered (Chapter 3). Neaira's case, however, illustrates the relatively rarity of such grants of freedom, as well as the often limited scope of the grant and the precariousness of freedom once attained. First, it is important to stress that, according to our source, Neaira was given the opportunity to purchase her freedom only due to the extraordinary goodwill of her owners who appear to have grown fond of her (after many years of sexually exploiting her) and were willing to do her a favor.[123] As a result, her owners offered to forgive one third of her purchase price if she could raise the remaining two thirds. Since Neaira was a valuable slave this meant that she had to raise 2,000 drachmas – a very considerable sum.

As we saw in Chapter 3, Neaira was a resourceful woman and she succeeded in raising her purchase price. She did so by canvassing her former clients and persuading them to donate towards her freedom. Putting together these contributions with money she had saved from her own earnings, she further appealed to one of her former clients, an Athenian named Phrynion, to make the actual purchase. As a slave, Neaira herself did not have the legal standing to make a purchase, even when it concerned "purchasing herself." The process of gaining freedom therefore took the form of a sale, but with the legal purchaser "buying" the slave "for the purpose of freedom" from funds gathered by the slave herself.[124] As such, the sale was a legal fiction and such sales for the purposes of freedom are sometimes referred to as fictive sales.[125] Such "sales" were witnessed by third parties who could later attest to the freedom of the former slave if it were ever challenged.[126] That such protections against reenslavement were needed is illustrated by the next phase of Neaira's life story.

Indeed, despite the willingness of her owners to allow her to purchase herself as well as her own success in both raising the funds and finding a sponsor to transact the sale, Neaira's freedom was precarious. She was in fact very nearly re-enslaved. Indeed, the Athenian Phrynion, who had contributed a portion of her purchase price and transacted the actual purchase from her former owners, claimed her as his slave when she deserted him and took up with another Athenian named Stephanus. Neaira was only saved from re-enslavement by Stephanus, who defended

---

[123] Pseudo-Demosthenes 59.30.   [124] Pseudo-Demosthenes 59.29–32.   [125] Kamen 2014.
[126] Neaira's sale, for example, was witnessed by the Athenian citizen Philagros of the district (deme) of Melite, who is called as a witness in the trial: pseudo-Demosthenes 59.32.

her freedom before the polemarch, the magistrate in charge of the affairs of non-citizen residents (metics) at Athens. Phrynion, however, did not give up in his attempt to re enslave Neaira and responded to Stephanus' support of Neaira's freedom by prosecuting Stephanus. When both sides submitted the dispute to private arbitration, it was decided that Neaira was in fact free but that she was required to spend alternate days living with each man, or to conform to whatever arrangement these men should agree between them.[127] Neaira's "freedom," therefore was not only precarious but also conditional upon this very significant restraint on her place and mode of residence.

As noted in Chapter 3, no fewer than sixty-three women number among the one hundred and fifty-eight (legible) individuals on the inscriptions recording the dedications of silver bowls in commemoration of the grant of freedom at Athens.[128] This number shows that there were a significant number of women who secured the resources to gain freedom. Many of these women appear to be textile workers (fifty-one), and it would be fascinating to know their personal stories. Unfortunately, the stone inscriptions reveal only their profession and the fact of their attainment of freedom. We may well admire their industry and yet also wonder whether there were limitations on their freedom and whether their freedom was as precarious as Neaira's appears to have been.

The slave-bankers Pasion and Phormion are further illustrations of slaves who were permitted to keep a portion of their earnings and used the money to purchase their freedom from their masters. While Pasion is certainly not typical in the extent of his wealth and his ultimate attainment of citizenship in addition to freedom, his life story as revealed in several law-court speeches suggests that he was rewarded for his extraordinary skill in banking operations with both a handsome salary and the opportunity to purchase his freedom.[129] Moreover, Pasion later offered his own slave Phormion the same opportunities to keep a share of his earnings and ultimately purchase his freedom.[130] The examples of Neaira, Pasion and Phormion suggest that it was only relatively "privileged" slaves who had the opportunity to purchase their freedom, both because of their ability to accumulate resources and due to the goodwill that their services generated in their owners.

---

[127] Pseudo-Demosthenes 59.45.
[128] Rosivach 1989, 366. Patterson (1982, 263) suggests that in most societies women, and particularly prostitutes, have a higher chance of gaining their freedom because of the frequency of sexual relations with the master.
[129] Demosthenes 36.43.   [130] Demosthenes 36.4.

While these examples illustrate grants of freedom that were extended during the lifetime of the owner, some slaves were freed only on the death of their owners. Demosthenes, for example, mentions that his father freed his trusted slave Milyas, the manager of his knife factory, only on his deathbed.[131] Moreover, literary accounts of the lives of some famous fourth-century philosophers suggest that some owners made provision for the freedom of their slaves in their wills.[132] For example, Aristotle freed some (not all) of his slaves, specifying different time frames for each. A slave girl named Ambracis is freed immediately upon his death, whereas three other slaves – Tycho, Philo and Olympios, as well as an unnamed child – are granted their freedom only upon the marriage of his daughter. With regard to his other slaves, Aristotle states, somewhat vaguely, that they are not to be sold and should be given their freedom "at the proper age" and "if they deserve it."[133] In the wills of other philosophers, moreover, freedom is granted only after a specified term of service following the death of the master and "if they are blameless."[134]

The practice of setting some conditions – such as a period of continued loyal service – on a grant of freedom is best known from the Hellenistic and Roman periods (see below), although it existed at least by the fourth century.[135] Moreover, it has given rise to some debate about whether such grants of conditional freedom created an in-between status of "partially free" individuals.[136] For current purposes, the key point is that by freeing a slave, fully or conditionally in his will, an owner maximized the incentive for the slave to work hard for the owner's entire lifetime and sometimes for some period afterwards. The owner thereby gained a potentially very long period of profit from his slave, who often will have used his prime working years in service to his master. By offering this incentive to hard work, the master thereby optimized his use of the slave, freeing him only in his later years when he was likely to be less productive anyway.

---

[131] Demosthenes 29.25.
[132] The authenticity of these wills is generally accepted: Harrison 1968, 183–84; Todd 1993, 127; Lewis 2015, 24. Klees (1998, 301), however, considers this testimony unrepresentative.
[133] Diogenes Laertius, *Lives of the Philosophers* 5.11–16.
[134] Diogenes Laertius, *Lives of the Philosophers* 5.55. This condition of "blamelessness" is paralleled in many of the grants of freedom from the second century BCE from Delphi: see e.g., *SGDI* 1755, 1764.
[135] Plato, *Laws* 915a, for example, provides penalties for a freedman who does not perform services.
[136] For a forceful argument that conditional freedom was not freedom or partial freedom but deferred freedom, see Sosin 2015. For the older view that such grants were equivalent to partial freedom, see Zelnick-Abramowitz 2005.

Of course, some slaves may still have been in their prime when freed, and these had the most to gain from this reward. Yet, as we saw in Neaira's case, the grant of freedom was not necessarily secure, and many slaves may have had to defend themselves against attempts to reenslave them.[137] In the law-court case on the disputed status of Pancleon (Chapter 4), for example, no fewer than three people tried to claim Pancleon as their slave, while Pancleon himself claimed that he was a free citizen. Another law-court speech mentions two cases in which it is alleged that men were executed for enslaving individuals who were actually free. According to this account, the Athenian people executed Menon the miller because he kept a free boy from Pellene (in the Peloponnesus) in his mill. Similarly, one Euthymachus was executed because he put a free woman from Olynthus in a brothel.[138] The fact that these two individuals were not Athenians but metics presumably made it easier for potential enslavers to assimilate them to slaves. The seriousness with which the Athenians took the crime of enslavement of the free, moreover, is indicated by the task given to magistrates responsible for enforcing the law to arrest "enslavers" (ἀνδραποδισταί).[139] Sadly, we cannot assume that all such cases of wrongful enslavement were checked, and many former slaves may have found themselves unable to defend themselves against re-enslavement.

Such outcomes were possible, in part because grants of freedom were largely private acts, with at most a few witnesses to support a claim to freedom if it were later contested.[140] For example, when Milyas' freedom was disputed, Demosthenes is able to offer only the testimony of some female slaves in his household to prove that his father had emancipated Milyas on his deathbed.[141] Some owners (possibly at the suggestion of their soon-to-be-freed favored slaves) apparently tried to buttress a grant of freedom by having it proclaimed publicly in the theater, thereby gaining thousands of witnesses to the act. According to the Athenian politician Aeschines, such announcements had become an inconvenience to the performances in the theater and were banned by the fourth century in Athens.[142]

---

[137] The Delphic inscriptions recording grants of freedom dating to the second and first centuries BCE almost always contain a clause asserting the inviolability of the newly freed person and providing procedures for redressing illegal reenslave ment. See e.g., *SGDI* 1685, 1686, 1688 etc.; with discussion in Zelnick-Abramowitz 2005, 292–300.
[138] Dinarchus 1.23.   [139] [Aristotle] *The Constitution of the Athenians* 52.
[140] Todd 1993, 126–27.
[141] Demosthenes 29.25. Similarly, Neaira's sale for the purpose of freedom is witnessed by a single individual (pseudo-Demosthenes 59.32).
[142] Aeschines 3.41–45.

Grants of Freedom to Slaves by the State in Times of Crisis

Another method of attempting to secure a grant of freedom was to enlist the support of the gods. One way masters did this was by "selling" their slave to a god. Just as in the case of the fictive sales discussed above, so called "sacral fictive sales" were not real sales but transactions through which a slave was "sold" for the purposes of freedom. The key difference in the case of sacred fictive sales was that the god served as "buyer" of the slave, and thereby became divine protector of the resulting freedom of the slave. Any attempt to enslave such a slave risked divine vengeance. Moreover, records of such "sales" were kept in temples and served as further proof of a grant of freedom. This method of publicizing grants of freedom goes back to at least the sixth century in Boeotia, but becomes prevalent in the Hellenistic and Roman periods.[143] Most strikingly, inscriptions on stone at the sanctuary of Apollo at Delphi dating to the period between 201 BCE and 100 CE record grants of freedom to over 1350 slaves.[144] Most of these record "sales" to the god Apollo, but some also record "sales" to private individuals for the purpose of freedom.[145] Either way, the god served as witness and guarantor of freedom of the former slave. Similarly, the records of the silver bowls dedicated by freedmen at the sanctuary of Athena on the Athenian acropolis not only created a public record of a former slave's free status, but enlisted the goddess herself as witness and by extension guarantor of this fact.

Despite the seemingly high number of slaves freed at Delphi, it is important to stress that only a small proportion of the tens of thousands of slaves who lived in classical Greece ever gained their freedom. Most toiled in slavery until they died, and only the few relatively favored slaves avoided this fate. Nevertheless, the offer of freedom was an important instrument in the slave-owner's toolbox, and one that the state itself took advantage of on occasion. It is to these state-initiated grants of freedom, and the ways that slaves took advantage of them, that this chapter now turns.

Grants of Freedom to Slaves by the State in Times of Crisis

We have already seen (Chapter 3), that Greek states sometimes called on slaves to serve as soldiers and rowers, and that they sometimes offered the

---

[143] Boeotia: Darmezin 1999; compare a fifth-century list on Chios: Robert 1938, 118–26.
[144] Grants of freedom from Delphi: *SGDI* 1684–2342. Other important records are found in Boeotia, Phocis, Locris, Thessaly and in the Peloponnesus (e.g., at Olympia and Tainaron). On grants of freedom recorded in sanctuaries, see Kamen 2014; Lewis 2015; with earlier references cited therein.
[145] For example, *SGDI* 1694 records the fictive sale of a female slave named Thraissa to the private individual Boethos.

reward of freedom and even citizenship in return. Typically, such appeals to slaves occurred in times of crisis, although arming slaves is surprisingly common in other historical periods and it makes some sense that states or factions within states might try to tap this large population in its war efforts.

Yet slaves had a potentially even more important asset in the state's self-preservation. Since slaves often lived and worked in close proximity to their owners, they often had intimate knowledge of their owner's affairs.[146] In particular, they were aware of any activities that might threaten the security of the state, such as political conspiracies or sacrilegious behavior that might bring the wrath of the gods down on the community. Obviously, states had a great interest in gathering such intelligence and were willing to offer great rewards in return. Indeed, some states offered slaves freedom, money and even citizenship in return for such information.[147] Moreover, while states incentivized slaves to report on their owners through such rewards, slaves themselves could in some cases take the initiative to exploit these opportunities, and potentially even blackmail their owners. The practice of offering freedom to slaves for informing on their owners, therefore, was a double-edged sword in that it gave slaves a bargaining chip in their relations with their owners. It is in any case remarkable that the state had the power to violate a citizen's property rights when the well-being of the state was under threat.

A few examples will illustrate these points. On the eve of the launching of an invasion of Sicily in 415, the Athenians woke up to find that some persons had mutilated the stone statues of Hermes, the god of travelers, that stood in various public and private spaces in the city. Determined to get to the bottom of this sacrilegious act that could threaten the success of the expedition, they passed a decree offering rewards to any citizen, foreigner or slave who might have information about the perpetrators of this act or any other act of impiety.[148] Two slaves, among other individuals, came forward and laid information against their owners. One Andromachus informed against his owner Alcibiades, and Lydus informed against his owner Pherecles.[149] Besides being granted immunity for their testimony, they were given a monetary reward and probably freedom as well. Indeed, it is clear from several other pieces of evidence that freedom was the standard reward for slaves for providing information. For example, a speaker in a law-court speech uses the assumption that his slaves would

---

[146] Hunter 1994. [147] OR 176; Osborne 2000, 83–84. [148] Thucydides 6.27.
[149] Andocides 1.12, 17.

denounce him and claim freedom, as proof that he did not commit an impiety.[150] Plato, furthermore, probably reflects Athenian law when he sets freedom as the reward for slaves who denounce their masters for unjust acts such as mistreatment of one's parents and failure to disclose the discovery of treasure.[151] These examples raise the question of the potential for slaves to take the initiative in denouncing their masters. Were slaves able to "police" their owners and even manipulate them into granting concessions or even freedom itself?[152]

Indications of the potential for slaves to use their ability to testify as a means to extract concessions from their owners can be found in the frequent accusations in law-court cases that an opponent had freed his slave in order to avoid a challenge to have the slave tortured for testimony.[153] While such a challenge could always be rejected by the slave's owner, as we saw in Chapter 4, such a refusal gave the appearance of having something to hide and hence guilt. One way to avoid such implications was to free a slave. Seen from the slave's perspective, this result could be the outcome of manipulation or suggestion by the slave.

It is important, however, not to exaggerate the power of the slave over her master through her testimony. As just noted, in private cases, owners had sole power to decide whether their slaves testified and owners could always reject challenges to have their slaves examined under torture for testimony. Moreover, public cases such as treason or impiety in which the state encouraged slaves to denounce their masters were relatively rare. Moreover, if a slave's testimony proved false and his master was exonerated, the slave risked severe punishment from his master and possibly execution by the state.[154] Nevertheless, warfare and public inquiries into acts that threatened the security of the state, not to mention misbehavior in private, represented opportunities for slaves to maneuver within the cracks in the ideology and practice of slavery in order to claim freedom.

Conclusion

In this chapter, we have examined the range of ways that slaves worked within the system of slavery in order to advance their interests, and conversely, the ways that slave-owners attempted to control their slaves. We have seen that slave tactics ranged from accommodation to modes of

---

[150] Lysias 7.16. [151] Plato, *Laws* 932d, 914a.
[152] This is the question that Hunter (1994) poses and answers insightfully in the affirmative.
[153] Lysias 4, 12, 14; Isocrates 17.50; Demosthenes 29.14. [154] Andocides 1.20.

covert and overt resistance. Moreover, while violent rebellion was rare, there were occasions when slaves took advantage of moments of crisis to flee their owners en masse and – in the case of the Spartan helots – engage in prolonged revolt. Comparative evidence explains this pattern by showing that the conditions for slave rebellion were largely present at Sparta but absent elsewhere.

Recognition of the rarity of full-blown slave rebellion in history cleared the way for examining the more common methods of coping with life in slavery, including the formation of slave communities and culture that expressed the hopes, fears and fantasies of the enslaved. Traces of slave culture were found in animal trickster fables, heroic slave narratives such as the tale of Drimakos and performative genres such as mimes. Each of these modes of expression articulated slaves' hopes of revenge and helped build a sense of self-worth and even superiority among slaves.

Finally, this chapter examined the sophisticated tactics used by some slaves to leverage Greek legal, political and religious institutions to improve their conditions in slavery or even escape slavery altogether. The ability of slaves to exploit these tactics was a consequence of the embeddedness of slaves in the fabric of Greek society, an embeddedness that allowed slaves ample opportunity to gain intimate knowledge of the laws and customs of their place of enslavement. Moreover, despite the attempts of slave-owners to deny the rationality and humanity of their slaves, slaves showed an almost uncanny ability to upset these ideological constructions of difference and exploit the very capacities that their owners simultaneously both denied and – in practice – often utilized. Indeed, it was this fault line in the system of slavery that provided the opening for the various techniques by which slaves attempted to make their life liveable.

CHAPTER 6

Why Should We Care?

> It is said that when Gandhi was asked by a reporter what he thought of Western Civilization, he replied, "I think it would be a good idea."[1]
>
> The past is never dead. It isn't even past.
> William Faulkner, Requiem for a Nun

It is fitting to end a study of slavery in ancient Greece by asking why – in the twenty-first century – we should care. This question was broached already in Chapter 1, but the answers sketched there lacked the support of the evidence and arguments presented throughout this book. It is now time to take stock and flesh out these justifications.

The first justification for this book was to give "historical due" to a segment of the population of ancient Greece that – although often briefly acknowledged – is seldom placed front and center of an historical study. Indeed, those books that do concern themselves with slavery tend to adopt the perspectives and experiences of slave-owners rather than slaves. By contrast, this book has attempted to recover the perspectives, agency and experiences of slaves themselves, from the moment of enslavement, through their laboring lives until their deaths or, in some cases, their attainment of freedom. This goal has required reading our sources "against the grain," as well as the use of evidence from other time periods to illuminate relatively scanty evidence from ancient Greece. It has often required frank admission of the inadequacy of our evidence and sometimes even liberal use of the imagination.

The result of these efforts has been first and foremost to reveal the great variety of experiences of slavery. We have encountered slaves who were whipped, tortured and chained. We have also encountered slaves who lived independently of their owners, were able to keep a portion of the fruits of

---

[1] This anecdote has been associated with Gandhi since the 1960s, and, although possibly apocryphal, is quite apt.

their labor and enjoyed a good, sometimes even very high, standard of living. Between these extremes existed the vast majority of slaves – the farm laborers, skilled craftsmen and the household slaves who labored day-in, day-out at the command of their owners. At Sparta and in many other city-states, the vast majority of slaves worked the land. In Athens, in addition to agricultural work, many slaves labored at specialized crafts such as metalworking, stonemasonry and carpentry. Some slaves even supervised other slaves as managers of estates, workshops or mining operations. Thousands of slaves spent their days laboring in the mines, washing the ore or stoking the smelting furnaces.

Our sources enable us to reconstruct vivid portraits of some slaves. The experiences of others can be sketched only in broad outline. Nevertheless, the attempt to describe the lives of tens of thousands of individuals who lived as slaves in ancient Greece is an important part of a full historical account of ancient Greece. Such an account acknowledges the true scale of human suffering that Greek "civilization" engendered. A full account of ancient Greece, in sum, acknowledges how Greeks conquered, captured and enslaved thousands of individuals, both fellow Greeks and non-Greeks. A full account of ancient Greece, moreover, acknowledges how Greeks deprived countless individuals of their freedom, forced them to work, and appropriated (stole) all or part of the fruits of their labor. A full account of ancient Greece, in other words, acknowledges the violence, suffering and injustice at the heart of the ancient Greek state.

A full account of ancient Greece also acknowledges the enormous contribution that slave labor made directly or indirectly to the features of Greek society that are so often heralded – its material prosperity, its sophisticated political systems, its military victories and its artistic and intellectual accomplishments. As we have seen, slave labor was central to agricultural production, manufacturing and commerce. Moreover, slaves were essential to the operation of the Athenian democracy – for example, they assisted magistrates, maintained public records and kept order in public spaces. More importantly, it was slave labor that provided citizens with the leisure to practice politics. In addition, slaves fought in the armies and rowed in the ships that won some of the most famous battles of antiquity – Marathon, Plataea, Salamis and Arginusae. Slaves sculpted the columns of the architectural marvels of ancient Greece, and painted the pots that are displayed in museums around the world.[2]

---

[2] See DuBois (2003, 59–81) for an excellent discussion of the ways that museums erase slavery from the history of ancient Greece.

When it comes to intellectual accomplishments – the poetry, the philosophy and the drama – it must at least be acknowledged that slaves enabled the leisure that allowed the free to develop such fields. A more generous assessment would allow for the influence of popular culture, including slave culture, on literature written by elites.[3] Not only does Plato give a laudatory account of the Thracian cult of Bendis, for example, at the beginning of his famed work the *Republic*, but his representation of Socrates often draws on themes from popular culture, including traditions about the slave Aesop.[4] A full account of ancient Greece, therefore, also brings to light the very significant contribution that slaves – many of them from lands further east – made to what we call "Greek" culture. Indeed, given that many slaves were brought to Greece from non-Greek lands, one might even ask in what sense "Greek civilization" was wholly "Greek."[5]

A second major goal of focusing on the experience of slaves in ancient Greece is to recover their voices and agency in the historical record. Indeed, integral to giving slaves their "historical due" is to grant them dignity as historical agents alongside their owners. While their choices were often constrained by their conditions of slavery, we have seen how slaves strategized, sometimes in ingenious ways, to increase their autonomy and improve their conditions in slavery, or even to escape slavery altogether. Such an approach acknowledges the intelligence of slaves, their ability to master not only the Greek language but also other aspects of the culture of their owners (e.g., religion and the law) in order to leverage them to their own advantage. As we have seen, Greek religion reflects these efforts in the existence of shrines that served as places of refuge for abused slaves. Greek laws reflect these efforts not only in acknowledging the right of slaves to seek refuge and transfer to a new master, but also in the ways in which the laws on such acts as damage and wounding reveal that slaves could and did act in their own interest against the will of their owners. The Athenian law on citizenship itself shows that slaves sometimes even tried to surreptitiously cross the most fiercely guarded of status boundaries – the boundary between citizen and slave. We cannot know how many slaves succeeded in passing as citizens, but the traces of such efforts suggest that some did.

Thirdly and finally, an inquiry into slavery in ancient Greece is justified by the light that it sheds on patterns of discriminatory thought in ancient

---

[3] Forsdyke 2012.
[4] Kurke 2011. For the *Life of Aesop* as a partial reflection of slave culture, see Forsdyke 2012.
[5] This question was raised provocatively by Bernal (1987) although he did not focus on slavery, but rather on broader patterns of migration and settlement from Egypt and Phoenicia beginning in prehistoric times.

and modern times. As we have seen, the Greeks justified the enslavement of individuals primarily on the basis of imagined physical, mental and moral qualities that they believed to be caused by environmental and cultural conditions, including political regime. Although these views developed into blatantly racist beliefs about the suitability of non-Greeks for slavery, the Greeks continued to enslave other Greeks as well as non-Greeks, and never justified slavery on the basis of superficial biological differences such as skin color. Indeed, because there was no obvious physical marker by which the Greeks determined who was a slave and who was not, they had to work hard to construct imagined differences such as poor posture, irrationality and "a slavish nature." In this sense, the justification for subjecting a portion of humanity to enslavement in ancient Greece was different from the dominant paradigm of biological racism, with its focus on skin color, that has characterized modern racist thought since the nineteenth century.[6]

The difference between ancient Greek and modern justifications of slavery, moreover, provides an instructive perspective on the artificiality of such ideologies and the ways that they can change over time. Indeed, ancient Greece is a startling example of how purportedly rational people – as the Greeks are conventionally judged to have been, and as we also pride ourselves on being – are capable of believing in wholly arbitrary and also wholly convenient constructions of difference. We are forced to ask ourselves how the Greeks could dismiss the individuals on whom they relied to run the machinery of the state, manage their businesses and build their temples – not to mention grow their food, manufacture their swords and care for their children – as not rational or needing guidance from the free? The fact that the Greeks justified the enslavement of individuals in ways that are so obviously faulty and self-serving cautions us to look carefully at our own conscious and unconscious biases and the ways that these biases undergird the differences of power and resources that continue to plague our own societies.

Finally, a study that places slaves front and center in the history of ancient Greece can play a role in confronting modern appropriations of the past to justify discriminatory beliefs. By demonstrating not only the arbitrariness and injustice of the subjection of some individuals to slavery but also the incredible resourcefulness of slaves in both enduring and resisting their enslavement, the history of slaves in ancient Greece refutes

---

[6] Other excellent explorations of racism in the ancient world include Isaac 2004; Lape 2010; McCoskey 2012.

easy assumptions about inferiority or unsuitability of certain groups for citizenship and full political enfranchisement. The views of Aristotle – and indeed the Greeks in general – have cast a long shadow over the modern world, from justifications of slavery in nineteenth century America to the far-right political groups of today who appropriate the example of ancient Greece to justify white supremacy.[7] An account of the past that grants slaves a central place in the legacy of ancient Greece can go some way to countering the false narratives upon which such appropriations are based.

---

[7] See Zuckerberg (2018) for a powerful critique of appropriations of (false ideas about) ancient Greece and Rome by white supremacists and other far-right groups.

Bibliographical Essay

For recent debate about definitions of slavery and slave societies, with review of previous scholarship on these questions, see N. Lenski and C. Cameron, eds., *What Is a Slave Society? The Practice of Slavery in Global Perspective* (Cambridge, 2018). For an original and still influential definition of slavery from a comparative perspective, see O. Patterson, *Slavery and Social Death* (Cambridge, MA, 1982). For a recent reassessment of Patterson's definition, see J. Bodel and W. Scheidel, eds., *On Human Bondage: After Slavery and Social Death* (Malden, MA, 2017). For modern legal definitions of slavery, see J. Allain, ed., *The Legal Understanding of Slavery: From the Historical to the Contemporary* (Oxford, 2012). On forms of slavery in contemporary times, see K. Bales, *Disposable People. New Slavery in Global Perspective* (Berkeley, 1999) and *New Slavery: A Reference Handbook* (Santa Barbara, 2000).

For a trenchant assessment of the methodological challenges and potential pitfalls of attempting to understand ancient slavery, see N. McKeown, *The Invention of Ancient Slavery* (London, 2007). For a similar methodological challenge from an historian of slavery in the American South, see W. Johnson, "On Agency," *Journal of Social History* 37 (2003): 113–24.

For an excellent recent overview of slavery in both ancient Greece and Rome, see P. Hunt, *Ancient Greek and Roman Slavery* (Malden, MA, 2018); see also J. Andreau and R. Descat, *Esclave en Grèce et à Rome* (Paris, 2006). Translated by M. Leopold as *The Slave in Greece and Rome* (Madison, WI, 2011). For a recent collection of essays by experts on various aspects of ancient (mainly Greek and/or Roman) slavery, see K. R. Bradley and P. A. Cartledge, eds., *The Ancient Mediterranean World*, Vol. 1 of *The Cambridge World History of Slavery* (Cambridge, 2011).

For studies of slavery focused on ancient Greece, see Y. Garlan, *Slavery in Ancient Greece*, rev. ed., trans. J. Lloyd (Ithaca, 1988); and H. Klees, *Sklavenleben im klassischen Griechenland* (Stuttgart, 1998). More recent studies include P. Ismard, *La Démocratie contre les experts: Les esclaves publics en Grèce ancienne* (Paris, 2015) (translated by J. M. Todd as *Democracy's Slaves: A Political History of Ancient Greece* (Cambridge, MA, 2017)); and P. Ismard, *La cité et ses esclaves: Institution, Fictions, Experiences* (Paris, 2019). For an insightful study of Greek slavery in its broader Mediterranean context, see D. M. Lewis, *Greek Slave Systems in their Eastern Mediterranean Context, c.800–146 BC* (Oxford, 2018). For more specialized studies of aspects of slavery in ancient Greece, see the Bibliography.

On slavery in ancient Rome, K. Bradley's *Slavery and Society at Rome* (Cambridge 1994) is still the most vivid and compelling general account. Bradley attempts to recover the experience of slaves themselves, and this current book was inspired partly by his ethical commitment to understanding slavery from the slaves' own perspective. See now also K. Bradley, *The Bitter Chain of Slavery* (Washington, DC, 2015). For a reading of slavery in Roman literature, especially comedy, see W. Fitzgerald, *Slavery and the Roman Literary Imagination* (Cambridge, 2000); and now A. Richlin, *Slave Theater in the Roman Republic: Plautus and Popular Comedy* (Cambridge, 2017).

For comparative studies of ancient and modern slavery, see C. Katsari and E. Dal Lago, eds., *From Captivity to Freedom: Themes in Ancient and Modern Slavery* (Leicester, 2008). D. Geary and K. Vlassopoulos, eds., "Slavery, Citizenship and the State in Classical Antiquity and the Modern Americas," special issue, *European Review of History* 16 (2009); and S. Hodkinson and D. Geary, eds., *Slaves and Religions in Greco-Roman Antiquity and Modern Brazil* (Newcastle Upon Tyne, 2012). On slavery in the American Old South, the work of Eugene Genovese on slave culture and slave rebellion is still enlightening: E. Genovese, *Roll, Jordan, Roll: The World the Slaves Made* (New York, 1974); E. Genovese, *From Rebellion to Revolution: Afro-American Slave Revolts in the Making of the Modern World* (Baton Rouge, 1979). W. E. B. Du Bois's *The Souls of Black Folk* (Chicago, 1904) is also a must read for anyone interested in slavery and its legacy in America. For excellent recent studies that shed important light on slave agency in various spheres, including the law, see W. Johnson, *Soul by Soul: Life Inside the Antebellum Slave Market* (Cambridge, MA, 1999); A. Gross, *What Blood Won't Tell: A History of Race on Trial in America* (Cambridge, MA, 2008); and D. Scharfstein, *The Invisible Line: Three American Families and the Secret Journey from Black to White* (New York, 2011).

For ancient ideologies of slavery and the influence of these (especially Aristotle) on modern ideologies of slavery, see P. Garnsey, *Ideas of Slavery from Aristotle to Augustine* (Cambridge, 1996); L. Hanke, *Aristotle and the American Indians: A Study of Race Prejudice in the Modern World* (Indiana, 1959); M. I. Finley, *Ancient Slavery and Modern Ideology*, ed. B. D. Shaw (Princeton, 1998); and R. de Bivar Marquese and F. Duarte Joly, "Panis, disciplina et opus servo: The Jesuit Ideology in Portuguese America and Greco-Roman Ideas of Slavery," in *Slave Systems: Ancient and Modern*, ed. E. Dal Lago and C. Katsari (Cambridge, 2008), 214–30.

Bibliography

Abbreviations

BNJ	I. Worthington, ed. *Brill's New Jacoby*. Leiden, 2005–.
Davies *APF*	J. K. Davies. *Athenian Propertied Families*. Oxford, 1971.
FGrH	F. Jacoby, ed. *Die Fragmente de griechischen Historiker*. Leiden, 1923–69.
IC	F. Halbherr and M. Guarducci, eds. *Inscriptiones Creticae*. Rome: Libreria dello Stato, 1935–50.
IG	*Inscriptiones Graecae*. 1873–.
K-A	R. Kassel and C. Austin, eds. *Poetae Comici Graeci*. 8 vols. 1983–2001.
LSCG	F. Sokolowski. *Lois sacrées des cités grecques*. Paris, 1969.
ML	R. Meiggs and D. M. Lewis, eds. *A Selection of Greek Historical Inscriptions to the End of the Fifth Century B.C.* Oxford, 1969.
OR	R. Osborne and P. J. Rhodes, eds. *Greek Historical Inscriptions 478–404 BC*. Oxford, 2017.
PMG	D. L. Page, ed. *Poetae Melici Graeci*. Oxford, 1962.
Pollux	I. Bekker, ed. *Iulii Pollucis Onomasticon*. Berlin, 1846.
RO	P. J. Rhodes and R. Osborne, eds. *Greek Historical Inscriptions 404–323 BC*. Oxford, 2003.
SEG	*Supplementum Epigraphicum Graecum*. Leiden, 1923–.
SGDI	J. Baunack, F. Bechtel, A. Bezzenberger, F. Blass, H. Collitz, W. Deecke, A. Fick et. al. *Sammlung der griechischen Dialekt-Inscriften*. Göttingen, 1899.

Works Cited

Akrigg, B. 2015. "Metics in Athens." In *Communities and Networks in the Greek World*, edited by C. Taylor and K. Vlassopoulos, 155–73. Oxford.

Akrigg, B. and R. Tordoff, eds. 2013. *Slaves and Slavery in Ancient Greek Comic Drama*. Cambridge.

Alcock, S. 2002. "A Simple Case of Exploitation: The Helots of Messenia." In *Money, Labour and Land: Approaches to the Economies of Ancient Greece*, edited by P. Cartledge et al., 185–99. London.
　　2003. "Researching the Helots: Details, Methodologies, Agencies." In *Helots and Their Masters in Laconia and Messenia. Histories, Ideologies, Structures*, edited by N. Luraghi and S. Alcock, 3–11. Cambridge, MA.
Allain, J., ed. 2012. *The Legal Understanding of Slavery: From the Historical to the Contemporary*. Oxford.
Anastasiades, V. I. and P. N. Doukellis, eds. 2005. *Esclavage Antique et Discriminations Socio-Culturelles*. Actes du XXVIII Colloque International du Groupement International de Recherche sur L'Esclavage Antique. Berlin.
Andrews, W. L. and H. L. Gates. 2000. *Slave Narratives*. New York.
Andreau, J. and R. Descat. 2006. *Esclave en Grèce et à Rome*. Paris. Translated by Marion Leopold as *The Slave in Greece and Rome*. Madison, WI: 2011.
Archer, L., ed. 1988. *Slavery and Other Forms of Unfree Labour*. New York.
Arnott, W. G. 1996. *Alexis: The Fragments*. Cambridge.
Asheri, D. et al. 2007. *A Commentary on Herodotus Books I-IV*. Oxford.
Austin, C. and S. D. Olson, eds. 2004. *Thesmophoriazusae*. By Aristophanes. Oxford.
Bäbler, B. 1998. *Fleissige Thrakerinnen und Wehrhafte Skythen. Nichtgriechen im klassischen Athen und ihre archäologische Hinterlassenschaft*. Stuttgart.
　　2005. "Bobbies or Boobies? The Scythian Police Force in Classical Athens." In *Scythians and Greeks: Cultural Interactions in Scythia, Athens and the Early Roman Empire*, edited by D. Braund, 114–22. Exeter.
Bain, D. 1981. *Masters, Servants and Orders in Greek Tragedy*. Manchester.
Bales, K. 1999. *Disposable People: New Slavery in Global Perspective*. Berkeley.
　　2000. *New Slavery: A Reference Handbook*. Santa Barbara.
Baptist, E. E. 2014. *The Half Has Never been Told: Slavery and the Making of American Capitalism*. New York.
Bernal, M. 1987. *Black Athena: The Afroasiatic Roots of Classical Civilization*. Vol. 1. New Brunswick.
Bergad, L. W. 2007. *The Comparative Histories of Slavery in Brazil, Cuba, and the United States*. Cambridge.
Bielman, A. 1994. *Retour à la liberté, Libération et sauvetage des prisonniers en Grèce ancienne, Recueil d'inscriptions honorant des sauveteurs et analyse critique. Études épigraphiques 1*. Athens.
Bivar Marquese, R. de and F. Duarte Joly. 2008. "Panis, disciplina et opus servo: The Jesuit Ideology in Portuguese America and Greco-Roman Ideas of Slavery." In *Slave Systems: Ancient and Modern*, edited by E. Dal Lago and C. Katsari, 214–30. Cambridge.
Bodel, J. and W. Scheidel, eds. 2017. *On Human Bondage: After Slavery and Social Death*. Malden, MA.
Bömer, F. 1960–1990. *Untersuchungen über die Religion der Sklaven in Griechenland und Rom*. Wiesbaden & Stuttgart.

Booth, J. Forthcoming. "Dethroning Justice: Building Post-Emancipation Societies through Law in the Atlantic World." PhD diss., Harvard University.

Bradley, K. R. 1987. *Slaves and Masters in the Roman Empire*. Oxford.

 1989. *Slavery and Rebellion in the Roman World, 140 B.C.–70 B.C.* Indiana.

 1994. *Slavery and Society at Rome*. Cambridge.

 2015. *The Bitter Chain of Slavery*. Washington, DC.

Bradley, K. R. and P. A. Cartledge, eds. 2011. *The Ancient Mediterranean World*. Vol. 1 of *The Cambridge World History of Slavery*. Cambridge.

Braund, D. 2008. "Royal Scythians and the Slave Trade in Herodotus' Scythia." *Antichthon* 42: 1–19.

 2011. "The Slave Supply in Classical Greece." In *The Ancient Mediterranean World*. Vol. 1 of *The Cambridge World History of Slavery*, edited by K. Bradley and P. A. Cartledge, 112–33. Cambridge.

Braund, D and G. R. Tsetskhladze. 1989. "The Export of Slaves from Colchis." *CQ* 39, no. 1: 114–25.

Bresson, A. 2007. *L'économie de la Grece des cités*. Paris.

Brown, C. L and P. D. Morgan, eds. 2006. *Arming Slaves from Classical Times to the Modern Age*. New Haven.

Burford, A. 1972. *Craftsmen in Greek and Roman Society*. Ithaca.

Burstein, S. 1984. *The Hellenistic Age from the Battle of Ipsos to the Death of Kleopatra VII*. Cambridge.

Bush, M. L., ed. 1996. *Serfdom & Slavery: Studies in Legal Bondage*. London.

Cambiano, G. 1987. "Aristotle and the Anonymous Opponents of Slavery." In *Classical Slavery*, edited by M. I. Finley, 22–41. London.

Canevaro, M. 2018. "The *graphe hybreos* against Slaves: The *Time* of the Victim and That of the *hybristes*." *Journal of Hellenic Studies* 138: 100–26.

Cartledge, P. A. 1979. *Sparta and Lakonia: A Regional History, 1300–362 BCE*. London.

 1985. "Rebels and Sambos in Classical Greece: A Comparative View." In *Crux: Essays in Greek History Presented to G.E.M. de Ste. Croix*, edited by P. Cartledge and F. Harvey, 16–46. London. Reprinted in P. A. Cartledge, *Spartan Reflections*, 127–52. Berkeley: 2001.

 1988. "Serfdom in Classical Greece". In *Slavery and Other Forms of Unfree Labor*, edited by L. Archer, 33–41. London.

 1993. "Like a Worm i' the Bud? A Heterology of Classical Greek Slavery." *Greece & Rome* 40, no. 2: 163–80.

 2002. *The Greeks: A Portrait of Self and Others*. New Ed. Oxford.

 2003. "Raising Hell? The Helot Mirage – a Personal Re-view." In *Helots and Their Masters in Laconia and Messenia: Histories, Ideologies, Structures*, edited by N. Luraghi and S. Alcock, 12–30. Cambridge, MA.

 2011. "The Helots: A Contemporary Review." In *The Ancient Mediterranean World*. Vol. 1 of *The Cambridge World History of Slavery*, edited by K. R. Bradley and P. A. Cartledge, 74–90. Cambridge.

Chaniotis, A. 1996. "Conflicting Authorities: Asylia between Secular and Divine Law in the Classical and Hellenistic Poleis." *Kernos* 9: 65–86.

Chatzidimitriou, A. 2005. "Distinguishing Features of Craftsmen, Professionals and Slaves." In *Esclavage Antique et Discriminations Socio-Culturelles*, edited by V. I. Anastasiades and P. N. Doukellis, 131–45. Berlin.

Christensen, K. A. 1984. "The Theseion: A Slave Refuge at Athens." *American Journal of Ancient History* 9: 23–32.

Clinton, K. 2008. *Commentary*. Vol. 2 of *Eleusis: The Inscriptions on Stone*. Athens.

Cohen, E. E. 1992. *Athenian Economy and Society: A Banking Perspective*. Princeton.

⎯⎯⎯. 2000. *The Athenian Nation*. Princeton.

⎯⎯⎯. 2006. "Free and Unfree Sexual Work: An Economic Analysis of Athenian Prostitution." In *Prostitutes and Courtesans in the Ancient World*, edited by C. A. Faraone and L. K. McClure, 95–124. Madison

Cottias, M., A. Stella and B. Vincent, eds. 2006. *Esclavage et Dépendances serviles*. Paris.

Cox, C. 2013. "Coping with Punishment: The Social Networking of Slaves in Menander." In *Slaves and Slavery in Ancient Greek Comic Drama*, edited by B. Akrigg and R. Tordoff, 159–72. New York.

Crenshaw, K. 1991. "Mapping the Margins: Intersectionality, Identity Politics and Violence against Women of Color." *Stanford Law Review* 43, no. 6: 1241–99.

Crowther, N. B. 1992. "Slaves and Greek Athletics." *QUCC* 40: 35–42.

Dal Lago, E. and C. Katsari, eds. 2008. *Slave Systems Ancient and Modern*. Cambridge.

Darmezin, L. 1999. *Les Affranchissements par consécration en Béotie et dans le monde grec hellénistique*. Paris.

De la Fuente, A. 2004. "Slave Law and Claims-Making in Cuba: The Tannenbaum Debate Revisited." *Law and History Review* 22: 339–69.

De Souza, P. 1999. *Piracy in the Greco-Roman World*. Cambridge.

Descat, J. 1994. *Les Pénestes de Thessalie*. Besançon.

Deshours, N. 2006. *Les Mystères d'Andania. Étude d'épigraphie et d'histoire religieuse*. Bordeaux.

Dover, K. J. 1978. *Greek Homosexuality*. London.

Du Bois, W. E. B. (1904) 1994. *The Souls of Black Folk*. Chicago. Reprint, New York: Dover. Citations refer to the Dover edition.

DuBois, P. 1991. *Torture and Truth*. New York.

⎯⎯⎯. 2003. *Slaves and Other Objects*. Chicago.

⎯⎯⎯. 2010. *Slavery: Antiquity and Its Legacy*. London.

Ducat, J. 1990. "Les Hilotes." Supplement, *Bulletin de Correspondance Hellénique* 20. Athens.

⎯⎯⎯. 1994. *Les Pénestes de Thessalie*. Paris.

Duchêne, H. 1986. "Sur la stèle d'Aulus Caprilius Timotheos, Somatemporos." *Bulletin de Correspondance Hellénique* 110: 513–30.

Ducrey, P. 1999. *Le traitement des prisonniers de guerre dans la Grèce antique des origines à la conquête romaine*. 2nd ed. Paris.

Dunbar, N., ed. 1995. *Aristophanes: Birds*. Oxford.
Eidinow, E. 2007. *Oracles, Curses and Risk among the Ancient Greeks*. Oxford.
Engerman, S. L. 1996. "Slavery, Serfdom and Other Forms of Coerced Labour: Similarities and Differences." In *Serfdom and Slavery: Studies in Legal Bondage*, edited by M. Bush, 18–41. London.
Ferguson, W. S. and A. D. Nork. 1944. "The Attic Orgeones and the Cult of the Heroes" *Harvard Theological Review* 37: i–iv + 61–174.
Finley, M. I. 1952. *Studies in Land and Credit in Ancient Athens*. New Brunswick. Reprint, 1984.
　　1962. "The Slave Trade in Antiquity: The Black Sea and Danubian Regions." *Klio* 40: 51–59. Reprinted in M. I. Finley, *Economy and Society in Ancient Greece*. Edited by B. D. Shaw and R. P. Saller. London, 1981.
　　1980. *Ancient Slavery and Modern Ideology*. London.
　　1981. *Economy and Society in Ancient Greece*. Edited by B. D. Shaw and R. P. Saller. London.
　　ed. 1987. *Classical Slavery*. London.
　　1998. *Ancient Slavery and Modern Ideology*. Edited by B. D. Shaw. Exp. ed. Princeton
Fischer, J. 2012. "Kinderleben und Kinderarbeit im klassischen Griechenland." In *Kindersklaven-Sklavenkinder: Schicksale zwischen Zuneigung und Ausbeutung in der Antike und im interkulterellen Vergleich*, edited by H. Heinen, 103–22. Stuttgart.
Fisher, N. R. E. 1993. *Slavery in Classical Greece*. London.
　　trans. 2001. *Against Timarchus*. By Aeschines. Oxford.
　　2005. "Hybris, Status and Slavery." In *The Greek World*, edited by A. Powell, 44–84. London.
　　2008. "'Independent' Slaves in Classical Athens and the Ideology of Slavery." In *From Captivity to Freedom: Themes in Ancient and Modern Slavery*, edited by C. Katsari and E. Dal Lago, 121–46. Leicester.
Fitzgerald, W. 2000. *Slavery and the Roman Literary Imagination*. Cambridge.
Fogel, R. W. and S. L. Engerman 1974. *Time on the Cross: The Economics of Negro Slavery*. New York.
Foley, H. 1994. *The Homeric Hymn to Demeter*. Princeton.
Forsdyke, S. 2001. "Athenian Democratic Ideology and Herodotus' Histories." *American Journal of Philology* 122: 329–58.
　　2005. "Revelry and Riot in Archaic Megara: Democratic Disorder or Ritual Reversal?" *Journal of Hellenic Studies* 125: 73–92.
　　2006. "Herodotus, Political History and Political Thought." In *The Cambridge Companion to Herodotus*, edited by C. Dewald and J. Marincola, 224-41. Cambridge.
　　2012. *Slaves Tell Tales and Other Episodes in the Politics of Popular Culture in Ancient Greece*. Princeton.
　　2019. "Slave Agency and Citizenship in Classical Athens." In *Symposion 2017: Gesellschaft für griechische und hellenistische Rechtsgeschichte*, edited by G. Thür, U. Yiftach, R. Zelnick-Abramovitz. Vienna. 345–66.

Forthcoming. "Slave Agency and the Law in Classical Athens." In *Voiceless, Invisible and Countless: Subordinate Experience in Ancient Greece, 800–300 BCE*, edited by S. Gartland and D. Tandy.

Foxhall, L. 2007. *Olive Cultivation in Ancient Greece*. Oxford.

Fragiadakis, C. 1986. *Die attischen Sklavennamen von der spätarchaischen Epoche bis in die römische Kaiserzeit*. Mannheim.

Frier, B. W. 1989. *A Casebook on the Roman Law of Delict*. Atlanta, GA.

Gagarin, M. 1996. "The Torture of Slaves in Athenian Law." *Classical Philology* 91: 1–18.

  1997. *Antiphon: The Speeches*. Cambridge.

  2010. "Serfs and Slaves at Gortyn." In *Zeitschrift der Savigny-Stiftung für Rechtsgeschichte* 127: 14–31.

Gagarin, M. and D. M. MacDowell, trans. 1998. *Antiphon & Andocides*. Austin, TX.

Gagarin, M. and P. Perlman. 2016. *The Laws of Ancient Crete c.650–400 BCE*. Oxford.

Gallant, T. W. 1991. *Risk and Survival in Ancient Greece: Reconstructing the Rural Landscape*. Stanford.

Garlan, Y. 1987. "War, Piracy and Slavery in the Greek World." In *Classical Slavery*, edited by M. I. Finley, 7–21. London.

  1988. *Slavery in Ancient Greece*. Translated by J. Lloyd. Rev. and exp. ed. Ithaca.

  2006. "L'anti-esclavagisme a-t-il existé en Grèce ancienne?" In *Esclavage et Dépendences serviles*, edited by M. Cottias, A. Stella and B. Vincent, 187–94. Paris.

Garland, R. 1987. *The Piraeus: From the First to the Fifth Century BC*. 2nd ed. 2001. Ithaca.

  1992. *Introducing New Gods: The Politics of Athenian Religion*. London

  2010. *The Eye of the Beholder: Deformity and Disability in the Greco-Roman World*. Bristol.

Garnsey, P. 1996. *Ideas of Slavery from Aristotle to Augustine*. Cambridge.

Gates, H. L. 1987. *The Classic Slave Narratives*. New York.

Gavriljuk, N. A. 2003. "The Graeco-Scythian Slave-Trade in the Sixth and Fifth Centuries BC." In *The Cauldron of Ariantas: Studies Presented to A. N. Shcheglov on His 70th Birthday*, edited by P. Guldager Bilde, J. Munk Hojte and V. F. Stolba, 75–85. Aarhus.

Geary, D. and K. Vlassopoulos, eds. 2009. "Slavery, Citizenship and the State in Classical Antiquity and the Modern Americas." Special Issue, *European Review of History* 16.

Genovese, E. D. 1974. *Roll, Jordan, Roll: The World the Slaves Made*. New York.

  1979. *From Rebellion to Revolution: Afro-American Slave Revolts in the Making of the Modern World*. Baton Rouge.

Glazebrook, A. 2011. "Porneion: Prostitution in Athenian Civic Space." In *Greek Prostitutes in the Ancient Mediterranean, 800 BCE–200 CE*, edited by A. Glazebrook and M. Henry, 34–59.

Glazebrook, A. and M. Henry, eds. 2011a. *Greek Prostitutes in the Ancient Mediterranean, 800 BCE–200 CE*. Wisconsin.
  2011b. Introduction to *Greek Prostitutes in the Ancient Mediterranean, 800 BCE–200 CE*, 3–13. Wisconsin.
Golden, M. 1981. "Demography and the Exposure of Girls at Athens." *Phoenix* 35: 316–31.
  1990. *Children and Childhood in Classical Athens*. Cambridge.
  1998. *Sport and Society in Ancient Greece*. Cambridge.
Goodheart, A. 2011. "The Shrug that Made History." *New York Times Magazine*, April 3, 59.
Gottesman, A. 2014. *Politics and the Street in Democratic Athens*. Cambridge.
Graham, A. J. 1992. "Thucydides 7.13.2 and the Crews of Athenian Triremes." *Transactions of the American Philological Association* 122: 257–70.
  1998 "Thucydides 7.13.2 and the Crews of Athenian Triremes: An Addendum." *Transactions of the American Philological Association* 128: 89–114.
Greco, E. and M. Lombardo, eds. 2005. *La Grande Iscrizione di Gortyna*. Centoventi anni dopo la scoperta. Atti del I Convegno Internazionale di Studi sulla Messarà. Athens.
Gross, A. 2000. *Double Character: Slavery and Mastery in the Antebellum Southern Courtroom*. Princeton.
  2008. *What Blood Won't Tell: A History of Race on Trial in America*. Cambridge, MA.
Gruen, E. 2011. *Rethinking the Other in Antiquity*. Princeton.
Habicht, C. 1957. "Samische Volksbeschlüsse der hellenistischen Zeit." *Mitteilungen des Deutschen Archäologischen Instituts, Athenische Abteilung* 72: 152–274.
Hall, J. 2002. *Hellenicity: Between Ethnicity and Culture*. Chicago.
Hanke, L. 1959. *Aristotle and the American Indians: A Study of Race Prejudice in the Modern World*. Bloomington.
Hansen, M. H. 1999. *The Athenian Democracy in the Age of Demosthenes*. Normon.
Hansen, W. 1998. *Anthology of Greek Popular Literature*. Bloomington.
Hanson, V. D. 1992. "Thucydides and the Desertion of Attic Slaves during the Decelean War." *Classical Antiquity* 11: 210–28.
Harris, E. M. 2002. "Workshop, Marketplace and Household: The Nature of Technical Specialization in Classical Athens and Its Influence on Economy and Society." In *Money, Labour and Land: Approaches to the Economies of Ancient Greece*, edited by P. Cartledge, E. E. Cohen and L. Foxhall, 67–99. London.
  2004. "Notes on a Lead Letter from the Athenian Agora." *Harvard Studies in Classical Philology* 102: 157–70.
  2006. *Democracy and the Rule of Law in Classical Athens*. Cambridge.
Harris, W. V. 1989. *Ancient Literacy*. Cambridge, MA.
Harrison, A. R. W. 1968. *The Law of Athens*. Vol. 1. 2nd ed. Oxford.
Hartog, F. 1988. *The Mirror of Herodotus: An Essay in the Representation of the Other*. Berkeley.

Harvey, F. D. 2007. "'Help! I'm Dying Here': A Letter from a Slave." *Zeitschrift für Papyrologie und Epigraphik* 163:49–50.

Heinen, H., ed. 2010. *Antike Sklaverei: Rückblick und Ausblick; Neue Beiträge zur Forschungsgeschichte und zur Erschließung der archäologischen Zeugnisse.* Stuttgart.

——— ed. 2012. *Kindersklaven-Sklavenkinder: Schicksale zwischen Zuneigung und Ausbeutung in der Antike und im interkulterellen Vergleich.* Stuttgart.

Himmelmann, N. 1971. "Archäologisches zum Problem der griechischen Sklaverei" *Akademie der Wissenschaften und der Literatur. Abhandlungen der Geistes- und Sozialwissenschaftlichen Klasse.* Wiesbaden. 615–59.

Hodkinson, S. 2000. *Property and Wealth in Classical Sparta.* London.

——— 2003. "Spartiates, Helots and the Direction of the Agrarian Economy: Towards an Understanding of Helotage in Comparative Perspective." In *Helots and Their Masters in Laconia and Messenia: Histories, Ideologies, Structures*, edited by N. Luraghi and S. Alcock, 248–85. Cambridge, MA.

Hodkinson, S. and D. Geary, eds. 2012. *Slaves and religions in Greco-Roman Antiquity and Modern Brazil.* Newcastle Upon Tyne.

Hopkins, K. 1978. *Conquerors and Slaves: Sociological Studies in Roman History.* Cambridge.

Hornblower, S. 1991. *Books I-III.* Vol. 1 of *A Commentary on Thucydides.* Oxford.

——— 2008. *Books 5.25–8.109.* Vol. 3 of *A Commentary on Thucydides.* Oxford.

Hunt, P. 1998. *Slaves, Warfare and Ideology in the Greek Historians.* Cambridge.

——— 2001. "Slaves and the Generals of Arginusae." *American Journal of Philology* 122: 359–80.

——— 2015. "Trojan Slaves in Classical Athens: Ethnic Identity among Athenian Slaves." In *Communities and Networks in the Greek World*, edited by C. Taylor and K. Vlassopoulos, 128–54. Oxford.

——— 2016. "Violence against Slaves in Classical Greece." In *The Topography of Violence in the Greco-Roman World*, edited by W. Riess and G. Fagan, 136–61. Ann Arbor.

——— 2018a. *Ancient Greek and Roman Slavery.* Malden, MA.

——— 2018b. "Ancient Greece as a Slave Society." In *What Is a Slave Society? The Practice of Slavery in Global Perspective*, edited by N. Lenski and C. Cameron, 61–85. Cambridge. Hunt forthcoming "The Gender Ratio in the Attic Stelai"

Hunter, V. J. 1994. *Policing Athens: Social Control in the Attic Lawsuits, 420–320 B. C.* Princeton.

——— 2000. "Introduction: Status Distinctions in Athenian Law." In *Law and Social Status in Classical Athens*, edited by V. Hunter and J. Edmondson, 1–29. Oxford.

Hunter, V. and J. Edmondson, eds. 2000. *Law and Social Status in Classical Athens.* Oxford.

Isaac, B. 2004. *The Invention of Racism in Classical Antiquity.* Princeton.

Ismard, P. 2015. *La Démocratie contre les experts: Les esclaves publics en Grèce ancienne.* Paris. Translated by J. M. Todd as *Democracy's Slaves: A Political History of Ancient Greece.* Cambridge, MA: 2017.

——— 2019. *La cité et ses esclaves: Institution, fictions, experiences.* Paris.

Jacob, O. 1928. *Les Esclaves publics à Athènes*. Liège.
James, C. R. L. 1963. *The Black Jacobins*. New York.
Jameson, M. 1977/78. "Agriculture and Slavery in Classical Athens." *Classical Journal* 73: 122–44.
Johnson, W. 1999. *Soul by Soul: Life Inside the Antebellum Slave Market*. Cambridge, MA.
　2003 "On Agency." *Journal of Social History* 37:113–24.
　2013. *River of Dark Dreams: Slavery and Empire in the Cotton Kingdom*. Cambridge, MA.
Jones, A. H. M. 1957. *Athenian Democracy*. Oxford.
Jones, C. P. 1987. "Stigma: Tattooing and Branding in Graeco-Roman Antiquity." *Journal of Roman Studies* 77: 139–55.
　2008. "Hyperides and the Sale of Slave Families." *Zeitschrift für Papyrologie und Epigraphik* 164: 19–20.
Jones, M. 2018. *Birthright Citizens: A History of Race and Rights in Antebellum America*. Cambridge.
Jones, N. F. 1999. *The Associations of Classical Athens: The Response to Democracy*. Oxford.
Jordan, D. R. 2000. "A Personal Letter Found in the Athenian Agora." *Hesperia* 69: 91–103.
　2003. "Slaves Among the Frogs." *L'Antiquité Classique* 72: 41-53.
Joshel, S. R. 2010. *Slavery in the Roman World*. Cambridge.
Joshel, S. R. and S. Murnaghan, eds. 1998. *Women and Slaves in Greco-Roman Culture: Differential Equations*. London & New York.
Jouanna, J. 1999. *Hippocrates*. Baltimore.
Kamen, D. 2011. "Reconsidering the Status of *khoris oikountes*." *Dike* 14: 43–53.
　2013. *Status in Classical Athens*. Princeton.
　2014. "Sale for the Purpose of Freedom: Slave Prostitutes and Manumission in Ancient Greece." *Classical Journal* 109: 281–307.
Kapparis, K. A. 1999. *Apollodorus 'Against Neaira' [D 59]*. Berlin.
Karanika, A. 2014. *Voices at Work: Women, Performance and Labor in Ancient Greece*. Baltimore.
Katsari, C. and E. Dal Lago, eds. 2008. *From Captivity to Freedom: Themes in Ancient and Modern Slavery*. Leicester.
Kazakévich, E. G. 2008. "Were the χωρὶς οἰκοῦντες Slaves?" *Greek, Roman, and Byzantine Studies* 48: 343–80.
Keesling, C. 2006. "Heavenly Bodies: Monuments to Prostitutes in Greek Sanctuaries." In *Prostitutes and Courtesans in the Ancient World*, edited by C. A. Faraone and L. K. McClure, 59–76. Madison.
Kennell, N. M. 2010. *Spartans: A New History*. Malden, MA.
Klees, H. 1998. *Sklavenleben im klassischen Griechenland*. Stuttgart.
Knigge, U. 2001. *The Athenian Kerameikos: History, Monuments, Excavations*. Athens.
Knight, F. W. and A. Hurley, eds. 2003. *Bartolomé de las Casas: An Account, Much Abbreviated, of the Destruction of the Indies. With Related Texts*. Indianapolis.

Kosmopoulou, A. 2001. "Working Women: Female Professionals on Classical Attic Gravestones." *Annual of the British School at Athens* 96: 281–319.

Kudlien, F. 1988. "Zur sozialen Situation des flüchtigen Sklaven in der Antike." *Hermes* 116: 232–52.

Kurke, L. 1996. "Pindar and the Prostitutes or Reading Ancient Pornography." *Arion* 4: 49–75.

2011. *Aesopic Conversations: Popular Tradition, Cultural Dialogue and the Invention of Greek Prose*. Princeton.

Kyrtatas, D. J. 2011. "Slavery and Economy in the Greek World." In *The Ancient Mediterranean World*. Vol. 1 of *The Cambridge World History of Slavery*, edited by K. R. Bradley and P. A. Cartledge, 176–93. Cambridge.

Langdon, M. 2015. "Herders' graffiti." In *Axon: Studies in Honour of Ronald S. Stroud*, edited by A. Matthiou and N. Papazarkadas, 49–58. Athens.

Lape, S. 2010. *Race and Citizen Identity in the Classical Athenian Democracy*. Cambridge.

Latte, K. 1920. *Heiliges Recht. Untersuchungen zur Geschichte der sakralen Rechtsformen in Griechenland*. Tübingen.

Lauffer, S. 1979. *Die Bergwerkssklaven von Laureion*. 2nd ed. Wiesbaden. First ed. published 1955/6.

Lenski, N. 2018. "Framing the Question: What Is a Slave Society?" In *What Is a Slave Society? The Practice of Slavery in Global Perspective*, edited by N. Lenski and C. Cameron, 15–57. Cambridge.

Lenski, N. and C. Cameron, eds. 2018. *What Is a Slave Society? The Practice of Slavery in Global Perspective*. Cambridge.

Levine, L. W. 1977. *Black Consciousness and Black Culture: Afro-American Folk Culture from Slavery to Freedom*. Oxford.

Lewis, D. M. 2013. "Slave Marriages in the Laws of Gortyn: A Matter of Rights?" *Historia* 62: 390–416.

2015. "Slavery and Manumission." In *Oxford Handbook of Ancient Greek Law*, edited by E. Harris and M. Canevaro, 1–32. Oxford.

2016a. "The Market for Slaves in the Fifth and Fourth Century Aegean: Achaemenid Anatolia as a Case Study." In *The Ancient Greek Economy: Markets, Households and City-States*, edited by E. Harris, D. M. Lewis and M. Woolmer, 316–36. Cambridge.

2016b "Review of P. Ismard *La Démocratie contre les experts. Les esclaves publics en Grèce ancienne*." *Classical Review* 66: 476–78.

2017. "Notes on Slave Names, Ethnicity and Identity in Classical and Hellenistic Greece." *Studia Źródłoznawcze. U Schyłku Starożytność* 16: 183-213.

2018. *Greek Slave Systems in Their Eastern Mediterranean Context, c.800–146 BC*. Oxford.

Lewis, S. 2002. *The Athenian Woman. An Iconographic Handbook*. London.

Long, T. 1986. *Barbarians in Greek Comedy*. Chicago.

Loomis, W. 1998. *Wages, Welfare Costs and Inflation in Classical Athens*. Ann Arbor.

Lovejoy, P. E. 2012. *Transformations in Slavery: A History of Slavery in Africa*. 3rd ed. Cambridge.
Luraghi, N. 2002. "Helotic Slavery Reconsidered." In *Sparta: Beyond the Mirage*, edited by A. Powell and S. Hodkinson 229–50. London.
 2003. "The Imaginary Conquest of the Helots." In *Helots and Their Masters in Laconia and Messenia: Histories, Ideologies, Structures*, edited by N. Luraghi and S. Alcock, 109–41. Cambridge, MA.
 2008. *The Ancient Messenians: Constructions of Ethnicity and Memory*. Cambridge.
Luraghi, N. and S. Alcock, eds. 2003. *Helots and Their Masters in Laconia and Messenia: Histories, Ideologies, Structures*. Cambridge, MA.
Mactoux, M. M. 1990. "Esclaves et rites de passage." In *Mélanges de l'Ecole française de Rome* 102: 53–81.
Maffi, A. 2014. "Identificare gli schiavi nei documenti Greci." In *Identifiers and Identification Methods in the Ancient World: Legal Documents in Ancient Societies III*, edited by M. Depauw and S. Coussement, 197–206. Leuven.
Masson, O. 1973. "Les noms des esclaves dans la Grèce antique." In *Actes du Colloque 1971 Sur L'Esclavage*, 9–23. Paris.
Mattingly, D. 2011. *Imperialism, Power and Identity: Experiencing the Roman Empire*. Princeton.
Maurizio, L. 1998. "The Panathenaic Procession: Athens' Participatory Democracy on Display." In *Democracy, Empire and the Arts in Fifth-Century Athens*, edited by D. Boedeker and K. Raaflaub, 297–318. Cambridge, MA.
Mayor, A. 2018. *Gods and Robots: Myths, Machines and Ancient Dreams of Technology*. Princeton.
McCoskey, D. E. 2012. *Race: Antiquity and Its Legacy*. London.
McKeown, N. 2007. *The Invention of Ancient Slavery*. London.
 2010. "Inventing Slaveries: Switching the Argument." In *Antike Sklaverei: Rückblick und Ausblick; Neue Beiträge zur Forschungsgeschichte und zur Erschließung der archäologischen Zeugnisse*, edited by H. Heinen, 39–59. Stuttgart.
 2011. "Resistance among Chattel Slaves in the Classical Greek World." In *The Ancient Mediterranean World*. Vol. 1 of *The Cambridge World History of Slavery*, edited by K. R. Bradley and P. A. Cartledge, 153–75. Cambridge.
Merola, F. R and A. S. Marino, eds. 1999. *Femmes-Esclaves: Modèles d'Interprétation anthropologique, économique, juridique*. Atti del XXI Colloquio internationale GIREA. Lacco Ameno-Ischia, 27–29 ottobre 1994. Naples.
Middleton, D. 1982. "Thrasybulus' Thracian Support." *Classical Quarterly* 32: 298–303.
Miles, T. 2017. *The Dawn of Detroit: A Chronicle of Slavery and Freedom on the Straits*. New York.
Mirhady, D. 1996. "Torture and Rhetoric in Athens." *Journal of Hellenistic Studies* 116: 119-31.

2000. "The Athenian Rationale for Torture." In *Law and Social Status in Classical Athens*, edited by V. Hunter and J. Edmondson, 53–74. Oxford.

Morris, I. 1998. "Remaining Invisible: The Archaeology of the Excluded in Classical Athens." In *Women and Slaves in Greco-Roman Culture: Differential Equations*, edited by S. R. Joshel and S. Murnaghan, 193–220. London & New York.

2011. "Archaeology and Greek Slavery." In *The Ancient Mediterranean World*. Vol. 1 of *The Cambridge World History of Slavery*, edited by K. R. Bradley and P. A. Cartledge, 176–93. Cambridge.

Morris, S. and Papadopoulos, J. 2005. "Greek Towers and Slaves: An Archaeology of Exploitation." *American Journal of Archaeology* 109: 155–225.

Morrow, G. 1939. *Plato's Law of Slavery and Its Relation to Greek Law*. Urbana, IL.

1960. *Plato's Cretan City: A Historical Interpretation of The Laws*. Princeton.

Mussche, H. 1998. *Thorikos: A Mining Town in Ancient Attica*. Ghent.

Naiden, F. S. 2006. *Ancient Supplication*. Oxford.

Natali, C. 2013. *Aristotle: His Life and School*. Princeton.

Northrup, S. 2013. *Twelve Years a Slave*. New York.

Ober, J. 2005. "Quasi Rights: Participatory Citizenship and Negative Liberties." In *Athenian Legacies: Essays on the Politics of Going On Together*, by J. Ober, 92–127. Princeton. Originally published in *Social Philosophy and Policy* 17 (2000): 27–61.

Oliver, G. 2009. "Honours for a Public Slave at Athens (*IG* ii² 502 + Ag. I 1947; 302/1 B.C.)." In *ΑΤΤΙΚΑ ΕΠΙΓΡΑΦΙΚΑ: ΜΕΛΕΤΕΣ ΠΡΟΣ ΤΙΜΗΝ ΤΟΥ Christian Habicht*, edited by A. A. Themos and A. Matthaiou, 111–24. Athens.

Olson, S. D., ed. 2007. *Broken Laughter: Select Fragments of Greek Comedy*. Oxford.

Osborne, R. 1985. *Demos: The Discovery of Classical Attica*. Oxford.

1987. *Classical Landscape with Figures*. London.

1991. "Pride and Prejudice, Sense and Subsistence: Exchange and Society in the Greek City." In *City and Country in the Ancient World*, edited by J. Rich and A. Wallace-Hadrill, 119–45. London.

1995. "The Economics and Politics of Slavery at Athens." In *The Greek World*, edited by C. A. Powell, 27–43. London.

2000. "Religion, Imperial Politics and the Offering of Freedom to Slaves." In *Law and Social Status in Classical Athens*, edited by V. Hunter and J. Edmondson, 75–92. Oxford.

2011. *The History Written on the Classical Greek Body*. Cambridge.

Palmieri, M. G. 2016. *Penteskouphia: immagini e parole dipinte sui pinakes corinzi dedicati a Poseidon*. Athens.

Panagopoulos, A. 1978. *Thucydides: Captives and Hostages in the Peloponnesian War*. Amsterdam.

Parker, R. 1996. *Athenian Religion: A History*. Oxford.

2005. *Polytheism and Society at Athens*. Oxford.

Parry, M. 2016. "Shackles and Dollars: Historians and Economists Clash over Slavery." *Chronicle of Higher Education*, December 8. https://www.chronicle.com/article/shackles-and-dollars/.
Patterson, C. 1985. "'Not Worth Rearing': The Causes of Infant Exposure in Ancient Greece." *Transactions of the American Philological Association* 115: 103–123.
Patterson, O. 1982. *Slavery and Social Death*. Cambridge, MA.
Pelling, C. B. R. 1997. "East Is East and West Is West – Or Are They? National Stereotypes in Herodotus." *Histos* 1: 51–66. https://research.ncl.ac.uk/histos/Histos_BackIssues1997.html.
Pickard-Cambridge, A. W. 1968. *The Dramatic Festivals of Athens*. 2nd ed. Oxford. Revised with a new supplement 1988.
Saunders, T. J., trans. 1970. *Laws*. By Plato. Harmondsworth.
Pritchett, W. K. 1971–1991. *The Greek State at War*. Berkeley.
Pulleyn, D. 1997. *Prayer in Greek Religion*. Oxford.
Research Network on the Legal Parameters of Slavery. 2012. "Bellagio-Harvard Guidelines on the Legal Parameters of Slavery." *Global Dialogue* 14.
Richlin, A. 2017. *Slave Theater in the Roman Republic: Plautus and Popular Comedy*. Cambridge.
Rihll, T. E. 2010. "Skilled slaves and the Economy: The Silver Mines of the Laurion." In *Antike Sklaverei: Rückblick und Ausblick; Neue Beiträge zur Forschungsgeschichte und zur Erschließung der archäologischen Zeugnisse*, edited by H. Heinen, 203–20. Stuttgart.
  2011. "Classical Athens." In *The Ancient Mediterranean World*. Vol. 1 of *The Cambridge World History of Slavery*, edited by K. R. Bradley and P. A. Cartledge, 48–73. Cambridge.
Robert, L. 1938. *Études épigraphiques et philologiques*. Paris.
Robertson, B. 2008. "The Slave-Names of *IG* i^3 1032 and the Ideology of Slavery at Athens." In *Epigraphy and the Greek Historian*, edited by C. Cooper, 79-109. Toronto.
Roger, J. 1945. "Inscriptions de la region du Strymon." *Revue Archéologique* 24: 37–55.
Rosivach, V. 1989. "Talasiourgoi and paideia in *IG* II^2 1553–1578: A Note on Athenian Social History." *Historia* 38: 365–70.
Roth, U. 2007. *Thinking Tools: Agricultural Slavery between Evidence and Models*. London.
Ste. Croix, G. E. M. de. 1981. *The Class Struggle in the Ancient Greek World from the Archaic Age to the Arab Conquests*. London. Corrected impression, 1983.
Saller, R. 1987. "Slavery and the Roman Family." In *Classical Slavery*, edited by M. I. Finley, 65–87. London. Also published in *Slavery and Abolition* 8: 65–87.
Scharfstein, D. 2011. *The Invisible Line: Three American Families and the Secret Journey from Black to White*. New York.
Scheibler, I. 1995. *Griechische Töpferkunst: Herstellung, Handel und Gebrauch der antiken Tongefässe*. Munich.

Scheidel, W. 2003a. "Helot Numbers: A Simplified Model." In *Helots and Their Masters in Laconia and Messenia: Histories, Ideologies, Structures*, edited by N. Luraghi and S. Alcock, 240–47. Cambridge, MA.

2003b. "The archaeology of ancient slavery" *Journal of Roman Archaeology* 16: 577–81.

Schmitz, W. 2011. "Der Verkauf einer Sklavenfamilie." *Zeitschrift für Papyrologie und Epigraphik* 179: 54–56.

2012. "'Sklavenfamilien' im archaischen und klassischen Griechenland." In *Kindersklaven-Sklavenkinder: Schicksale zwischen Zuneigung und Ausbeutung in der Antike und im interkulterellen Vergleich*, edited by H. Heinen, 63–102. Stuttgart.

ed. 2016. *Antike Sklaverei zwischen Verdammung und Beschönigung: Kolloquium zur Rezeption antiker Sklaverei vom 17. bis 20. Jahrhundert*. Stuttgart.

Schofield, M. 2016. *Plato Laws*. Cambridge.

Schumacher, L. 2001. *Sklaverei in der Antike: Alltag und Schicksal der Unfreien*. Munich.

Scott, J. C. 1985. *Weapons of the Weak: Everyday Forms of Peasant Resistance*. New Haven.

1990. *Domination and the Arts of Resistance: The Hidden Transcript*. New Haven.

Scott, R. 2012. "Under Color of Law: Siliadin v. France and the Dynamics of Enslavement in Historical Perspective." In *The Legal Understanding of Slavery: From the Historical to the Contemporary*, edited by J. Allain, 152–64. Oxford.

Sharfstein, D. 2011. *The Invisible Line: Three American Families and the Secret Journey from Black to White*. New York.

Shaw, B. 2001. *Spartacus and the Slave Wars: A Brief History with Documents*. Boston.

Sinn, U. 1990. "Eine sakrale Schutzzone in der korinthischen Peraia." *Mitteilungen des Deutschen Archäologischen Instituts, Athenische Abteilung* 105, 53–116.

1993. "Greek Sanctuaries as Places of Refuge." In *Greek Sanctuaries: New Approaches*, edited by R. Hägg and N. Marinatos, 88–109. London.

Sickinger, J. 1999. *Public Records and Archives in Classical Athens*. Chapel Hill.

Sokolowski, F. 1954. "The Real Meaning of Sacral Manumission." *Harvard Theological Review* 47: 173–81.

Sommerstein, A., ed. and trans. 1996. *Frogs*. By Aristophanes. Warminster.

Sosin, J. 2015. "Manumission with Paramone: Conditional Freedom?" *TAPA* 145: 325–381.

Szegedy-Maszak, A. 1981. *The Nomoi of Theophrastus*. New York.

Taylor, C. 2015. "Social Networks and Social Mobility in Fourth-century Athens." In *Communities and Networks in the Greek World*, edited by C. Taylor and K. Vlassopoulos, 35–53. Oxford.

Taylor, C. and K. Vlassopoulos, eds. 2015 *Communities and Networks in the Greek World*. Oxford.

Tchernetska, N., E. Handley, C. Austin and L. Horváth. 2007. "New Readings in the Fragment of Hyperides' Against Timandros from the Archimedes Palimpsest." *Zeitschrift für Papyrologie und Epigraphik* 162: 1–4.

Thalmann, W. G. 1998. *The Swineherd and the Bow: Representations of Class in the Odyssey*. Ithaca.

Thompson, F. H. 2003. *The Archaeology of Greek and Roman Slavery*. London.

Todd, S. 1993. *The Shape of Athenian Law*. Oxford.

   1994. "Status and Contract in Fourth-Century Athens." In *Symposion 1993*, edited by G. Thür, 125–40. Cologne.

Tomlin, R. S. O. 2003. "The Girl in Question: A New Text from Roman London." *Britannia* 34: 41–51.

Trevett, J. 1992. *Apollodorus, the Son of Pasion*. Oxford.

Tsetskhladze, G. R. 2008. "Pontic Slaves in Athens: Orthodoxy and Reality." In *Antike Lebenswelten: Konstanz – Wandel –Wirkungsmacht*, edited by P. Mauritsch, W. Petermandl, R. Rollinger and C. Ulf, 309–319. Wiesbaden.

Twitty, A. 2016. *Before Dred Scott: Slavery and Legal Culture in the American Confluence, 1787–1857*. New York.

Van Wees, H. 2003. "Conquerors and Serfs: Wars of Conquest and Forced Labour in Archaic Greece." In *Helots and Their Masters in Laconia and Messenia: Histories, Ideologies, Structures*, edited by N. Luraghi and S. Alcock, 33–80. Cambridge, MA.

   2004. *Greek Warfare: Myths and Realities*. Bristol.

Versnel, H. 1993. *Transition and Reversal in Myth and Ritual*. Vol. 2 of *Inconsistencies in Greek and Roman Religion*. Leiden.

Vlassopoulos, K. 2007. "Free Spaces: Identity, Experience and Democracy in Classical Athens." *Classical Quarterly* 57: 33–52.

   2009. "Slavery, Freedom and Citizenship in Classical Athens: Beyond a Legalistic Approach." *European Review of History* 16: 347–63.

   2010. "Athenian Slave Names and Athenian Social History." *Zeitschrift für Papyrologie und Epigraphik* 175: 113–44.

   2015. "Plotting Strategies, Networks and Communities in Classical Athens." In *Communities and Networks in the Greek World*, edited by C. Taylor and K. Vlassopoulos, 101–27. Oxford.

Vlassopoulos, K., ed. Forthcoming. *The Oxford Handbook of Greek and Roman Slaveries*.

Watson, A. 1987. *Roman Slave Law*. Baltimore.

Webster, J. 2001. "Creolizing the Roman Provinces." *American Journal of Archaeology* 105: 209–25.

Westermann, W. L. 1955. *The Slave Systems of Greek and Roman Antiquity*. Philadelphia.

Whitehead, D. 1977. *The Ideology of the Athenian Metic*. Cambridge.

   2000. *Hypereides: The Forensic Speeches*. Oxford.

Wiedemann, T. and J. Gardner, eds. 2002. *Representing the Body of the Slave*. London.

Wimja, S. M. 2014. *Embracing the Immigrant: The Participation of Metics in Athenian Polis Religion (5th–4th Century BC)*. Stuttgart.
Wrenhaven, K. L. 2009. "The Identity of the 'Wool Workers' in the Attic Manumissions." *Hesperia* 78: 367–86.
  2012. *Reconstructing the Slave: The Image of the Slave in Ancient Greece*. Bristol.
Yetman, N. R. 2002. *When I Was A Slave: Memoirs from the Slave Narrative Collection*. New York.
Zelnick-Abramowitz, R. 2005. *Not Wholly Free: The Concept of Manumission and the Status of Manumitted Slaves in the Ancient Greek World*. Leiden.
  2013. *Taxing Freedom in the Thessalian Manumission Inscriptions*. Leiden.
Zuckerberg, D. 2018. *Not All Dead White Men: Classics and Misogyny in the Digital Age*. Cambridge, MA.

Index

Abydus, 71
Acarnania, 169
accommodation
  by slaves, 173, 175, 201, 202–3
accountants
  slaves as, 138
Achilles, 176
Achilles Tatius
  Leukippe and Kleitophon, 229, 230
Acte, 184
Aegina, 55, 90
Aeschines, 32, 60, 88, 161, 170, 172, 242
Aesop, 249
  fables, 207
  Life of Aesop, 72, 73, 77–8, 104, 204, 205, 209, 232
Africa
  slave trade, 57
agency
  of slaves, 4, 77, 151, 223–35, 247, 249
agriculture
  and slave labor, 103–7
Alcibiades, 64, 68, 84, 244
Alke, 153
American South, 216, 220, 232
Amphipolis, 72
Anatolia, 55, 57, 71, 95
Andania, 229
Andocides, 80, 84
animal husbandry
  and slave labor, 107–9
Anthesteria, festival of, 182
Antigenes, 142
Antiphanes, 80
Apollo
  festival of, 183
  sanctuary of, 243
Apollodorus
  son of Pasion, 147, 150, 203
Archippe, 147
  wife of Pasion, 147

archivists
  slaves as, 138
Arginusae
  Battle of, 159
Aristagoras, 63
Aristophanes, 75, 76, 81, 128, 170
  Acharnians, 106
  Horai, 231
  Knights, 228
Aristotelian
  Constitution of the Athenians, 189
Aristotle, 93, 170, 241, 251
  Rhetoric, 25, 206
  theory of natural slavery, 21–31, 162, 164
Artemis
  sanctuary of, 229
associations
  of slaves, 179
Astarte, 154
asylum. *See* sanctuaries
Athena
  sanctuary of, 243
Athenogenes, 141
Athens
  size of slave population, 90–1
Atotas, 123, 173–5
Aulos Kapreilios Timotheos, 72
baking
  and slave labor, 155
Bales, Kevin, 20
bandits, 53, 57
banking
  and slave labor, 141–50, 180

Behistun Inscription, 71
Bendis. *See* Thrace
Black Sea, 55, 56, 71, 95, 180
Boeotia, 71, 243
branding
  of slaves, 83, 167–8, 213
Brasidas, 158, 217

271

breeding
  of slaves, 65–6, 237
Brer Rabbit, 207
brothels. *See* prostitution
building accounts, 110–11
burial. *See* tombstones
business
  and slave-agents, 141–50
Byzantium, 71

Cappadocia, 55, 95
Caria, 55, 82, 96
Caribbean, 216, 220, 221
carpentry
  and slave labor, 110
Caucasus, 58
ceramics. *See* pottery
Chaeronea, 59, 91
chaining
  of slaves, 202, 235
charcoal maker, 115
childcare
  by slaves, 132
children, 98
  and slave labor, 156–7
  of slaves, 66–8
Chios, 57, 71, 90, 157, 158, 188, 213, 216, 221
Choës
  festival of, 140, 182
Cilicia, 63
citizen
  status distinctions in law, 189–90
citizenship
  and slaves, 249
  grant of, 147
  grants of, 149
  law of Pericles, 190
Cittus, 147
civic cult. *See* religion
civil war
  in ancient Greece, 213
  American, 214
Clazomenae, 71
coffle, 71
coinage
  Athenian law on, 196
  slave as minters and testers of, 136
  slaves as minters and testers of, 145
Colchis, 57, 71, 95
comedy
  and slaves, 106
commerce
  and slave labor, 141–50
communication
  between slaves, 214–15, 235

control
  of slaves, 201, 235–43
cooking
  and slave labor, 127, 156
Corcyra, 158, 214
Corinth, 71, 150
Cos, 231
Council
  of 500, 139
craftsmen. *See* manufacturing
Crete, 69, 96
critics
  of slavery, 164–5
cults. *See* religion
cultural dislocation
  of slaves, 83–9
culture
  of slaves, 168–81
Cybele, 154
Cylon, 227
Cyrus
  brother of Artaxerxes II, 87
  brother of King Artaxerxes II, 55
Cyzicus, 71

Daos, 103, 105, 171, 178, 179
debt bondage, 41, 47
Deceleia, 91, 124, 213
deference
  of slaves towards masters, 207
Delos, 71
Delphi, 153, 243
Demeter
  festival of, 129, 184, 185
  sanctuary at Eleusis, 111
  sanctuary of, 140
Demosthenes, 60, 82, 85, 88, 90, 112, 149, 172, 178, 196, 241
  ownership of slaves, 32
Dionysus
  festival of, 127, 140, 182
Drimakos, 188, 201, 209–10, 215
dye-making
  by slaves, 112

Egypt, 153, 211, 230
Eleusinian Mysteries, 185, 187
Eleusis, 54
enslavement
  trauma of, 70–1
Ephesus, 71, 229
Ephors, 219
Erechtheum
  building records, 110

ethnicities
  of slaves in ancient Greece, 92–8
ethnicity
  of slaves, 168–81
Eumaeus, 7
Eupolis
  Cities, 229, 231
Euripides, 66, 70, 164
  Medea, 9–10
exposure
  of children and slavery, 68
  of infants, 151

fables, 207
Finley, M. I., 48
flight
  of slaves, 201, 211–16
food
  of slaves, 235
freed slaves, 107, 175, 177, 178
  and reenslavement, 242
freedom
  grants of, 116, 145, 146, 147, 149, 150, 151, 155, 156, 157, 158, 174, 202, 213, 238–45
Fugitive Slave Act of 1850, 215
Fulling, 114
furniture-making
  and slave labor, 174

gender
  and slavery, 150
  of slaves in ancient Greece, 98–100
Genovese, 220
Getas, 107, 128
goldsmiths, 116
Gordion, 57
Gorgias, 103
Gortyn, 46, 233
  laws, 31
grave monuments. *See* tombstones
gravestones
  of slaves, 179

Haiti, 221
Halicarnassus, 69
helot
  revolts of, 201
helots, 109, 159, 160, 185, 216, 228
  as slaves or serfs, 42–5
  ethnicity of, 92
  numbers of, 91–2
  population size, 220
  religion of, 185–6
  revolt of, 215, 216, 217
Heracles
  sanctuary of, 230, 231
herdsmen, 107
Hermes
  festival of, 183
  mutilation of, 244
hero cult
  and slaves, 188
Herodotus, 56, 63, 88, 230
hidden transcripts, 207–10
Hippocrates
  Airs, Waters, Places, 163–4
Homer
  Iliad, 173, 176
  Odyssey, 7–9, 109
Homeric Hymn to Aphrodite, 89
Homeric Hymn to Demeter, 53
hoplites, 157
  slaves as, 157–8
house-born slaves, 65–8, 171, 202
household
  and slave labor, 125–34
  ritual introduction of slaves to, 83, 182
housing
  of slaves, 237
hubris
  law of, 36–8, 63, 198, 229
Hunt, Peter, 157, 231
Hyacinthia, festival of Apollo at Sparta, 183
hybridity
  and slave identity, 175
Hykkara, 52, 59, 63, 71
Hyperides, 79, 91

Illyria, 95
impiety, 245
indentured servitude, 41, 47
independent slaves, 4, 115, 118–19, 137, 155, 175, 197, 202, 238
intersectionality
  and slave identity, 175

Jamaica, 220
James, C. R. L, 57
Johnson, Walter, 232

Kinadon
  conspiracy of, 220
Klarotae, 45
Knemon, 107
Komon, 112
Kronia, festival of, 183

L'Ouverture, Toussaint, 221
Laconia, 109
Lampis, 143

language
  of slaves, 2, 61, 85, 86–9, 148, 168–81, 214–15
Laurion, 91
Laurium, 178, 181, 221
law
  ancient Greek
    of slavery, 31–9
  and judicial torture of slaves, 245
  contemporary
    of slavery, 18–19
  judicial torture of slaves, 131, 143, 147, 195–6
  of damage, 223–7
  of wounding, 223–7
  punishments for slaves, 196–7
  regulating sale of slaves, 74
  slavery as legal penalty, 69
  slaves' manipulation of, 223–35
  slaves' lack of legal rights, 34, 194–5
  slaves' manipulation of, 201
law courts
  and slave clerks, 139
leatherworkers, 116
leatherworking
  and slave labor, 110, 174
Lemnos, 79, 89
Lenski, Noel, 49
Lesbos, 57
Lesis, 1, 114, 122, 157
Leucas, 87, 169
Leuctra
  battle of, 221
literacy. *See* language
Lydia, 55, 58, 82, 95
Lydos, 179
Lysias, 151, 185, 187
  On the Murder of Eratosthenes, 129

Macedonia, 85, 95, 98
Macronians, 87, 181
malnutrition
  of slaves, 168
Manes, 171, 178, *See* names
Mannes, 176
manufacturing
  and citizen labor, 110
  and slave labor, 110–19, 148
  effect of labor on the body, 113
  of couches, 112
  of knives, 112
  of shields, 112
manumission. *See* freed slaves
Marathon, 158
  Battle of, 248
maroon communities
  of slaves, 201, 216

marriage
  of former slaves, 148
  of slaves, 66–8, 194
Melos, 62, 68, 84
Men
  Phrygian god, 176
Men, Phrygian god, 178
Menander, 69, 106, 128
  Aspis, 10–12
  Bad-Tempered Man, 103
Messenia, 95, 109, 186, 215, 218, 221, 229
metalworking
  and slave labor, 110
metic, 118, 141, 143, 151, 185, 187
metics, 69, 111, 112, 177, 242
  status distinctions in law, 193
Metroön, 138
Midas, 141
Miletus, 63
milling
  and slave labor, 155, 242
  as punishment for slaves, 155
mills
  and slave labor, 125–7
Milyas, 112, 116, 241, 242
mimes, 208, 210
mining, 119–25
  and slave labor, 81, 91, 130, 173–5, 176, 178
Moschion, 112, 205
Mount Ithome, 215
murder
  of slaves, 36

names
  of slaves, 76, 93–6, 171–3
Naucratis, 153
naval warfare
  and slave labor, 158–9
Neaira, 82, 99, 150–2, 157, 173, 239–40, 242
New Orleans, 76, 78
Nicarete, 150
Nicias, 63, 64, 82, 91, 119, 122
Nicobulus, 142
Notion, 58
noxal surrender, 223

occupation
  as marker of slave status, 174, 177
Old Oligarch. *See* Xenophon (pseudo-)
Olynthus, 62, 85
opponents. *See* critics
oracles
  and inquiries by slaves, 187
Orlando, Patterson, 40–1
overseers
  of slaves, 104, 107, 115, 203, 205, 238

Pan, 179
Panathenaic Festival, 184, 194
Pancleon, 193, 242
Pantaenetus, 142
Paphlagonia, 55, 95, 123, 173
Pasion, 146–50, 180, 202, 203, 240
passing
  of slaves as citizens, 190–2, 249
  of slaves as free and/or citizens, 38–9, 151, 152, 153
  slaves passing as metics, 193
Patterson, Orlando, 19–20, 50
Pausanias
  Spartan regent, 227
Peace of Nicias, 59, 62
Pelasgians, 89
Peloponnesian War, 158, 159
penal servitude, 41
Pendeskouphia, 120
Penestae, 45
Perinthus, 56, 71
perioikoi, 220
Persia, 63, 72
Persian Wars, 158
Phano, 173
Phoenicia, 95, 146, 180
Phormion, 143, 170, 180, 203, 240
Phrygia, 55, 57, 63, 89, 95, 102, 176, 178
Phryne, 153
Phrynion, 151
Piraeus, 146, 177
pirates, 53, 57, 60
Pittacus, 126
Pittalacus, 138, 140, 202
Plataea, 158
  Battle of, 248
Plato, 12, 22, 65, 88, 171, 177, 211, 221, 235
  Laws, 200, 205, 213, 223–5, 245
  Republic, 249
Plutarch, 122
  Life of Theseus, 229
policing
  by slaves, 135
Pollux, 45
population size
  of slaves in ancient Greece, 89–92
porters
  slaves as, 127
Poseidon
  sanctuary of, 230
  sanctuary of (at Tainaron), 185, 228
pottery
  and slave labor, 110
prices. *See* sale
Propontis, 71

Propontis (Sea of Marmara), 56
prostitution
  and slave labor, 150–4, 156, 239–40, 242
  male, 154
public executioner
  slave as, 135
public slaves, 202
public works
  and slave labor, 140
publicly-owned slaves, 4, 80, 91, 134–41
punishment
  as tool of control of slaves, 236–8
  of slaves, 130, 201, 224
Pylos, 217

quarrying
  and slave labor, 119–25

race. *See* racism
racism, 4, 6–7, 249–51
raiding
  as part of military campaign, 58
ransoming
  of war captives, 59–61
rebellion. *See* revolt
religion
  and slave resistance, 186–8, 201
  and Spartan helots, 185–6
  of slaves, 177–9
  slaves and civic cult, 184–5
  slaves and household cult, 182–4
resistance
  by slaves, 13, 173, 175, 201
  low-level acts of, 203–7
  of slaves in speech, 210
Reverent Goddesses
  sanctuary of, 227
revolt
  of slaves, 201, 216–22
rewards
  as tool of control of slaves, 238–43
  for the capture of runaway slaves, 211
  of slaves as incentive to good behavior, 235–6
  to slaves, 202
Rhodopis, 153

Sabazius, Phrygian god, 179
Salamis
  Battle of, 248
salary
  of slaves, 137, 202, 238, 240
sale
  of slaves, 52, 53, 73–8, 81, 141, 201, 231–5
  of slaves as punishment, 238
  of slaves to a god, 243

sale (cont.)
  prices of slaves, 81–3, 151
  separation of families through sale, 79–80
Samos, 153, 229
sanctuaries, 4, 37
  and transfer of slaves to new masters, 227–35
  as refuges for slaves, 227–35
Sappho, 153
Scione, 62
scribes
  slaves as, 138
Scythia, 71, 83, 95
Scythian archers, 81, 90, 135
Sepúlveda, Juan Ginés de, 27
serfdom, 41
Seuthes, 55
sexual assault
  of slaves, 65, 68, 130, 152
shoe-making
  and slave labor, 174
Sicilian Expedition, 60, 61–2, 64, 244
Sicily, 52, 125
slave market, 76, See sale:of slaves
slave society
  definition, 48
slave trade, 55, 56, 74, 94
slave-owners
  liability for offenses committed by slaves, 34–6
slavery
  archaeological evidence for, 12
  comparative approaches, 6, 15–17
  inscriptional evidence, 14–15
  justifications of, 13, 162–8, 205, 249
  modern definitions, 18–21
slaves
  as security for loans, 34
  contributions to society and culture, 3–4
  terminology of, 24, 29
Socrates, 113, 117, 135, 153, 177, 211, 235, 249
Solon, 170
Sophocles, 67, 68
Sosias, 82, 123, 173, 178
Sounion, 81, 192
Sparta, 158, 160, 183, 201, See helots
  earthquake in, 217
Sphacteria, 59
Stelae Atticae, 33, 65, 79, 96–8, 174
Stephanus, 150
steward
  slaves as, 104
stone-masonry
  and slave labor, 110
Strabo, 57
symposia
  male drinking-parties, 154

Syracuse, 71, 159
Syria, 63, 80, 82, 95, 146
Syros, 171, 179, See names

tales
  told by slaves, 207–10
tanning (hides)
  and slave labor, 174
tattooing
  and slaves, 167–8
textile production
  and slave labor, 112, 113, 115, 117–18, 133, 240
Thebes, 221
theft
  by slaves, 205–6
Theodote, 153
Theophrastus, 173
Thermopylae
  Battle of, 159
Theseus
  sanctuary of, 228–9, 234
Thesmophoria, festival of Demeter, 184
Thessaly, 71
Thorikos, 54, 71, 81
Thrace, 55, 56, 57, 71, 72, 79, 82, 83, 94, 102, 158, 178
  cult of Bendis at Athens, 93, 177, 249
Thucydides, 52, 64, 91, 124, 158, 176, 213, 221, 227, 228
Timarchus, 112, 115, 117, 140
tombstones
  of slaves, 123, 132, 173, 178, 183
Torone, 62
trade. See commerce
transfer
  to a new master, 223–7
transport
  of slaves, 71–3
treason, 245
trickster tales, 207
Trojan War, 174
Troy, 89

Valladolid, 26
vase painting
  and the representation of slaves, 157, 166–7
Virginia, 72
Vlassopoulos, K., 93, 96, 110, 171–2, 188, 235, 253
voices
  of slaves, 1, 7

warfare
  and slave labor, 157–9, 194, 217, 243
  enslavement of captives, 61–3
weapons of the weak, 203–7
weavers. See textile production:and slave labor

wet nurses
    slaves as, 65, 131
whipping
    of slaves, 1, 38, 86, 114, 146, 147, 168, 196, 202, 235
women. *See* gender
wood-cutting
    and slave labor, 176
wool-workers. *See* textile production and slave labor
work
    slow-downs, 204
    songs, 125

workshops. *See* manufacturing

Xanthias, 127, 171
Xenocles, 114
Xenophon, 12, 55, 68, 87, 91, 113, 117, 120, 130, 138, 170, 178, 211, 235
    On Household Management, 103, 203, 236
Xenophon (pseudo-), 118, 161

Zeus, 209
    festival of (at Olympia), 184
    household worship of, 182
    oracle of (at Dodona), 187